Greetings!

Welcome to Moon Rock Books. That Amazon.com has banned *NO-BODY DIED AT SANDY HOOK* (2015) less than a month after it had been approved for sale appears to be on a par with Nazi book burning. There are multiple reasons to conclude that this was a blatantly political action to suppress research on Sandy Hook supporting conclusions that disagree with the government's official account.

Consider, for example, that the book had to satisfy Amazon's guidelines to have been accepted in the first place. The notification of suppression which I received did not specify which guidelines it had been found to violate, which is absurd if they were banning it for violating its guidelines, since they would have to know which guidelines it had violated—yet they were unable to tell me, even after inquiry.

Dr. Eowyn (of *fellowshipoftheminds.com*) has determined that Amazon had 20 books on Sandy Hook available online, but only one was banned. The reason is not in doubt: the other 19 were consistent with or supported the government's account. The sole exception was suppressed in an extraordinary measure to deny the public information that would better enable the people to understand what happened on 14 December 2012, which appears to have been an elaborate hoax.

The 13 contributors to the book, including six (current or retired) Ph.D. college professors, concluded that it had been a drill, that no one had died, and that it was done to promote the Obama administration's gun control agenda. We included an interview with Paul Preston, a Los Angeles school safety expert, who reached out to his contacts in the Obama Department of Education, who confirmed that it was a drill, that no one had died, and that it was done to promote gun control.

It may come as no surprise but Jay Carney, former Press Secretary for President Obama, joined Amazon as Senior Vice President when he left the White House. Jeff Bezos, its owner, is a Bilderberger and recently purchased *The Washington Post*. Although I was initially skeptical, I now believe that this book ban may go down in history along with the suppression of *THE PENTAGON PAPERS* (1971). Thank you for the courage and integrity to consider "the other side of the story." Everyone deserves to know the truth.

—JIM

JAMES H. FETZER, Ph.D.
McKnight Professor Emeritus
University of Minnesota Duluth
http://www.d.umn.edu/~jfetzer

Nobody Died at Sandy Hook

It was a FEMA Drill to Promote Gun Control

Also by Mike Palecek

Fiction:

SWEAT: Global Warming in a small town,
and other tales from the great American Westerly Midwest
Joe Coffee's Revolution
The Truth
The American Dream
Johnny Moon
KGB
Terror Nation
Speak English!
The Last Liberal Outlaw
The Progressive Avenger
Camp America
Twins
Iowa Terror
Guests of the Nation
Looking For Bigfoot
A Perfect Duluth Day
American History 101:
Conspiracy Nation Revolution
One Day In The Life of Herbert Wisniewski
Operation Northwoods: . . . the patsy
Red White & Blue

Non-Fiction:

Cost of Freedom (with Whitney Trettien and Michael Annis)
Prophets Without Honor (with William Strabala)
The Dynamic Duo: White Rose Blooms in Wisconsin,
Kevin Barrett, Jim Fetzer & the American Resistance
And I Suppose We Didn't Go To The Moon, Either? (with Jim Fetzer)
Nobody Died At Sandy Hook (with Jim Fetzer)

Nobody Died at Sandy Hook

It was a FEMA Drill to Promote Gun Control

Jim Fetzer and Mike Palecek
Editors

MOON ROCK BOOKS

SAVE THE WORLD/RESIST THE EMPIRE SERIES

The Dynamic Duo: White Rose Blooms in Wisconsin
And I Suppose We Didn't Go to the Moon, Either?
Nobody Died at Sandy Hook

MIKE PALECEK, CHUCK GREGORY, JIM FETZER
SERIES EDITORS

———

Nobody Died at Sandy Hook
It Was a FEMA Drill to Promote Gun Control

JAMES H. FETZER, PH.D. & MIKE PALECEK

FIRST EDITION: OCTOBER 2015
BANNED EDITION: DECEMBER 2015

ISBN: 978-0-692-59494-0

Ordering more copies: Order more copies of *Nobody Died at Sandy Hook* from MOON ROCK BOOKS, 6256 Bullet Drive, Crestview, FL 32536 or *MoonRockBooks.com*.

MOON ROCK BOOKS
6256 Bullet Drive, Crestview, FL 32536
www.MoonRockBooks.com

Cover design and layout by Ole Dammegård

CONTENTS

CONTENTS (continued)

PREFACE

Some Conspiracy theories Are True

by Mike Palecek

"What can government do about conspiracy theories? Among the things it can do, what should it do? We can readily imagine a series of possible responses. (1) Government might ban conspiracy theorizing. (2) Government might impose some kind of tax, financial or otherwise, on those who disseminate such theories. (3) Government might itself engage in counter-speech, marshaling arguments to discredit conspiracy theories. (4) Government might formally hire credible private parties to engage in counter-speech. (5) Government might engage in informal communication with such parties, encouraging them to help. Each instrument has a distinctive set of potential effects, or costs and benefits, and each will have a place under imaginable conditions. However, our main policy idea is that government should engage in cognitive infiltration of the groups that produce conspiracy theories, which involves a mix of (3), (4) and (5).

" … One line of thinking denies that conspiracy theories matter. There are several possible reasons to think so. First, conspiracy theories may be held by only a tiny fraction of the population. Perhaps only a handful of kooks believe that U.S. government officials had any kind of role in the events of 9/11.

" … Government agents (and their allies) might enter chat rooms, online social networks, or even real-space groups and attempt to undermine percolating conspiracy theories by raising doubts about their factual premises, causal logic or implications for political action."

— "Conspiracy Theories," Cass R. Sunstein, Adrian Vermeule, Jan. 15, 2008

"More than a year and a half after Adam Lanza brutally murdered 26 women and children at the Sandy Hook Elementary School in Newtown, parents and relatives of the victims still relive the terror of that fateful day along with the daily anguish and torment they suffer over the loss of their loved ones. Worse, they have to suffer the onslaught of delusional conspiracy theorists, commonly called hoaxers, who claim Sandy Hook was a "false flag" event concocted by the government as a pretext to gun confiscation."

— Lenny Pozner, *Hartford Courant*, July 25, 2014

Well, then, let us begin at the beginning.

This is where it starts and ends.

Right here.

If Lenny Pozner is right then I am wrong.

If his son Noah was murdered by Adam Lanza at Sandy Hook School on Dec. 14, 2012, then this book is a bust, worse than that, much worse.

But I do not think that is the case.

We are saying that Sandy Hook did not happen as we have been told.

We also think the Boston Marathon bombing did not happen as we have been told.

We think these events are part of a pattern that stretches at least as far back as the murder of John F. Kennedy, likely farther.

These "false flag" events are part of a conspiracy, a vast conspiracy.

You have been taught to laugh now.

But there is nothing funny here.

Some of those who have spoken the truth are no longer here.

Their chairs at the Thanksgiving adult big table are empty.

Their relatives have sent them to Siberia with a roll of their eyes.

So, let us begin. ...

... Okay, here we go, scooch up to the samovar,

maybe leave your hat and boots on, fill your peasant hands with a warm drink, and listen for the sound of hoofbeats on the ice.

The New American Dream means never having to say some question or idea is not valid.

We are allowed to ask any questions that we have, there are no wrong questions. There is no hidden black military budget, there are no UFO files Americans cannot see, no JFK documents that will not be opened during our lifetimes, no destroyed RFK murder photos by the L.A. police, no evidence from Ground Zero taken away before we can even look at it — we are not the U.S.S.R. of the 1960s — this is supposed to be America. That is our dream, to become America, The New America, the real hope of the world.

We have a dream, of bringing the United States politicians, journalists and generals who have brought about this long war and debacle to trial — and put on TV just like O.J. — every afternoon — so every American can watch, just like the McCarthy Hearings and the JFK funeral procession.

What we need is a New American Dream.

Not of new homes and toasters and microwaves, but of becoming the type of country we always thought we were.

Right now we live on lies. We subsist on lies, but it's not really living.

9/11 was an inside job.

Bush, Cheney, Rice, Powell, Rumsfeld, Ashcroft, Obama, Bill Clinton, Hillary Clinton, Joe Biden.

They all know that.

What we need in America is a Truth Commission like they had in South Africa to heal their broken country. We need to put certain people on the stand and we need to be allowed to ask questions.

Our country is surely broken as well.

The troops are not protecting us. That is someone's spin on the day's news, somebody's advertising slogan, someone else's sermon.

The troops serve the empire. They are not heroes. They kill and plunder for the empire. American bases overseas serve nobody but the empire. The heroes in our country are the protesters, the ones who go face to face with the empire, those in the Plowshares Movement, for one example.

You have to know that Barack Obama knows the whole truth about the 9/11 attacks. He is complicit. He has lied. He has continued the wars everywhere based on a lie. And he knows he is lying.

He lied right to our faces on national television when he said that Osama bin Laden had been killed, and buried at sea.

Osama bin Laden was buried at sea, and Jessica Lynch was rescued heroically, the U.S.A. does not torture, Iraq had weapons of mass destruction, George Bush won the 2000 election, see, there is a plane there in that hole in Shanksville, it went all the way into that hole and no, there is no blood and no bodies and no luggage scattered, or plane parts, and Osama bin Laden was buried at sea.

Remember the anthrax letters, which said "Are You Afraid?" Those were not written with a rock and chisel like Fred Flintstone from the recesses of some cave in Afghanistan. Those letters came from persons within our own government.

Like a horror movie and the killer is in the same house with us.

These killers are right here, with us and "they" want us to be afraid.

We cannot be afraid.

And now for a word from National Public Radio, Good ol' Reverend Bob, Miss Thompson, Your 5th Grade Teacher, The Police, The Tired Old Editor Strolling Down The Street After A Long Day At The Office, The Democratic

Party, The American Legion, The Boy Scouts and Mom & Dad — all the people you trust to tell you the truth.

No plane hit the Pentagon, nobody died at Sandy Hook. Nobody died at the Boston Bombing.

The War on Terror is a fake. These phony-baloney weekly shootings are someone's idea of public policy.

If a plane would have hit the Pentagon, we would have seen that short film one thousand times by now on Chevrolet commercials and Miller Beer commercials and on commercials somehow juxtaposing the Pentagon, puppy pellets, the Pittsburgh Pirates and the Pope-Mobile.

So.

No plane hit the Pentagon.

And because we know that from the lack of Pope-Mobile prevarications, we can be sure that Bush, Rove, Rumsfeld, etc. all are liars and murderers.

And we can include a bunch more folks in there as well. Bill Clinton, Hillary Clinton. The nice Obama family across the street.

They all know the truth and refuse.

Refuse.

To tell us.

And that's the truth and I don't care what happens to me, it's just important that you know.

This has been a word from National Public Radio, Good ol' Reverend Bob, Miss Thompson Your 5th Grade Teacher, The Tired Old Editor Strolling Down The Street After A Long Day At The Office, The Police, The Democratic Party, The American Legion, The Boy Scouts and Mom & Dad — all the people you trust to tell you the truth.

A TRUTH Series
SAVE THE WORLD: Resist The American Empire

You have trusted these people to tell you the truth, but all they have done is lie.

This is the truth. This book. This series of books.

Right at the end of your nose.

You hold it in your hands.

This book is the third in the truth series.

The first, "The Dynamic Duo: White Rose Blooms in Wisconsin, Kevin Barrett, Jim Fetzer & The American Resistance," was also published by Chuck Gregory's CWG Press.

The second, "And I Suppose We Didn't Go To The Moon, Either?" dealt with the alleged moon landings, the alleged Holocaust, and the probability that Paul McCartney died long ago.

The fourth will tell the truth about the alleged Boston Marathon bombing.

There will be a fifth, with new information on the events of Sept. 11, 2001.

C'mon ... Teachers, priests, ministers, coaches, parents, please start telling the truth.

We can handle the truth. In fact, without the truth, we cannot live. * We will die. * Slowly, and then all at once. * We will collapse and that will be that. * It will be over. * A dusty pile of rubble and Ho Ho's and lies. *

In this book we seek to catalogue and examine just one of the many hoax events, terror events that have occurred in America since the attacks of Sept. 11, 2001.

We seek to point a finger at these events, put a spotlight on them in the dark and ask, "What Is That?"

We believe they are not occurring organically.

We believe they are being seeded by elements within the United States government, and growing, spreading like pernicious weeds toward some end that for sure someone has envisioned, but that, at this point, we have not quite figured out.

History is important.

We really do need to know where we have been in order to see where we are going.

The terms conspiracy theory, conspiracy theorist, tin-foil hat are all widespread in our society. They are derogatory terms, meant to ridicule, meant to throw up dust and smoke while the perpetrators make their getaway.

The heroes of our country are not the soldiers and politicians and journalists you see paraded down main streets, in the newspapers, across television screens.

The real heroes are the protesters, and, I believe, especially the citizen journalists who have taken it upon themselves to find out the truth about our country, the ones who have written this book.

It started long ago, with Penn Jones, Jr., probably way before that.

But Jones, who operated a small newspaper in Texas, took his calling seriously and worked to delve into the facts of the murder of John F. Kennedy, as Walter Cronkite, Dan Rather and hundreds, thousands of other "journalists" chose to turn away, to build careers, make money, run for cover.

There are many who would dismiss what we say here.

They might offer "where is your proof?"

In these pages you will find the proof that our country is overcome, in need of a truth commission. Our country is indeed broken, just as South Africa in the days of apartheid, in need of a healing ceremony. Not a giant flag unfurled from sideline to sideline across a sports stadium, but something real, something true, something to build upon, not sand, but rock.

THE WIDESPREAD DECEPTION

The Heritage Foundation published on April 25, 2012, "50 Terror Attacks Foiled Since 9/11."[1]

Key Points

-The death of Osama bin Laden marked an important victory in the long war on terrorism. One year later, however, Congress and the Administration must remember that the war is not won. The nation and its leaders must be mindful of the requirements of the continued fight against terrorism at home and abroad.

-Since 9/11, at least 50 *publically* known attempted terrorist attacks against the U.S. have been foiled — of these, at least 42 could be categorized as homegrown plots.

-With the global operating environment for terrorist networks becoming increasingly hostile, homegrown terrorism has become more appealing to al-Qaeda and other terrorist networks.

-The U.S. must not only continue its reliance on existing counterterrorism and intelligence tools, such as the PATRIOT Act, but also enhance cooperation among federal, state, and local authorities, as well as build mutual trust and partnerships with Muslim communities throughout the U.S.

... *This, from the Heritage Foundation,* is part of the widespread deception, burning and out of control, like west coast wildfires, threatening to engulf the countryside.

John Avlon, writing in *The Daily Beast,* tell us "there have been at least 45 jihadist terror attacks plotted against Americans since 9/11 — each of them thwarted by a combination of intelligence work, policing and citizen participation." [1A]

The young, hip editor at *Time Magazine* talks about the glory of the new One World Trade Center, showing our strength, resurgence.

The Sandy Hook file is finally released, showing incredible fictional detail and yet no names of the deceased.

The "backstory" on the Tsarnaevs, the patsies in the Boston Marathon bombing event, runs in a hundred big city newspapers, hits the street in the morning edition, and finally, at long last, the writers in Langley can get some needed sleep.

With this series we cut a firebreak in this calculated confusing conflagration.

It stops here.

As we will show: the "Boston Bombing," the Sandy Hook School Shooting, both fake.

We are here to stop it.

It must be stopped.

There is a "they" out there, somewhere.

And there is a you and me and together are us — and we are going to stop them.

It begins here, with this book, with words, with learning, with heart.

Such as the White Rose Resistance fought Nazi Germany hand-to-hand with words, with writing, to save their countrymen, their nation.

"I'M NOT SUPPOSED TO BE INVOLVED IN THIS"

Most of us do not have inside information, have not had the privilege of sitting close-by and smelling the cigar smoke of the actual plotters, but once in a while we catch a hint of a loose whiff on the wind.

An article that ran in *The Rock Creek Free Press,* written by Sheila Casey, included an interview conducted by the CIT (Citizens Investigation Team) with an insider in the attack on the Pentagon, Lloyde England, the cab driver whose cab was allegedly speared through the front windshield by one of the light poles said to have been sheared off by the plane that hit the Pentagon. [2]:

England: "You gotta understand something. When people do things and get away with it, you … eventually it's gonna come to me, and when it comes to me, it's gonna be so big, I can't do nothing about it."

England: I wasn't supposed to be involved with this, this is too big for me, man, this is a big thing. This is a world thing happening, I'm a small man … I'm not supposed to be involved in this. This is for other people, people who have money and all this kind of stuff.

Interviewer: Your point that these people who have all the money …

England: This is their thing.

Interviewer: This is their event.

England: This is for them.

Interviewer: Meaning they're doing it for their own reasons …

England: (with conviction) That's right. I'm not supposed to be in it.

Interviewer: They must have planned it.

England: It was planned.

England: You know what history is? It's not the truth. It's "his story." Has nothing to do with the truth." [2]

Another example of us perhaps getting our noses in behind the curtain like a dog under the circus tent is in listening to the recording of flight attendant Ceecee Lyles, apparently speaking to her husband from the doomed United Airlines Flight 93, sneaks in a word at the end.

"It's a frame." [3]

YOU HAVE TO BEGIN TO WONDER

Yes, when one starts to name and name and name the fakeries, then one is going to hear snickers about Elvis.

But when a person begins to understand, he has to wonder about very nearly everything the United States government, the CIA, the FBI, the NSA does, behind their massive modern walls, with the billions of dollars that we give to them.

"It's the CIA."

"That was done by the CIA."

It's so easy to type that, to say it.

But what does it really mean?

Who is the CIA? Where is the CIA?

It is a real place, with real people, headquartered in Langley, Virginia, near Washington, D.C.

The rest you will know when it is time.

Until then you may believe in them, just as you do the Boston Red Sox and the mountains of County Cork where you are allegedly from, though you have seen neither in all your life, and it's getting late.

And because by now you are open to believing some things not mentioned by Brian Williams or his successors on the NBC Nightly News, you have to also wonder about the Haymarket bombs, because you know how they think, what they are capable of. [4]

To not consider the possibilities — or probabilities — is to be reckless, lazy, playing loose with your child's future.

You also have to wonder about the explosion precluding the Palmer Raids. [5]

From the comments section of an article on *Veterans Today*:

Leif Oldhart

March 31, 2011 - 6:07 pm

"Speaking of false flag terrorism, NEVER FORGET Haymarket Square, where during a peaceful public assembly in favor of the eight-hour day, the powers that be had someone lob a bomb at the police. In the resulting riot, eleven people died and hundreds were injured. Seven cops died, so the nasty "anarchists" responsible were arrested and railroaded. Several were executed, including a newspaperman named August Spies (sounds like spees).

"The Haymarket Square "Anarchist" Terror Bombing may be the seminal act of false flag terrorism in US history. So it would be a good idea to learn what you can about it. Google is a pretty good place to start." [6]

BUT WHERE IS THE PROOF!

Someone might easily ask, again, and, justifiably, again and again — where is the proof?

Where is the game-changer? There are many hints, but where is the rock-solid, clamp on the handcuffs stuff?

9/11. The actor immediately telling us what happened on national TV. The Pentagon with no debris. The Dancing Israelis. The "hole" in Shanksville. The "hole" in the Pentagon. Building 7 going down when it had not been hit. Who told the fighter jets not to respond? Just look at how the buildings came down. Look at how the national television commentators immediately began naming Osama bin Laden. Look at how George W. Bush just sat there in that elementary school. The list goes on.

Boston. The photographs showing the fake blood, the fake victims getting into place. The backpacks on the backs of the agents in the street and sidewalk. The woman tossing something to the old man in the street, the runner, the "bomb" goes off, he reaches for it, misses, falls to the street, the cops run up, the photographer snaps the photo, but the blood sack the man missed does not get blood into the picture, the photo is on the cover of *Sport Illustrated* anyway.

There are many others: hints in movies, books, the "Dark Knight".

And just wondering what do you think about this in *The Big Lebowski*?

As kids, the Coen brothers attended Camp Herzl in Wisconsin. Theodore Herzl is the founder of modern political Zionism. (Silverstein, Dancing Israelis, hmm, hmmm, hmm)

One of the characters in *The Big Lebowski* quotes Herzl: "If you will it, it is no dream, Theodore Herzl," says Walter Sobchak upon entering the bowling alley carrying a Pomeranian in a carrier.

The Big Lebowski was filmed from January to April 1997. It was set in the early 1990s.

In the opening scene, the main character "The Dude," played by Jeff Bridges, writes a check for half and half at Ralph's Grocery for sixty-nine cents while in the background George H.W. Bush is talking on a small black and white television saying about the Iraq invasion of Kuwait: This will not stand.

The date on The Dude's check for sixty nine cents: Sept. 11, 1991, ten years to the day.

That's not proof of anything, but why did it happen?

Coincidence.

Okay. If you feel that way, fine.

I'll mark it zero. Are you happy now?

It's a league game.

But do you also see what happens when you find a stranger in the Alps?

MORRIS BERMAN, HOWARD ZINN, NOAM CHOMSKY

During an acceptance speech on June 22, 2013 for the Neil Postman Award for Career Achievement in Public Intellectual Activity, Morris Berman mentioned that of the 315,000,000 people in the United States, maybe 200,000 read alternative websites. He praised the alternative websites and their reporters. [7]

And yet during his talk Berman does not mention the real truth, just as these alternative websites. Why?

Alternative to what, I might wonder.

Is he not aware?

Does he just believe the government truth? I doubt that. Has he not "had time" to study, as Howard Zinn once said:

"I don't know much about the situation and the truth is, I don't care that much about it, that's passed, that's a diversion from what we really have to do," adding that debating who was behind 9/11, "gets in the way of dealing with the immediate situation". [8]

During a 2006 Internet forum event, Noam Chomsky claimed that the 9/11 truth movement peddled "arcane and dubious theories" and had distracted activists from pursuing "crimes that are far more serious than blowing up the WTC ..." [9]

AND NOW, FOR THE SPORTS AT SEA ...

When I first heard about Osama bin Laden having been buried at sea I was pulling out of the driveway of a group home in Duluth after doing the overnight shift. I listen to sports talk radio when I drive and the morning show was detailing the news break, I assume with straight faces.

When I heard about the Boston bombings I was headed to Norfolk, Nebraska to pick up my sister Donna to take a trip to Fort Collins to visit my other sister, Connie, actually for the funeral of her husband, Jack, a longtime Fort Collins radio personality and manager, reporter. I heard the Minneapolis sports talk crew droning in somber tones about the bombings and the number of limbs missing, the wheelchairs. And, if you still listen daily, as I do, you get updates from these guys, the number of missing limbs, the wheelchairs.

"They" are able to put the lie everywhere immediately. And they keep it going, everywhere, all the time. That is power.

But, we fight back.

Mark Lane fought the lies of the Warren Commission almost immediately. David Ray Griffin fought the lies of the 9/11 Commission. Many others fought too.

Luke Rudkowski and We Are Change ask unwanted questions, as do Jim Fetzer, Kevin Barrett, James Tracy. Many others do, too.

— "We Are Change Confrontations" [10]

— "Top Ten Reasons Sandy Hook Was An Elaborate Hoax" [10]

— "U.S. Needs Pro-Democracy Revolution" [10]

— "State Propaganda, Historical Revisionism, and Perpetuation of the 9/11 Myth" [10]

The cover story dives deep. Roots are planted.

First the event happens, the play is staged, the media takes its cue, the public is engaged, and then the detailed fake back-story is added and then it can finally be said: this indeed happened as we said, please go about your day, move along. The dissidents are laughed at, sneered at, corralled into a corner.

— "Police File On Newtown Yields Chilling Portrait" [11]
— Kevin Barrett: NY Times DC correspondent covers up 9/11 [12]
— "Guardians of the National Mythos" [13]

UNLIKELY SOURCES OF DISINFORMATION

We hear what we hear from the standard ops, Fox News, Rush Limbaugh, but we are shocked when we hear the same from some we thought might possibly be on our side: Maddow, Goodman, Stewart, Maher, The Progressive, The Nation, National Public Radio.

And we realize how much we are up against.

It's too much.

Maybe a change of scenery would be good, get off the damn computer, join a church, hit the driving range, move to Canada, Mexico, get to know the grandkids, those old friends you argued maybe too hard against, was it four years ago? Five? Forty? No.

That can't be.

But you can't get into Canada because you burned your draft card live on the local public access channel some time ago, and you need to be here when the guy comes to fix the garbage disposal, and there's the grandchild's kindergarten graduation coming.

You stay.

IT GOES WAY, WAY BACK, it seems

As Kevin Barrett says, "the terms "conspiracy theory" and "conspiracy theorist" were virtually unheard-of until the mid-1960s, when the CIA issued a memorandum to its thousands of Operation Mockingbird media assets telling them to attack JFK assassination researchers using those words. That memo is preserved as CIA Document 1035-960, released in response to a 1976 FOIA request by none other than the New York Times. [14]

Two-time Medal of Honor recipient Major General Smedley Butler:

"I spent 33 years and four months in active military service and during that period I spent most of my time as a high class muscle man for Big Business, for Wall Street and the bankers. In short, I was a racketeer, a gangster for capitalism. I helped make Mexico and especially Tampico safe for American oil interests in 1914. I helped make Haiti and Cuba a decent place for the National City Bank boys to collect revenues in. I helped in the raping of half a dozen Central American republics for the benefit of Wall Street. I helped purify Nicaragua for the International Banking House of Brown Brothers in 1902-1912. I brought light to the Dominican Republic for

xix

the American sugar interests in 1916. I helped make Honduras right for the American fruit companies in 1903. In China in 1927 I helped see to it that Standard Oil went on its way unmolested."

In his series, "Ten False Flags That Changed The World," [15] Joe Crubaugh tells us about "Remember The Maine," The Reichstag Fire, The Myth of Pearl Harbor, Operation Northwoods, The Gulf of Tonkin, The September 11, 2001 Attacks, and others.

Even *The New York Times* admits that we have discovered the terrorists, and they are us.

"Terrorist Plots, Helped Along by the FBI" [16]

THE STRATEGY OF TENSION, TOWARD WHAT END?

"You had to attack civilians, the people, women, children, innocent people, unknown people far removed from any political game. The reason was quite simple: to force ... the public to turn to the state to ask for greater security." — *A defendant*, from Operation Gladio

Maybe that's what's happening here.

Because something's happening here.

Certainly things are different than the 1960s, when we thought we were really getting things done: ending war, ending poverty, ending racism. Who has time for anything like that now? We are busy. Busy paying bills. Busy. Busy.

In a piece on *Veterans Today*, Gordon Duff argues that what we are facing is Operation Gladio on steroids or at least espresso. ("The Gift That Keeps On Giving" [17])

"Who Knew?"

"The War of the Worlds" provided a template, a track record of what the public could be convinced of by the media. Whether intended or not by Orson Welles.

And Richard Dolan says that even though we try, it's going to be pretty tough for anyone to get to the bottom of the real history of the United States.

"... our best estimates of U.S. archival system tell us that probably more than 50 percent of all U.S. government documents are classified ... which means that ... so, if you were an historian trying to put together a history of this government, of the United States, you could argue that more than half of the history of that government is secret." [18]

Maybe the JFK assassination was part of Operation Northwoods.

Maybe Operation Northwoods continues to this day.

Just sayin'.

My post titled "Boston Wrong" got this response from a website named after the White Rose student resisters of Nazi Germany:

"Mike Palecek, you are being removed from this group for rules violation. Your promoting a softly written right wing conspiracy ideology in many of your writings and that is something this group will not abide and THIS sir, is frankly offensive."

And this from Eric of the Lake Superior Writers group:

I disagree with your writing Mike. However I'd love to see you share it face to face with people who lost family on 9/11. And with those who are missing arms and legs and family members in Boston. That would be a hoot.

Me: *Eric, hello and thanks for comment. I do think that people died on 9/11. I just don't think it was perpetrated by Muslims with box cutters. The government story is a lie. With Boston, I don't think anyone died or lost limbs. I respectfully submit that in this case it would be helpful if you would do a little more study. I know how that sounds, but if you could go here and read I do think it would help. (memoryholeblog – James Tracy)*

Eric: *I swore to support and defend the Constitution from all enemies foreign and domestic. You are exercising your right to look just as ridiculous as you want. I wish you had a larger forum so more people could hear your opinions.*

Me: *If you are serious about that you need to look at the Bushes, Clinton, Obama. These are your/our real enemies.*

Eric: *Sorry, I have to go back to actual studying. Plus, I misplaced my tin-foil hat.*

And in response to a portion of a piece where I asked why liberal bloggers do not seem to want to "go there" on 9/11, Boston, Sandy Hook, etc., I got this from Mark Karlin, a liberal blogger for Buzzflash/Truthout.

"I see no reason to talk about 9/11 conspiracy theory. * The world is imploding. * The corporations run the world economy. * We have a duopoly party running our nation. * Most of us are getting poorer and poorer. I'll write till I die, but what is writing about 9/11 now going to do to save the Earth?"

… And, so … I'm trying to understand why people don't understand.

This quote was not sent to me by Karen Kwiatkowski. I found it somewhere, but it helps me to understand a little what is going on.

"I have been told by reporters that they will not report their own insights or contrary evaluations of the official 9/11 story, because to question the government story about 9/11 is to question the very foundations of our entire modern belief system regarding our government, our country, and our way of life.

"To be charged with questioning these foundations is far more serious than being labeled a disgruntled conspiracy nut or anti-government traitor, or even being sidelined or marginalized within an academic, government service, or literary career."

"To question the official 9/11 story is simply and fundamentally revolutionary. In this way, of course, questioning the official story is also simply and fundamentally American."

"Communist" used to be a pretty sharp dagger to be able to pull out and do some damage, and then it was "liberal."

Now conspiracy theorist or tin-foil hat carries the load, the punch the old-timers do not pack anymore.

Some say that "conspiracy theorists" need or desire or get satisfaction from the psychological warm, fuzzy of being in the know, fighting the power.

That's true.

That does feel good. *Mmmm-hmmm.*

Like a "sow-*na*."

Why would one not want to know what's going on.

Then why do some people "know" and some do not?

Coincidence? Serendipity?

I don't know.

Life experience, curiosity, you talked to this person, read this book, saw this video, maybe something like that. Desire to know what's going on.

I do not think it's a desire to know or think that people do bad things.

There are also many frustrations that go along with the warm, fuzzy of "being in the know."

There are so many people who do not know, who refuse to know and there is the frustration of living with that.

There is also the knowing that people are dying, living in poverty, being cheated out of decent lives, for whole generations, and that it is not just a matter of the curvature of the earth or coincidence, or "we tried, we did the best we could, but, well, sorry."

It's a matter of planning for certain people to die and live in poverty and some to live in unbelievable wealth.

The "knowing" goes something like this.

Knowing that the buildings on 9/11 were not brought down by fire and gravity.

Knowing that the evidence shows that nobody died at Sandy Hook, as wild as that sounds. The grieving parents are actors, the school was not a functioning school, only a stage, Gene Rosen, Wayne Carver are insanely ridiculous. Of course there's more, following, here, in this book in your hands.

Knowing about Oklahoma City that more bombs were found inside the building, knowing about the death of Officer Terry Yeakey.

Knowing about Boston would mean knowing about the photographic evidence of the backpacks of the "security" details, the photographic evidence showing that the injuries were faked.

And then, join the club.

Whether you want to or not, now you can see that the Bushes, Obama, Clinton, Biden, etc. etc., and Cooper, Maddow, Morgan, Williams, Lauer, etc., etc. are either CIA operatives or paid off by the CIA or whatever.

And that is the real world.

Take off your tin-foil hat. You don't need it anymore. You are living in reality.

There Is Only You

Once we thought we had hope.

We had Michael Moore.

We had pissed-off Republicans and that's always a good thing. We had Jon Stewart and Stephen Colbert from the home team fighting for the loose puck against the boards.

We had National Public Radio, The Progressive, The Nation, CommonDreams.org, Colbert at the Washington Reporters dinner, McNeil & Lehrer, Woodward & Bernstein, Peter Matthiessen ... the list is long and goes on and on.

But really it does not. It stops as it starts.

There is no list.

Not of big-time, powerful progressives telling the truth.

There is only Bill Hicks.

And you.

But he is dead.

And there was Jim Garrison.

And George Carlin did what he could.

We have a litany of heroes and we are thankful for that.

And there are these writers in this book and a hundred more like them around the world. But will that be enough? The world is big and it is so difficult to reach so many people when you cannot get on TV, in the big daily newspapers, on the popular liberal websites (Daily Kos: You are banned for saying 9/11).

For lack of just a few honest persons we have lived in Disneyland since at least 1963.

And now we have a new, advanced nano-termite, the kind that has been bred lately, they come up with terms like "cognitive infiltration."

Cass Sunstein, an academic and Washington, D.C. and elsewhere bigshot says that conspiracy theorists are dangerous, take up valuable time I guess, and need to be stopped by playing mind games, black ops in Bemidji. They do it elsewhere, have for decades. Why not here?

Especially here.

There is hope.
As with anything, you won't find it the first place you look. There is no hope in Michael Moore or Amy Goodman or Matt Rothschild or Jon Stewart, Rachel Maddow, Ruth Conniff.
Russ Baker? Chris Hedges?
Hmmm.
If it were me, I would go to the bottom of the barrel. That's where the good stuff is, the juice.
Hope is in the comments section.
Of James Tracy's Memory Hole Blog, the articles of Gordon Duff, Jim Fetzer and Kevin Barrett on Veterans Today. There are many people out there like you.
And so, we are not doomed.
Well, maybe not so fast.
Anyway, we've got good company.

Example:
APRIL 19, 2014 AT 1:23 AM
Excellent article, as usual, thanks. I can't help thinking that what we see today is actually relatively old. In my lifetime many have complained about the lies of the "press". This didn't begin with Kennedy, although that operation may have been the first leap into "in your face" boldness on their part.

For some time there was a certain concern to maintain at least the semblance of objectivity. Not anymore.

When I was young I remember people talking of the Soviet Union, of TASS and Pravda and how "those people are fed on lies". Naturally, the implication was that we were not. After all, the way it was supposed to work in a "democracy" was that we were "informed voters" and our government was responsive to our wishes.

How were we to be "informed" if our "news" could not be trusted? The major changes that I see are in the utter lack of pretext any longer for truth telling or "reporting". Coupling that with the technology of digital photography has enabled them to literally manufacture "reality" without having to actually go out and get the action shots needed to support their narrative.

Now, when their patrons want a meme, they simply manufacture one. When actual events occur they simply spin those in any direction they are told to. It isn't uncommon to flip through "news" channels and find the readers presenting the same material verbatim.

Aynesworth is obviously a classic "Mockingbird" graduate. In many ways the internet has enabled us to offer a curative solution for this. I suspect this presents a problem for them. As they lose viewers and the alternative media gains acceptance, they will, no doubt, take measures.

And a comment on the Citizens From Legitimate Government website:
These false-flag operations are concrete evidence of deeply malicious and dangerous private networks operating from within the depths of the national security state, which serves as the 'muscle' for the corporate elite.

These attacks were all designed to terrorize the community and to pave the way for new authoritarian legislation. All bore characteristics of a sophisticated, well-executed operation carried out with military precision by professionals likely working for a covert section of the military/intelligence community or a private contractor (Craft International, Blackwater, Booz Allen Hamilton). All were attributed to men whose level of professionalism is far below what was required.

Many of these men had ties to the U.S. Military and U.S. Intelligence. Most ended up dead, while the exceptions sat meekly in the interrogation room, under the control of the intelligence agencies, and, then, the courtroom, as a show trial (the verdict already decided by the media) ensured they would never be heard from again.

There are virtually always additional suspects (professionals) who are initially reported and seen by eyewitnesses but who disappear from all official reports. There is little evidence connecting the accused to the crime, and they are usually simply a decoy who is maneuvered into the wrong place at the wrong time.

There is nearly always a training exercise running shortly before, during, or scheduled for after the "attack." It always eerily mirrors what reportedly happened. Using a training exercise to provide "cover" for preparations or execution of a covert operation is an age-old technique of military deception.

The information flow is often heavily manipulated for the purpose of ensuring that damaging information is suppressed and to maximize the propaganda. The latter is accomplished through the airing of fake interviews, with actors posing as witnesses, authorities and grievers. It also often involves airing fake video footage or photographs of the event. This requires the full collaboration of the mainstream media and those few corporations that own it.

What all of this represents is a full-scale psychological warfare campaign against the international public. It is designed to sew fear throughout the community, thus resulting in submission to authority. It is a "strategy of tension" that has been in operation for quite some time now. [20]

We are all patsies now.
Though we owe apologies to Lee Harvey Oswald, Osama bin Laden, James Earl Ray, Mark David Chapman, John Hinkley, Jr., Sirhan Bishara Sirhan, those guys with three names, and some with two as well: Timothy McVeigh, Adam Lanza, James Holmes.

Who else? There are more.

They came for them and we watched TV, we cheered the fighters flyover the ball game, we ate strawberry swirl ice cream and watched American Idol, went back for more, we worked religiously and we went to church with reckless abandon.

And some day, a Tuesday morning or Wednesday afternoon, nondescript, they will come for us.

False flags make sense.

They make all things possible.

Three dead teenagers means it makes sense for Israel to invade Gaza. A missing plane and then that plane crashes in the Ukraine with dead bodies and it makes sense to somebody to do something. Gives them license.

"A" follows B, C.

And we all say, oh, yeah, yep, okay.

That's why "they" do it.

"... That's not the way the world really works anymore. We're an empire now, and when we act, we create our own reality. And while you're studying that reality — judiciously, as you will — we'll act again, creating other new realities, which you can study too, and that's how things will sort out. We're history's actors ... and you, all of you, will be left to just study what we do." — Karl Rove

Children "die" at Sandy Hook, people "die" at the Boston Marathon, in a theater in Aurora, Colorado, a federal building in Oklahoma City, in some giant buildings in New York City.

And then, yes, it makes sense. Now we can do that. Before we couldn't, but now we can.

Let's go.

Let's roll.

Let's boogie.

Why can't people just live.

Why can't we all just be good to each other, take what we need and give some to somebody else.

Why do some people have to be Karl Rove, Dick Cheney, George Bush, Bill Clinton, Hillary Clinton, Barack Obama.

Why?

That's a hard question, the why.

Or not.

There is a photo in an article on Veterans Today that is interesting. (July 25, 2014)

It shows the photographer from *The Newtown Bee* newspaper taking the photo of the children being evacuated from the Sandy Hook school. That photo ran on the front page of *The New York Times* and the *Los Angeles Times*, and elsewhere.

It's a photo of her taking the photo in a casual setting, setting up the photo, setting it up to be iconic.

This shows that the photo was a setup.

It shows that Sandy Hook was a setup.

It is the thread that starts the shredding, that unravels the United States, the bad part, the criminal, the treasonous. Sure, there is still a big, good part.

This article, set of articles, by Jim Fetzer and others on Sandy Hook is bigger than the Watergate reporting by Woodward & Bernstein, and more truthful.

It shows that President Barack Obama, that pillar of anti-terror and hunting down the bad guys, is a terrorist.

He surely knows about all of this, as does his Head of the Department of Justice, Eric Holder.

This means that the Department of Homeland Security is a terrorist organization.

Terror At The Marathon

The Boston Globe of course ran a big special section in Metro: "Globe coverage of the April 15, 2013 bombings at the Boston Marathon and the events that followed."

It also featured an iconic photo of an older runner on the ground and three police officers standing over him after coming to his aid. That photo also was featured on the cover of *Sports Illustrated.*

Great shot, probably award-winning. Would have been better with some cherry-red blood, though. It's got green and some red, but blood would really pop.

There was supposed to be blood, I think.

There is a video that shows someone running just in front of him tossing something back to that old man just as the bomb goes off, a packet of some sort. But, alas, he fumbles with it and does not get the nice cherry red on his legs as the Globe photographer, ready and steady, rushes up, and we are left with what might have been.

But then again, why wouldn't the old man have just carried the packet with him rather than have it tossed? But it remains that something is tossed to him as the bomb goes off, he tries to catch it, does not, falls down, gets on the cover of *Sports Illustrated.*

His back is to the camera, but it's still *Sports Illustrated,* man.

The old man is only one of so many Boston "victims," who like World Cup soccer players, are flopping all around the sidewalk with wide mouths and looking for who is noticing out the corner of their eyes.

That Globe special section has it all. We are not left to wonder. It's in your local newspaper. The rest of the story, the way it is.

"Trauma survivor now acting as a beacon of inspiration"

"Officer wounded in shoot-out heads home"

"Tsarnaev indicted on 30 counts"

"Times Square was next target, officials say"

"Tsarnaev friend tells of beliefs in conspiracies"

"Russians secretly recorded Tsarnaev calls, talks of jihad"

The Official Story of Sandy Hook
From "Swallowing The Camel":

On the morning of December 14, 2012, 20-year-old Adam Lanza shot and killed his mother, Nancy Lanza, in the home they shared in Newtown, Connecticut.

He then drove his mother's Honda Civic to Sandy Hook Elementary School with four semi-automatic firearms licensed to Nancy.

He took three of the guns with him when he entered the school.

Using a Bushmaster XM15-E2S rifle, he shot his way into the locked building at approximately 9:35 AM local time. Between that time and about 9:49 AM, he killed principal Dawn Hochsprung, school psychologist Mary Sherlach, teacher Natalie Hammond, first-grade teacher Victoria Soto, teacher's aide Anne Marie Murphy, substitute first-grade teacher Lauren Rousseau, and 20 students who were 6 years old or younger.

Six-year-old Dylan Hockley was autistic. Lanza shot all but two of his child victims multiple times; 6-year-old Noah Pozner was shot 11 times. All of the staff members died trying to stop the gunman or shield their students. Ms. Murphy covered Dylan Hockley's body with her own. Throughout the school, teachers and faculty members hid children in closets and bathrooms, thereby saving an untold number of lives.

Six children fled Ms. Soto's classroom and escaped from the school, making their way to the driveway of a home owned by Gene Rosen.

Before police could reach him, Lanza returned to Soto's classroom and shot himself in the head with a Glock 10mm.

His motivation remains obscure, but Lanza reportedly suffered mental and emotional problems that left him socially isolated and unable to work full-time or complete college.

Around the time of the massacre, Nancy Lanza told friends she was considering leaving New England and attempting to enroll Adam in college for a third time.

Adam had access to the weapons because his mother was an avid collector who had taught both of her sons how to shoot.

(http://swallowingthecamel.wordpress.com/2013/08/16/sandy-hook-truth-9-months-later/)

Journalism 101, 101.1, 101.2

Jim Fetzer, Kevin Barrett, Sophia Smallstorm, James Tracy, Gordon Duff, Wolfgang Halbig, and others have been doing real reporting, real journalism in the U.S.A., which has been missing since Penn Jones, Jr. ran the weekly in Midlothian, Texas.

I so admire Penn Jones, Jr.

I would like to share an email exchange I had awhile back with an editor of a small daily newspaper in northern Minnesota, Bill Hanna of the *Mesabi Daily News* of Virginia, Minnesota.

I was thinking that I would like to see if there would be any part-time reporting work I might be able to do, so I sent out email notes to the area papers.

Bill Hanna said:
Mike:
Would you be open at all to a full-time opportunity of reporting/editing?

Bill,
I might be.
What do you have?
Could we talk about it in person?
Maybe next Monday or Tuesday? Could I come up and visit?

Mike:
Nothing definite.
Just doing some adjusting in newsroom.
Always willing to talk to anyone.
Just curious why you got out of business. It's been quite a while now and changes have been big.

And so I told him ...

Then ...

From Bill Hanna:

Mike:
Certainly respect anyone's opinions.
But with such advocacy don't see you as a fit in a very good small daily newspaper. We are about good community journalism, not novels or anti-war views or chasing 9/11 theories or blaming the media.
Thanks for your comments and good luck. - Bill

Well, thanks to Penn Jones Jr., at least the entire history of American journalism, small town and big town, has not been a disgrace.

And I think it also bears mentioning at this point that the German journalists who supported and carried out the Nazi propaganda were also put on trial at Nuremberg.

... And that exchange with Bill Hanna, longtime American journalist, reminds me of who I am, why I'm doing this, reminds me of the day that I quit the *Ainsworth Star-Journal* after my column was canceled because I said I do not support the troops of Desert Storm.

... Did you see the piece in *The Chronicle of Higher Education* about how the CIA helped to fund the Iowa Writers Workshop in order to influence creative writing in America to fit the American Cold War stance?

Have you heard of Project Mockingbird? Do you read newspapers anymore? Watch the News on TV, listen to the news on your local radio station?

Is there anywhere, any place left to go in America?

Well, it's all closing in, been closing in for years, closing up, tight.

Okay now... quickly ... we need to get to the real book, enough window-dressing.

David Swanson, Daily Kos, Mathew Rothschild, Chris Matthews, Bill Moyers, Garrison Keillor, Geneva Overholser, Ruth Conniff, Eric Alterman, Maureen Dowd, Jeremy Scahill, Arianna Huffington, Glenn Greenwald, James Fallows, Amy Goodman, Chris Hedges, Jon Stewart, Stephen Colbert, Rachel Maddow — and there are hundreds more names that go here ... liberal members of the mainstream media — please tell me why you do not tell the truth about 9/11, Boston, Sandy Hook, as you must know ... not that I assume I know the answer ... I think I do, but I might be wrong ... I want to know and I am not being sarcastic, not yet, not now ... I am pleading here, asking for knowledge, to know ...

Why, though you claim boldly to be a real journalist, and by that I assume that you are not a CIA or FBI agent in journalist disguise — why you do not go after the biggest, blockbuster stories of ours or any other generation.

And the underlying story — that you won't touch this with a twelve-foot pole — is also one of the most un-talked about big stories of our time.

Please, contact me, Mike Palecek, at nwestiowa@gmail.com to arrange to be on The New American Dream Radio Show and let's talk about it.

"Waterboarding Anderson Cooper," sponsored by Mr. Bubble
If we are going to torture people who we say we think are terrorists but we know are not really terrorists because we did 911, there are no terrorists,

no Al Queda, no reason for war, and really no information we can gain, other than to perpetuate the lie, go deeper into the story of the lie, build and embellish the lie fable — then why not also waterboard people who we know are terrorists, who were in fact *our* terrorists, who helped us to lie a long time ago and overturn our own country — And! And!

This terrorist is one of those who really is there, who really knows the truth — and what he knows is actually real — no need to fake kill him and fake bury him at sea –One or two or maybe three quick sessions — which are not really such a big deal anyway, right? Would change the course of this whole country.

Just one little Goon Afternoon live on national TV.

The Committee To Waterboard Anderson Cooper — CIA agent fake reporter, who knows what is really happening.

… Reporters used to be on our side, like Penn Jones Jr. and the little Texas weekly he operated. They are not anymore. The CIA has money and they figured it out. Money sells, it works, that's how things operate.

Bob Woodward, from the office of naval intelligence, Dan Rather, Tom Brokaw, Peter Jennings: pour a bucket of water on his grave, *that* son of a bitch; Peter Matthiessen, started the Paris Review to spy on Americans in France for the CIA, it likely goes on much further than we dare to imagine. William Buckley, also CIA. Those are just the ones we know of, the tip of the iceberg, as they say.

Read Carl Bernstein's article in Rolling Stone, Google Operation Mockingbird. … etc. etc.

We are The Committee To Waterboard Anderson Cooper — it's not really that bad anyway — endorsed by Allen Dulles, Dick Cheney, George Bush, George Bush, John Yoo, Barrack Obama, two jugglers, one hot air balloonist, three that we know of night shift welders, thirty-three dental hygienists, and millions of folks like you.

Sponsored by Mr. Bubble … gets you so clean your mother won't know you.

Coming soon:

Waterboarding Ruth Paine, Thane Eugene Caesar, Lon Horiuchi, H. Wayne Carver, Gene Rosen, and Robbie Parker.

Noteworthy:
The conspiracy theory CIA memo
The Global Terrorism Database
Teaching Terror in School

The conspiracy theory CIA memo

IA Document 1035-960
Concerning Criticism of the Warren Report
1. Our Concern. From the day of President Kennedy's assassination on, there has been speculation about the responsibility for his murder. Although this was stemmed for a time by the Warren Commission Report, (which appeared at the end of September 1964), various writers have now had time to scan the Commission's published report and documents for new pretexts for questioning, and there has been a new wave of books and articles criticizing the Commission's findings. In most cases the critics have speculated as to the existence of some kind of conspiracy, and often they have implied that the Commission itself was involved. Presumably as a result of the increasing challenge to the Warren Commission's report, a public opinion poll recently indicated that 46 percent of the American public did not think that Oswald acted alone, while more than half of those polled thought that the Commission had left some questions unresolved. Doubtless polls abroad would show similar, or possibly more adverse results.

2. This trend of opinion is a matter of concern to the U.S. government, including our organization. The members of the Warren Commission were naturally chosen for their integrity, experience and prominence. They represented both major parties, and they and their staff were deliberately drawn from all sections of the country. Just because of the standing of the Commissioners, efforts to impugn their rectitude and wisdom tend to cast doubt on the whole leadership of American society. Moreover, there seems to be an increasing tendency to hint that President Johnson himself, as the one person who might be said to have benefited, was in some way responsible for the assassination.

Innuendo of such seriousness affects not only the individual concerned, but also the whole reputation of the American government. Our organization itself is directly involved: among other facts, we contributed information to the investigation. Conspiracy theories have frequently thrown suspicion on our organization, for example by falsely alleging that Lee Harvey Oswald worked for us. The aim of this dispatch is to provide material countering and discrediting the claims of the conspiracy theorists, so as to inhibit the circulation of such claims in other countries. Background information is supplied in a classified section and in a number of unclassified attachments.

3. Action. We do not recommend that discussion of the assassination question be initiated where it is not already taking place. Where discussion is active [business] addresses are requested:

a. To discuss the publicity problem with [?] and friendly elite contacts (especially politicians and editors), pointing out that the Warren Commission made as thorough an investigation as humanly possible, that the charges of the critics are without serious foundation, and that further speculative discussion only plays into the hands of the opposition. Point out also that parts of the conspiracy talk appear to be deliberately generated by Communist propagandists. Urge them to use their influence to discourage unfounded and irresponsible speculation.

b. To employ propaganda assets to [negate] and refute the attacks of the critics. Book reviews and feature articles are particularly appropriate for this purpose. The unclassified attachments to this guidance should provide useful background material for passing to assets. Our ploy should point out, as applicable, that the critics are (I) wedded to theories adopted before the evidence was in, (I) politically interested, (III) financially interested, (IV) hasty and inaccurate in their research, or (V) infatuated with their own theories. In the course of discussions of the whole phenomenon of criticism, a useful strategy may be to single out Epstein's theory for attack, using the attached Fletcher [?] article and Spectator piece for background. (Although Mark Lane's book is much less convincing that Epstein's and comes off badly where confronted by knowledgeable critics, it is also much more difficult to answer as a whole, as one becomes lost in a morass of unrelated details.)

4. In private to media discussions not directed at any particular writer, or in attacking publications which may be yet forthcoming, the following arguments should be useful:

a. No significant new evidence has emerged which the Commission did not consider. The assassination is sometimes compared (e.g., by Joachim Joesten and Bertrand Russell) with the Dreyfus case; however, unlike that case, the attack on the Warren Commission have produced no new evidence, no new culprits have been convincingly identified, and there is no agreement among the critics. (A better parallel, though an imperfect one, might be with the Reichstag fire of 1933, which some competent historians (Fritz Tobias, A.J.P. Taylor, D.C. Watt) now believe was set by Vander Lubbe on his own initiative, without acting for either Nazis or Communists; the Nazis tried to pin the blame on the Communists, but the latter have been more successful in convincing the world that the Nazis were to blame.)

b. Critics usually overvalue particular items and ignore others. They tend to place more emphasis on the recollections of individual witnesses (which are less reliable and more divergent -- and hence offer more hand-holds for criticism) and less on ballistics, autopsy, and photographic evidence. A close examination of the Commission's records will usually show that the conflicting eyewitness accounts are quoted out of context, or were discarded by the Commission for good and sufficient reason.

c. Conspiracy on the large scale often suggested would be impossible to conceal in the United States, esp. since informants could expect to receive large royalties, etc. Note that Robert Kennedy, Attorney General at the time and John F. Kennedy's brother, would be the last man to overlook or conceal any conspiracy. And as one reviewer pointed out, Congressman Gerald R. Ford would hardly have held his tongue for the sake of the Democratic administration, and Senator Russell would have had every political interest in exposing any misdeeds on the part of Chief Justice Warren. A conspirator moreover would hardly choose a location for a shooting where so much depended on conditions beyond his control: the route, the speed of the cars, the moving target, the risk that the assassin would be discovered. A group of wealthy conspirators could have arranged much more secure conditions.

d. Critics have often been enticed by a form of intellectual pride: they light on some theory and fall in love with it; they also scoff at the Commission because it did not always answer every question with a flat decision one way or the other. Actually, the make-up of the Commission and its staff was an excellent safeguard against over-commitment to any one theory, or against the illicit transformation of probabilities into certainties.

e. Oswald would not have been any sensible person's choice for a co-conspirator. He was a "loner," mixed up, of questionable reliability and an unknown quantity to any professional intelligence service.

f. As to charges that the Commission's report was a rush job, it emerged three months after the deadline originally set. But to the degree that the Commission tried to speed up its reporting, this was largely due to the pressure of irresponsible speculation already appearing, in some cases coming from the same critics who, refusing to admit their errors, are now putting out new criticisms.

g. Such vague accusations as that "more than ten people have died mysteriously" can always be explained in some natural way e.g.: the individuals concerned have for the most part died of natural causes; the Commission staff questioned 418 witnesses (the FBI interviewed far more people, conduction 25,000 interviews and re interviews), and in such a large group, a certain number of deaths are to be expected. (When Penn Jones, one of the originators of the "ten mysterious deaths" line, appeared on television, it emerged that two of the deaths on his list were from heart attacks, one from cancer, one was from a head-on collision on a bridge, and one occurred when a driver drifted into a bridge abutment.)

5. Where possible, counter speculation by encouraging reference to the Commission's Report itself. Open-minded foreign readers should still be

impressed by the care, thoroughness, objectivity and speed with which the Commission worked. Reviewers of other books might be encouraged to add to their account the idea that, checking back with the report itself, they found it far superior to the work of its critics.

The Global Terrorism Database
(http://www.start.umd.edu)

At START, National Consortium for the Study of Terrorism and Responses To Terrorism, you can find all sorts of stuff, a list of terror actions, lists of terror groups.

You will find a PDF file: Integrated United States Security Database (IUSSD): Data on the Terrorist Attacks in the United States Homeland, 1970 to 2011.

(http://www.start.umd.edu/sites/default/files/files/publications/START_IUSSDDataTerroristAttacksUS_1970-2011.pdf)

And to think that it's all based in lies. I think they do this because if there is so much information and such a nice website, it has to be true.

Much the same for the *Washington Post* in-depth articles about the Tsarnaev brothers and their history. If there is some guy who knew them when they said this or that back then, then the whole lie we are asking you to believe is true.

I know, right?

College Terrorism 101
(Or Nothing Is Over Until We Say It's Over ... Was It Over When The Germans Bombed Pearl Harbor? Hell No! ... And It Ain't Over Now!)

Kevin Barrett and James Tracy, university professors, have both been hounded because of their attempts to teach critical inquiry into important topics.

Here is an example from the "other side".

Why is it allowed?

TERRORISM SINCE 9/11 The American Cases
March 2014

"This book includes a detailed discussion, each organized in a similar manner, of the cases that have come to light of Islamist extremist terrorism since 9/11, whether based in the United States or abroad, in which the United States itself has been, or apparently has been, targeted. It mostly springs from papers generated in honors seminars I conducted at Ohio State University. I have added an introduction as well as a headnote for each case. Since we plan to update, revise, and correct, and then to re-post from time to time, each case study and each headnote is dated and carries its own individual pagination. — John Mueller

"Included in this study, then, are cases of four types:

1) Islamist extremist conspiracies or connections that, in the view of the authorities, might eventually develop into plots to commit violence in the United States,

2) Islamist extremist terrorist plots to commit violence in the United States, no matter how embryonic, that have been disrupted,

3) Islamist extremist plots to commit violence in the United States that were essentially created or facilitated in a major way by the authorities and then rolled up by arrest when enough evidence was accumulated—including in some cases having the would-be perpetrator actually push the button that he mistakenly believed would set off an explosion, and

4) Cases in which an Islamist extremist terrorist or terrorist group actually commits, or tried to commit, violence in the United States."

http://politicalscience.osu.edu/faculty/jmueller/SINCE.pdf

James Tracy, on his website Memory Hole Blog, mentioned Attorney General Eric Holder's concern with "homegrown extremists":

"Eric Holder wants to convey his all-consuming concern over 'lone wolf homegrown violent extremists' who have 'domestic concerns.' *http://memoryholeblog.com/2014/07/15/americas-real-homegorwn-extremists/*

Tracy was writing about a Holder appearance on a TV news show, ABC This Week with George Stephanopoulos, to talk about these domestic threats that "keep him up at night," specifically the Tsarnaev brothers and the individuals involved in the Las Vegas shooting of two police officers.

In the article Tracy goes on to discuss the anomalies of the Las Vegas event.

• Government "fusion centers" are a part of the Department of Homeland Security's vast network to fight so-called terrorism.

Fusion center:
A fusion center is an information sharing center, many of which were jointly created between 2003 and 2007 under the U.S. Department of Homeland Security and the Office of Justice Programs in the U.S. Department of Justice.

They are designed to promote information sharing at the federal level between agencies such as the Central Intelligence Agency (CIA), Federal Bureau of Investigation (FBI), U.S. Department of Justice, U.S. military, and state- and local-level government. As of July 2009, the U.S. Department of Homeland Security recognized at least 72 fusion centers. Fusion centers may also be affiliated with an Emergency Operations Center that responds in the event of a disaster.

The fusion process is an overarching method of managing the flow of information and intelligence across levels and sectors of government to integrate information for analysis.[1] That is, the process relies on the active involvement of state, local, tribal, and federal law enforcement agencies — and sometimes on non-law enforcement agencies (e.g., private sector) — to provide the input of raw information for intelligence analysis. As the array of diverse information sources increases, there will be more accurate and robust analysis that can be disseminated as intelligence.

We also find a senate report that says fusion centers are a waste of time, there is no domestic terrorism.

"A two-year senate investigation found that "the fusion centers often produced irrelevant, useless or inappropriate intelligence reporting to DHS, and many produced no intelligence reporting whatsoever."[2][3] The report also said that in some cases the fusion centers violated civil liberties or privacy.[4]"

Okay, Let's Make A List
Wikipedia has a long list for "Terrorism in the United States," beginning with the lynching of a slavery abolitionist in 1837.

The list *(http://en.wikipedia.org/wiki/Terrorism_in_the_United_States)* includes references to Ted Kacynski, John Brown, John Wilkes Booth, McKinley, anarchist bombings, Orlando Letelier, David Gunn, Medgar Evers, Alan Berg, The Earth Liberation Front, and many others.

It also includes groupings of terrorism by type: KKK, Christian extremism, anarchism, leftist militancy, black militancy, Puerto Rican nationalists, and more.

So, there is a lot to choose from and where do we begin?

Well, my time is short and I've already talked too long, so I must begin and end with government false terrorism, false flags.

Definition of False Flag
"False flag terrorism" occurs when elements within a government stage a secret operation whereby government forces pretend to be a targeted enemy while attacking their own forces or people. The attack is then falsely blamed on the enemy in order to justify going to war against that enemy. Or as Wikipedia defines it:

False flag operations are covert operations conducted by governments, corporations, or other organizations, which are designed to deceive the public in such a way that the operations appear as if they are being carried out by other entities. The name is derived from the military concept of flying false colors; that is, flying the flag of a country other than one's own. False flag operations are not limited to war and counter-insurgency operations, and have been used in peace-time; for example, during Italy's strategy of tension.

The term comes from the old days of wooden ships, when one ship would hang the flag of its enemy before attacking another ship in its own navy. Because the enemy's flag was hung instead of the flag of the real country of the attacking ship, it was called a "false flag" attack.

It's All About Me
The mind of an American rules the world.

The President? Warren Buffett? Tiger Woods? Katie Couric? Jon Stewart? The Michelin Man?

No, stupid, it's you.

You are king of the world, god, superman, King Midas, all that.

It's you.

You are more than just a legend in your own mind.

You are The Man.

And when the CIA through the CIA propaganda machine called Radio Free Europe or the American Free Press tells you the Russians are coming or the criminals are coming or terrorists or the Iranians or Iraqis of Afghans on nuclear-powered blue donkeys or big bees, and you believe it — well, then, Zeke, that's how the world will go.

You are powerful, the most powerful yahoo who has ever lived in the history of living.

And you are an idiot.

And the world is going to burn.

You are not an idiot-on-purpose, but an idiot none-the-less.

The CIA, the persons in the CIA, are smart.

But they are evil.

The actual Evil Empire.

And they control you.

The most powerful person in the world.

If you were not an idiot they could not do that.

But you are an idiot.

And that's a bummer, man.

That's a bummer.

... Do you read comment sections that follow most articles on the internet.
I do.

Sometimes they are very instructive.

These comments followed an article that spoke about two candidates in Arkansas who both believe that Sandy Hook was a hoax.

Let's listen in, be a fly on the wall in the kitchen on a hot summer morning in Arkansas.

It could be fun.

We might learn something.

"This is absolutely shameful. I'm an Arkansan now living in New York. My husband works with the father of one of the children who died in that massacre. To deny what happened there is absolutely disgusting."

"Another pair of crawly-bottom mouth breathers. Wonder how much they'll get from the money slingers."

"These people are scum. And the people who vote for them are scum."

"These guys wouldn't have to go very far to check out their claim. Jesse Lewis, a six-year-old "alleged" victim had (has?) relatives in NW Arkansas. Go find one of them and ask if Jesse is still alive. Dare you."

"Amazing that we live in an era where facts don't matter. The mass media's unwillingness to call anything a lie is partially to blame."

"Just no words....... I MEAN REALLY?"

"This subject got me to thinking about similar hoaxes. Max alluded to one of them. The moon landing never happened. It was just a plot to sell Tang. Certain Iranians and the KKK also tell us that the Holocaust never happened. That was an evil ploy to build sympathy for the Jews for their annexation of some prime real estate in the Middle East. You know how Jews are... If course if the Holocaust is fictional, you would wonder whether or not the whole context of it was all made up. World War II? How about World War I? All this supposedly happened before I was born. How could I confirm it!? Maybe the newspapers just hated Germans and Japs. Makes sense to me. Civil War? Doubtful. Slavery? Laughable, couldn't possibly be truth -- just an excuse for welfare queens and affirmative action...and Obama. It's hard to know for sure about anything unless you were actually there at the time. There are very few truths of which we can be absolutely certain. One of them is that Jesus Christ died for your sins 2014 years ago so that 7 or 8 of us can go to Heaven some day and that Jesus' dad ordered us to stone gays to death with stones about a thousand years prior to that. Other than that, we can know very little for an absolute fact."

"i like them to have seen the look on my 17 yr old cousins face and the 4 funerals we saw when we visited her in newton,ct on dec.19,2012. plus all the new media from new york city that was present throughout the town. she was in school at the high school; which was across the parking lot from sandy hook."

"Now let me get this straight ... these people who pretend to see and talk to Jesus missed 2 weeks, at least, of non-stop TV coverage...67 dozen clips of little body bags being loaded in ambulances & hearses? They believe in some ghosts that no one has ever laid eyes on in over 2000 years ... but they don't believe 20 little grade school kids were slaughtered by a crazy man with super powerful weapons that never should be allowed in private homes. Wonder if these 2 guys believes bullets actually come from the muzzle of a gun? Do they believe guns are real? Do they think it might hurt to be shot...even with just a 22 ... do they think bullets bounce off human skin ... even little girl skin? Do they understand firearms at all? Do they not also think firearms are dangerous and can kill? Maybe if someone shot them they'd smarten up ... they'd not be having any grey area if they experienced bright red blood gushing out of their bodies. I never heard of anyone so stupid they had to be shot to learn a lesson but these guys might be setting a new trend in ignorance. Anyone who votes for them when the election comes should be fenced off from the rest of the community too. What kind of human votes for candidates this dog-stupid? ... my apologies to dogs. You don't have to have kids to still be super upset about the massacre at Sandy Hook but let me tell you as a parent, I doubt there's anything that would make me suddenly get real unfriendly faster than an idiot saying the massacre at Sandy Hook didn't happen. Are we sure we're sure about America being a good country? And if so, what are we basing that assumption on?"

"If one (such as Trump) believes a 6 week old Kenyan kid could sneak himself and his parents into Hawaii AND post date his birth certificate into public records, with the master plan of world domination 50 years later, faking a mass elementary shooting is small potatoes! Too bad the magical Kenyan infant hadn't spoken to infant Ted Cruz and found out an American Mother is all you need to be a citizen. When I was 6 weeks old all I thought about was titties, sleeping and crapping (not much different 50 years old). Only Bill Clinton and Barack Obama were able to scheme stealing the POTUS intrauterine. What next? Obama packed the Boston Pressure Cooker Bomb for those fellows? Obama is loosing his touch, those Eastern European brothers botched the marathon unpleasantry by getting caught!
Ignorant people are gullible ... and we have lots of ignorant people."

"My Lord has everyone gone Bonkers ... Saying Sandy Hook was a Hoax. What do you think the Families of all the victims would think? If this is the way you think we do not need any of you in any position. ED Moser you need to re think what you said, NO a matter of fact keep thinking it and you will never win. Get a life people. Check your facts before opening your mouths."

"Since these two jokers lack the intelligence (and courage) to travel to Sandy Hook and conduct an unfettered investigation, perhaps they can get to a nearby gun-control hoax, in Jonesboro. If they were to go there, I would recommend flak jackets (preferably faulty ones made by a company connected to Cheney), an escort of fast-retreating local journalists, and a medical team of first-year health administration students on standby. I'm certain that as soon as these would-be politicians started asking relatives if the Westside Middle School massacre was a hoax orchestrated by gun control fanatics, the relatives would be exercising their perceived 2nd Amendment rights. Here are two articles obviously planted by George Soros and Islamic Jihadists to cunningly disarm."

"Jesus wept."

"We moved here from California six years ago and love it. Really friendly people, lots of whom, when they hear California, will mention the Breakfast State: full of nuts and fruit. That always makes me give them a huge smile. Nuts and fruit indeed."
(www.arktimes.com/ArkansasBlog/archives/2014/06/16/sandy-hook-massacre-a-hoax-two-arkansas-candidates-seem-to-think-so)

American History 101
Lee Harvey Oswald did not kill John F. Kennedy
Sirhan Sirhan did not kill Robert F. Kennedy
James Earl Ray did not kill Martin Luther King, Jr.
Timothy McVeigh did not blow up the Oklahoma City Murrah Federal Building on his own
Osama bin Laden was not buried at sea, did not plan, take part in the attacks of Sept. 11, 2001
The U.S. Government burned children alive on purpose at Waco
Senator Paul Wellstone was assassinated in a plane crash in the north woods forest near Eveleth, MN because he opposed the coming war on Iraq
Adam Lanza did not kill anyone, if he even existed
Nobody died at Sandy Hook.
Nobody died at Boston.

There are many lies that make up official United States History 101.
Not all are exactly false flags, but the lies, the lies.
One of big, interesting questions for me is how do they do this? Internally and also intellectually ... it's fascinating ... a mystery ... also the mystery of the liberal pundits - big names who either won't say anything or attack the conspiracy theorists.
Kevin Barrett told me: *Well, they are psychopaths, that's how.*
But that doesn't do it for me. There is more than that.
"They are all just crazy."
I would say they are probably not all crazy, probably none of them are

crazy. That's more in the direction of what I really feel, believe.

I think it is more in line with what someone once said about the banality of evil.

Of course, it's in all of us, but still.

I think what happens, perhaps, is that people do evil while believing they are doing good.

Or maybe it's for the money.

Maybe the excitement.

Something to do. I know from experience that Tuesday afternoons almost never end.

The power.

Hmmm.

It's all so very interesting and so very frustrating, seemingly impossible to get to, the inner workings of how these things happen, why, by whom, how and when and where are they planned, carried out, covered up.

You have to agree that it's fascinating.

Jon Rappoport was on James Tracy's radio show, and he said this, in talking about how "they" do what they do, how they create this world where we have these people on the Arkansas blog and the people next to us in church and at the stoplight not knowing, like The Truman Show, what reality really is.

Rappoport is talking about the mindset of these actual planners, maybe Karl Rove, maybe Rahm Emmanuel, maybe some smart guys in a nice office with lots of windows in Utah, who all go to the same church and play on the same summer softball team in Bluffdale.

"... how am I going to frame reality today so that the population receives it and accepts it so that there really is no difference between what they perceive and the reality that I am inventing for them, the painter. It's a marriage. It isn't just the painting I am painting, it's also the embrace of the painting by that individual."

(Jon Rappoport on James Tracy radio show, Checkin' It Out ... http:// memoryholeblog.com/2014/07/13/journalism-education-and-the-matrix/)

And maybe there you have it.

Remember The White Rose: Sophie, Hans, Alexander, Kurt, Christoph, Willi.

Be The White Rose.

Notes

[1] The Heritage Foundations published on April 25, 2012 "50 Terror Attacks Foiled Since 9/11."
http://www.heritage.org/research/reports/2012/04/fifty-terror-plots-foiled-since-9-11-the-homegrown-threat-and-the-long-war-on-terrorism
[1A] John Avlon, The Daily Beast, Sept. 8, 2011, "Forty-Five Foiled Terror Plots Since 9/11
http://www.thedailybeast.com/articles/2011/09/08/9-11-anniversary-45-terror-plots-foiled-in-last-10-years.html
[2] Sheila Casey, Rock Creek Free Press, April 2009, "Eyewitnesses Contradict Pentagon Story" – Lloyde England, taxi cab driver whose cab was said to have been hit by a light pole sheered off by the plane that hit the Pentagon.
[3] Ceecee Lyles airphone call allegedly from UA93
https://www.youtube.com/watch?v=LiX7mNV4ab0
[4] Haymarket bombs
http://www.deathandtaxesmag.com/67874/republican-lawyer-recommended-false-flag-operation-to-discredit-wisconsin-unions/
[5] "The Mother of All Black Ops: The Palmer Raids Were Another Mass Deception of the American People … "
http://9-11themotherofallblackoperations.blogspot.com/2010/03/palmer-raids-were-another-mass_11.html
[6] "Western Governments Admit Carrying Out 'False Flag' Terror", Veterans Today
http://www.veteranstoday.com/2011/03/28/western-governments-admit-carrying-out-false-flag-terror/
[7] "In Praise of Shadows": Morris Berman's acceptance speech for the 2013 Neil Postman Award
http://www.teemingbrain.com/tag/morris-berman/
[8] 911: Say It Ain't So, Howard Zinn!
http://www.globalresearch.ca/9-11-say-it-ain-t-so-howard-zinn/13488
[9] Howard Zinn: "I Don't Care" If 9/11 Was An Inside Job, Prison Planet,
http://www.prisonplanet.com/howard-zinn-i-dont-care-if-911-was-an-inside-job.html
[10] We Are Change Confrontations
https://www.youtube.com/playlist?list=PLECC886187911762D
[10] Jim Fetzer: Top Ten Reasons Sandy Hook Was An Elaborate Hoax
http://www.veteranstoday.com/2014/01/07/top-ten-reasons-sandy-hook-was-an-elaborate-hoax/
[10] Kevin Barrett: U.S. Needs Pro-Democracy Revolution"
http://www.presstv.com/detail/2014/04/18/359029/us-needs-prodemocracy-revolution/
[10] James Tracy: State Propaganda, Historical Revisionism, and Perpetuation of the 9/11 Myth"
http://memoryholeblog.com/2012/05/06/state-propaganda-historical-

revisionism-and-perpetuation-of-the-911-myth/

[11] "Police File On Newtown Yields Chilling Portrait"
http://bigstory.ap.org/article/police-file-be-released-newtown-shooting-0

[12] Kevin Barrett/NY Times DC correspondent covers up 9/11
http://www.presstv.ir/detail/2013/12/27/342150/nyts-dc-correspondent-covers-up-911/

[13] "Guardians of the National Mythos"
http://memoryholeblog.com/2014/04/18/guardians-of-the-national-mythos/#more-10670

[14] Kevin Barrett, Press TV, "DC Correspondent Covers Up 9/11"
http://www.presstv.com/detail/2013/12/27/342150/nyts-dc-correspondent-covers-up-911/

[15] Ten False Flags That Changed The World, Joe Crubaugh, *joecrubaugh.com/blog/2007/01/18/10-false-flags-that-changed-the-world/*

[16] Terrorist Plots, Helped Along by the FBI [15]
http://www.nytimes.com/2012/04/29/opinion/sunday/terrorist-plots-helped-along-by-the-fbi.html?pagewanted=all&_r=0

[17] Duff, "Gladio, The Gift That Keeps on Giving," Veterans Today
http://www.veteranstoday.com/2014/03/07/gladio-the-gift-that-keeps-on-giving/

[18] "Tin Foil Hat or Not," by Gordon Duff, Veterans Today
http://www.veteranstoday.com/2014/02/09/tin-foil-hat-or-not/

[19] Comments Section, Memory Hole Blog
[ ] *lophatt* says:
APRIL 19, 2014 AT 1:23 AM
http://memoryholeblog.com/2014/04/18/guardians-of-the-national-mythos/comment-page-1/#comments

[20] Comments for "False Flag Stew"
http://www.legitgov.org/False-Flag-Stew

Contributors

Dennis Cimino has extensive engineering and support experience with military electronics, predominantly US Navy Combat Systems, was the Navy's top EMI troubleshooter before he went to work for Raytheon in the 1980s. He has collaborated with Jim Fetzer on many articles about "false flag" attacks, including (with regard to Sandy Hook), "The Nexus of Tyranny: The Strategy behind Tucson, Aurora and Sandy Hook" (30 January 2013), "Sent worldwide, Shannon Hicks' 'iconic' photo was faked" (18 July 2014), and "Sandy Hook, Stephen Sedensky, William Shanley and the Elaborate Hoax" (28 July 2014). He has also published extensively on various aspects of 9/11. His articles on the Pentagon, for example, include "The 'official account' of the Pentagon is a fantasy" (2012), "9/11: A World Swirling in a Volcano of Lies" (14 February 2014) and "Reflections on the Pentagon: A Photographic Review" (16 August 2014), and "Limited Hangouts: Kevin Ryan, A&E911 and The Journal of 9/11 Studies" (with Jim Fetzer, 14 August 2014).

Dr. Eowyn, Ph.D., professor emeritus of political science at a U.S. university and author of university press books and countless peer-reviewed articles, maintains the site *fellowshipoftheminds.com*, where more than 80 articles on Sandy Hook are archived, including (among her more recent) "BBC admits but will not investigate why pic of Sandy Hook's Noah Pozner is among Peshawar massacre victims" (7January 2015), "Sandy Hook: The boys who were evacuated TWICE" (26 January 2015), "Citizen speaks out on Sandy Hook hoax at Connecticut State committee hearing" (6 March 2015), "Former state trooper Wolfgang Halbig files Sandy Hook lawsuit" (8 March 2015), "Sandy Hook families sue Lanza estate, as Newtown demolishes the Lanza home" (18 March 2015), "Sandy Hook dad Lenny Pozner's website redirects to Obama regime's NSA" (7 July 2015), and "Sandy Hook families each gets $94k to settle lawsuits against Lanza estate" (21 August 2015).

Jim Fetzer earned his Ph.D. in the history and philosophy of science. A former Marine Corps officer, he has published widely on the theoretical foundations of scientific knowledge, computer science, artificial intelligence, cognitive science, and evolution and mentality. McKnight Professor Emeritus at the University of Minnesota Duluth, he has also conducted extensive research into the assassination of JFK, the events of 9/11 and the plane crash that killed Sen. Paul Wellstone. The founder of Scholars for 9/11 Truth, his latest books include *The Place of Probability in Science* (with Ellery Eells, 2010) plus *And I Suppose we didn't go to the moon, either?* (2015), which was his 30th. He has also published more than 30 articles about Sandy Hook.

Sterling Harwood, J.D., Ph.D. has served as a practicing attorney in San Jose, CA since 1998. He has tenure as an adjunct Professor at Evergreen Valley College after teaching at: Cornell Law School, Lincoln Law School, San Jose State University, Illinois State University, San Jose City College, and Hobart and William Smith Colleges. His books include: *Crime and Punishment: Philosophic Explorations* (with Michael J. Gorr, 2000), *Business as Ethical and Business as Usual* (1996), *Judicial Activism: A Restrained Defense* (1996), and *Controversies in Criminal Law* (with Michael J. Gorr, 1992). Since 1989 he has published dozens of essays in legal, moral and political philosophy. His most recent essays are "Did 'Tricky Dick' Land Men on the Moon?" and "The Beatles' Greatest Mystery" in *And I suppose we didn't go to the moon, either?* (2015).

Nicholas Kollerstrom, Ph.D., has two history of science degrees, one from Cambridge 1968, plus a Ph.D. from London, 1995. An honorary member of staff of UCL for 11 years, he was in 1999 elected as a Member of the New York Academy of Sciences. A Fellow of the Royal Astronomical Society, he has several dozen articles on the history of astronomy in academic journals. His book, *Terror on the Tube* (3rd edition, 2011), establishes that the accused Islamic youth were innocent of the 2005 London bombings. *Breaking the Spell: The Holocaust, Myth and Reality* (2014), demonstrates that the official narrative of WWII cannot be sustained. He contributed four chapters to *And I suppose we didn't go to the moon, either?*. His latest book, *The Life and Death of Paul McCartney 1942-66: A Very English Mystery* (2015), has just appeared.

Vivian Lee, Ph.D., the *nom de plume* of a tenured professor at an American university whose research interests include war, psyops, and propaganda, with a current focus on false flag terrorism and shootings along with the media's role in these staged events. The Sandy Hook and Boston Marathon narratives figure prominently due to their significant impact on US national policy, their importance for the conditioning of the public mentality, and the boost they have given to the production, dissemination, and acceptance of fake news worldwide. She has updated and revised the original "Top Ten Reasons: Sandy Hook was an Elaborate Hoax" (7 January 2014), of which she was the lead author with Sofia Smallstorm, James Tracy, Jim Fetzer and other members of the Sandy Hook Research Group, for publication here.

Mike Palecek lives in Saginaw, Minnesota, west of Duluth. A writer, he is a former federal prisoner for peace and the Iowa Democratic Party candidate for the U.S. House of Representatives, 5th District in the 2000 election, gaining 65,000 votes on an anti-war platform in a conservative district. A former award winning reporter, editor, publisher in Nebraska, Iowa, Minnesota. The small newspaper that Mike & Ruth Palecek owned and operated in Byron, Minnesota, won the MNA Newspaper of the Year Award in 1993. He co-hosts "The New American Dream" radio show and has published over a dozen books that offer fictional but insightful studies of the American character and the plight in which we find ourselves in the world today. Mike is the founder of Moon Rock Books and the co-editor of this volume.

Allen William Powell, born in the United Kingdom, has retired and resides in Canberra, AU. When he appeared on "The Real Deal Ep. #81 Explosive New Revelations about Sandy Hook" hosted by Jim Fetzer, it became apparent that one of the leading experts on mischief in Connecticut resided half-way around the world. He has made several additional appearances, including "The Real Deal Ep. 83 Allen Powell does the Boston bombing", "The Real Deal Ep. 87 The Lanza Home: A Prop for Sandy Hook", and "The Real Deal Ep. 96 More Sandy Hook", which are accessible via a search using their titles. His contributions here, "Ch. 7 (with Kelley Watt), "Fixing a Prop: Furnishing the Lanza Home" and "Ch. 8 Setting the Stage: Refurbishing the School", are going to qualify as the most brilliant studies published on Sandy Hook, which provide unexpected but decisive proof that this was a staged event.

James Tracy, Ph.D., Associate Professor in the School of Communication and Multimedia Studies at Florida Atlantic University in Boca Raton, has been on the faculty since 2002. He received his doctorate from The University of Iowa, specializing in the areas of political economy of the news media and media history and criticism, and has published numerous academic journal articles and book chapters in these areas. In early 2013, major Western news outlets attacked Tracy for public commentaries on journalistic coverage of the Sandy Hook school massacre and Boston Marathon bombing events, which he had circulated via alternative media. Because of the considerable publicity, Florida Atlantic's administration embarked on formal disciplinary measures against Tracy, later proven baseless and rescinded.

He maintains *memoryholeblog.com*, where his studies of Sandy Hook and other events, such as the Boston bombing, are very popular and widely read.

Kelley Watt became a Sandy Hook skeptic a month after it was presented as a "live" event on national television. Owning a residential/commercial cleaning service for 18 years prompted her calls to several Connecticut state agencies (Connecticut's Environmental Protection Agency, Connecticut State Police and the Connecticut Major Crimes Squad) to whom she addressed the question, "Who received the contract to clean up the blood (bio hazard) at Sandy Hook?" None of them had an answer to this simple question, when their responses was either "We don't know" or the priceless response of Lt. Paul Vance, "What blood?" She then began making several hundred phone calls to the Chief Medical Examiner and to the Town Clerk's Office, for example, asking basic questions. Rather than being helpful they were rude and would state, "This really happened; how dare you say it didn't". With hundreds of people in Connecticut saying the same thing,"This really happened", and becoming defensive, I knew something was not right with what we were being told. I then contacted all the Connecticut news outlets numerous time sand again was met with hostility and threatened with legal action if I called asking any more questions. It was a combination of these attempts I made to find the answers that led me to question and disbelieve everything surrounding this event.

Jim Fetzer

PROLOGUE

Thinking about Sandy Hook: Reality or Illusion?

by Jim Fetzer

"It ain't what we don't know that hurts us; it's what we think we know that ain't so."—Will Rogers

The Sandy Hook experience has divided Americans, most of whom have been convinced by media coverage that it was a real event, where a young man massacred 20 children and six adults before killing himself.

Another substantial segment of the US population has taken a closer look at the evidence and drawn the conclusion it was a hoax, where no children really died: it was an elaborate psy-op to promote gun control.

Sandy Hook has become a celebrities cause

Americans are hard pressed to sort these things out, because they are hit with a blizzard of reports that appear to confirm the official account, leaving them in the predicament of not being able to tell if it was real or fake.

It matters even more today because gun control has become one of the defining issues of politics in America, where leading Democrats (Barack Obama and Hillary Clinton) are using their authority as President (in the first instance) to issue Executive Orders constraining our 2nd Amendment

3

rights and (in the second) threatening to impose liability laws upon their manufacturers for their use by those who buy them. Ben Carson, on the Republican side, has observed that Jews would have been better able to fend off The Third Reich had they not been disarmed; and Matt Drudge has challenged the President to demonstrate his sincerity by giving up his (heavily armed) Secret Service protection.

The appeals to Sandy Hook (shooting 20 children), the Charleston shooting (of nine blacks) and the Oregon shooting (where college students were asked their religion and those responding "Christian" were shot in the head) has struck some observers as appearing to be calculated to instill fear into specific targeted subpopulations of the American community: parents, blacks and Christians, for example, where it's as though we were experiencing *a series of psy-ops* to convince the public that we ought to give up our guns. That troubles many, because disarming populations has all-too-often occurred to set the stage for tyranny in world history past. What if Sandy Hook was *only an illusion?*

Probabilities vs. Certainties

Knowledge of historical events (based upon documents and records, photos and videos and witness testimony, for example) can never be "definitive and certain". You only know *your own origin in life* (where and when you were born and the parents who brought you into this world) on the basis of information that could have been faked. Even DNA comparisons can be invalid or mistaken on purpose or by accident. Your belief about *today's day/month/year* is something else of which you have no direct and certain knowledge but rather have a host of sources of information, such as newspapers and television reports, which collectively confirm your belief but could be fabricated or faked, but which are *almost always* accurate and true.

The occurrence of an elaborate hoax intended to fool the people does not occur often, but there can be no doubt that it does sometimes occur. *The Warren Report* (1964), for example, provides an indictment of Lee Harvey Oswald as the lone assassin of JFK, where the evidence for that conclusion was carefully selected and, in some cases, completely fabricated.

The backyard photographs were faked, for example, and the home movies of the assassination were edited. That he had been captured in a famous photo taken during the shooting was suppressed. (Check out *The Great Zapruder Film Hoax* (2003) or many articles about JFK at *jamesfetzer.blogspot.com* for abundant proof, if you like.) These things can and sometimes do happen. And one of them happened here.

If you only read the government's account, you might very well be convinced that JFK had been killed by Lee Oswald. And if you only paid attention to the mass media, you would probably believe that 20 children died at Sandy Hook. Once you acknowledge that some of the evidence has been fabricated or faked, however, the case begins to assume a completely different character. This does not mean we cannot know what happened in this instance, but *it should not have been necessary to frame a guilty man.* New evidence or alternative hypotheses may thus require us to revise our position by rejecting hypotheses we previously accepted, accepting hypotheses we previously rejected and leaving others in suspense. We now know more about Sandy Hook.

Inference to the best explanation

The principle known as "inference to the best explanation", has the potential to turn every American into a critical thinker in comparing alternative hypotheses. In relation to Sandy Hook, there are two alternatives, which have consequences that would also be true (or probably true) if they were true and others that would be false (or probably false) if they were not (setting the alleged suicide by Adam Lanza to the side):

(h1) Sandy Hook was a real event, where 20 children and 6 adults were killed at a school;

(h2) Sandy Hook was an elaborate hoax, where a drill was conducted and no children died.

But the key to understanding is making an appraisal of which of these hypotheses is better supported by the evidence. We can think of the evidence as *effects* of one or another hypothesis *as their cause.* When one hypothesis makes the effects *more probable* than the other, it is more likely to be true and the alternative false. *For the shooting to have been real, the school had to have been operational in 2012; yet we have indication after indication that it had been abandoned by 2008 (which you will discover in Chapters 2 and 3),* including not only its deplorable physical condition (both inside and out), but also that it was not in compliance with both federal and state laws required in accordance with the Americans with Disabilities Act:

Here is a photograph of the school taken on the day of the shooting. Notice that the handicapped parking areas are not properly demarcated with white paint and blue markings. There are no "above grade signs with white lettering against a blue background" that bear the words, "handicapped parking permit required" and "violators will be fined", which means that Sandy Hook Elementary School was non-ADA compliant. That day, CNN was mixing images from other schools with those from Sandy Hook:

Analogously, *we know from past experience that the names, ages and sex of victims of crimes are almost invariably printed in newspaper accounts of crimes. In this case, however, the final reports coming from the Connecticut authorities did not include them.* That is a very odd aspect of this event, but an attempt has been made to explain it away on the ground of preserving the privacy of the families of the victims. But if there were victims, their families already know they are dead. There is no evident benefit to the families, if it was real, but a major element of the cover up, if it was not.

From the date of the event, we have a photograph taken from a CT State Police chopper at 9:15 AM/ET, which is 20 minutes *before* the first 911 call came in; there was no surge of EMTs into the building to rush those little bodies off to hospitals, where doctors could pronounce them dead or alive; virtually all of the emergency vehicles were kept at the Firehouse, which became the center of activity as opposed to the school; the parents were not even allowed to identify their children, which was done using photos. As a parent myself, I can emphasize that there is no way I could have been kept from viewing the body of a child of mine, where the conduct of the "parents" in this case is unlike that of any parents I have ever known, where these many oddities are confirmed by Chapter 5.

Other circumstantial anomalies

If the school had been abandoned, then the shooting has to be an illusion, since there would have been no students present for Adam Lanza to shoot. And if that were the case, then we might not be surprised if any number of measures were taken at the time by authorities to suppress relevant information (and thereby making it unavailable) or by otherwise circumventing what would have been the ordinary and normal procedures of investigation and administration by local and state authorities. But the measures that were taken were rather extraordinary, including these examples:

the Attorney General of Connecticut argued against releasing the 911 calls, where the court ruled against him;

the Clerk of Newtown entered into secret negotiations with the state legislature to avoid issuing death certificates;

a special panel of the state legislature recommended that any state employee who released information about Sandy Hook other than via Freedom of Information Act request be prosecuted as an E-felony with a five year sentence; and,

those who were hired to participate in the demolition of the school building were required to sign life-time gag orders that prohibit them from talking about what they saw or did not see during its destruction.

Each of these qualifies as a "fact" insofar as its truth can be confirmed by research you can conduct yourself. Admittedly, if all the information accessible via the Internet about Sandy Hook were fabricated or faked, then that would not be the case.

But I know of no one who seriously contests any of these points. So ask yourself, *what is the probability that these five claims (if we also include the missing names, ages and sex from the final report) would be true if Sandy Hook had been a real event?* And by comparison, *what is the probability these five claims would be true if Sandy Hook had been a hoax? Which hypothesis is more likely to be true?*

7

The Governor's Press Conference

The day of the shooting, Governor Dan Malloy and his Lt. Governor held a press conference, during which he observed that they had been "spoken to" that something like this might happen. That got me thinking about, "something like this"? What could that mean.

There are only two alternatives:

> *(a) that he had been told there would be a shooting in a school in his state, in which case he, as governor, should have warned school districts to be on high alert and make sure it did not happen, which he did not do; or,*

> *(b) that he had been told they would be taking an abandoned school and using it as a prop for a drill, which would be presented to the public as real to promote an aggressive gun-control agenda, which is the case here.*

And when I looked into recent visits with the Governor to determine by whom he might have been "spoken to", I discovered that Attorney General Eric Holder had met with him on 27 November 2012 to discuss "Operation Longevity", a special interest of the Attorney General and the President of the United Staes for promoting gun control. Mark my words. The evidence presented here demonstrates that the school was closed by 2008; that there were no students to evacuate; that Adam Lanza appears to have been a work of fiction; and that *the teachers, the parents, the Newtown School Board, the State Police, the Medical Examiner and the Governor were in on the hoax.*

We have the FEMA manual

Our collaborative research, you will find for yourself, is extensive, thorough and detailed—and leaves this matter resolved beyond any reasonable doubt. We have 50 photos that show the preparation of the Lanza home as a prop and another 50 documenting the refurbishing of the school as a stage (in Chapters 7 and 8). Doubt in this case would be reasonable were there *a reasonable alternative explanation.* But, as you are about to discover, there is none here.

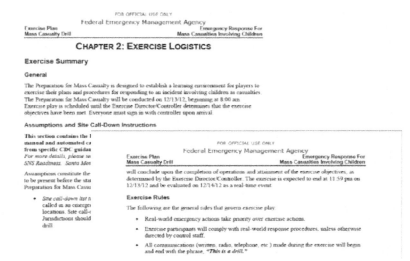

And I am not just talking about the sign, *"Everyone must check in"*, the *Port-a-Potties*, the boxes of bottled water and pizza cartons at the Firehouse, the name tags on lanyards and parents bringing their children to (what was supposed to be) a child shooting massacre! **WE HAVE THE FEMA MANUAL.** *It stipulates that everyone must register and that refreshments and restrooms will be provided. Some participants did not realize that the official event was not until the 14th:* We now know why some of the donation pages went up a day early and why Adam Lanza was recorded as having died on the 13th! Don't take my word for it, because *you can read it for yourself.* I included it here as *Appendix A.*

The Requirement of Total Evidence

Indeed, scientific reasoning specifically and rational inquiries generally must satisfy *the requirement of total evidence: in the search for truth, reasoning must be based upon all of the available relevant evidence,* where evidence is relevant when its presence or absence (or truth or falsity) makes a difference to the outcome, typically on the basis of considerations of *probability.*

According to the official report on Sandy

Hook by Danbury States Attorney Stephen Sedensky (to which we refer as "T*he Sedensky Report*"), there were 489 children present that day. Minus 20 murdered, there ought to have been 469 to evacuate (as well as around 70 more teachers, administrators and staff). But we have no pictures of their evacuation. What we have instead this "iconic" photograph (above):

It has sometimes been said that *"You can't prove a falsehood true!"* But that assertion overlooks the role of false clams and fabricated evidence. We have here a photograph purporting to show a string of children being led away from the school to safety by a policewoman on the scene. This photo was published on the front page of virtually every newspaper in the world—and shown endless times on television. It was undoubtedly the single most important form of proof in convincing the public around the world that Sandy Hook was real.

But there is a catch: *the photograph was staged!* And we know that not on the basis of the weaker evidence that there are too many leaves on the trees and no frost for this to be a 28 degree day in December but because Shannon Hicks *took a second photograph!*

Rearranging the kids to get a better shot

It's bad enough that we have a series of parents looking on, some with their arms cross or their hands in their pockets—which is certainly not what we would expect in an emergency situation. It gets much worse when you realize that the police woman has stopped the children to rearrange them to get "a better shot"! Here's a comparison that shows what was going on and demonstrates—as conclusively as anyone could have the right to expect— that the first photograph was staged to create the false impression that there

was an emergency and that these kids needed to be removed from a threat at the earliest possible opportunity—which would not leave time to stop and rearrange them as follows:

We not only know that Shannon Hicks was "in on the game" by taking these photos (as early as in October) in preparation for this elaborate charade but we also know that there was no evacuation. The claim is sometimes made that "You can't prove a negative!" But that turns out to be false. *When evidence that ought to be present if an hypothesis were true is not present, then the absence of evidence qualifies as evidence of absence.* Suppose you were told there is an elephant in your living room. If you go there and find no indications of the presence of an elephant, you are completely justified in inferring that there is no elephant in your living room.

If the 469 kids who should have been there, had this this event been real, were not there, you are completely justified in inferring that it was not real.

An evacuation would have looked something like this, with strings of children led by other police officers or teachers performing their duty under stress.

But we have DashCam footage at the locations in the parking lot where, according to official police records, the evacuation was taking place—*and there is nothing there!* Just as the absence of signs of the presence of an elephant in your living room is proof of the absence of an elephant, the absence of signs of the presence of children undergoing evacuation is proof that no evacuation was taking place.

More parking lot anomalies—and a stunner!

Inspection of the vehicles in the parking lot in front of the school shows that they are parked in the wrong direction (which should have been nose-in), given the arrangement for driving into the lot. The image itself suggests of a group of drivers methodically filling up the lot with used or abandoned cars, driving straight into the designated parking places without regard for how they should have been arranged.

Once again we ask, *"What is the probability that the lot would be filled with cars parked in the wrong direction, if this had been a real event? What if this had been a drill?"* Truly stunning, however, is the discovery of a series of photographs that display setting the stage early in the morning for the events that would transpire this day, including this one from Chapter 8:

Notice that the windows of Classroom 10 are not shot out and the flag is up. Wayne Carver can be seen behind the man in the blue evidence suit. This photograph is taken from one of the elevated cameras we have discovered that were mounted around the parking lot to record the drill. The mortuary tent is not there yet, which makes this early morning. *Could we have more decisive proof?* When an hypothesis has been confirmed by abundant evidence and no alternative explanation is reasonable, it has been established "beyond a reasonable doubt".

Hypothesis (h1), that Sandy Hook was real, has been falsified and (h2), that this was an elaborate hoax, has been proven beyond any reasonable doubt.

Benefits to the participants

The benefits to those who participated in the Sandy Hook hoax have been substantial. The donation sites created by "families of the victims" have hauled in over $27,000,000 or in excess of $1,000,000 per family. Other substantial grants have been given to alleviate the pain and suffering of those who responded to the event. On Friday, 12 December 2014, for example, Senators Richard Blumenthal (D-CT) and Chris Murphy (D-CT) and Representative Elizabeth Esty (CT-5) announced a $775,914 grant from the Department of Justice's Office for Victims of Crimes and their families, firs responders and members of Newtown community in the wake of the shooting to "help fund continued mental health services and other support services", which sounds like a lot for participating in a charade.

Other pay-offs, bribes and hush-money—*and under the circumstances, is there anything more appropriate to call it?*—are documented in Chapter 5. When debate was taking place over the choice between refurbishing the old school or constructing a new one, *The Newtown Bee* published about the presence of asbestos, lead and PCBs in the building, which had no doubt factored in the earlier decision to abandon the school in 2008. Newtown received $50,000,000 to build a brand new K-4 elementary school. I surveyed the cost of comparable cost for K-4 schools across the nation and discovered they average $7,000,000, which reflects the generous benefits that a community might accrue from cooperating covertly with the federal government in the pursuit of its political agenda.

The gun control agenda

We are told that fewer guns means less crime. But when you look into serious studies of crime rates in relation to gun laws, that is not what you

The Newtown Bee

Since 1877 – Best for Local News and Advertising

Widespread Haz-Mat Presence Would Have Hampered Sandy Hook Renovations
By John Voket
Monday, December 2, 2013

Long before the first environmental contractors started reporting higher than expected levels of lead, asbestos, and PCBs in construction debris at Sandy Hook School, a panel of town officials and residents in a subsequent referendum had already endorsed razing and replacing the aging elementary school building.

According to Public Building & Site Commission Chairman Robert Mitchell, the town and its residents made the right choice. Mr Mitchell said in a facility update he plans to deliver to his commissioners on December 3, that had the town decided to reoccupy the school on Dickinson Drive, it would have faced a daunting and possibly insurmountable challenge regarding the presence of hazardous materials.

The report states that during a review of materials found throughout the school, one assessment "indicated that should we have determined to keep and renovate the school, it would not have been possible to keep the original building in any cost-effective manner."

Mr Mitchell told *The Newtown Bee* that the expense for identifying, removing and processing the heightened amount of materials found during demolition required nearly double what was originally budgeted for that aspect of the project. Much of the information in the PBSC report has already been advanced to town officials by First Selectman Pat Llodra, who noted the hazmat issues during recent Legislative Council, Board of Finance, and Board of Selectmen meetings.

On November 20, she told the council that the Sandy Hook School building was essentially gone except for subsurface materials, which have subsequently been removed. During that meeting, Mrs Llodra echoed Mr Mitchell's assessment.

"Had we made the choice to renovate instead of demolish, we would have found ourselves in a difficult circumstance," she said of the school, which was completed in 1956. So much

Photo: Courtesy Reuters

The Sandy Hook School demolition site was nearly clear by the time this aerial photo was taken on November 13. Local officials have since indicated that the extensive degree of hazardous materials on the site would have prevented or significantly hampered efforts to reoccupy the building, which was the site of the 12/14 tragedy. Construction of a new school on the site was approved by voters in October, and will commence in the coming months.

Share

E-mail this story Print this story
Save this story

discover. Appendix D, for example, "Comparing Murder and Homicide Rates before and after Gun Bans", suggests something closer to the opposite is the case, contrary to our president's claims.

Barack Obama himself praised the sweeping gun confiscation that took place in Australia in the late 1990s and said:

"Couple of decades ago, Australia had a mass shooting, similar to Columbine or Newtown," Obama said. "And Australia just said, well, that's it, we're not doing, we're not seeing that again, and basically imposed very severe, tough gun laws, and they haven't had a mass shooting since."

And while they haven't seen a mass shooting since, local officials say that gun violence on the continent is much worse than it was before the tougher gun policies went into effect.

Meanwhile, the one thing that the President failed to recognize is that gun crime in the U.S. is on the decline.

According to a PEW research study, gun crime is down 49% since 1993. Another study by the Bureau of Justice Statistics showed that non-fatal gun crime is actually down 70% since the same time.

Even the President's own study performed by the Center for Disease Control reached a similar conclusion: "Firearm-related death rates for youth ages 15 to 19 declined from 1994 to 2009," the report states. "The number of public mass shootings of the type that occurred at Sandy Hook Elementary School accounted for a very small fraction of all firearm-related deaths."

What these studies show is there's a clear agenda being carried out by the Mainstream Media to make it seem like mass shootings are the norm. As soon as a mass shooting happens, it reverberates through all the major news networks for weeks, much like an echo after the initial shot.

Because of this, much of the nation seems to believe that gun violence, particularly school shootings, is on the rise even with **evidence that points to the contrary.**

The reasons behind this aggressive behavior by the administration, even when gun violence has been falling in the United States, involves deep questions about the role of DHS in our society and why America has been devolving into a totalitarian state. I was born a year-and-a-day before Pearl Harbor, as my father used to put it; and I would never have imagined in my wildest dreams that the United States of American could descent into a bottomless pit of lies, deceit and deception.

Faking a school shooting to instill fear into a population for political purposes is an act of terrorism, where it has become clear that this instance was brought to us by officials at every level of Connecticut government from the teachers and reporters to the State Police and the Newtown School board to the Governor and the Attorney General and the President himself. And this is the ugly legacy of Barack Hussein Obama.

Part I

Early indications something was wrong

1

Medical Examiner: More Questions than Answers

by James F. Tracy, Ph.D.

"[My staff] and I hope the people of Newtown don't have it crash on their head later"

–Connecticut Medical Examiner D. Wayne Carver II, MD, December 15, 2012

Inconsistencies and anomalies abound when one turns an analytical eye to news of the Newtown school massacre. The public's general acceptance of the event's validity and faith in its resolution suggest a deepened credulousness borne from a world where almost all news and information is electronically mediated and controlled.

The condition is reinforced through the corporate media's unwillingness to push hard questions vis-à-vis Connecticut and federal authorities who together bottlenecked information while invoking prior restraint through threats of prosecutorial action against journalists and the broader citizenry seeking to interpret the event on social media.

Along these lines on December 19 the Connecticut State Police assigned individual personnel to each of the 26 families who lost a loved one at Sandy Hook Elementary. "The families have requested no press interviews," State Police assert on their behalf, "and we are asking that this request be honored.

[1] The de facto gag order will be in effect until the investigation concludes—now forecast to be "several months away" even though lone gunman Adam Lanza has been confirmed as the sole culprit.[2]

With the exception of an unusual and apparently contrived appearance by Emilie Parker's alleged father, victims' family members have been almost wholly absent from public scrutiny.[3] What can be gleaned from this and similar coverage raises many more questions and glaring inconsistencies than answers. While it sounds like an outrageous claim, **one is left to inquire whether the Sandy Hook shooting ever took place—at least in the way law enforcement authorities and the nation's news media have described.**

The accidental Medical Examiner

An especially important yet greatly underreported feature of the Sandy Hook affair is the wholly bizarre performance of Connecticut's top medical examiner H. Wayne Carver II at a December 15 press conference. Carver's unusual remarks and behavior warrant close consideration because in light of his professional notoriety they appear remarkably amateurish and out of character.

H. Wayne Carver II has an extremely self-assured, almost swaggering presence in Connecticut state administration. In early 2012 Carver threatened to vacate his position because of state budget cuts and streamlining measures that threatened his professional autonomy over the projects and personnel he oversaw.

Along these lines the pathologist has gone to excessive lengths to demonstrate his findings and expert opinion in court proceedings. For example, in a famous criminal case Carver "put a euthanized pig through a wood chipper so jurors could match striations on the bone fragments with the few ounces of evidence that prosecutors said were on the remains of the victim."[4] One would therefore expect Carver to be in his element while identifying and verifying the exact ways in which Sandy Hook's children and teachers met their violent demise.

Yet the H. Wayne Carver who showed up to the December 15 press conference is an almost entirely different man, appearing apprehensive and uncertain, as if he is at a significant remove from the postmortem operation he had overseen. The multiple gaffes, discrepancies, and hedges in response to reporters' astute questions suggest that he is either under coercion or an imposter. While the latter sounds untenable it would go a long way in explaining his sub-pedestrian grasp of medical procedures and terminology.

With this in mind extended excerpts from this exchange are worthy of recounting here in print. Carver is accompanied by Connecticut State Police Lieutenant H. Paul Vance and additional Connecticut State Police personnel. The reporters are off-screen and thus unidentified so I have assigned them simple numerical identification based on what can be discerned of their voices.

Reporter #1: So the rifle was the primary weapon?
H. Wayne Carver: Yes.
Reporter #1: [Inaudible]
Carver: Uh (pause). Question was what caliber were these bullets. And I know—I probably know more about firearms than most pathologists but if I say it in court they yell at me and don't make me answer [sic]—so [nervous laughter]. I'll let the police do that for you.
Reporter #2: Doctor can you tell us about the nature of the wounds. Were they at very close range? Were the children shot at from across the room?
Carver: Uhm, I only did seven of the autopsies. The victims I had ranged from three to eleven wounds apiece and I only saw two of them with close range shooting. Uh, but that's, uh y'know, a sample. Uh, I really don't have detailed information on the rest of the injuries.
[Given that Carver is Connecticut's top coroner and in charge of the entire postmortem this is a startling admission.-JT]
Reporter #3: But you said that the long rifle was used?
Carver: Yes.
Reporter #3: But the long rifle was discovered in the car.
State Police Lieutenant Vance: That's not correct, sir.
Unidentified reporter #4: How many bullets or bullet fragments did you find in the autopsy. Can you tell us that?
Carver: Oh. I'm lucky I can tell you how many I found. I don't know. There were lots of them, OK? This type of weapon is not, uh ... the bullets are designed in such a fashion that the energy—this is very clinical. I shouldn't be saying this. But the energy is deposited in the tissue so the bullet stays in [the tissue].
[In fact, the Bushmaster .223 Connecticut police finally claimed was used in the shooting is designed for long range field use and utilizes high velocity bullets averaging 3,000 feet-per-second, the energy of which even at considerable distance would penetrate several bodies before finally coming to rest in tissue.]
Reporter #5: How close were the injuries?
Carver: Uh, all the ones (pause). I believe say, yes [sic].
Reporter #6: In what shape were the bodies when the families were brought to check [inaudible].
Carver: Uh, we did not bring the bodies and the families into contact. We took pictures of them, uhm, of their facial features. We have, uh, uh—it's easier on the families when you do that. Un, there is, uh, a time and place

for the up close and personal in the grieving process, but to accomplish this we thought it would be best to do it this way and, uh, you can sort of, uh ... You can control a situation depending on the photographer, and I have very good photographers. Uh, but uh—

Reporter #7: Do you know the difference of the time of death between the mother in the house and the bodies recovered [in the school].

Carver: Uh, no, I don't. Sorry [shakes head excitedly] I don't! [embarrassed laugh]

Reporter #8: Did the gunman kill himself with the rifle?

Carver: No. I—I don't know yet. I'll-I'll examine him tomorrow morning. But, but I don't think so.

[Why has Carver left arguably the most important specimen for last? And why doesn't he think Lanza didn't commit suicide with the rifle?]

Reporter #9: In terms of the children, were they all found in one classroom or—

Carver: Uhm ... [inaudible] [Turns to Lieutenant Vance] Paul and company will deal with that.

Reporter #9: What?

Carver: Paul and company will deal with that. Lieutenant Vance is going to handle that one.

Reporter #10: Was there any evidence of a struggle? Any bruises?

Carver: No.

Reporter #11: The nature of the shooting; is there any sense that there was a lot of care taken with precision [inaudible] or randomly?

Carver: [Exhales while glancing upward, as if frustrated] Both. It's a very difficult question to answer ... You'd think after thousands of people I've seen shot but I ... It's ... If I attempted to answer it in court there'd be an objection and then they'd win—[nervous laughter].

[Who would win? Why does an expert whose routine job as a public employee is to provide impartial medical opinion concerned with winning and losing in court? Further, Carver is not in court but rather at a press conference.]

Reporter #12: Doctor, can you discuss the fatal injuries to the adults?

Carver: Ah, they were similar to those of the children.

Reporter #13: Doctor, the children you had autopsied, where in the bodies were they hit?

Carver: Uhm [pause]. All over. All over.

Reporter #14: Were [the students] sitting at their desks or were they running away when this happened?

Carver: I'll let the guys who—the scene guys talk—address that issue. I, uh, obviously I was at the scene. Obviously I'm very experienced in that. But there are people who are, uh, the number one professionals in that. I'll let them—let that [voice trails off].

Reporter [#15]: How many boys and how many girls [were killed]?
Carver: [Slowly shaking his head] I don't know.

More unanswered questions and inconsistencies

In addition to Carver's remarks several additional chronological and evidentiary contradictions in the official version of the Sandy Hook shooting are cause for serious consideration and leave doubt in terms of how the event transpired vis-à-vis the way authorities and  major media outlets have presented it.

It is now well known that early on journalists reported that Adam Lanza's brother Ryan Lanza was reported to be the gunman, and that pistols were used in the shooting rather than a rifle. Yet these are merely the tip of the iceberg.

When did the gunman arrive?

After Adam Lanza fatally shot and killed his mother at his residence, he drove himself to the elementary school campus, arriving one half hour after classes had commenced. Dressed in black, Lanza proceeds completely unnoticed through an oddly vacant parking lot with a military style rifle and shoots his way through double glass doors and a brand new yet apparently poorly engineered security system.

Further, initial press accounts suggest how no school personnel or students heard gunshots and no 911 calls are made until *after* Lanza begins firing *inside* the facility. "It was a lovely day," Sandy Hook fourth grade teacher Theodore Varga said. And then, suddenly and unfathomably, gunshots rang out. "I can't even remember how many," Varga said.[5]

The recollection contrasts sharply with an updated version of Lanza's arrival where at 9:30AM he *walked up to the front entrance and fired at least a half dozen rounds into the glass doors. The thunderous sound of Lanza blowing an opening big enough to walk through the locked school door caused Principal Dawn Hochsprung and school psychologist Mary Scherlach to bolt from a nearby meeting room to investigate. He shot and killed them both as they ran toward him.*

Breaching the school's security system in such a way would have likely triggered some automatic alert of school personnel. Further, why would the school's administrators run *toward* an armed man who has just noisily blasted his way into the building?

Two other staff members attending the meeting with Hochsprung and Scherlach sustained injuries "in the hail of bullets" but returned to the aforementioned meeting room and managed a call to 911.[6] This contrasted with earlier reports where the first 911 call claimed students "were trapped in a classroom with the adult shooter who had two guns."[7] Recordings of the first police dispatch following the 911 call at 9:35:50 indicate that someone "thinks there's someone shooting in the building."[8] There is a clear distinction between potentially hearing shots somewhere in the building and being almost mortally caught in a "hail of bullets."

How did the gunman fire so many shots in such little time?

According to Dr. Carver and State Police, Lanza shot each victim between 3 and 11 times during a 5 to 7 minute span. If one is to average this out to 7 bullets per individual—excluding misses—Lanza shot 182 times, or once every two seconds. Yet according to the official story Lanza was the sole assassin and armed with only one weapon. Thus if misses and changing the gun's 30-shot magazine at least 6 times are added to the equation Lanza must have been averaging about one shot per second—extremely skilled use of a single firearm for a young man with absolutely no military training and who was on the verge of being institutionalized. Still, an accurate rendering of the event is even more difficult to arrive at because the chief medical examiner admittedly has no idea exactly *how* the children were shot or whether a struggle ensued.

Where is the photo and video evidence?

Photographic and video evidence is at once profuse yet lacking in terms of its capacity to demonstrate that a mass shooting took place on the scale described by authorities. For example, in an era of ubiquitous video surveillance of public buildings especially no visual evidence of Lanza's violent entry has emerged. And while studio snapshots of the Sandy Hook victims abound there is little if any eyewitness testimony of anyone who's observed the corpses except for Carver and his staff, and they appear almost as confused about the conditions of the deceased as any layperson watching televised coverage of the event. Nor are there any routine eyewitness, photo or video evidence of the crime scene's aftermath—broken glass, blasted security locks and doors, bullet casings and holes, bloodied walls and floors—all of which are common in such investigations and reportage.

Why were medical personnel turned away from the scene?

Oddly enough medical personnel are forced to set up their operation not at the school where the dead and injured lay, but rather at the fire station several hundred feet away. This flies in the face of standard medical operating procedure where personnel are situated as close to the scene as possible. There is no doubt that the school had ample room to accommodate such personnel. Yet medical responders who rushed to Sandy Hook Elementary upon receiving word of the tragedy were denied entry to the school and forced to set up primary and secondary triages off school grounds and wait for the injured to be brought to them.

Shortly after the shooting "as other ambulances from neighboring communities rolled up, sirens blaring, the first responders slowly realized that their training would be tragically underutilized on this horrible day. 'You may not be able to save everybody, but you damn well try,'" 44 year old emergency medical technician James Wolff told NBC News. "'And when (we) didn't have the opportunity to put our skills into action, it's difficult.'"[9]

In light of this, who were the qualified medical practitioners that pronounced the 20 children and 7 adults dead? Who decided that none could be revived? Carver and his staff are apparently the only medical personnel to have attended to the victims—yet this was in the postmortem conducted several hours later. Such slipshod handling of the crime scene leaves the State of Connecticut open to a potential array of hefty civil claims by families of the slain.

Did a mass evacuation of the school take place?

Sandy Hook Elementary is attended by 600 students. Yet there is no photographic or video evidence of an evacuation on this scale. Instead, limited video and photographic imagery suggest that a limited evacuation of perhaps at most several dozen students occurred.

A highly circulated photo depicts students walking in a single file formation with their hands on each others' shoulders and eyes shut. Yet this was the image of a drill that took place prior to the event itself.[10. See Correction] Most other photos are portraits of individual children.

Despite aerial video footage of the event documenting law enforcement scouring the scene and apprehending one or more suspects in the wooded area nearby the school,[11] there is no such evidence that a mass exodus of children from the school transpired once law enforcement pronounced Sandy Hook secure. Nor are there videos or photos of several hundred students and their parents at the oft-referenced fire station nearby where students were routed for parent pick up.

Sound bite prism and the will to believe

Outside of a handful of citizen journalists and alternative media commentators Sandy Hook's dramatically shifting factual and circumstantial terrain has escaped serious critique because it is presented through major media's carefully constructed prism of select sound bites alongside a widespread and longstanding cultural impulse to accept the pronouncements of experts, be they bemused physicians, high ranking law enforcement officers, or political leaders demonstrating emotionally-grounded concern.

Political scientist W. Lance Bennett calls this the news media's "authority-disorder bias." "Whether the world is returned to a safe, normal place," Bennett writes, "or whether the very idea of a normal world is called into question, the news is preoccupied with order, along with related questions of whether authorities are capable of establishing or restoring it."[12]

Despite Carver's bizarre performance and law enforcement authorities' inability to settle on and relay simple facts, media management's impulse to assure audiences and readerships of the Newtown community's inevitable adjustment to its trauma and loss with the aid of the government's protective oversight—however incompetent that may be—far surpasses a willingness to undermine this now almost universal news media narrative with messy questions and suggestions of intrigue. This well-worn script is one the public has been conditioned to accept. If few people relied on such media to develop their world view this would hardly be a concern. Yet this is regrettably not the case.

The Sandy Hook tragedy was on a far larger scale than the past year's numerous slaughters, including the Wisconsin Sikh temple shooting and the Batman theater shooting in Colorado. It also included glaringly illogical exercises and pronouncements by authorities alongside remarkably unusual evidentiary fissures indistinguishable by an American political imagination cultivated to believe that the corporate, government and military's sophisticated system of organized crime is largely confined to Hollywood-style storylines while really existing malfeasance and crises are without exception returned to normalcy.

If recent history is a prelude the likelihood of citizens collectively assessing and questioning Sandy Hook is limited even given the event's overtly superficial trappings. While the incident is ostensibly being handled by Connecticut law enforcement, early reports indicate how federal authorities were on the scene as the 911 call was received. Regardless of where one stands on the Second Amendment and gun control, it is not unreasonable to suggest the Obama administration's complicity or direct oversight of an incident that has in very short order sparked a national debate on the very topic—and not coincidentally remains a key piece of Obama's political platform.

The move to railroad this program through with the aid of major media and an irrefutable barrage of children's portraits, "heartfelt" platitudes and ostensible tears neutralizes a quest for genuine evidence, reasoned observation and in the case of Newtown honest and responsible law enforcement. Moreover, to suggest that Obama is not capable of deploying such techniques to achieve political ends is to similarly place ones faith in image and interpretation above substance and established fact, the exact inclination that in sum has brought America to such an impasse.

Notes

[1] State of Connecticut Department of Emergency Services and Public Protection, "State Police Investigate Newtown School Shooting" [Press Release] December 15, 2012.
[2] State of Connecticut Department of Emergency Services and Public Protection, "Update: Newtown School Shooting" [Press Release], December 19, 2012.
[3] CNN, "Family of 6 Year Old Victim," December 14, 2012, "Sandy Hook School Shooting Hoax Fraud," Youtube, December 17, 2012.
[4] *Hartford Courant*, "Finally 'Enough' For Chief Medical Examiner" [Editorial], January 30, 2012.
[5] John Christofferson and Jocelyn Noveck, "Sandy Hook School Shooting: Adam Lanza Kills 26 and Himself at Connecticut School," *Huffington Post*, December 15, 2012.
[6] Edmund H. Mahoney, Dave Altmari, and Jon Lender, "Sandy Hook Shooter's Pause May Have Aided Escape," *Hartford Courant*, December 23, 2012.
[7] Jaweed Kaleem, "Sandy Hook Elementary School Shooting: Newtown Connecticut Students, Administrators Among Victims, Reports Say," *Huffington Post*, December 14, 2012.
[8] RadioMan911TV, "Sandy Hook Elementary School Shooting Newtown Police / Fire and CT State Police," Youtube, December 14, 2012. At several points in this recording audio is scrambled, particularly following apprehension of a second shooting suspect outside the school, suggesting a purposeful attempt to withhold vital information.

[9] Miranda Leitsinger, "You Feel Helpless: First Responders Rushed to School After Shooting, Only to Wait," *US News on NBC*, December 20.

[10] *http://thenetng.com/wp-content/uploads/2012/12/Sandy-Hook-Elementary-School-600×400.jpg. 12/25/12 Note that this photo of approximately fifteen children allegedly being evacuated from Sandy Hook Elementary* was *reportedly produced on December 14. See Connor Simpson, Alexander Abad-Santos et al, "Newtown School Shooting: Live Updates,"* The Atlantic Wire, *December 19, 2012. Still, the paltry number of children confirms the claim that little photographic evidence exists of Sandy Hook's 600 students being moved from the facility on December 14. This photo was from a Tweet of a Sandy Hook drill published by the school's slain principal Dawn Hochsprung titled, "Safety First." See Julia La Rouche, "Principal Killed in Sandy Hook Tweeted Picture of Students Practicing an Evacuation Drill,"* Business Insider, *December 16, 2012. [**Editor's note**: See the Prologue and Ch. 6, among others.]*

[11] Rob Dew, "Evidence of 2nd and 3rd Shooter at Sandy Hook," *Infowars Nightly News*, December 18, 2012, *http://www.youtube.com/watch?v=8nCFHImNeRw*. A more detailed yet less polished analysis was developed by citizen journalist Idahopicker, "Sandy Hook Elem: 3 Shooters," December 16, 2012. See also James F. Tracy, "Analyzing the Newtown Narrative: Sandy Hook's Disappearing Shooter Suspects," Memoryholeblog.com, December 20, 2012.

[12] W. Lance Bennett, *News: The Politics of Illusion* 9th Edition, Boston: Longman, 2012, 47.

NOTE: Andrew Whooley provided suggestions and research for this article, which originally appeared as *"The Sandy Hook Massacre: Unanswered Questions and Missing Information"* (24 December 2012), on *memoryholeblog.com*.

2

Six Signs Sandy Hook Elementary School was Closed

by Dr. Eowyn, Ph.D.

The alternative media have blogged and made countless YouTube videos on what Wolfgang Halbig calls "things that don't make sense" about the Sandy Hook Elementary School (SHES) shooting massacre of 20 first-graders and 6 adults on December 14, 2012, in Newtown, Connecticut.

Some of those "things that don't make sense" are emergency medical helicopters not being called to the scene, parents showing no grief, donation websites with creation dates that preceded the massacre, government's continuing refusal to release the death certificates and burial sites of the alleged victims, and homes with a sale transaction date of 12/25/2009 and a $0 sale price.

Recently, I undertook a review of the "things that don't makes sense," which led me to conclude that the crux — the decisive and most important issue — of whether the massacre actually happened is this:

Was Sandy Hook Elementary School (SHES) operational on December 14, 2012, or had it long been abandoned?

If the school already was closed, no children or teachers would be there on December 14 to be gunned down by Adam Lanza.

Here's the evidence supporting the contention that SHES had long been abandoned:

29

1. What school's neighbors said

In an interview with Halbig on Truth Radio Show on March 21, 2014, Infowars reporter Dan Bidondi said (5:45 mark), "The school's been closed down for God knows how long. [Neighbors] can't understand why there were kids in that building because it was condemned."

2. Reports of shes being contaminated with asbestos. requiring expensive repairs

SHES was built in 1956. Several reports in local newspaper *The Newtown Bee* indicate that years before the massacre, SHES was in a state of disrepair and contaminated with environmental toxins.

As examples, in 2002, Consulting Engineering Services recommended to the school district that SHES be "worked on in 2010 over a nine-month period" to upgrade and renovate its heating and ventilation system at a cost of $4.5 million. Two years later, in 2004, the Newtown Board of Education was told "there were serious problems with the Sandy Hook elementary school roof." Four years later, in 2008, there was yet more bad news: SHES was contaminated with asbestos. **(Remember that 2008 date.)**

On October 5, 2013, nearly 10 months after the massacre, a city referendum passed by over 90% in support of the demolition and rebuilding of SHES with a generous $49.25 million grant from the State of Connecticut. The reason given for the demolition was "asbestos abatement". On Dec 2, 2013, Newtown's Public Building and Site Commission Chairman Robert Mitchell issued a report to justify the already-approved demolition.

Consigli Construction's drawing of the new $50 million replacement Sandy Hook Elementary School

He said that "had the town decided to reoccupy the school on Dickinson Drive, it would have faced a daunting and possibly insurmountable challenge regarding the presence of hazardous materials" because the school was contaminated by not just asbestos, but also PCBs under the flooring and in the foundations and footings.

Just think: If the city already knew in 2008 that the school was contaminated with asbestos and, in 2013, used the contamination to justify tearing it down, why would the same asbestos-contaminated school be safe for children and teachers to inhabit from 2008 through 2012? If SHES had remained open, wouldn't the school district be sued for endangering public health?

It makes more sense that the school was shut down in 2008 and remained closed, until the massacre provided Newtown with the financial means — a windfall of $50 million from the state — to tear down the school and build a swanky, state-of-the-art replacement.

3. Photographic evidence of an abandoned school

Crime scene photos of the exterior and interior of SHES — from the website of the State of Connecticut's Department of Emergency Services and Public Protection, and from a batch of photos that Halbig obtained via Connecticut's Freedom of Information Act (FOIA), some of which are posted on Jim Fetzer's blog — are consistent with the appearance of an abandoned school.

Moss and grime covered the school building; repairs were left undone.

Especially noteworthy, as pointed out by Jim Fetzer, is a dangerous, exposed metal rod on an exterior staircase (see #3 in photo below):

Classrooms and hallways were used for storage, jammed with furniture and office supplies. If those rooms and hallways were actually in an operational school, then SHES was in clear violation of the fire safety code.

Then there is this photo of a pile of dust underneath an alleged bullet hole in a wall outside Room 1C, which looks suspiciously like the debris from someone drilling a pretend "bullet" hole into the ceramic wall-tile.

I've painted red circles around the "bullet" hole and the little pile of drilled dust underneath.

4. Absence of handicapped parking spaces and signage

But we don't need crime scene photos for visual indicators of a long abandoned school. The many aerial photographic and video images of Sandy Hook Elementary School's parking lot taken by news media on the day of the massacre would suffice, such as the one from a CNN news video.

Although the CNN image on the next page shows a wheelchair symbol painted on a parking space closest to the school's front door, it is not painted

BREAKING NEWS
POLICE: SHOOTINGS TOOK PLACE IN TWO ROOMS AT SCHOOL
School's principal and psychologist among the dead CNN

in the now-familiar blue and white colors that have become ubiquitous certainly by 2012.

As an example, an August 22, 2011 article by Debbie Moore for *My Parking Sign* stated:

> *Americans with Disabilities Act signed in 1990 ... details guidelines for every public area that needs to provide with ample accessibility options for the disabled....*
>
> *ADA states the following rules that need to be followed while posting accessibility signs in designated areas –*
>
> *The international symbol of accessibility should be posted on all accessible parking spaces marking the reserved spot. The accessibility symbol is the well-known picture of a person using **a wheelchair on top of a blue background.***
>
> *Van-accessible parking spaces to have additional 'text' or 'sign' below the accessibility symbol to mark the van-accessible area specifically.*
>
> ***Signs should be placed** at such a height (**at least 60 inches above surface**) that they do not get obscured by any parked vehicles or other obstructions. ADA handicap parking signs (commonly known as Access Signs) posted must be viewable from the drivers' seat of the vehicle and located right in view of parking spaces."*

But aerial images of SHES's parking lot, including the CNN image, show no blue-and-white signage for designated handicap parking spaces, which would make the school in violation of the Americans with Disabilities Act of 1990 and the subsequent ADA Amendments Act of 2008 that broadened the meaning of disabilities.

Indeed, Connecticut General Statutes, Sec. 14-253a(h), clearly states that "Parking spaces designated for persons who are blind and persons with disabilities on or after October 1, 1979, and prior to October 1, 2004, shall be as near as possible to a building

entrance or walkway and shall be fifteen feet wide including three feet of cross hatch, or parallel to a sidewalk on a public highway."

Referring to that Connecticut state law, a 2009 ordinance of the town of Monroe, CT,about 9 miles from Newtown, specified that "**Exterior accessible parking spaces [for the handicapped] shall be** located on the shortest route . . . and **identified by both a standing sign and painted on the pavement.**"

But aerial views of SHES's parking lot show no handicap standing signs or the distinctive blue-and-white handicap sign colors.

5. Absence of internet activity 2008-2012

Arguably, the most compelling evidence that SHES had long been abandoned before the 2012 massacre is the testimony from the Internet Archive's Wayback Machine of the school's lack of of Internet activity from the beginning of 2008 through all of 2012.

The Wayback Machine is a digital archive of the Internet which uses a special software to crawl and download all publicly accessible World Wide Web pages. It was Jungle Server_who first discovered that the Wayback Machine shows an absence of Internet activity from SHES since 2008 — the same year when the school was found to be contaminated with asbestos.

To verify Jungle Surfer's claim, I searched for SHES's website, *http:// newtown.k12.ct.us/~sh*, on the Wayback Machine, the result of which is below,

showing the school's lack of Internet activity from the beginning of 2008 to mid-2013. By mid-2013, we are told SHES temporarily had relocated to the nearby town of Monroe, about 9 miles from Newtown.

6. Halbig's FOI hearing

On April 24, 2015, more than two years after Halbig first asked questions about Sandy Hook by phoning and writing letters to Connecticut officials invoking the FOIA, the state finally granted him the first of two hearings before the State of Connecticut Freedom of Information Commission. The respondents were the Newtown Police Department, First Selectman Patricia Llodra, the Town of Newtown, and Newtown's Board of Education. They were represented by attorney Monte Frank, a gun-control activist who founded Team 26, a cycling group that lobbies for gun control.

The purpose of the hearing was to determine if Newtown improperly withheld documents requested by Halbig. Halbig claims that he had requested the following documents from the respondents, but was denied — the denial being a violation of FOIA:

SHES maintenance work orders, including:

1. Copies of all maintenance work orders submitted by SHES principal Dawn Hochsprung (one of Lanza's alleged victims who, strangely, was interviewed by The Bee about the massacre) **or her designee to the school district maintenance department** for any repairs, new classroom doors or painting **from July 1, 2012 through December 13, 2012.**

2. Copies signed by Hochsprung or her designee **showing the date of completion of the repairs together with time stamps showing job completion.**

2. Copies of all emails to and from Hochsprung and her assistant to various school district departments, e.g., food services provider, **from May 1, 2012 through December 13, 2012.**

The requested documents presumably could prove that the school was operational on the day of the massacre.

In a post on April 25, 2015, an anonymous contributor to *SandyHookFacts. com*, a blog that claims to debunk Sandy Hook "conspiracy theorists," triumphantly crowed that the FOI hearing was a "total failure" for Halbig because attorney Frank said time-stamped SHES maintenance work orders signed by Hochsprung or her designee had been made available to Halbig six months before the hearing.

SandyHookFacts.com is much too hasty and mistaken in its crowing, for in a memo on June 25, 2015, titled "Transmittal of Proposed Final Decision," the State of Connecticut Freedom of Information Commission (FOIC) states the following:

> *"it is found that the respondents, through counsel, informed the complainant [Halbig] that the respondents maintained 45 records responsive to the complainant's request described in paragraph 2(a)(i), above, and that they would be provided upon payment of the copying fee. [...]*
>
> *It is found that the respondents' counsel also informed the complainant that his **request described in paragraph 2(a)(i)**, above, was vague, overly broad, and that it was not a request for 'specific documents and **would require research and analysis not required under the FOI Act.**'"*

Most importantly, the FOIC states:

> *"It is found that . . . the respondents, through counsel, also informed the complainant that **the town had no records responsive to the request described in paragraph 2(a)(ii)**, above."*

Note that paragraph 2(a)(i) in the FOIC memo is 1A in this post (see above), i.e., copies of all maintenance work orders submitted by SHES principal Dawn Hochsprung or her designee to the school district maintenance department for any repairs, new classroom doors or painting from July 1, 2012 through December 13, 2012.

Note that paragraph 2(a)(ii) in the FOIC memo is 1B in this post, i.e., copies signed by Hochsprung or her designee showing the date of completion of the repairs together with time stamps showing job completion.

By saying that "the town had no records responsive to the request described in paragraph 2(a)(ii)," the FOIC means the town of **Newtown does not have documents signed by Hochsprung or her designee showing the date of completion of the repairs [to SHES] together with time stamps showing job completion.**

Furthermore, the FOIC memo also states:

> *"It is found that the respondents' counsel also informed the complainant*

that his request described in paragraph 2(b)(i), above, was vague, overly broad, and that it . . . 'would require research and analysis not required under the FOI Act.'"

Note that FOIC's paragraph 2(b)(i) is document 2 in this post, i.e., copies of all emails to and from Hochsprung and her assistant to various school district departments, e.g., food services provider, from May 1, 2012 through December 13, 2012.

In other words, Newtown cannot produce evidence that in the months preceding the massacre from May 1, 2012 through December 13, 2012, repairs were made on Sandy Hook Elementary School or that Hochsprung had exchanged emails with school district departments.

The reason is a simple one: the school was not operational, having been closed down for years, most probably since 2008 when it was discovered to be contaminated with asbestos.

This chapter originally appeared as *"Sandy Hook Hoax: 6 Signs that School was Closed before Massacre"* (9 September 2015), *fellowshipoftheminds.com.*

Dr. Eowyn

3

Wolfgang Halbig goes for the Jugular in his FOIA Hearing

by Jim Fetzer , Ph.D.

Wolfgang Halbig, a former Florida State Trooper, school principal and nationally recognized school safety expert, may be the leading researcher into the Sandy Hook affair. After filing complaint upon complaint about the failure of responses to his FOIA (Freedom of Information Act) requests, he was granted ahearing, which was initially scheduled for March 31, 2015. Wolfgang waited, but the time came and went. It was re-booked for April 24th and has taken place. Here is an exclusive interview withWolfgang by MBC (Media Broadcasting Center), where a video recording of the hearing and a panel discussion of what had transpired during the hearing with many serious students of Sandy Hook follows (search by title on YouTube):

For those who are less familiar with the background of the Sandy Hook hoax, here is a summary of key aspects, which include ample proof that the school had been closed by 2008, which included that it was not compliant with Connecticut laws implementing the *Americans with Disabilities Act,* where there is a complete absence of the familiar white-and-blue parking areas and corresponding signage, where the exterior of the building is in deplorable condition and the inside was being used for storage (search by title on YouTube):

Among our most important discoveries has been the FEMA manual for the Sandy Hook event (Appendix A), which specifies that a rehearsal will be conducted on December 13, 2012, with the event going "LIVE" on the 14th, which explains why Wolf has been unable to obtain information about the *Port-A-Potties*, which on its face seems very obscure, but where releasing the documents he has requested would reveal that they were delivered on the 13th, which blows the cover for the whole event. *Bear in mind that, while we*

already know that it was a scam, Wolf is proceeding to establish that point as a matter of law.

Photos from "The Crime Scene"

One of Wolf's successes has been to gain access to dozens and dozens of photographs taken of the school the day after the alleged shooting. MBC has included them with its broadcast, where I am offering a sample of what they tell us about the condition of the school, both inside and out. These photographs provide further substantiation of my inference that the school had been closed by 2008, which I published (with Amanda) in "Sandy Hook Elementary School: Closed in 2008, a stage in 2012". The building is covered with moss and grime, with many indications of repairs left undone:

The interior shots provide even more damning proof that the school had long-since been abandoned, with loose electrical chords dangling, unkempt offices and rooms, with materials stored everywhere. Anyone who reviews these photos should have a more profound appreciation for the points that I made in "Sandy Hook: Ten More Proofs that Vitiate the 'Official Account'" and in "Sandy Hook Elementary School: Closed in 2008, a stage in 2012", at least one of which remains accessible on YouTube today:

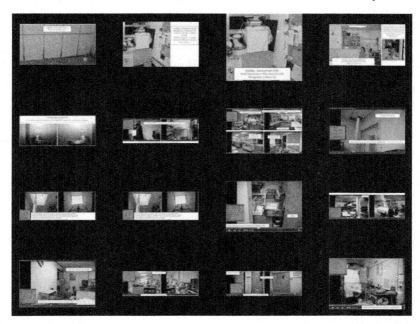

The FOIA Hearing (April 24, 2015)

Kelley Watt has summarized the event as follows: On Friday, April 24, 2015, Wolfgang had his long overdue and awaited hearing before the Freedom of Information Commission. The Commissioner is a Governor Malloy appointee. The discussion dealt with the consent agenda regarding the Super Bowl permission by Dawn Hochsprung (*"the hoax was sprung in the dawn"*), documents for which Wolf had requested. Monte Frank, an attorney, was present representing the School Board, the Newtown Police and the Town of Newtown.

Frank claimed Wolf had the documents he needed and had requested but Wolf stood firm and stated he wanted permission slips of children to sing, authorization from Dawn and the school board approving the field trip and those documents he did not receive. Wolf also took issue with documents

41

regarding Chatfield's regarding the *Porta-A-Potties* and who called for them; he wanted but did not receive the documents from the school board or the school. The school would have to have been the party ordering them, since they are on their property.

Wolf then brought up the fact that there were no documents pertaining to communications between Connecticut Trooper One and the Newtown police. Chief Kehoe of the Newtown Police Department has claimed there were no communication logs, yet it was the Newtown police who asked for Trooper One helicopter to help search for a shooter or multiple  shooters in the woods behind the school. (Search YouTube by title.)

Then it was the man in charge of maintenance for Sandy Hook schools who garnered laughter from the crowd when he stated *he had read the work orders but didn't know if they existed.* The FOIA requests that Wolf received had two unsigned signature lines at the bottom stating that the work had been done and signed off on by a supervisor; however, this man stated that they were not signed and that they just signed off verbally.

When asked when the new security system was installed, he stated it was last updated in 2007! This was new information to all researchers and when Wolf was asked why he thought there was a new system, Wolf said every news outlet in America reported that the school had a new system and that the school principal, Mrs. Hochsprung, had sent out letters to parents describing the new security upgrades.

Monte said it was "hearsay" and he objected to it being in the record based on hearsay. The question also arose during the hearing why, after the first 911 calls were made, the police records indicate the incident was "moderate" rather than an emergency, where the unknown person in the vicinity was said to be "unwanted". Most of the meeting consisted of Monte Frank objecting to things, asking that things not be put in the record, and contending that most of the items Wolf was pursuing were irrelevant.

Wolf visits with Governor Malloy

After the meeting it was decided to take Wolf over to the state legislature in order to go to Malloy's office and ask him a question. They had to park a mile away but they went to the Governor's office and Wolf made a request of his aide, *"Can you ask Malloy who spoke to him during the press conference he referenced that, 'The Lt. Governor and I have been spoken to that something like this may be played out in our state'?"* And you can watch and hear the Governor make precisely that remark in this video (search YouTube by title):

Much to Wolf's amazement, the Lt. Governor and Malloy walked right by Wolf, so Wolf said, *"Hello, I am Wolfgang Halbig. Can I ask you a question?"* Malloy said *"Sure."* So Wolf asked who had spoken to him in advance apprising him that something like this might happen in your state. Governor Malloy's response was *"I never said that!"*, which was rather astonishing, since

the Governor's press conference the day of the event was recorded and widely publicized at the time. Wolf now has his denial on film! (Search YouTube by title.)

Governor Malloy blundered here, no doubt because he did not want to admit that the person who had warned him "something like this might happen" appears to have been Attorney General Eric Holder, who visited with the governor on November 27, 2012, which was only a few weeks before the event at Sandy Hook would go down. Yet the governor made no effort to warn Connecticut school districts to enhance their security due to an imminent threat. I surmise he was in fact told they were going to take an abandoned school and conduct a drill and present it as real to promote the administration's anti-gun agenda.

Conclusion and Discussion

The room was full of Wolf's supporters. Wolf was told subpoenas were irrelevant because it was not a courtroom, where Monte Frank told Pat Llodra and the head custodian they did not have to obey the subpoenas and not to show up. It was reported that Monte was trembling. They ran out of time so the hearing will be held at a later date to finish up. I just listened to the hearing once and I think this all pretty accurate. Wolf's attorney did a great job considering she believed at first this really happened. I wonder what she thinks now! Thus concludes Kelley Watts summary of the initial hearing. But many of Wolf's supporters joined him in a round-table discussion of what he had accomplished thus far:

While many other photos and videos of the deplorable condition of Sandy Hook Elementary School may be found in "Sandy Hook Elementary School: Closed by 2008, a stage in 2012", I would like to offer a few examples of the photos that are now in the public domain, which illustrate the key point--reinforced by the report that the school's security system had most recently been updated in 2007!--by examples of the deplorable state of the school inside and out, where it was clearly being used for storage and was not operating at the time, one of which I have taken from that article for inclusion here:

Exhibit (1): Absence of compliance with Americans with Disabilities Act:

Exhibit (2): Presence electrical hazards for teachers, staff and students alike:

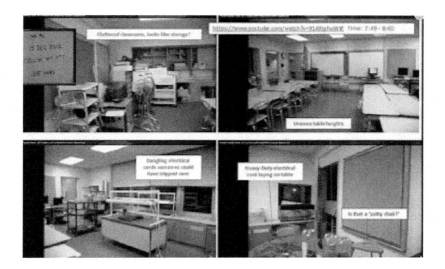

Exhibit (3): Absence of wheelchair accessibility and of proper maintenance:

Exhibit (4): Presence of stored items of every shape, kind and description:

If these are not compelling, there are many more. You will find gutters in need of repair, walls covered with moss, leaks and stains that require

attention, classrooms filled with boxes and miscellaneous stuff, which have now been released because of Wolfgang's heroic actions. I have no doubt that his approach is going to drive legal nails into the coffin of the Sandy Hook hoax, where I encourage everyone to visit his site and contribute to his cause. He is a good and decent man, whom I personally support 100%.

This chapter originally appeared as *"SANDY HOOK: Wolfgang Halbig goes for the jugular in FOIA Hearings"* (8 May 2015), on *jamesfetzer.blogspot. com.*

4

Shannon Hicks denies staging her fake "iconic" photograph

by Jim Fetzer, Ph.D. & Dennis Cimino

"I am not in that photo. I took that photo. And I took it while covering the evacuation of SHES on Friday, December 14, 2012"–Shannon Hicks

The photograph to which Shannon Hicks, Associate Editor of *The Newtown Bee*, refers is one that I (with Dan Cady) published in *"The Sandy Hook 'Smoking Gun': Game, Set, Match!"*, which seems to be one in a series of staged photographs.

What became of her?

Among the features that suggest they were staged is that, in the one to which she refers, a little girl is at the front of the conga line of students led by a police woman in uniform. But she is missing in Shannon's "iconic" photograph.

If this was taken in real time under emergency conditions, how could she have taken more than one? And, as we explain below, the white arrow is not in the same position in the two photos, which suggests the second was taken later.

And there is no sense of urgency about any of this. You have bystanders–whom Shannon Hicks claims were parents picking up their children–but does anyone buy that? And there should have been around 469 students and 83 faculty and staff to evacuate: *Where are they?*

47

The "Smoking Gun"

Perhaps the most extraordinary proof that the Sandy Hook "shooting" was a fabricated event in which no children died is the "iconic" photograph that was taken by Shannon Hicks, Associate Editor of *The Newtown Bee*, which **Dennis Cimino and I have subjected to an extensive and detailed analysis**. It is the only photo we have of any children being evacuated from the school:

Shannon Hicks—Newtown Bee/AP

The following photos were taken on Dec. 14, 2012.
Connecticut State Police lead a line of children from the Sandy Hook Elementary School in Newtown, Conn.

Hicks claims to have taken this on 14 December 2012 during the evacuation of children from Sandy Hook Elementary School (SHES). Rather to our astonishment, Dan Cady, *"The Sun and Sandy Hook"*, had published another photograph on 14 January 2013, more than a year-and-a-half prior to the efforts of Dennis Cimino and me to establish when her photograph was actually taken. Notice the absence of any frost on the ground or exhaust from their breathing, which will become important.

On the basis of a shadow analysis, Dan concluded that the Shannon Hicks' photograph was taken at 9:45 AM on 12 November 2012, over a month before Sandy Hook. But shadow

analysis turns out to be surprisingly complex and, given the distribution of the vehicles in the photo and such, **it would not surprise me if it had been taken in much closer proximity to the event.** It is less important when the photograph was taken than that we now have a second photo at approximately the same time.

Notice how many indications are present that this photo was staged. There was no emergency in progress, the people behind the woman in the center (closest to the children, whom Dan Cady has identified as Lisa Terifay) appear part of a drill by their body language, where the conga line sequence in the first photo is *missing the girl in the front, meaning Hicks' claim that she took that photo under emergency conditions is indefensible: they staged multiple shots and selected the one that they thought was best.*

Dan Cady has conjectured that Shannon Hicks is taking the picture of the conga line and the parents. It is his guess that Lisa Terifay (near center, blue sweatshirt, clear line of sight to the kids, in front of Shannon) took the photo that got the most attention. A relative of mine with a keen eye, however, has observed, on the basis of the location of the (driving direction) white arrow, that the "iconic" photo was taken later and from a different position, reinforcing that the photo was staged. And facebook commentator, Lisa Spears, has noticed that **the cars there on 14 December 2012 don't look the same as in Hicks' photograph.**

William Shanley and Shannon Hicks

William Shanley, a film maker of some note who resides in Connecticut, was so incensed by this discovery that he wrote to Shannon Hicks about it, where she has now asserted that she had also taken the second photo above (which appears to have been taken prior to her "iconic" image) and that she is therefore not in the photograph itself, implying that Dan Cady's conjecture was wrong:

William was not satisfied and wrote back his strongly expressed dissatisfaction that what she was telling him was true. The key point here, I think, is not whether Shannon Hicks was in the second of these photographs that has now emerged but whether the first–the "iconic" photograph–was of a real event (a *bona fide* shooting in which 20 children died) or was instead staged (during a drill):

Dennis and I believe that his photograph not only proves the "iconic" Shannon Hicks' photograph was staged but that the entire episode–the

-------- Original Message --------
Subject:RE: Sandy Hook Smoking Gun
Date:Thu, 24 Jul 2014 08:36:48 -0400
From:Shannon Hicks <Shannon@thebee.com>
To:William Shanley <wbs2012@zoho.com>

Mr Fetzer's claim that the photo you sent in your first mail, which he also used as part of his recent post, is a photo of me taking photos at Sandy Hook Elementary School on December 14, 2012 is wrong, just like most of Mr Fetzer's claims.

I am not in that photo.

I took that photo. And I took it while covering the evacuation of SHES on Friday, December 14, 2012.

-----Original Message-----
From: William Shanley [mailto:wbs2012@zoho.com]
Sent: Thursday, July 24, 2014 8:34 AM
To: Shannon Hicks
Subject: Sandy Hook Smoking Gun

http://www.veteranstoday.com/2014/07/22/the-sandy-hook-smoking-gun-game-set-match/

See attached.

William Shanley

William Shanley   8:17 AM (2 minutes ag
to Shannon, me

You can communicate with Mr. Fetzer directly about this. Wm.

On 7/24/14, 8:52 AM, Shannon Hicks wrote:
That is not a photo of a drill.

No one is taking a photo in that picture. Those are people watching for their children or siblings to emerge from the school.

That is a photo that I took during the evacuation on Friday, December 14, 2012, as I just told you less than ten minutes ago.

-----Original Message-----
From: William Shanley [mailto:wbs2012@zoho.com]
Sent: Thursday, July 24, 2014 8:49 AM
To: Shannon Hicks
Subject: Re: Sandy Hook Smoking Gun

This is a photo of the drill in which a photographer is taking the iconic photo. If you are not in the photo, then you lied about taking the picture, for as you see on close examination they were taken at the same time. Your paper will be facing all sorts of lawsuits for propagating this fraud. Besides criminal aspects, knowing producing a defective news product, although it is a civil crime, the damages will be enormous. So if you did not take the picture, then who did? How much money have you been paid by the drill organizers? As a first responder? You've got a hole lot of explaining to do. There was no evacuation of 600 students, no buses, etc., etc.

alleged shooting at the school–about which so many have published so much–was indeed an elaborately fabricated event in which no children died (as Paul Preston has reported has even been confirmed by officials in the Department of Education) to promote Barack Obama's anti-gun agenda.

Enter Dan Hennen

Imagine our surprise when I (Jim) discovered (among the comments on my "Smoking Gun" article) one from Dan Hennen, which provided a link that I had initially overlooked. When I followed the link, I was taken to a web page with the following (now familiar) photograph, accompanied by a caption stating, *"Picture at Sandy Hook taken on October 17, 2012, during emergency drill at the school"*, which reinforces the question it raises:

Bear in mind, *Shannon Hicks has acknowledged that she took this photograph.* If we take for granted that she took it as well as her "iconic" photograph, then when was it taken? She appears to be compounding the fraud by reaffirming that she took it "during the evacuation" of students at SHES. But we and others have noted before the absence of evidence that any evacuation took  place, including that those 469 students are nowhere to be seen.

As C.W. Wade and others who are attempting to defend the indefensible have observed, Shannon Hicks claims to have taken hundreds of photos at Sandy Hook, including of the evacuation. **There are not "hundreds" but 21–and no "evacuation" photos beyond those we have already seen.**

There are some photos of kids walking along Dickinston Drive (who are not K-4th graders) and others beside a car, but those are not "evacuation photos". This must be "the new math"–and confirms there was no "evacuation" because it was a drill, not a shooting.

Resolving the date

We now have at least three dates attributed to this photograph: the official date of 14 December 2012 (by Shannon Hicks and the NENPA, presumably, which made her "Photographer of the Year" for taking it); on 12 November 2012 (by Dan Cady); and on 17 October 2012 during a drill conducted at SHES (by Dan Hennen). It's obvious that this photograph was staged, as can also be seen from this photo on that day with frost on the ground and exhaust from the cold:

We have no frost on the ground or visible exhalation from the cold in the Shannon Hicks' photograph, which makes the date of 14 December 2012 no longer even remotely plausible. We should be able to narrow it down between 12 November 2012 and 17 October 2012, where we are inclined to believe that it was taken during the earlier drill as Dan Hennen reported. But it cannot be an authentic photograph taken on 14 December 2012. And other photos afford more evidence that this was a drill:

What is this officer doing *running away from the scene of the crime*, for example? He ought to be assisting in dealing with the threat from the alleged shooter. If there was one, there might have been more. And notice the officer whose silhouette can be seen in the background in front of the school. He appears more concerned with what's going on in the parking lot than with what's going on inside the school. And for good reason: *there was nothing going on inside the school!*

Shannon Hick's "iconic" photograph was thus an essential element of **(what can only be described as)** *an act of terrorism.* The events reported to have occurred at SHES on 14 December 2012 instilled fear into the hearts and minds of every American–parents and children alike–in order to make the people more amenable to manipulation to promote a political agenda. It was despicable conduct and a grotesque form of treason for which Barack Obama and Eric Holder bear ultimate responsibility.

This chapter originally appeared as *"Shannon Hicks denies staging her fake 'iconic' photograph"* (24 July 2014), in *veteranstoday.com*.

Part II

How we know
Sandy Hook was an illusion

5

Top Ten Reasons: Sandy Hook was an Elaborate Hoax

by Vivian Lee, Ph.D.

"It is an old maxim of mine that when you have excluded the impossible, whatever remains, however improbable, must be the truth."
–Sherlock Holmes ("The Adventure of the Beryl Coronet")

Figure 1. Gene Rosen Fox News live interview of December 18, 2012, now known to have been filmed in front of a green screen, with the "everyone must check in" sign inserted in the background.[1]

This article was first published in January 2014 at *Veterans Today*, a little over one year after the alleged Sandy Hook Elementary School shooting of December 14, 2012.[2] Much research on Sandy Hook has been done since the time of its publication, but the original "top ten reasons" that discredit the official story are still as valid as ever. They form the basis for all further research and, as such, are offered here in a revised and updated version. Means of accessing the videos from the online article are given in the notes.

As the article was being written, *The New York Times*, our nation's newspaper of record, published a story on Connecticut's "final report" on the Newtown shooting (December 27, 2013).[3] In this article we are told that although the report contained "hundreds of photographs, hours of video, and voluminous crime scene reports… care was taken to conceal the most graphic crime scene images." Not only that—the final report does not even include the names, ages, or sex of the alleged shooting victims (Figure 2). There was no actual identification of any of the dead.[4] Even the *News–Times* of Danbury, CT, found it unsatisfying.[5]

Redaction Index

#	Statute	Brief Description
01	CGS § 1-210(b)(3)(B)	Identity of minor witnesses
02	CGS § 1-210(b)(11)	Names/addresses of students enrolled in public school
03	CGS § 1-210(b)(2)	Personnel/medical/similar files, invasion of personal privacy
04	CGS § 1-210(b)(3)(A)	Identity of confidential informant/witness
05	n/a	Court order of J. Blawie dated March 27, 2013
06	CGS §1-210(b)(27)	Visual image depicting a homicide victim
07	CGS § 29-28(d)	Pistol permit information
08	CGS § 19a-411	Records of OCME examinations/findings
09	CGS § 1-200(5)	Items not meeting the definition of public record, including but not limited to seized physical evidence
10	CGS § 1-210(b)(3)(c)	Signed statements of witnesses
11	18 USC 2724	Information protected by the Federal Driver's Privacy Protection Act
12	US/CT Constitutions	Right to privacy (US Const. Amend. 14) and/or Victim Rights (CT Const. Art. 1 Sec 8b)
13	CGS § 1-210(b)(3)(E)	Investigatory techniques not otherwise known
14	CGS § 1-210(b)(19)	Safety risk to persons and/or buildings
15	CGS § 29-164f	COLLECT (Connecticut On-Line Law Enforcement Communications Teleprocessing) system records
16	28 USC 534	NCIC (National Crime Information Center) Records
17	CGS § 1-210(b)(3)(H)	Uncorroborated allegations subject to destruction pursuant to CGS 1-216
18	CGS § 1-210(b)(5)(A)	Trade secrets and/or proprietary information
19	CGS § 1-210(b)(5)(B)	Commercial and/or financial information given in confidence, not required by statute
20	CGS § 1-210(b)(3)(F)	Arrest/investigatory files of a juvenile compiled for a law enforcement purpose
21	31 USC 5318(g)(2)	Records protected by the Bank Secrecy Act
22	31 CFR 103.18(e)	Records protected by Federal regulations promulgated under the Bank Secrecy Act
23	CGS § 1-210(b)(1)	Preliminary drafts and/or notes
24	CGS § 1-210(b)(17)	Educational records not subject to disclosure pursuant to 20 USC 1232g
25	n/a	Code not used
26	CGS § 12-15	Tax returns and return information
27	CGS § 1-210(b)(10)	Communications privileged by common law and/or general statutes
28	CGS § 1-17a	Photo/computerized image in connection with state-issued identification
29	CGS § 1-210(b)(3)(d)	Information prejudicial to a prospective law enforcement action
30	Public Law 112-55	BATFE Records

Figure 2. Sandy Hook Elementary School Shooting Reports, Redaction Index (2013 final report).

The New York Times was not worried, however, proceeding once again to retail the official story, seemingly satisfied that in place of the redacted pages are "detailed descriptions," "eyewitness accounts," and "snapshots" of emergency workers dashing around and supposedly interacting with the school's teachers.[6] According to *The Times*, the report "did not appear to alter the broader understanding of the shooting"—the official version, that is, which the paper has promoted relentlessly despite massive evidence to the contrary. In this gross dereliction of duty, *The Times* has displayed not only its journalistic incompetence but, more grievously, its complicity in the perpetration of the Sandy Hook hoax.

This pattern of deceit extended to the Newtown Clerk's secret arrangements with the state legislature to avoid releasing death certificates to the public, attempts to withhold the 911 calls, and gag orders that were imposed on those responsible for tearing down the school building itself. In a letter accompanying the report, Reuben F. Bradford, the Commissioner of Connecticut's Department of Emergency Services and Public Protection, stated that "the names and contextually identifying information of involved children" were removed, including descriptions and images of the children, their clothing, and their belongings. "All visual images depicting the deceased have been withheld," he added, "as well as written descriptions whose disclosure would be highly offensive to a reasonable person and would violate the constitutional rights of the families."[7]

According to Bradford, the investigation was "unparalleled in the one hundred and ten year history of the Connecticut State Police. Tens of thousands of hours were spent by investigators from all over the country tracking down leads, processing evidence, and doing everything within their collective ability to provide answers for the questions that remained in the wake of the terror that morning." With the issuing of the "final report," the investigation "has been closed for administrative purposes." However, this so-called investigation did nothing to reveal the truth of the matter but rather was part of the conspiracy to conceal the reality of the event from the public.

The basic principle that applies here is inference to the best explanation.[8] Consider the totality of the evidence in this case. *Is the evidence more probable on the hypothesis that Sandy Hook was a real event or that it was instead an exercise (a "drill"), which was presented as though it was a real shooting?* The hypothesis that confers the highest degree of probability based on the evidence is preferable. Despite the exhaustive investigation allegedly carried out by the Connecticut State Police, the official scenario is not feasible in terms of the evidence. Here are the "top ten" reasons that support the conclusion that the Sandy Hook shooting was staged and not real, where no children or adults appear to have died.

1. Proof of death has been suppressed

Twenty-eight people allegedly died: 27 children and adults, including Adam Lanza, at the school, and his mother, Nancy Lanza, in her home at 36 Yogananda Street, Newtown. However, there is no direct proof of anyone's death: no photographic evidence or video footage was released to confirm the official story that these 28 persons actually died. In fact, no video surveillance footage shows anything—not even Adam shooting out the front plate-glass window or walking through the halls like Rambo, even though the school had supposedly updated its security system at the start of the 2012–2013 academic year.[9]

Figure 3. Sandy Hook Elementary, alleged bullet hole
(2013 final report, Walkley scene photos).

The best the authorities could come up with was a heavily redacted "final report" (December 2013) that includes numerous photos of the inside of the school, with a few dings identified as bullet holes, several bullets and casings on the floor, and hundreds of black (redacted) images with white numbers, which we are supposed to associate with dead people (Figures 3–4).

Figure 4. Sandy Hook Elementary, redacted image
(2013 final report, Meehan autopsy photos)

Compounding the situation, the parents were not allowed to view their children's bodies to identify them. Instead, they were reportedly shown photographs of the deceased. This was done, according to the Medical Examiner, Wayne Carver, in order to "control" the situation. But what was there about the situation that required "control"? No normal parent would have agreed to accept the death of a child without viewing the body. James Tracy has published a discussion of the medical examiner's performance (Figure 5).[10] According to Carver:

> Uh, we did not bring the bodies and the families into contact. We took pictures of them, uhm, of their facial features. We have, uh, uh—it's easier on the families when you do that. Uh, there is, uh, a time and place for the up close and personal in the grieving process, but to accomplish this we felt it would be best to do it this way and, uh, you can sort of, uh … You can control a situation depending on the photographer, and I have very good photographers. Uh, but uh—[11]

Figure 5. Medical Examiner Wayne Carver's press conference of December 15, 2012

Remarkably, the state has done its best to avoid releasing the death certificates and even recordings of the 911 calls. Death certificates were eventually "released" but not to the public or those who might want to investigate the case further; only a short, general summary was available.[12] On June 5, 2013, Connecticut passed legislation (Public Act 13–311) blocking disclosure of photos or video images of (all) homicide victims, along with other records.[13] According to Gov. Dannel Malloy, who signed the bill hours after it was passed, "all families have a right to grieve in private."[14] The final version did not cover the 911 recordings, which were ordered released in late 2013, after Judge Eliot Prescott ascertained that "no children are identified by name, no callers indicate that they can see a child being shot, and the only injury described is that of an educator's being shot in the foot."[15]

Moreover, the victims' funerals were all "closed casket," although the funeral of Noah Pozner supposedly included a private viewing before the public ceremony. As recounted in interviews with the families, the circumstances of their last encounters with their children (or with their caskets) are strange to say the least. The "love fest" at the white coffin of Grace McDonnell was detailed on CNN for Anderson Cooper (Figure 6). [16]

Figure 6. Chris and Lynn McDonnell interviewed by Anderson Cooper, December 18, 2012.

Veronique Pozner gave her account of her last look at her son Noah to the *Jewish Daily Forward* on December 26, 2013 (Figure 7):

Veronique asked the medical examiners not to autopsy her son; she felt that his body had suffered too many indignities. At his funeral, Noah was dressed in a suit and tie. A Jewish friend of Veronique's at work enjoined Rabbi Praver to allow him to be wrapped in a blue tallis, even though he had not yet had a bar mitzvah.

The family placed stuffed animals, a blanket and letters to Noah into the casket. Lastly, Veronique put a clear plastic rock with a white angel inside—an "angel stone"—in his right hand. She asked the funeral director to place an identical one in his left, which was badly mangled.

Just before the ceremony, Connecticut Governor Dannel Malloy came to the funeral home to pay his respects. Veronique took him by the arm and brought him to the casket. Noah's famously long eyelashes—which she spoke about in her eulogy—rested lightly on his cheeks and a cloth covered the place where the lower half of his face had been. "I just needed it to be real for [the governor]," she

Figure 7. Veronique Pozner interview of December 26, 2012, Jewish Daily Forward.

says. "This was a live, warm, energetic little boy whose life was snuffed out in a fraction of a second because our schools are so defenseless."[17]

2. Emergency protocols were not followed

There is no evidence of any frantic effort to save lives or remove bodies to hospitals. Instead the scene outside the school looked calm and largely bloodless—with police and other personnel milling around casually and a severe shortage of dead or injured victims. One Sandy Hook researcher decided to call Lt. Paul Vance to ask who cleaned up the blood, which would have been considered a bio-hazard, and got the reply, "What blood?" "Kelley from Tulsa" discusses this with James Fetzer on the "The Real Deal" on December 9, 2013.[18] Kelley was onto a real issue: under the EPS' Medical Waste Tracking Act of 1988, a paper trail must kept by all parties involved in the cleanup and must be tracked all the way to the incinerator with names and dates.[19]

In a Mass Casualty Incident (MCI) like Sandy Hook, the proper protocol is START triage (Simple Triage and Rapid Treatment) using tarps of different colors with the aim being to save lives and get the injured to the hospital for treatment (Figure 8).[20] Red tarps indicate that "immediate" treatment is needed, yellow that treatment may be "delayed," green that the injuries are "minor," and black tarps signify "deceased."

Figure 8. START triage set up after a train crash in Los Angeles

Outside Sandy Hook Elementary, tarps were laid out, but not even the black tarps for the dead were used, much less the red ones for those who needed immediate treatment (Figure 9). As Sofia Smallstorm has documented, nothing at all like this occurred at Sandy Hook: the appropriate protocols were not followed.[21]

Figure 9. START tarps outside Sandy Hook Elementary with no victims.

Sandy Hook Fire Chief Bill Halstead was ready to help the victims but could recall only two wounded people (Figure 10).[22] A few survivors were reportedly taken to the hospital, but, oddly, these people were never interviewed. There were no first-hand accounts that proved anyone was killed or injured. Nonetheless, by the afternoon of December 14, Lt. Vance had

TRAGEDY AT SANDY HOOK
NEWS 8 | Bill Halstead
Sandy Hook Fire Chief

Figure 10. Sandy Hook Fire Chief Bill Halstead, in an interview on December 18, 2012, says he got word that "no one else would be coming out of the building."

confirmed that 18 children were pronounced dead at the scene, two children were removed to an area hospital and died at the hospital, and seven adults were pronounced dead at the scene, including the shooter.[23]

No emergency vehicles were present at the school or even lined up in the fire lane for a rescue attempt—the parking lot was filled with parked cars, police cars and possibly media vehicles. Such rescue activity as occurred was centered, not on the school premises, but at the nearby Firehouse. Emergency vehicles at the Firehouse were jammed together impeding access to the school, in case anyone might have thought about attempting a rescue.

Figure 11. Crowds circling around and through the Sandy Hook Firehouse.

The scene at the Firehouse was quite peculiar, with people milling around and circling through the building, walking out one door and into another, to give the impression of lots of people and lots of action (Figure 11).[24]

But it was all in accordance with FEMA manuals for drills.

3. Drill protocols were followed instead

We are now living in a security state, and the school system is among its beneficiaries. While we used to have occasional "fire drills," we now have "lockdown drills" implemented by school districts, with some states requiring a set number of drills by law. Private security firms, which operate for profit, now conduct "crisis preparedness assessments" at the taxpayer's expense.[25] Larger scenarios are also developed as active-shooter drills, in which local law enforcement can take part in storming a school in pursuit of an active-actor-shooter.

One such plan available on the web is "Operation Closed Campus," developed in Iowa following guidance set forth by the Homeland Security Exercise and Evaluation Program (HSEEP) of the US Department of Homeland Security.[27] According to protocol, everyone at the drill must check in, identification badges

Figure 12. Lt. Paul Vance discussing an active shooter drill he was supervising at Oxford High School, Oxford, CT, in August 2007.[26]

are issued to personnel and observers, and drinking water and restrooms are available. Personnel include the director, staff, controllers, evaluators, actors, media personnel and "players" (agency employees) both in uniforms and civilian clothes.

Figure 13. "Gunshot wound victim" being made up for an active-shooter drill that took place in 2014 in Contra Costa County, CA.[28]

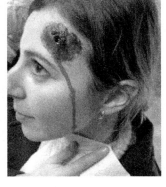

This protocol appears to have been followed at Sandy Hook, where many participants wore ID/identification badges on lanyards, a huge check-in sign is visible in one Gene Rosen interview, water is available in quantity at the Firehouse (Figure 14), and even Port-a-Potties are at the ready.[29] The check-in sign was inserted via green screen, however, shown in an interview held days after the event, so its presence is controversial (see Figure 1).

Figure 14. Sandy Hook Firehouse on December 14, 2012, with drinking water for the participants, according to drill protocol.

An emergency preparedness drill took place on December 14, 2012 (9:00 am – 4:00 pm ET), in Bridgeport, CT, which is a 20 minute drive from Sandy Hook. The course, "Planning for the Needs of Children in Disasters," was run by the Connecticut Department of Emergency Services and Public Protection/Emergency Management and Homeland Security.[30] And a FEMA Mass Casualty Drill, "Emergency Response for Mass Casualties Involving Children," was scheduled to take place on December 13 or 14, 2012 (location unspecified). The exercise was to target the following capabilities: Mass Prophylaxis, Mass Death of Children at a School by Firearms, Suicide or Apprehension of Unknown Shooter, Use of Media for Evaluation, and Use of Media for Information Distribution.[31] This may have been the script for the Sandy Hook "shooting." [Editor's note: See Appendix A for the Sandy Hook FEMA drill manual.]

The Sandy Hook "massacre" appears to have been an Integrated Capstone Event (ICE), an exercise run by FEMA to coordinate federal, state and local emergency response teams in the case of a mass-casualty event.[32]

As such, it would have utilized actors and media partners to simulate a tragedy in order to train participants, and also to observe the reaction of the citizenry.

4. There was foreknowledge of the event

The Connecticut state emergency system was taken over long before the "massacre" occurred, with a frequency change implemented five hours in advance of the "shooting." Normal police and EMS dispatch protocol, using the Alpha Phonetic System for communications between officers and dispatchers, was replaced with staged transmissions by non-trained personnel.[33]

In addition, tweets about the shooting began before it occurred,[34] a tribute was apparently uploaded one month before the event, and web pages honoring the victims, including a Facebook page R.I.P. Victoria Soto, were established before they had "officially" died (Figure 15).[35]

Figure 15. R.I.P. Victoria Soto facebook page, with "Joined Facebook December 10".

And photos of the "evacuation" and "shooting" scene by *Newtown Bee* photographer Shannon Hicks were taken before December 14, 2012 (see below). A Sandy Hook timeline has been reconstructed at *memoryholeblog. com*, detailing major developments and highlighting the numerous inconsistencies in reports by the media.[36] [Editor's note: See Appendix C.]

5. There were contradictory reports about the weapons

According to initial reports, weapons used in the shooting included four handguns recovered at the scene, the only guns taken into the school (NBC). Then an AR–15 was said to have been found in the trunk of Lanza's car (NBC). Then it was reported that Lanza may have carried only two handguns and that a rifle was also found in the school (NBC).

Wayne Carver, the Medical Examiner, said that all the victims were shot with the "long weapon."[37] Lt. Paul Vance then said that a Bushmaster AR–15 assault weapon with high capacity magazines was used "most of the time" and that Lanza was carrying "many high-capacity clips" for the weapon (Huffington Post).

In January 2013, Connecticut state police released a statement indicating that they had found three guns inside the school: a Bushmaster .223 caliber XM 15–E2S semi-automatic rifle with high capacity 30 round clips, a Glock 10mm handgun, and a Sig Sauer P226 9mm handgun (Figures 16–18).

Figure 16. Bushmaster allegedly found inside the school (2013 final report, Walkley scene photos).

Figure 17. Glock and clip allegedly found inside the school (2013 final report, Walkley scene photos).

Figure 18. Sig Sauer and clip allegedly found inside the school (2013 final report, Walkley scene photos).

The police said they also found an Izhmash Saiga–12 12-gauge shotgun in Lanza's car (NBC). This is presumably the gun shown in a video aired on the night of December 14, 2012, by NBC (Figure 19). An evidence collection team and a policeman are shown finding the shotgun in the trunk of Lanza's Honda Civic— the policeman handles the gun without gloves and ejects the ammunition on the spot, destroying evidence in the process.[38] Some have seen two long guns in the trunk in the NBC video: the 12-gauge shotgun and the Bushmaster rifle.[39]

Figure 19. Policeman ejecting ammunition from a long gun found in the trunk of Adam Lanza's car on December 14, 2012.

Lt. Vance then asserted that Lanza had killed all his victims with the .223-caliber semi-automatic rifle (ctpost.com). Regarding the confusion, Vance told reporters, "It's all these conspiracy theorists that are trying to mucky up the waters."

Perhaps "The Top Prize for Fantastical Reporting" goes to Fox News, however, which announced that a 12-gauge shotgun along with two magazines containing 70 rounds of Winchester 12-gauge shotgun rounds had been found in the glove compartment of Adam Lanza's Honda Civic—that's right, *in the glove compartment.*[40]

6. Adam Lanza cannot have done the shooting

Adam Lanza, reportedly a frail young man weighing 112 pounds with Asperger's Syndrome, is said to have carried massive weaponry on his person when he shot his way into the Sandy Hook school and proceeded to kill 26 people and then himself. This after

Figure 20. A young Adam Lanza, who supposedly "fell off the face of the earth" around 2009, with no record of his activities since that time (CNN).

he supposedly killed his mother before driving to the school. It should of course be noted that Adam Lanza was initially listed in the Social Security Death Index as having died on December 13, 2012, one day before the alleged shooting.[41]

According to State's Attorney Stephen Sedensky, Lanza killed his 26 victims with the Bushmaster .223-caliber rifle and then killed himself with his Glock 10mm handgun.[42] Lanza was also allegedly carrying three 30-round magazines for the Bushmaster as well as a Sig Sauer 9mm handgun (see above). The victims were supposedly shot multiple times each in a fusillade of bullets from these military-style weapons. In order to wreak this havoc, he fired more than 150 rounds, and he carried more rounds in addition. Lanza was reportedly found dead wearing a bulletproof vest and military-style clothing (AP).

As Mike Powers, a professional military investigator and ballistics expert, has observed, this young man of slight build could not have carried all these heavy, bulky weapons and ammunition on his person. Furthermore, since first responders were supposedly inside the school within seven minutes, there was not enough time for Lanza to have carried out the shooting as reported. In an interview with Joyce Riley, Powers states that Lanza could not have fired so many times continuously without destabilizing himself from the intense noise from the Bushmaster. As a novice, he could not have shot an AR–15 with such speed and accuracy, supposedly changing magazines 4–5 times without a stoppage.[43] For a real person shooting an AR–15 and what it entails, see Redsilverj's "Sandy Hook Hoax Ultimate Case Closed" (Figure 21):

Figure 21. A skilled marksman shooting off 100 rounds from an AR–15.[44]

According to Lt. Vance on the night of the shooting, one victim survived. So in less than seven minutes—or less than five minutes according to the media—Lanza killed 26 people and then himself, producing only one injured victim. This is a 96% kill ratio, which is unheard-of accuracy among the most experienced marksmen. Mike Powers thinks the whole scenario is a physical impossibility. He is not even convinced that Adam Lanza was a real person.

Oddly, considering the horrifying details of the alleged massacre, as well as Adam's own suicide by shooting himself in the head with the Glock handgun, the 2013 final report photos show no obvious traces of blood or gore on Adam's clothes, hat, gloves, or shoes (Figure 22).

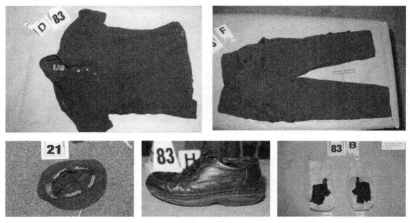

Figure 22. Some of Adam Lanza's alleged clothing removed from his body for photography (2013 final report, Walkley scene photos).

The final travesty involves the weapons and other paraphernalia that were allegedly found in the Lanza house.[45] [Editor's note: See Chapter 6.]

The "arsenal" supposedly included guns, Samurai swords, knives, a bayonet and more than 1,000 rounds of ammunition, according to search warrants released. Other items of interest were ear and eye protection, binoculars, holsters, manuals, paper targets, a military-style uniform, and Lanza's NRA certificate (Fox). Lanza had reportedly compiled a spreadsheet 7 feet long and 4 feet wide in 9-point type detailing 500 victims of other mass murders (CBS). We are supposed to believe this, and, at the same time, that Adam Lanza was a shy, quiet kid who didn't like noise and chaos, as promoted by the PBS Frontline Special, "Raising Adam Lanza."[46]

7. Key participants displayed inappropriate behavior

There are many bizarre media reports and interviews of those associated with the "shooting." Many of the participants seem to be actors (or intelligence operatives). Some examples:

Wayne Carver—Medical Examiner Wayne Carver's surreal press conference is one of the most startling of all the media offerings. Widely available on youtube, this event shows H. Wayne Carver II, a public official of some standing, clowning and acting outlandish—grinning strangely, making irrelevant comments, and basically appearing unknowledgeable and unprofessional (Figure 23).[47]

Figure 23. Dr. H. Wayne Carver II, entertainer.

Robbie Parker—Perhaps the most infamous press conference is that of Robbie Parker, the alleged father of victim Emilie Parker, speaking on a CNN report of December 15, 2012. He chuckles as he walks up to the camera (Figure 24), then gets into character by hyperventilating, and finally feigns distress as he talks about his daughter—reading from a cue card—and about the fund set up to help raise money "for Emilie."[48]

Figure 24. Robbie Parker, walking up to the camera for his interview.

The families—In addition to Robbie and Alissa Parker, other parents and family members take their turn in the spotlight, including (but not limited to) Mark and Jackie Barden, Jimmy Greene and Nelba Marquez–Greene, Ian and Nicole Hockley, Neil Heslin (alleged father of Jesse Lewis), Chris and Lynn McDonnell, Veronique Pozner, Carlee Soto, and David and Francine Wheeler.[49] Anderson Cooper is the interviewer in two notable instances: his conversation with the McDonnells mentioned above, and an interview with Veronique Pozner, remarkable for its green-screen effects such as Anderson's disappearing nose (Figure 25).[50]

Figure 25. Anderson Cooper during a green-screen interview of Veronique Pozner.

The school nurse—Numerous reports offer detailed and totally fictitious information, some of which was later abandoned in favor of more tenable versions. On the evening of December 14, a USA Today reporter said she had spoken with the school nurse (not identified by name), whom she had met on the street (Figure 26). The nurse told her that the gunman had come into her office, "they met eyes, she jumped under her desk," and he walked out. The nurse said that the gunman was the son of the kindergarten teacher, who was known to her and "an absolutely loving person." It later developed that Nancy Lanza had not been a kindergarten teacher at all, and that neither Nancy nor Adam had any proven connection to Sandy Hook school whatsoever.[51]

Figure 26. USA Today reporting a fabricated story about the school nurse, the gunman, and his mother the kindergarten teacher at Sandy Hook Elementary.

Dawn Hochsprung—In an embarrassing fiction, *The Newtown Bee* reported on December 14, 2012, that Dawn Hochsprung, the Sandy Hook school principal, told the paper that a masked man had entered the school with a rifle and started shooting multiple shots—more than she could count—that went "on and on." Of course, Dawn Hochsprung was allegedly killed by Adam Lanza and so could not easily have provided this statement. In fact, Dawn was said to have acted heroically, dying while lunging at the gunman—although one wonders who witnessed and reported this act of heroism. On December 17, 2012, *The Bee* retracted the report and apologized:

> An early online report from the scene at the December 14 shootings at Sandy Hook Elementary School quoted a woman who identified herself to our reporter as the principal of the school. The woman was not the school's principal, Dawn Hochsprung, who was killed in the Friday morning attack. The quote was removed from subsequent online versions of the story, but the original story did remain in our online archive for three days before being deleted. We apologize for whatever confusion this may have caused our readers and for any pain or anguish it may have cause [sic] the Hochsprung family.[52]

Gene Rosen—Gene Rosen is one of the most prolific of the Sandy Hook media stars, giving animated and conflicting statements to a series of reporters (in English and Spanish). Considered a "good Samaritan" by the mainstream media, Gene supposedly harbored six children who ran away from the school, rode to his house on a school bus, sat down on his lawn and proceeded to cry and tell him that their teacher, Miss Soto, was dead. Strangely, Rosen took the children inside and gave them some toys to play with, instead of calling 911 like any normal person.[53]

The Gene Rosen videos are important for the official narrative, in that they corroborate many of its details: the staccato gunfire (and thus a semiautomatic weapon) and hearsay evidence from the children (Lanza had a big gun and a little gun, Vicki Soto was killed, etc.). These incriminating videos are some of the best evidence that the Sandy Hook shooting was a hoax.

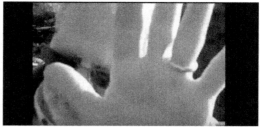

Figure 27. Gene Rosen signaling to a "reporter" that he wants to start over, after bungling his lines in a practice interview.

8. Photos at scene and of victims look staged or fake

Many of the photos released to the public look staged or fake; here are some notable examples:

Shannon Hicks photo of children being evacuated from the school— The only photo we have seen of any children being evacuated from the school was apparently taken earlier in the fall during a drill—no coats, smiling faces, leaves remaining on a few trees.[54] Shannon Hicks of *The Newtown Bee* took the "iconic" photo (Figure 28) and claimed to have taken many others of the event—although no other children being evacuated were seen in those released to the media. Hicks reportedly took the famous photo "as an associate editor" and then, when another editor arrived, "changed into her firefighting gear and tried to help." This heroic account was promoted by NPR on December 16.[55]

Figure 28. Shannon Hicks' photo for The Newtown Bee of children supposedly being evacuated from Sandy Hook Elementary on the morning of December 14, 2012.

An analysis of the Hicks "iconic" photo has shown that it was not taken around 10:00 am on the morning of December 14, 2012—the shadows are wrong for that time of day, no one's breath has condensed into visible vapor (although the recorded temperature was 28 degrees F and frost appears on the ground in other photos), the markings on the parking lot are wrong, the positions of the vehicles and traffic cone do not match, etc.[56] A recent sun-shadow analysis shows that the photo was taken at around 11:10 am, not at 10:09 am as alleged by Hicks, and clearly not on the cold morning of December 14.[57]

Indeed, another photo appeared (Figure 29), showing what appears to be a preliminary staging for the famous "iconic" photo released worldwide. Here also is the line of students but in a somewhat different order. In addition, several onlookers stand in the foreground; the woman at center may have been snapping photographs, although there is certainly someone else taking pictures here—the photographer who captured this second image.

Figure 29. Staging of the "evacuation" photo, with children in a different arrangement than in the final version.

Shannon Hicks was named Photographer of the Year by the New England Newspaper and Press Association (NENPA) in February 2014, as well as receiving a first place award for Spot News Photo "for her iconic image of young students being led from Sandy Hook School by law enforcement responders."[58] However, it has now emerged that Shannon Hicks uploaded a slideshow of 20 photographs to YouTube the day before the alleged shooting—including the staging shot (Figure 29) among others. This slideshow was available by the evening of December 13, 2012, but released on December 14 as photos taken on that date, as documented by QKultra (Figure 30).[59]

Figure 30. "Newtown Bee Stinger."

Photo of shattered plate glass window at entrance to Sandy Hook Elementary—Several photos from Connecticut's December 2013 final report show the plate glass window that Adam Lanza allegedly shot out with his Bushmaster, and through which he entered the premises. But how did he get past the furniture, with all his weaponry, without moving anything out of position?[60] Not only did Lanza squeeze through this hole and edge carefully through the narrow space between the couch and table, but so did ten policemen, all with their guns and gear, according to sworn affidavits.[61] Yet nothing was pushed aside, and the magazine rack looks like it was moved carefully away from the window (Figure 31).

Figure 31. Window with shattered glass, supposedly blown out by "the shooter," next to the front lobby doors (2013 final report, Walkley scene photos).

Many of the photos from the December 2013 final report look staged, such as those showing small numbers of bullets scattered over the school floor, or the unlikely shots of Adam Lanza's clothing (see Figure 22 above).

Just as insidious are photographs of the children who allegedly died at Sandy Hook, many of which were demonstrably altered via Photoshop. Most of the individual images of the children released to the media are peculiar—numerous images have a curiously similar background of green foliage, and several look outdated and may be old photos.

Parker family photos—Some of the most problematic involve the Parker family, several of which show evidence of tampering. In two notorious photos, Emilie's red-and-black dress appears in both: once worn by Emilie in a Photoshopped family photo (Figure 32) and then supposedly worn by her younger sister Madeline for the photo-op with Barack Obama (Figure 33).

Figure 32. Photoshopped image of the Parker family, showing the two youngest girls missing their legs and Emilie, at right, apparently added to the image.

Victoria Soto photos—Photos of Victoria Soto have emerged as Photoshopped creations. Images of Soto were inserted into photographs in which she did not originally appear, and several shots of her face were created from a single photo.[62]

The well-known photograph of Soto's class of first grade students is an elaborate composite, released in a small format, low quality image (Figure 34). Soto is wearing the exact same outfit seen in another photo with green foliage background, although there she faces the other direction; that image was merely flipped and inserted into the class picture.

In doing so the creators had to reconstruct her right hand and did so poorly, cutting off her thumb with a vertical line. Ann Marie Murphy was also inserted, and her hand too is problematic.

The hands of the children are blurry, their eyes are fuzzy, and square and rectangular defects appear on their faces—all unnoticeable in a small image but readily seen when enlarged (Figure 35 on the next page).[63]

Figure 33. President Obama with children from the Parker family (and others), in which Emilie's sister Madeline is supposedly wearing her red-and-black dress.

Figure 34. Photograph of Victoria Soto's first grade class, a Photoshopped composite.

Figure 35. Soto's class photo with defects visible in enlarged images (Megatronics Media).

Allison Wyatt/Lily Gaubert—In a likely sloppy slip-up, a photo of a real child, Lily Gaubert (Figure 36, left), who is apparently alive and well, was promoted in the media as an image of Allison Wyatt (Figure 36, right), an alleged victim. Lily's mother supposedly discovered the error and made it public via Flickr.[64]

Figure 36. Lily Gaubert (left) and Allison Wyatt (right).

Adam Lanza—The ridiculously fraudulent photographs of Adam Lanza clearly do not depict a real person:[65]

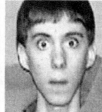

Figure 37. Adam Lanza, four fake photos.

9. The crime scene was completely destroyed

As with Ground Zero after 9/11, Sandy Hook Elementary and all the evidence have been completely obliterated; *$50 million in CT state funds* were allocated for the demolition and rebuilding of Sandy Hook school. This would never have been tolerated if an actual crime had been committed—at least one that was meant to be investigated.[66] The demolition of the school has been completed and rebuilding is in progress.

Figure 38. Demolition of Sandy Hook Elementary nearing completion (November 13, 2013)

Employees who worked on the project were required to sign non-disclosure agreements.[67] They were not only prohibited from removing anything from the site, but they were forbidden from discussing publicly anything they may have observed or not observed during the demolition, such as an absence of bullet marks on the walls or blood on the floor of the classrooms.

Researchers have speculated that the Sandy Hook Elementary School was not a working school in December 2012, and may have been closed for years.[68] Photos indicate the deplorable physical condition of the school and its grounds, as well as loads of junk in rooms, halls, and closets, more appropriate for a storage facility—but with classrooms staged to look real. Sandy Hook Elementary was indeed dilapidated, nothing like the marvelous school that people say drew parents to the Newtown community.

The new Sandy Hook School has been designed (Figure 39) and is in the process of being built. The building is scheduled for completion by 2016, in time for the 2016–2017 school year, according to the official project website.[69] In FAQ at the website, the question is asked, "Why was the decision made to build a new school and not just renovate?" The response:

Analysis of the renovate vs. build new by the Advisory Committee showed that costs to renovate this 56 year old building, bring it up to code, eliminate the portables, make it energy efficient, provide necessary safety features, and more, generated a cost almost at the same level of new building construction.[70]

This is underscored by an article in the *Newtown Bee*, clear acknowledgment that Sandy Hook Elementary was old, unsafe, and not up to code at the time of the alleged shooting.[71]

Figure 39. Design for the new Sandy Hook School, Svigals + Partners, LLP (design team) and Consigli Construction Co., Inc. (construction manager), scheduled for completion in 2016.

10. Deceased children sang at the Super Bowl

Research has resulted in a "Sandy Hoax Surprise," a convincing youtube video by QKultra identifying eight alleged Sandy Hook victims and six brothers of victims singing in the Newtown children's choir at the 2013 Super Bowl, February 3, 2013.

Figure 40. "Sandy Hook Elementary School Chorus" sings "America the Beautiful" at Super Bowl XLVII, along with Jennifer Hudson and Sabrina Post of Encore Productions.[72]

Identified here are Charlotte Bacon, Olivia Engel, Josephine Gay, Grace McDonnell, Emilie Parker, Caroline Previdi, Avielle Richman, and Benjamin Wheeler, along with victims' brothers Guy Bacon, Jake Hockley, Freddy Hubbard, Jack McDonnell, Walker Previdi, and Nate Wheeler.[73]

Figure 41. Screen capture from "Sandy Hoax Surprise."

One more victim has been identified since the original video, Noah Pozner,[74] making a total of 15 out of the 26 children in the choir who were from the Sandy Hook "families." The newly recognized victims are all older than they appear in the photos released at the time of the "shooting," giving credence to the theory that the victims' photos we were shown were outdated images.

The children in the Newtown choir, whoever they are, seem quite happy to be singing at the Super Bowl, smiling and running across the field after the event—giving no sign of the trauma they had suffered less than two months prior. So are the dead children actually alive? One can only hope.

Cui bono?

The evidence thus demonstrates that (1) proof of death was suppressed, (2) emergency protocols were not followed, (3) drill protocols were followed instead, (4) there was foreknowledge of the event, (5) there was confusion over the weapons supposedly used, (6) Adam Lanza cannot possibly have carried out the shooting as claimed, (7) strange and inappropriate behavior was displayed by officials, witnesses, and relatives, (8) many odd photos of the participants and premises were released, (9) the crime scene was destroyed under conditions of secrecy, and (10) as many as nine of the children who were supposedly murdered appeared on television singing at the Super Bowl seven weeks later.

With the possible exception of (5) and (9), all these features yield a low probability that Sandy Hook was a massacre but a high probability that it was *a staged psy-op tied to a drill.*[75] Some of them are decisive by themselves, such as (1), (2), (3), (4), and (6)—not to mention (10). And nothing else about this event supports the conclusion that it was real as reported. Although this may be hard to believe for some—"no one could have faked a massacre like this," "we watched the funerals on TV," or "there were too many people involved and someone would have spilled the beans"—the evidence is conclusive. To return to the maxim of Sherlock Holmes, "when you have excluded the impossible, whatever remains, however improbable, must be the truth."

So who did it and why? The "shooter" Adam Lanza had no apparent motive, as even the 2013 final report acknowledged:

Why did the shooter murder twenty-seven people, including twenty children? Unfortunately, that question may never be answered conclusively... there is no clear indication why he did so, or why he targeted Sandy Hook Elementary School.

But all good detectives will look for a motive when investigating a crime. When considering *cui bono* (who benefits), a large amount of money is at stake–and much of it has already been distributed.

Follow the money

First of all, the construction industry got a boost, with the **$50 million** in Connecticut state funds allocated for the destruction of *Sandy Hook School* and rebuilding of a new school on the premises. [76] And this from a state with a projected budget deficit of $1.1 billion for the 2015–2016 fiscal year. [77]

The *Sandy Hook School Support Fund* raised approximately **$12 million** and distributed it to the Newtown– Sandy Hook Community Foundation, overseen by Ken Feinberg, "a victim compensation master with a national reputation," according to United Way of Western Connecticut. [78] *And the Support Fund/United Way posted its condolences on December 11, 2013, which was three days before the actual event.* The Sandy Hook School Support Fund paid **$281,000** to each of the *victims' families*, as well as **$20,000 each** to the families of 12 children who reportedly witnessed the shootings but survived, and **$150,000** to two teachers who were injured. [79]

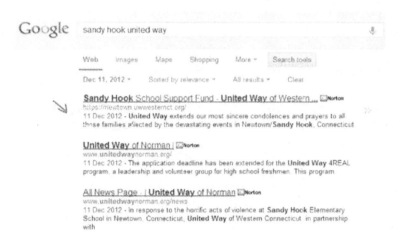

Figure 42. Google search page listing the United Way document date as December 11, 2012. [80]

The families have also raised additional funds through private organizations with their own websites—some of which were apparently advertised on the web in advance of the shooting. These include efforts such as 26 Miles for Caroline (Previdi), the Musical Benefit for Catherine Hubbard Foundation, Ben's Lighthouse (Benjamin Wheeler), and Noah's Ark of Hope

(Noah Pozner). All of the victims, both children and adults, have had memorial funds established in their names to collect money.[81]

"Sandy Hook Promise," which actively solicits money "to protect children and prevent gun violence by providing awareness, education, and programs in the areas of mental health, mental wellness, and gun safety," currently boasts over 434,000 people who have made the "Sandy Hook Promise" to turn the "tragedy into a moment of transformation."[82] Nicole Hockley and Mark Barden are staff members. As part of their fund- raising efforts, the group sells car decals, wrist bands, T-shirts, and OPI limited-edition Sandy Hook Green nail polish. The latest estimate of funds available to Sandy Hook Promise is **$3 million**.

Figure 43. OPI's Limited-edition Sandy Hook Green Nail Polish for a donation of $26 to Sandy Hook Promise.

The federal government has also forked over a lot of taxpayer money, including a **$150,000** federal grant to Newtown to pay for two "school resource officers" (aka police), **$1.5 million** from the US Department of Justice Office for Victims of Crime, and **$2.5 million** in federal funds from the DOJ to compensate the Connecticut State Police, the town of Newtown, the town of Monroe, and other partner agencies. In June 2014, the DOJ gave Newtown another **$7.1 million** for mental health counseling for families, law enforcement, and first responders.[83] In December 2014, another **$775,914** was donated by the DOJ Office for Victims of Crimes for Sandy Hook victims, their families, first responders, and members of the Newtown Community.[84]

In addition, the US Department of Education has awarded a total of **$3.2 million** to the Newtown Public School District under Project SERV (School Emergency Response to Violence) to help with ongoing recovery efforts following the shooting.[85] This total of **$15.2 million** in hush money is sure to keep the lid on things for now.

The latest edition of the video "We Need To Talk about Sandy Hook," lists a total of **$131,009,229** in grants and donations, including the **$50**

million for the new school,[86] but this is only a partial accounting. Indeed, the total amount of money raised to date cannot easily be calculated. A 2014 Connecticut report on charitable donations lists organizations such as The Animal Center, Inc., Newtown Forest Association, Inc., Sandy Hook Arts Center for Kids, and Angels of Sandy Hook Bracelets, all raising funds for Sandy Hook Elementary.

Gun control

The issue of gun control gained ground after the Sandy Hook "shooting," with widespread coverage in the mainstream press, expertly juxtaposed with maudlin stories about the fallen children to tug at the nation's heartstrings.[87] The families have been out in force, appearing on television and in print, lobbying for gun control in the states and the US capitol. By now, their stories are known to everyone in America.

In late February 2013, New York Mayor Michael Bloomberg, a relentless gun-control advocate, used his clout to meet separately with Vice President Biden and several senators. At the same time, Neil Heslin, father of alleged victim Jesse, testified tearfully at a Senate hearing on the banning of assault weapons.[88] Publicity surged in late March, when authorities allegedly found a huge cache of guns, ammunition, and exotic weaponry in the Lanza home, publishing a detailed list and photos (see above, reason #6).[89]

On April 2, 2013, the United Nations "Arms Trade Treaty" regulating the international trade in conventional arms was passed by the General Assembly.[90] On April 8, 2013, 12 parents of the Sandy Hook "victims" flew with President Obama to Washington, D.C., aboard Air Force One to lobby congress on gun-control legislation put forward by the White House—which ultimately failed.[91] The continuing media blitz has created an impression that the Sandy Hook hoax was all about gun control. Meanwhile, however, the gun industry has benefited immensely.

Figure 44. "The Newtown 12": Sandy Hook parents deplaning from Air Force One on April 8, 2013.

The New York Times reported in 2013 that around 1,500 state gun bills had been introduced in the year following the shooting, with 109 becoming law. However, nearly two-thirds of these laws ease legal restrictions and support the rights of gun owners.[92] This may have been an unintended consequence of an intentional plan. Nonetheless, it is not clear that the Sandy Hook event was carried out solely with the aim of passing gun-control legislation. More plausibly it was a Gladio-type operation—implementing a strategy of tension with real and simulated events in order to control and oppress the population.[93]

It does appear that the government is out to disarm the American public, if not by legal means then ultimately by seizure. The efforts of "the families" at promoting gun-control legislation may merely be a pretext, a prelude to accustom us to the idea; the increasing number of false-flag shootings may eventually be used as grounds to round up weapons. This would involve a beefed-up security apparatus, which is already in progress.

The security state

The already immense and rapidly growing "security industry" has also benefitted from the Sandy Hook "massacre," as we, the citizens of the United States, lose more of our Constitutional rights (see above, reason #3). Efforts[94] to increase security in schools—and even arm teachers—are underway. This suggests an orchestrated charade in which more gun violence is partnered with more guns in society, but held only by the approved authorities.

The Sandy Hook families have pushed continually for increased security measures along with gun control legislation, starting right after the "shooting."[95]

Some are now directly involved with security companies, such as the Gay, Parker, Mattioli, and Rekos families, which are affiliated with "Safe and Sound," a non-profit started by Michele Gay and Alissa Parker, mothers of alleged victims Josephine Gay

Figure 45. NaviGate Prepared, a "sponsor" of Safe and Sound, affiliated with the Gay, Parker, Mattioli, and Rekos families.

and Emilie Parker (who, by the way, were both identified in the children's choir that sang at the 2013 Super Bowl). Safe and Sound is partnered with NaviGate Prepared, a for-profit "school safety emergency response system," as well as with several other "sponsors."[96]

Mental health screening and treatment

In a 2015 TEDxTalk, Nicole Hockley relates gun violence to mental health issues, another pervasive concern of the Sandy Hook parents. After reciting the statistics on shooting deaths, she urges us to learn how to "identify children who may be troubled and get them help…to insure that those that are crying out for help on social media are properly investigated before they hurt themselves or someone else…" We can find out about all the actions that we can take, "focused on identification and intervention," at the Sandy Hook Promise website.[97]

Figure 46. Standing ovation for Nicole Hockley's TEDx Talk at the University of Nevada, Reno.

This is part of a more subtle but insidious effort to promote mental health screening and the consequent treatment (medication) of the "mentally unstable" in our society, based upon an event that did not take place.[98]

We are asked to consider Adam Lanza's "mental illness," which was supposedly "completely untreated," based on unverified information in a November 2014 report of the State of Connecticut's Office of the Child Advocate.[99]

We find that Adam had Autism Spectrum Disorder, Anxiety, and Obsessive Compulsive Disorder, as well as possible undiagnosed Anorexia, and was deprived of recommended services and drugs. It is here that we learn Adam was 6 feet tall and weighed 112 pounds. The report resulted in numerous recommendations, based on the fictional medical and psychological evaluation of Adam Lanza, including universal mental-health screening for children ages birth to 21, and the evaluation of children by the school system. The report exposes one purpose

of the Sandy Hook event: a "dramatically intensified bureaucratic and quasi-scientific control over the everyday lives of children alongside the continued erosion of the family itself."[100]

Trauma-based mind control & "The Revelation of the Method"

Beyond all these agendas, the Sandy Hook "massacre" was an exercise in trauma-based mind control, employed with increasing frequency in the US (and throughout the world) since the mega-trauma of 9/11. As with 9/11, the official Sandy Hook narrative is nothing like what really happened, as proven again and again by an army of independent researchers. The official version is recounted in detail at Wikipedia—the go-to source for the propaganda that the intelligence state wishes to convey.[101]

This false and illogical account is transmitted through all forms of media—TV, radio, newspapers, websites, and magazines, many of which have been taken over in toto by the intelligence services since 9/11. The evolving account has become so confusing, with its inconsistencies and contradictions, that most people find it easier to accept the official story and go about their business—resulting in a nation of people who can no longer think for themselves, even when confronted with the obvious.

On the most basic level, mass terror and tragedy are used to frighten the public into acquiescence, causing people to band together as a community and turn to their leaders for guidance. Thus the seemingly endless series of violent assaults in the form of terrorist attacks, lone-wolf shootings, and white-on-black police killings, all to keep us focused on these horrifying acts and not on the looting of the US treasury or illegal foreign wars. Perhaps the most significant achievement of the Sandy Hook event was the creation of a terrifying crisis *that did not actually occur*—but was vividly portrayed in the media—allowing the perpetrators both to achieve their objectives and to gauge the public's response.

Would-be investigators have also been taken in—chasing red herrings, delving deeply into individual facets of the mystery, and grasping at anomalies in an effort to solve the crime. We too are manipulated, as the perpetrators allow details to emerge—The Revelation of the Method—and watch our reaction.[102] Thus Governor Malloy's statement that "the Lieutenant Governor and I have been spoken to in an attempt that we might be prepared for something like this playing itself out in our state,"[103] or Wayne Carver's "I hope the people of Newtown don't have it crash on their head later." Likewise the "Please Check In" sign (Figure 1), Gene Rosen's practice interview (Figure 27), and memorial websites posted before the date of the tragedy (Figure 42).

Part of this ploy is the ridicule of the populace, a "macabre nose-thumbing at our complete indifference to our mental enslavement,"[104] such as the smiling relatives and weird interviews, Noah Pozner shown among photos of the victims of a Taliban attack in Pakistan, the myriad police photos providing no evidence, and—the ultimate joke on every sentient person—the students alive and well and singing at the Super Bowl. Such stunts are intentional, and are not only fun for the perpetrators but are seen to enhance their power.

In the face of this brutal violence, we are told to *choose LOVE*. This was expressed by the resigned and even cheerful parents and other participants in their interviews, even though their relatives and friends had died in a horrific bloodbath only one or two days earlier. This has also occurred with other recent manufactured acts of terror, such as the Boston Marathon Bombing and the recent Charleston church shooting. People *choose love*, resilient communities magically bond together, and everyone moves on to the healing process—immediately.[105]

Such hoaxes involve government at the highest levels, as shown by Obama's visit to Newtown (and Boston and Charleston),[106] the use of Air Force One to fly the families to Washington, D.C., and Francine Wheeler's White House Weekly Address (April 13, 2013).[107] Such government complicity has been demonstrated for the assassination of JFK, the attacks of 9/11, and beyond. In the face of such vast conspiracies, it is hard to know how to view the world.

When one understands the Sandy Hook psy-op, however, things come into focus. When contemplating our current predicament—the incessant "mass shootings" and their promotion in the media, the trashing of the constitution and rise of the security state, and the use of false flags and fake data to direct policy on everything from "climate change" to the "war on terror"—we can study the lessons of Sandy Hook, and navigate accordingly.

Vivian Lee, is the nom de plume *of a Sandy Hook researcher and professor at an East Coast University.*

Notes

1 *http://video.foxnews.com/v/2043823745001/man-comforts-sandy-hook-students-he-found-in-his-driveway/?#sp=show-clips.* "The Sandy Hook HOAX and Gene Green Screen." *https://www.youtube.com/watch?v=jViclRKcM7A.*

2 The article was removed from VT in May 2015 but has been reposted at the site. Original URL: *www.veteranstoday.com/2014/01/07/top-ten-reasons-sandy-hook-was-an-elaborate-hoax/.* New URL: *http://www.veteranstoday.com/2015/05/01/top-ten-reasons-sandy-hook-was-an-elaborate-hoax/.* I wish to acknowledge here the co-authors of that article—James Fetzer, James Tracy, Sofia Smallstorm, and members of the Sandy Hook research group—as well as QKultra, Redsilverj, the participants in "We Need To Talk about Sandy Hook," and many other researchers who have worked on the Sandy Hook event.

3 Sandy Hook Elementary School Shooting Reports, Department of Emergency Services and Public Protection. *http://cspsandyhookreport.ct.gov/*

4 Sandy Hook Elementary School Shooting Reports. Redaction index. *http://cspsandyhookreport.ct.gov/cspshr/Redaction_Index.pdf.*

5 "Final Sandy Hook Report Still Leaves Questions." *http://www.newstimes.com/news/article/Final-Sandy-Hook-report-still-leaves-questions-5106788.php.*

6 "Final Report on Sandy Hook Killings Sheds New Light on Gunman's Isolation." *http://www.nytimes.com/2013/12/28/nyregion/with-release-of-final-sandy-hook-shooting-report-investigation-is-said-to-be-over.html.*

7 State of Connecticut, Department of Emergency Services and Public Protection, Office of the Commissioner, letter from Commissioner Bradford. *http://cspsandyhookreport.ct.gov/cspshr/Sandy_Hook_Cover_Letter.pdf.*

8 James Fetzer, "Thinking about 'Conspiracy Theories': 9/11 and JFK." *http://www.d.umn.edu/~jfetzer/fetzerexpandedx.pdf.*

9 "Principal Outlined New Security Procedures at Sandy Hook Elementary School." *http://www.courant.com/breaking-news/hc- security-letter-newtown-shootings-20121214-story.html.*

10 "The Sandy Hook Massacre: Unanswered Questions and Missing Information." *http://memoryholeblog.com/2012/12/24/the-sandy-hook-massacre-unanswered-questions-and-missing-information/.*

11 For the full press conference, see "Medical Examiner FULL Press Conference – Sandy Hook School Mass Shooting."*https://www.youtube.com/watch?v=zE0OT5od9DA.*

12 The alleged death certificates of Adam Lanza and Noah Pozner were released in 2014 by one Lenny Pozner. Adam Lanza was initially listed as dying on December 13, 2012, according to www.geneaologybank.com following the Social Security Death

Index, and Noah Pozner was later pictured in a collage of the dead in a massacre in Peshawar, Pakistan on December 16, 2014. For this interesting story, see James Tracy, "Sandy Hook Victim Photo Used to Memorialize Pakistani Schoo. Massacre." *http://www.globalresearch.ca/sandy-hook-victim-photo-used-to-memorialize-pakistani-school-massacre/5422691.*

13 Public Act No. 13-311: "An Act Limiting the Disclosure cf Certain Records of Law Enforcement Agencies and Establishing a Task Force Concerning Victim Privacy under the Freedom of Information Act.". *https://www.cga.ct.gov/2013/act/pa/pdf/2013PA-00311- R00SB-01149-PA.pdf.*

14 "Malloy Signs Bill To Withhold Homicide Photos, Other Records, after Newtown." *http://www.courant.com/politics/hc-secret-foi- newtown-0605-20.30604-story. html.*

15 "Judge Orders Release of Sandy Hook 911 Recordings." *http://www.nytimes.com/2013/11/27/nyregion/judge-orders-release-of- sandy-hook-911-recordings.html.*

16 "McDonnell Parents Live through Grace." Interview of Chris and Lynn McDonnell on Anderson Cooper 360. *https://www.youtube.com/watch?v=ToQNVJE4xgk.*

17 "Noah Pozner's Family Remembers and Mourns." *http://forward.com/news/168277/noah-pozners-family-remembers-and-mourns/.*

18 "The Real Deal." *http://radiofetzer.blogspot.com/search?updated-min=2013-01-01T00:00:00-08:00&updated-max=2014-01-01T00:00:00-08:00&max-results=50.*

19 U.S. Environmental Protection Agency, "Medical Waste Tracking Act of 1988." *http://www.epa.gov/osw/nonhaz/industrial/medical/tracking.htm.*

20 S.T.A.R.T. Simple Triage and Rapid Treatment. *http://www.emsconedonline.com/pdfs/starttriage.pdf.*

21 "Unraveling Sandy Hook in 2, 3, 4, and 5 Dimensions." *https://www.youtube.com/watch?v=m1yfJDCMU64.*

22 "Sandy Hook Fire Chief Remembers Tragedy." *https://www.youtube.com/watch?v=3j3i3A7m8jk.*

23 "Tragedy in Connecticut: 20 Children, 6 Adults Killed at Elementary School. *http://www.npr.org/sections/thetwo- way/2012/12/14/167248541/developing-shooting-at-elementary-school-in-newtown-conn.*

24 "Sandy Hook Hoax—Walking in Circles around Sandy Hook Firehouse." *https://www.youtube.com/watch?v=TZRa5_DHgl4.*

25 James Tracy, "Nationwide Post-Sandy Hook Terror Drills." *http://www.globalresearch.ca/nationwide-post -sandy-hook-terror- drills/5346612.*

26 "Oxford CT High School Shooting Drill." *https://www.youtube.com/*

Vivian Lee, Ph.D.

watch?v=CnqKikVbHeM.

27 "Operation Closed Campus," Pottawattamie County, Iowa, 2011 Full Scale Exercise (FSE). *http://static.infowars.com/2011/03/i/general/ExPlan_03222011.pdf.*

28 "Lamorinda Active Shooter Drill, CERT Disaster Response Team, Contra Costa County, CA, December 17, 2014. *http://lamorindacert.org/lamorinda-active-shooter-drill/.*

29 "Sandy Hook Hoax—The FEMA School Shooting Handbook Says." *https://www.youtube.com/watch?v=i0782lVrxg8.*

30 *http://www.ct.gov/demhs/ical/eventDetail_page.asp?date_ID=CAC9C6C9CD83CDC9C7.*

31 Federal Emergency Management Agency, Mass Casualty Drill, Exercise Plan. The date December 14, 2012, is listed on the title page, but December 13, 2012, is given on pp. 12, 14-15 of the document. See James Tracy, "FEMA/DHS 12/14/12 Plan for 'Mass Death of Children at a School by Firearms." *http://memoryholeblog.com/2014/10/08/femadhs-12142012-pla n-for-ma ss-death-of- children-at-a-school-by-firearms/. [Editor's note: The rehearsal was on the 13th, going LIVE on the 14th. See Appendix A.]*

32 *https://cdp.dhs.gov/training/integrated-capstone-event/.*

33 Dennis Cimino with Jim Fetzer, "The Nexus of Tyranny: The Strategy behind Tucson, Aurora, and Sandy Hook." *http://www.veteranstoday.com/2015/05/01/the-nexus-of-tyranny-the-strategy-behind-tucson-aurora-and-sandy-hook/.*

34 "Sandy Hook Early Birds," Jennifer Lake's Blog. *https://jenniferlake.wordpress.com/?s=sandy+hook+tweets.* It is still unclear whether the time stamps on these early tweets reflect Eastern or Pacific Standard Time.

35 "Sandy Hook RIP/Donation Webpages Created BEFORE the Massacre." *http://fellowshipoftheminds.com/2013/01/08/sandy-hook-ripdonation-webpages-created-before-the-massacre/.* "Sandy Hook Update: United Way of Western Holds Back Donations?" *http://www.insanemedia.net/sandy-hook-update-united-way-of-western-holds-back-donations/2266.* Evidence from web pages showing foreknowledge of the event is discussed in detail in "We Need to Talk about Sandy Hook—NEW 2015." *https://www.youtube.com/watch?v=oD0z275nQnM.*

36 "Sandy Hook School Massacre Time Line." *http://memoryholeblog.com/2013/01/06/sandy-hook-school-massacre-timeline/.*

37 Supran. 11.

38 "Police Find Long Gun in Trunk of Car in Sandy Hook Parking Lot: Newtown Connecticut School Shooting." *https://www.youtube.com/watch?v=wLrxSgkqJQc.*

39 "PROOF Sandy Hook Massacre: Both Long Guns Found in Trunk of Car." *https:// www.youtube.com/watch?v=KNsFAbGTdKk.*

40 "Newtown Gunman Spent More Than 150 Rounds, Killed Victims within 5 Minutes." *http://www.foxnews.com/us/2013/03/28/warrants-to-be-released-in-newtown-investigation/?test=latestnews.*

41 "SSDI Says Adam Lanza Died a Day before Sandy Hook Massacre." *http:// fellowshipoftheminds.com/2013/01/20/ssdi-says-adam-lanza-died-a-day-before-sandy-hook-massacre/.*

42 The Report of the State's Attorney (pp. 1-2). *http://www.ct.gov/csao/lib/csao/ Sandy_Hook_Final_Report.pdf.*

43 "Joyce Riley Interviews Mike Powers Sandy Hook Investigation (edited version no commercials)." *https://www.youtube.com/watch?v=_AP0QDUpHFE.*

44 "Sandy Hook Hoax Ultimate Case Closed (Redsilverj)." *https://www.youtube. com/watch?v=3B3kC-zQfR.*

45 "Guns, Knives, Ammo and Gear: Adam Lanza's Arsenal, Item by Item." *http:// usnews.nbcnews.com/_news/2013/03/28/17501802-guns-knives-ammo-and-gear-adam-lanzas-arsenal-item-by-it em?lite.*

46 "Raising Adam Lanza," Frontline in association with Hartford Courant, February 19, 2013. *http://www.pbs.org/wgbh/pages/frontline/raising-adam-lanza/.*

47 "Sandy Hook Medical Examiner Wayne Carver Is a Very Funny Guy." *https:// www.youtube.com/watch?v=5wHkWBq-FCs.*

48 "Sandy Hook School Shooting Hoax Fraud Robbie Parker Actor Exposed Smiling Laughing Then Fake Crying." *https://www.youtube.com/watch?v=oMINqFGNr-w.*

49 "The Happy Sandy Hook Actors." *https://www.youtube.com/ watch?v=bhTqMoccVmY.*

50 "Anderson Cooper Disappearing Nose and Unedited Sound Clicks from Editing Mistake at CNN."*https://www.youtube.com/watch?v=rxAWy_bUuio.*

51 "Reporter Claims To Talk to Sandy Hook Nurse." *https://www.youtube.com/ watch?v=CilfQSYNC5g.*

52 "Retraction and Apology," The Newtown Bee, December 17, 2012. *http:// newtownbee.com/news/news/2012/12/17/retraction-and- apology/4588.*

53 "Sandy Hook HOAX: Gene Rosen's NONSENSE Analyzed." *https://www. youtube.com/watch?v=mgq6SVbIbAI.*

54 A drill was supposedly held at the school in October 2012, as publicized in a photo tweeted by Principal Dawn Hochsprung. *http://memoryholeblog.com/2013/01/01/ sandy-hook-the-illusion-of-tragedy/*. However, this alleged drill does not present the same scenery as that of the Hicks photo.

55 "The Story behind a Striking Image of the Scene at Sandy Hook." *http://www.npr. org/sections/thetwo- way/2012/12/16/167395779/the-story-behind-a-striking-image- of-the-scene-at-sandy-hook,*

56 Dennis Cimino with Jim Fetzer, "Sent Worldwide, Shannon Hicks' "Iconic" Photo Was Faked." *http://www.veteranstoday.com/2015/05/01/sent-worldwide- shannon-hicks-iconic-sandy-hook-photo-was-faked/*. See also "Shannon Hicks Denies Staging Her Fake "Iconic" Sandy Hook Photograph." *http://www.veteranstoday. com/2015/05/01/shannon-hicks-denies-staging-her-fake-iconic-sandy-hook- photograph/*. For temperatures in Newtown on December 14, 2012, see *http://www. wunderground.com/history/airport/KDXR/2012/12/14/DailyHistory.html?req_ city=Newtown&req_state=CT&req_statena me=Connecticut*. The temperature at 10:00 am was 28 degrees F, at which breath condenses to form visible vapor. *http:// www.sciencebits.com/ExhaleCondCalc*.

57 "Sandy Hook Fraud—Sun Shadow Analysis 2.0—100% Proof." *https://www. youtube.com/watch?v=rhSyzhsaBDI*. According to Time magazine, Hicks said she took the "iconic" photo at 10:09 am. *http://time.com/3449676/the-story-behind-the- iconic-photograph- from-sandy-hook/*.

58 "Bee Honored with NENPA Awards, Hicks Named Photographer of the Year." *http://www.newtownbee.com/news/news/2014/02/13/bee-honored-nenpa-awards- hicks-named-photographer/190795*.

59 "Newtown Bee Stinger." h*ttps://www.youtube.com/watch?v=anuWlH6fn84*. For Shannon Hicks' slideshow of December 13, 2012, see *https://www.youtube.com/ watch?v=fmSBqLoXqA0*. In light of this discovery, one might wonder whether the "iconic" photo was taken on December 13, but this is unlikely, since temperatures that day were cold enough so that the students' breath would have condensed no matter what time the photo was taken. *http://www.wunderground.com/history/airport/ KDXR/2012/12/13/DailyHistory.html?req_city=Newtown&req_state=CT&req_ statena me=Connecticut*.

60 Although it has sometimes been unclear who shot out the plate glass window, as late as December 28, 2014, The New York Times reported that "the Newtown killer had entered Sandy Hook by shooting through a window." *http://www.nytimes. com/2014/12/28/technology/out-of-tragedy-a-protective-glass-for-schools.html*.

61 "Critical Thinking and Sandy Hook: Pictures of Lily." *https://sandehook.wordpress. com/2014/01/05/pictures-of-lily/*.

62 See for instance "Sandy Hook Photoshop Exposé Victoria Soto—Redux." *https:// www.youtube.com/watch?v=rHSIwED7wco*.

63 "Hard Proof—Sandy Hook Class Picture Deception." *https://megatronicsmedia. wordpress.com/2013/04/28/hard-proof-sandy-hook-class-picture-deception/.*

64 "Media Using Sandy Hook Victim Photo of Girl That Is Still Alive!!!! MOTHER SPEAKS OUT." *https://www.youtube.com/watch?v=VEqrUbac2yo.*

65 "No Conclusive Evidence That Adam Lanza Existed—Mike Powers Investigator." *https://www.youtube.com/watch?v=wD1ELUjMBtY.*

66 James Tracy, "The Sandy Hook Massacre: School Building Is Now Slated for Demolition. Why?" *http://www.globalresearch.ca/the-sandy-hook-school-massacre-school-building-is-now-slated-for-demolition-why/5353205.*

67 James Tracy, "The Sandy Hook Massacre: School Demolition Crew Sworn to Silence." *http://www.globalresearch.ca/the-sandy- hook-masssacre-school-demolition-crew-sworn-to-silence/5354593.*

68 James Fetzer (with Amanda), "Sandy Hook Elementary School: Closed in 2008, a Stage in 2012."*http://www.veteranstoday.com/2015/05/01/sandy-hook-elementary-school-closed-in-2008-a-stage-in-2012/.*

69 "The New Sandy Hook School," official project website for the design and construction of the new Sandy Hook School. *http://www.sandyhook2016.com/index. html.*

70 *http://www.sandyhook2016.com/faq.html.*

71 :Widespread Haz–Mat Presence Would Have Hampered Sandy Hook Renovations." *http://www.newtownbee.com/news/news/2013/12/02/widespread-haz-mat-presence-would-have-hampered-sa/179316.*

72 "Sandy Hook Students & Jennifer Hudson Sing at the Super Bowl 2013—America the Beautiful." *https://www.youtube.com/watch?v=GbYNa_OzrKM.*

73 "Sandy Hoax Surprise." *https://www.youtube.com/watch?v=Uv4-5yQ L3-Q.*

74 "'Sandy Hook Victims ALIVE at…' The YouTube account associated with this video has been terminated due to multiple third- party notifications of copyright infringement."

75 Supra n. 8.

76 "State Pledges $50 Million for New Sandy Hook School." *http://www.ctpost.com/ news/article/State-pledges-50-million-for-new- Sandy-Hook-4585207.php.*

77 "Estimates Show Future Budget Deficits for State." *http://www.wfsb.com/ story/23986662/estimates-show-future-budget-deficits-for-state.*

78 "Newtown–Sandy Hook Community Foundation, Inc., 1st Distribution Committee." http://www.nshcf.org/1st-distributio n. "United Way of Western Connecticut Response to the December 14 Tragedy." *http://www.uwwesternct.org/sandyhook.*

79 "Newtown Families of Sandy Hook Elementary School Massacre To Get $281,000 Each of $7.7 Million Donations."*http://www.nydailynews.com/news/national/ newtown-families-281k-7-7-million-donations-article-1.1397274.*

80 The United Way December 11 document date is covered in detail in "We Need To Talk About Sandy Hook—NEW 2015." *https://www.youtube.com/ watch?v=oD0z275nQnM.* The United Way condolence page now reads December 15, 2012. *http://www.unitedway.org/blog/united-way-establishes-fund-to-support-newtown.*

81 In January 2013, a list of funds was published in the Danbury News-Times: *http://www.newstimes.com/newtownshooting/article/Foundations-and-memorials-for-Sandy-Hook-victims-4208239.php.*

82 *www.sandyhookpromise.org*

83 James Tracy, "Obama DOJ in $7.1 Million Sandy Hook Payout." *http:// memoryholeblog.com/2014/06/17/obama-doj-in-7-1- million-sandy-hook-payout/.*

84 "Esty, Blumenthal, Murphy Announce $775,000 Federal Grant to Newtown." *http://newtownbee.com/news/news/2014/12/12/esty- blumenthal-murphy-announce-775000-federal-gra/245261.*

85 "US Education Department Awards $1.3 Million Grant to Newtown, Conn., to Further Support Recovery Efforts." *http://www.ed.gov/news/press-releases/us-education-department-awards-13-million-grant-newtown-conn-further-support-rec.* "US Department of Education Awards Additional $1.9 Million Grant to Newtown, Connecticut, To Further Support Recovery Efforts." *http://www.ed.gov/news/press-releases/us-department-education-awards-additional-19-million-grant-newtown-connecticut-f.*

86 "We Need to Talk about Sandy Hook—NEW 2015 Documentary." *https://www. youtube.com/watch?v=wGkKzGMdOVw.*

87 "Massacre at School Sways Public in Way Earlier Shootings Didn't." *http://www. nytimes.com/2013/01/18/us/poll-shows-school- shooting-sways-views-on-guns.html.*

88 "Bloomberg Goes to Washington to Push Gun Laws, but Senate Has Other Ideas." *http://www.nytimes.com/2013/02/28/us/politics/bloomberg-goes-to-washington-to-push-gun-laws-but-senate-has-other-ideas.html.*

89 Supra n. 45, and see "Newtown Killer's Obsessions, in Chilling Detail." *http:// www.nytimes.com/2013/03/29/nyregion/search-warrants-reveal-items-seized-at-adam-lanzas-home.html.*

90 The treaty entered into force on December 24, 2014. *http://www.un.org/ disarmament/ATT/.*

91 "Newtown 12: Sounds of Silence Echoing in Washington." *http://go.bloomberg. com/political-capital/2013-04-08/newtown-12-sounds-of-silence-breaking-in-washington/.* "Senate Blocks Drive for GunControl." *http://www.nytimes. com/2013/04/18/us/politics/senate-obama-gun-control.html.*

92 "State Gun Laws Enacted in the Year Since Newtown." *http://www.nytimes.com/ interactive/2013/12/10/us/state-gun-laws-enacted- in-the-year-since-newtown.htm*l.

93 James Tracy, "Mass Traumatization and the Body Public." *http://memoryholeblog. com/2013/07/02/mass-traumatiz ation-and-the- body-politic/.*

94 "Report Sees Guns As Path to Safety in Schools." *http://www.nytimes. com/2013/04/03/us/nra-details-plan-for-armed-school-guards.html.* "A Missouri School Trains Its Teachers To Carry Guns, and Most Parents Approve." *http://www. nytimes.com/2013/04/15/us/missouri-school-trains-teachers-to-carry-guns.html.*

95 "Family of Noah Pozner Calls for New Laws to Avert School Violence, Hold Gun Owners Accountable." *http://articles.courant.com/2013-01-13/news/hc-newtown-pozner-family-gun-recommendations-20130113_1_gun-violence-gun-owner-law-enforcement.*

96 *http://www.safeandsoundschools.org/our-team-safe-and-sound-schools/; www. navigateprepared.com.*

97 "Preventing Gun Violence without Just Talking about the Gun." *http://tedxtalks. ted.com/video/Preventing-Gun-Violence-Without.*

98 "In Gun Debate, No Rift on Better Care for Mentally Ill." *http://www.nytimes. com/2013/04/13/us/politics/senators-make- bipartisan-push-for-mental-health-care. html.*

99 "Adam Lanza's Mental Problems 'Completely Untreated' before Newtown Shootings, Report Says." h*ttp://www.nytimes.com/2014/11/22/nyregion/before-newtown-shootings-adam-lanzas-mental-problems-completely-untreated-report-says.html.* Report of the Office of the Child Advocate. *http://www.nytimes.com/ interactive/2014/11/22/nyregion/report-on-adam-lanza.html.*

100 Vivian Lee and James Tracy, "CT Report Lays Groundwork for Nationwide Psychiatric Surveillance."*http://memoryholeblog.com/2014/11/23/ct-report-lays-groundwork-for-psychiatric-panopticon/.*

101 Vivian Lee, "Convicted on Wikipedia." *http://memoryholeblog.com/2013/10/06/ convicted-on-wikipedia/.*

102 Michael A. Hoffman II, Secret Societies and Psychological Warfare (Coeur

d'Alene, Idaho, 2001), 51-53.

103 "Sandy Hook—Press Conference—Gov. Dan Malloy." *https://www.youtube. com/watch?v=d7m5qIYYNnQ.*

104 Hoffman, op cit., 52.

105 James Tracy, "Newtown World Order Religion." *http://memoryholeblog. com/2013/04/14/newtown-world-order-religion/.*

106 "'These Tragedies Must End,' Obama Says." *http://www.nytimes.com/2012/12/17/ us/politics/bloomberg-urges-obama-to-take- action-on-gun-control.html.*

107 "Mother of a 6-Year-Old Boy Killed at Newtown Delivers the White House's Weekly Address." *http://www.nytimes.com/2013/04/14/us/politics/mother-of- newtown-victim-gives-white-houses-weekly-address.html.*

6

Even Obama officials confirmed that it was a drill

by Jim Fetzer, Ph.D.,
(with Sofia Smallstorm & Paul Preston)

"I have a lot of sources in regards to as to what's going on with the president and the administration and so on, and every one of my sources said it was a false flag"--Paul Preston

Sofia Smallstorm, who produced and directed the documentary, "Unraveling Sandy Hook", which many regard as the best video study of the Sandy Hook event, recently interviewed a Los Angeles school expert, Paul Preston, about

Sandy Hook and his knowledge of what had transpired.

Governor Malloy had held a press conference that day, explaining that he and the Lt. Governor had been "spoken to" that *something like this might happen*, which raised the question, what "something like this"? Did he mean he had been told a school shooting massacre would take place? or a drill that would be presented as a real event?

Remarkably, we now have confirmation from an unexpected source. Paul Preston had obtained information from officials in the U.S. Department of Education of the Barack Obama administration, who confirmed to him *on the basis of their own personal knowledge* that:

(1) it had been a drill;
(2) no children had been killed; and,
(3) it had been done to promote an anti-gun agenda.

Given his background of 41 years in the California public school system (from custodian to district superintendent) and having served as a teacher, coach, vice-principal and principal before retiring in 2012 as the superintendent of two charter schools, I thought what he had to say about Sandy Hook deserved widespread dissemination.

So when we did a two-hour show on Revolution Radio, "False Flags (9/11, Sandy Hook and the Boston bombing)" on 30 May 2014, as the third segment, I included the second 30-minutes of Sofia's interview with Paul Preston, which is archived on "The Real Deal", *radiofetzer.blogspot.com*.

Because Preston is also highly trained in school safety issues and had himself organized drills of many kinds, including active-shooter drills, what he has to say is especially telling. He has a website of his own at www. *Agenda21Radio.com*, which he created to alert listeners to the perils of Agenda 21.

Transcript of 30-minute clip of Sofia Smallstorm interviewing Paul Preston

Transcription by Jeannon
S = Sofia Smallstrom
P = Paul Preston

S – Welcome back everyone to the Speed of Light on the Pure Momentum Network. This is Sofia Smallstorm and we're listening to a very interesting discussion – Paul Preston, school principal, school safety

consultant, teacher, coach, and superintendent. He has been in the California system for 41 years. He is now retired. So Paul, let's continue. Can we get a little bit into Sandy Hook now and what set off your antenna about it?

P – Well, you know I've been involved in many many situations at schools that have been, you know, emergency type situations and was involved even to some degree with the Columbine situation in that we had an individual who was trying to blow up the school, our school, at the time. In a similar fashion to what was a predicted bomb threat that occurred at Columbine three days before the Columbine shooting, and that's how we kind of got in touch with the Columbine people. They got in touch with us because it turned out to be a similar neo-Nazi group that was related to the Trenchcoat Mafia, of all people.

And so learning and watching and seeing all these incidences play out, all these school shootings, I took an enormous interest in because we were doing a study trying to determine because the neo-Nazis we had been working with in our school along the same time of the Columbine incident were telling us that there was going to be some big event take place. And so our staff, myself, we all wanted to sit down and figure where this was all going to and we studied a lot of the Nazi websites and so on, and we figured out that yes, something big was going to happen.

Well then Columbine happened. So we watched with a lot of intensity--especially under my own circumstances--and also by watching the videos and replays of the other active shooter situations, I became sort of a specialist in that and applied it to my own active-shooter training that I was doing and conducting with my own people.

S – Right. And now can we get into Sandy Hook?

P – Well yes. Of all the hundreds of hours that I spent watching these scenarios and investigating and reporting on them on my radio show, the first thing I noticed when I heard about Sandy Hook when I turned on the TV like everybody else …now I have always told everybody when you're seeing these things play out in real time, the best news reporting is what's happening in real time – that day of, you know, the moments that are around the incident. But document for yourself what's going on because you'll never see it again.

And the first thing that caught my eye as I was watching everything play out was the lack of intensity with which people were moving and that really disturbed me. It hit me within the first few minutes, watching the video, the helicopters flying around and so on. Things just didn't seem to be right, like I would always understand in an incident command system. People weren't rushing around. People weren't panicking. They ran that one guy off into the woods and then they arrested him. They took him away and there was no connectedness to that.

I was also wondering why all the emergency equipment wasn't around the school. And I didn't see any students either and that really bothered me.

S – So, it was almost like too slow motion for a real event. Not enough panic. Not enough chaos. You had mentioned chaos earlier being a part of these real situations. And a lot of support people rushing around like press and police but not running fast enough, not running with intensity and alarm and panic and concern, I think.

P – None of that was there.

S – Yes. So all right, and then what did you start thinking?

P – Well, just within the first 10 or 15 minutes, it just all looked too staged to me, and I know about staging these things since I've staged a number of them. And, like I said, then when you stage something there's a complete lack of intensity as you would have in a real scenario when there's panic really taking hold of people and they're really afraid and they're screaming and yelling and so on.

But the one thing that really bothered me was where were the kids. You know they had how many hundreds of kids there at the school. I didn't see them.

S – Right.

P – And there was lack of accounting for them. And right away – and I'll juxtaposition this with the situation that happened in Pennsylvania. You saw the kids right away. I know it's a high school, but you know, you saw the kids right away and you saw their plan of evacuation of the school unfolding.

Now this is where it really falls apart with Sandy Hook for me. saw...I saw no evidence of a real plan of student evacuation taking place. And that stuck in my head like crazy when I was in the moments watching this whole thing play out in real time.

S – That's very interesting. No evidence of a real plan. Because only someone...I mean everybody had their own response to it. Some of us were already clued in from previous kinds of situations. All this has got to be not what they're telling us it is. But you come from the industry, the business, and you felt that there is… I would say you knew … It probably was not even a feeling. It was like, you know, set in stone in your head. Where's the plan? I don't see the plan playing itself out. Right?

P – I saw some of your evacuation centers and I saw some of your colored tarps on the ground, the colored taps and so on, but even that was pretty odd because normally if you have the tarps out there…in every active shooter situation you have ever see, there's somebody on the tarp or there's been some help that's been given to somebody when somebody has been wounded, but none of that was even evident. And I don't see anybody trying to rush to anybody's help at all in a mass casualty situation.

See, when you don't see that…I mean…I'll go back to the example that I have before about the 13 who overdosed. We had people everywhere, and we had people everywhere until everybody was safe, which was 35, 40 minutes, almost an hour. And that was never happening there at Sandy Hook. You didn't see the mass of people doing that.

S – Yes, it's more like the press filled in for that missing element. The press sounded more concerned and panicked on TV as they reported but the actual participants were not so …And we got, you know, long after the fact we got the supposed 911 calls, we got various people giving their versions of it on television as they got interviewed. But we didn't see it on the ground. And so how long did you watch it for? Over a period of days, weeks? And what were your thoughts?

P – You know, I make it a study. I study these things intensely, and what really, what really put me over the top was the next morning with Robbie Parker going out there, and I saw that clip as it happened. And I said there's something really wrong here.

And that's when I started thinking about the …the actors. You can actually rent these actors out. In fact they put these things up for training all the time.

And I just said 'this is not…first of all, his demeanor was terrible. I would never go out…and I know sometimes this happens but…to send a parent out to talk to the press in that fashion about the daughter that he just lost. None of that seemed to be appropriate. None of it seemed to fit. And his behavior with the smiling laughing thing and getting into character that you could see. I said ' hmmm, I'm not buying this. I'm just not buying it.'

S – Yes, I know. Very few other people did. So, did you contact anyone? Did you speak to anyone? I don't mean officially but in your own network of friends.

P – Yes.

S – And what were their thoughts.

P – Almost everybody was unanimous that it was a false flag.

S – And when did you start looking it up on the Internet because I think people started posting immediately. You know, they were making YouTubes. The community began to express online. So when did you start looking into all of that?

P – We–a side note to this is that I have a lot of sources in and around and in that area. I have a lot of sources in regards to as to what's going on with the president and the administration and so on, and every one of my sources said it was a false flag.

S – Now these are quasi-official… what kind of sources are these?

P – Let me say that they are sources that are very close to this administration who know what's going on.

S – Really. So they are really like almost insiders then?

P – Oh yes.

S – And they all….they say it was a false flag because they figured it out like you did, or they have actually factual knowledge of such..

P – They had factual knowledge of such. That's part of the plan.

S – I see. And so how much were they willing to tell you, and what else were they willing to tell you? Anything?

P – Oh, they told me quite a bit, and some of it I can't reveal to you, but it fits the narrative of the anti-gun movement and the disarmament of America and that's what the focus was.

S – And you realized that that's part of the broader picture? That's the Agenda 21 society?

P – Absolutely.

S – So do you want to tell us a little but about that or do you want to stick with the Sandy Hook material? I'll let you decide.

P – Well, let's go ahead with the Sandy Hook material and then we can jump into that.

S – OK, so we're past Robbie Parker now, and what about the funerals? You must have known then that …Did you have any concept about victims or no victims, et cetera?

P – Well, that whole thing was pretty shaky. What was really starting to filter into the system and was just confirming what I was already being told about these charity sites that had been developed. By the way, they were put up the day before the shooting. And I had gotten some screen shots, and I had confirmed with my sources. Some of them were thinking that it was a very sloppy operation actually.

But there were reassurances to me that there really were no victims and that everything's being staged.

And of course the funerals to me…you go and look at the whole funeral process. It looked like they were all staged, from the Robbie Parker one in Utah, or the Sarah Parker one with the Parker family.

And then I started getting information from people that actually had attended that funeral who lived in Utah and said that was something very funny about it.

S – Now I would like to ask you whether your sense is that these are real families even, or are they patched together?

P – Well, you know, that's a good question because, you know, the thing that rolls around in my head, you know, the actors type of thing, you know. You know because you can put families together and these acting programs will do that under certain training scenarios. And so, it's a good question. It really is a fair question to ask whether or not they were real families.

S – And then of course because they continue to speak and organize and be called upon to comment, they have to be formed into these family groupings over time. And remain grouped like that whether they are truly married or not.

You know, here's one thing that I noticed. When you see a couple, if they seem really like an odd couple, then that kind of strikes you as weird. And I saw that. I saw a very odd coupled-ness with lots of these Sandy Hook families. It seemed to me, why would this person marry this person and live with them? They're so totally different. That happens sometimes but in this context it really jumped out at me...myself anyway. I didn't know if you noticed that...

P – It' difficult to say, you know, when you saw them together whether they are natural families or not. That's...I'm suspicious of that. And like I say, I'm suspicious because I know that you can put these families together, you know, with some of these acting companies out there. And that just kind of blends in with what I was already being suspicious about.

And so, there's a lot of things that would go into the details of examining this. And I've see a lot of the pictures and so on, and some of the pictures don't match up, especially the one of the Parkers in the White House. And it looks like to me that's Sarah Parker sitting there that's, you know, supposed to be a victim.

S – There's no Sarah Parker...

P – Which one is it...maybe it's not the Parker...

S – Oh, you mean with Obama...

P – Yes, right.

S – Emily or Madeline ...those are the two older sisters, and a lot of people felt that that was Emily Parker leaning on Obama.

P – Yes, that was Emily Parker...

S – Have you seen the Super Bowl video?

P – Yes, I have seen that.

S – Well, there is a girl who looks a lot like an older Emily Parker in that video. So if that was Emily at the White House, or actually I think…I don't know if it was at the White House…but with Obama, she couldn't be six in one picture and then just a month or two later, twelve or thirteen.

P – Right.

S – That's where we have to make a decision.

But what did you think of all the photographs of the children? Did you notice anything – the portraits that we were shown that these were the victims? Did you notice anything about those portraits?

P – No, other than some of the malformations of different parts of their bodies – seemed to be a pretty obvious thing.

The whole thing …when you take a look at the totality of this, in my opinion, it's very sloppily done.

S – Why would it have been sloppily done though?

P – Well, you know, when …and again, it's kind of like sometimes there's order that comes out of chaos. And when you have these chaotic situations, people want to put things back together as best they possibly can to feel more comfortable or to recover from it. And I didn't see any of that. I don't know if that makes any sense to anybody. People don't want to have that chaos. They want to heal. They want to come back together. They want to solve a problem so that they can move forward.

And that's part of what happens when you do these drills is that you take a day or so and you talk about what happened so that you can improve upon and make it better. People do that naturally even when there's chaos and there's an emergency situation because they want to seek normalcy again.

I didn't see the same kind of emotions, if you will, or the same kind of communications between parents, kids, that you would normally see in these situations. It just didn't look…it looked phony to me.

S – So you mean the community itself, they did not try to repair in the organic way…?

109

P – I would say that is true, from the parents to the kids, to the entire community.

S – What do you think of this privacy issue that has been bandied about by the authorities, that all the privacy needs to be respected, and you can't reveal this or that…?

P – That to me just adds more fuel to the fire because that's not what you do in the normal situation of an incident command system. You get the facts out because you know oftentimes when you get the facts out, you're also looking for criminal behavior, and the more information that you can get out that that's way, the better.

And I'm certainly not buying the notion that the parents weren't allowed to see the kids.

S – The bodies, identifying the…

P – I just…that to me… that should be a red flag to anybody who has looked in to Sandy Hook. The parents weren't allowed to do that. What's up with that?

S – And what did you think of the coroner's behavior at his press conference?

P – Well there's many things about him. I just …I …first of all, I didn't understand why all of a sudden there's 26 bodies and then there's no coroner or doctor who's looked at the bodies and they're declared dead. And then all of a sudden the coroner comes out and everybody says that there was an automatic gun or a handgun that was used, and the coroner, on his own, comes out and says 'oh no, that was an AR15 that was used.'

So there's a lot of confusion, you know, about that coroner, his report, his reporting out. Nothing seems very clear and concise to me. And you know I would argue that, you know, as I looked at him and watched what was going on, he seemed to be just answering questions on the fly without a lot of knowledge behind the questions.

S – And this suggested to you that this was a sloppily created event?

P – Absolutely.

S – And would you say that that was because of the portent of the whole thing that they…there were people involved in this…let's say Dr. Carver, the coroner, who had some idea, if it was a scripted event, it was going to go big, and really big? So do you think that the sloppiness of it was because in being organized, it's very difficult to juggle how people are going to perform given that they know how big this thing could get?

P – Well, you know, what happens is that you…if you're going to do these things and carry it through with the lie, everybody's got to be telling the same lie at the same time all the time.

And I think with my judgments about the parents and the kids, and seeing them lie, I was seeing a big lie being perpetrated right in front of me because nothing seemed to be consistent. And like you said, which I thought was interesting, is that oftentimes the media would fill in a lot of the blanks for you.

A classic example of the blanks comes up when you talk about where are the kids that are evacuating the school. There were helicopters that were circling overhead. They certainly would have been able to show, you know, hundreds of kids exiting the school.

That was never shown. But you did see a picture out in a parking lot, which by the way if you take a long look at this picture of all these kids being led out, about 15 or 20 kids being led out by teachers and adults from this parking lot, if you take a look at the parking lot from the aerial  views, you can see that there are different cars in the parking lot in that area. So obviously that was done during some sort of drill. That's my opinion. And it didn't match with what was going on at the time. So nothing is matching in real time for me. That's just another thing.

But where are the kids? Where were the kids? They weren't present. They just weren't there. So that's the kind of stuff that wasn't worked out and, you know, they were doing things on the fly. That's why I say…I would say it was very amateur, very amateurish as to what was going on.

S – Which is surprising because given the powers that would have designed this thing – that it would be so amateur – but...

You are familiar with the character, Gene Rosen?

P – Gene Rosen – which one was ...?

S – Gene Rosen was the man who was very close to the school and he took the kids in and offered them juice and cookies, and he gave many different...he recounted his rescuing or fielding of these kids differently in many interviews. So can you comment on that?

P – I can comment on this because this points to this proves my point that these kids ...did they get off a bus? Where did they go? OK, I think that one of the stories was that the kids got off the bus and they made their way to his house, and there was all this panic or whatever was going on. OK, there's something really wrong with that picture to begin with.

First of all, when you're doing these scenarios and this school had to have been trained for this because FEMA requires these trainings, and if you're getting safety monies from the federal government, which every school does, they have to follow the proper protocols and that's the proper release of the students to their parents.

S – Right. He said, that children showed up on his lawn and they were with a bus driver, in one story. In another story, they were just there by themselves and they were repeatedly babbling that their teacher was dead. So what...would the protocol be that the children...the children, according to the story, left the school on their own.

P – Well, that to me, that's very suspicious in and of itself.

S – Right, I mean the cops had not gotten there in the first five minutes. Apparently some of them could still hear shooting going on, and how did the kids get out and just run down the road, you know?

P – All that seems to be ...and again, I want to go into the thing about the incident command system, evacuation, walk-outs and so on. None of that fits that protocol. None of it.

The story of Gene Rosen or any of that stuff — None of that fits. That to me is just more evidence that there were no students other than the actor students that were there.

S – Then what was the purpose of having the Gene Rosen player?

P – Diversion.

S – From what?

P – A diversion from the other realities going on and to add more hype about the story. It's the same thing about the guy that was chased through the woods. You know, they had a couple of guys that were chased through the woods. What were they all about?

And there were no answers about any of that, about where they came from and even my people couldn't come up with an answer about that. Some of my people say it was very sloppily done.

S – These are your insider people, right?

P – Right.

S – Now did you see any of the videos of the people circling through the firehouse?

P – Yes.

S – And did that strike you … what did you think of that?

P – Well, I had already come to my conclusion that this was a drill, and again, being very suspicious of the Obama administration, Diane Feinstein, Second Amendment issues, using Agenda 21 in particular, I had not see that until quite some time afterwards, maybe a couple of weeks after. We were engaged in our own things that we were doing in terms of investigations and stuff like that. We're pretty intense about what we're doing here on Agenda 21 Radio, and we have some very highly placed sources of information that comes to us and which we're very grateful for.

I, for one reason or another, hadn't seen that video maybe two or three weeks until after the incident.

There's more evidence right there because what in the world were all those people doing there to begin with? You see, if you're doing an incident command situation, there's a place for those people and those people can be moved on rather than seeing that circus that was going on, which is what that was. That was all staged.

S – Right. And these were far too many adults, no children whatsoever, no panic. And to me the people that were there--they weren't dressed for December. So some people have suggested that that particular drill, the circling in and out of the firehouse, took place a lot earlier, and it matches the time frame and the clothing of the children evacuated from the school. They did not have their coats.

And I was going to ask you, is it normal when there's an emergency for the teacher to evacuate the children without letting them get their coats, or would they take the extra time and say 'Children, go put your coats on as fast as you can.' How does that work?

P – Well no. If there's a signal to get them out of the building, and there's always a signal of some sort to get them out of the building safely, they go directly out. Period. End of subject.

And if they can get their coat, that's great, but the safety thing is to get them away from where there potentially is a threat and that would be the key thing. And again, you pointed to something else and I brought this up earlier about the drill that we used to run and people would always, you know, screw up the drill because they would knock on the door in an active shooter situation and the teacher would open the door.

Well, you know, how does that all play out? I was looking at things pretty much in real time within minutes of news being broadcast as it was happening from a helicopter. Now I am a real-time kind of guy. So I'm looking at maybe 15 minutes into the shooter, maybe 20 minutes into the shooter situation. I'm looking at clear video of the campus and so on. I'm not seeing anything happening.

Where are the kids? The kids aren't there.

S – Right.

P – And they should be released or what's going on with them?

S – And there were some people said that they were in closets for up to four hours. That doesn't make any sense either.

P – That does not many any sense to me because what happens, and again it goes back to the police, and back to Columbine, they will go in and check every nook and cranny. And quite frankly, I know how that's done. We used to do that. We always used to look and check to see where people were.

S – Right. And you would not miss large adults hiding in small closets.

And the idea of Kaitlyn Roig and some of these teachers bundling up all their kids into the bathroom and having a few sit on the toilet...I even heard the toilet roll holder, my God, that's pretty tough to do even for a six year old. But what do you think of that? That doesn't make sense to me.

Sofia Small-storm, "Unraveling Sandy Hook in 2, 3, 4 and 5 dimensions"

P – Well, you know, we tell people in an active shooter situation to seek...to hide or ...if there is a shooter there to take the challenge. We used to do these things where we had these dummy books and we'd bring in an active shooter as the stage person and throw books at them, you know, because that really throws them off. You're taught those kinds of little techniques to throw the active shooter off.

But I can imagine some people getting holed up in a closet or something like that if they haven't been able to lock the door. And that's one of the things we tell our people all of the time. Lock the door. And we made sure in all schools, and all schools should have the, the doors should have the inside key on them, you know, so you can use an inside key on them also as we could on the outside.

S – So we have a couple of minutes left of this first hour. Do you have anything to say about Adam Lanza – fiction, non-fiction, real?

P – Well, just on the surface of it, and again I would throw out I'm highly specialized trained in drugs and alcohol recognition, obviously looks like he has some meds onboard just by the look. But you know if you couch that along the same lines that that this may be a fictional event, that he's a fictional character, which fits his description of what I see there.

And of course if you're doing a fictionalized event like this, you want to have the most crazed individual that you can have looking at you through the picture there, and that's exactly what you have. That's my speculation. I think that's what they wanted. That's what they did.

And he has a history and what is the history? We're not real clear on the history. You know, first of all, they found out that he's got his brother's driver's license. Then there's some confusion. And you know it one of these kind of scenarios that just didn't quite fit.

And as a school person that to me was one of the big pieces of evidence. Why does he have his brother's license? And then they made contact his brother that I guess was in New Jersey some place, wherever he was, and there was an investigation. That all seemed to be tracking with me as a distraction about what was really happening at the school.

See, the more they under this situation… this is just my speculation – the more they could distract from the actual Sandy Hook school site itself and stage things away from there, the more they could sell the story of Sandy Hook on the whole.

S – That's a very very good point, Paul. Excellent. And we should add that the mug shot that they gave us of Adam Lanza was very painterly. It wasn't even a photo, and it did have that, you know, ghoulish expression on it to make us think this is a real lunatic.

But we are now at the end of our first hour and I really really thank you, Paul Preston, for being with us. And we will take up a second hour discussion in the Members Section. So this is Sofia Smallstorm thanking everyone for listening to this first hour and please do come to PureMomemtum.net and join us for the second hour in the Members Section with Paul Preston, 41 years in the public schools and someone who has been through a lot of staging of drills and has a lot of drill understanding and experience.

This chapter originally appeared under the title, *"Sandy Hook Redux: Obama officials confirm that it was a drlll and no children died", veteranstoday.com* (13 June 2014)

7

Fixing a Prop:
Furnishing the Lanza Home

by Allan Powell (with Kelley Watt)

To make the purpose of this chapter clear immediately at the outset, the Sandy Hook Elementary school and the Lanza Home were set up and stage-managed to support a false story that Adam Lanza killed his mother Nancy Lanza in their home and then went

to an Elementary School and killed 26 people.

There are hundred of images on the Internet that show both sites in gradual states of preparation to serve as a stage (in the case of the school) and as a prop (in the case of the Lanza home), which display its preparation over time with different states of tidiness.

Social engineering requires psychological operations presented to the public as factual phenomena. It stands to reason therefore that individuals willing to conduct these psychological operations have to be trained in the presentation of the same. Both the Lanza home and the Sandy Hook school are instances of presentations of this kind and of the training of DHS personnel in producing them.

The Lanza home

The story through the media is that the Lanza home was left in a state that Adam Lanza left it in until police officers entered that afternoon. That is false. The Lanza home was set up to resemble a home of a mentally deranged twenty-year-old who killed his mother and drove a Honda to kill over two-dozen at the school.

The images available on the Internet and from the evidence released by the Connecticut State Police show that the home was stage-managed with props to create a location to support a false media story. From the evidence of these images, one or more may have stayed at the home for several days.

The photos in this chapter show various stages of preparation of the house as a prop for the story of Adam Lanza the shooter. There are different takes on the décor of Adam Lanza›s bedroom for instance: messy, "normal" and pristine.

Exhibit 1: Adam's bedroom "messy"

Note the books in the television stand in no order.

* And the boxes have yet to be unpacked [where the asterisked comments are from Kelley Watt.]

Exhibit 2: Adam's bedroom "neat"

One of course has to ask why these two different states for one room exist as evidence retained by police and where--in chronological order--one follows the other.

If the room was found as messy and the result of action by those

government officers in the house was to render it to a different state other than that found, those officers are not acting in accord with the principles of forensic science but with the propagandist principle of public deception. They are setting a scene.

There are no evidence markers in either image and it is hard to imagine why any investigation of the dead shooter›s room would forward any evidence for clearing up any issues which could be in contention in a trial especially given that the shooter was dead.

* Note the glider pad under the leg of the headboard in order to move the bed around for picture-perfect staging.

* There is no blanket or electric blanket on bed despite 28 degrees outside.

* There is no bulletin board, sports memorabilia, ipads, ipods, headphones, stereo equipment, trashcan, trophies, pictures, magazines, caged pets (such as a snake or hampster) plants, shoes or shirts, video games or flat screen TV. These items are typical in the room of a 21-year old.

Exhibit 3: The "computer room" neat

* White cord running across the floor; sides of the computer taken apart; two bowls on table with white cloth draped over it, to the left of brown desk; trash can is located on side of desk; computer chair has no dust on legs. Cardboard boxes are stashed on the bottom shelf of black table. No medicine bottles or papers on desk. No box of "stuff" next to screwdriver on the floor.

Exhibit 4: The "computer room" messy

* Trash can is now on desk rather than on the floor next to file drawer; computer chair is moved; water bottle on desk and hand weight on top of desk. Cardboard boxes stacked on top of one another. Sheet of paper--*which is an*

evaluation form for those managing the arrangement, which will appear in many of these exhibits--on top of desk. The sides of the computer tower are now not taken off and strewn on floor.

Exhibit 5: Another "computer room" scenario

* Computer chair now in front of desk; screwdriver on floor; the cardboard boxes have been moved; small speakers behind cereal bowls.

Nothing on bottom of black shelf holding TV. Headphones on desk. Box of stuff with evidence marker is on the floor. White cloth on floor.

Exhibit 6: Now with a stash of pills

Here's an image with a good sized stash of pills on the desk. The pills have no evidence marker. The story is that Adam Lanza wouldn't take his meds, so what is this stash about? How did the photo come about? Why would forensics teams set up evidence like this in cross contamination of different areas of the house?

That is not what they do and they keep different types of evidence from different locations at a crime scene separate for study usually in a laboratory. They do not lump a whole bunch of items together to present a manipulated scene to persuade others of a thematic context.

Other images in the police evidence file show the desktops with only a dozen or so items. This image appears to be one of several mock-ups, probably by intelligence agents on a training course/drill.

* Stacked cardboard boxes now missing along with the screwdriver and box of "stuff" that was next to the screwdriver. Trash can now behind file drawer; desk chair is missing; cereal bowls are now on desk; the table they were on now missing.

* Small speakers behind cereal bowls are now facing backwards on desk; hand weight now on file cabinet and flat screen is turned sideways. White cloth that was on the floor is now missing. The sides of the computer tower that had been taken off are now gone, while medicine bottles appear on the desk.

Exhibit 7: The "boiler room" in one of its guises

The most inexplicable area in the house is what I shall call «the boiler room». There are at least four different images of this area which are completely contradictory to each other.

* Hoover box is front and center, white plastic table is upright. Adam's bed linens are under laundry basket; the green wire rack is in front of white box with pink pillow on floor behind it. The brown bookcase to the right of green wire rack. Painter's paper on floor. (Stuff behind the "black oil tank" changes in other photos of «the boiler room».)

Exhibit 8: Another "boiler room" arrangement

The contents of the boiler room here are arranged differently and are differ in number, position and category to the items in Exhibit 7.

* Now there is a book on top of the brown book case behind the green wire rack; the Hover box is moved and on its side; the brass magazine rack is in front of green wire rack; the United Van Lines box is front and center.

Exhibit 9: The "boiler room" rearranged again

Again the arrangement is different here. There is no explanation for this in the context of forensic investigation. None of the activity of re-arranging the boiler room--whoever undertook it--in any manner advances any precision in establishing a point in evidence or establishing a fact either in the positive or negative. The question then arises of what will explain the existence of different settings of the boiler room?

Training for creating misleading evidence is the only answer I can think of. In faking propaganda events, those who leave their integrity at the door have to be trained to do it and that appears to be the function of these attempts at fakery. Where it falls down, of course, is when other dullard public servants are clumsy enough to allow this kind of image to make its way to the public.

* The magazine rack is now on top of book case. United Van Lines box is gone and another box is in its place. Hoover box is now upright; pink pillow is no longer behind green wire rack and now, by the side of plastic movable cart, a plastic bin appears on the floor behind the black oil tank. An evaluation sheet is on top of the black garbage bag.

Exhibit 10: Another view of the boiler room

Just in case you notice something that we may have missed.

Exhibit 11: The "Adam Lanza rifle"

According to the official narrative, Adam shot his mother Nancy

four times, three in the eye one in the forehead. Four flattened 22 slugs (plus one fragment) were in the evidence, all flattened as if shot into ballistics gel (see below).

This image of the Savage shows what one would presume to be bloody matter on the carpet beside it at the muzzle and perhaps a few specks more.

Exhibit 12: Another view of "Adam's rifle"

Another image doesn't show the same matter on the carpet. Note too that Nancy is supposed to have been shot in the eye three times, yet the immediate surroundings including the carpet, the headboard and the bed itself do not indicate that any brain matter or blood were

expelled forward out of the eye socket from the three shots.

The shots did not penetrate the back of the skull. There's no cranial matter evident in any images around the bed except for what looks like some minimal and feint blood splash on the wall. Nancy didn't bleed much according to the images for having four shots to the head.

The general rule with headshots is that the heart keeps pumping blood because of which wounds evince a large quantity of blood. Four small spots of less than a quarter of an inch in diameter each are found on the bedside cabinet items. This is inconsistent with three wounds to the eye and a wound to the forehead.

Exhibit 13: The boxed "Adam Lanza rifle"

The Savage 22lr (long rifle) is boxed and cable-tied in this image before being used as a prop along with a magazine and (oddly) two expended cartridges. It looks like a factory boxed item. That is how the stage-managers received the rifle from FEMA to use in the sham setting.

Here it's in the box. In other photos, it›s on the floor. But the Savage couldn›t have been both boxed and on the floor when they found it. And if it was still in the box, Adam could not have used it to shoot his mother.

If the forensics team were transporting it to another location, they would have used a large plastic bag. This is another case of incompetent stagers of a hoax taking unnecessary images or of at least allowing the image to come into the public domain.

Exhibit 14: Used cartridges to plant as props?

The origin of these used shell casings is not obvious. If would seem odd for them to have been supplied with the rifle.

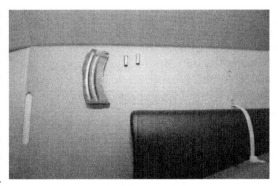

Live cartridges were also found and both were used for placement by the bed. These are clearly props for the staging of a murder which did not take place.

Exhibit 15: The blood on the tip of the barrel

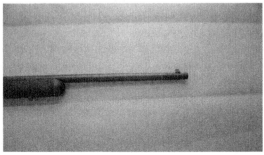

There's pretend blood on the muzzle but

it›s not very convincing. Note too that the rifle is now in a third location for image capturing.

Exhibit 16: Slugs purported shot into Nancy

The four flattened slugs (plus a fragment) that were purportedly shot into Nancy›s cranium all sustain uniform damage and look like they were actually fired into some form of ballistics retardant (or gel) rather than an anything-but-uniform

complex of skin, skull and brain in the head of a human being.

Exhibit 17: The Nancy Lanza bedroom

This DHS/FEMA image shows Nancy's bedroom with a pomegranate-seed colored stain on the bed. It is not the color of dried human blood or of brain matter. A pillow with a slight red stain lies on the floor against the double-mirror chest of drawers. There is no

corpse wearing polka-dot pyjamas.

None of these stains appear to be blood or brain matter. They are some kind of red matter applied to simulate blood. Again few and small splashes of the red liquid appear on the wall where the direction they indicate it as having travelled is forward *toward the lit lamp*. The stain on the bed indicates the red liquid there as having travelled *away from the lamp*. The red bed stain is slightest a the furthest point from the lamp.

The refection of the top of the bed in the mirror in the left of the picture does not reflect any red stain anywhere on the bed. The angle of view shows the end of the curtain closest to the bedhead wall. The part of the bed reflected in the mirror is that closest to the mirror, which is the right side. No red stains are evident.

The reason that the red stain evidence is inconsistent with a shooting death having occurred on the bed is that no shooting death occurred in the room. No evidence from the Connecticut State Police shows any image of any corpse on the bed. The reason for this is that there never was a corpse of a person who had been shot on the bed.

The evidence does show, however, that there were three pillows on the bed: a white one, a light blue one and a green-and-orange striped pillow. They were captured in the first four images taken by the forensic team (or police) as they entered the bedroom.

These same clumsy State government fakers have allowed the images which indicate that no corpse was in the bed to be come public on the Internet. The following five images are from the Connecticut State Police evidence made freely available to the public on a Connecticut State Government site.

* Notice the evaluation form on the foot chest. No blanket or electric blanket on the bed despite 28 degrees that morning. Notice the moving pad under the leg of the footboard--just as we saw in Adam's bedroom.

Exhibit 18: Peering into Nancy's bedroom

This image shows a view into the bedroom with the Savage rifle in the distance. No evidence markers for the rifle or the magazine are on the carpet; therefore, we can presume this is prior in time to those images. If one downloads the image and magnifies it, there is no blood or brain matter on what can be seen of the bed.

One should notice that the area of focus for this forensic officer is the floor, not the "corpse" on the bed of which they would have been well aware of by this point. The focus is on the floor because another element of this hoax involves a forced entry scenario, which will be discussed later.

* The Central Vacuum hose and toilet cleaner in the foreground suggest that a Maid Service has already been called, which would not appear to be consistent with proper forensic practice.

Exhibit 19: Taking a closer look

Here is an enlargement of Exhibit 18. One might be fooled into thinking one is viewing a body and that the conveniently placed ironing board and iron are concealing a head of a corpse, but that is not the case.

No part of this image contains any red stain much less a blood stain visible ever in the dark as it is. Nothing on the bed at this point discloses any murder having taken place let alone any victim on the bed.

Exhibit 20: The top portion of bed from side

Here is another enlargement of another image available on the same site referred to earlier. The iron is no longer obscuring the top of the bed. There is a green-and-orange pillow, a white pillow, a piece of scarlet cloth and a bundle of cloths in the middle. No polka-dot body in pyjamas is in sight.

From the lie of the coverlet, the fake corpse appears to have no feet. This first entry to the bedroom is at least three hours after Adam Lanza supposedly shot his mother. All blood by this time would be dark brown not scarlet. If the scarlet coloured material is intended to simulate blood, it has defied the law of gravity as a liquid and has failed to flow down on to the bedsheet.

127

No arms, hands, head, feet, face nor legs are discernible in this image. The curtains are closed in this photograph, yet open in others. This image is contrived to come across as uninformative yet realistic as the imagination of the scene-setters has allowed. It falls far short of reality.

In setting up this room, as in all the other rooms, the participants were graded. The graders were dumb enough to leave their evaluation forms.

Exhibit 21: Nancy Lanza's dressing table

This image was captured too casually because it shows the top of the bed reflected in the mirror on the left with no red colouring at all. No corpse, no head, but a cross section of the bed, which Exhibit 17 shows as having red staining. That staining is not evident here. Not even the faked material appear to be in place. The colour and configuration of the bedframe and of the chest appear different to other images of them.

* The evaluation form is now missing from the chest in the mirror reflection.

Exhibit 22: Nancy's bed with stains concealed

Ask yourself why a forensic photographer would take an image of a bed with the purported blood stain covered up? Was he queasy? Was he trying to conceal disturbing proof of a murder?

What complete nonsense. The job of a forensic photographer is to document images as they are originally found, not to create a more acceptable image that won›t upset the impressionable.

* The lamp is turned off in this picture. The sheets have been removed. No blood visible anywhere.

Exhibit 23: The Lanza family dining room

Notice the evaluation form in the dining area.

* Three candle holders on the table; no chair pads on chairs; boxes in dining room. No plants, framed art or area rugs. Cheap dining room curtains and curtain rods for a house appraised for over $500,000 owned by the ex-wife of an executive for finance at GE who was reported to have purchased the home new in the 1990's.

Exhibit 24: The photographer catches himself

One of the photographers and stager managers catches himself in a reflection in the mirror.

We have several others, where their reflections were apparently not noticed by those filing the photos.

* Mattresses are stacked on top of one another in the dining room. Candle holders are missing from table and moved to sideboard.

Exhibit 25: Here's another from the bedroom

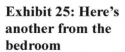

Exhibit 26: Here's one taken from above

This odd shot appears to be a different man than the one reflected in Exhibit 24. None of them seem to be wearing protective gear, which suggests that they are not forensic experts but photographers recording the home as it was being furnished.

Exhibit 27: The lounge area of the Lanza home

* Coffee table in the middle of the room rather than near the sofa or chairs. No coffee table books, candlesticks, candy bowl, magazines, magnifying glass, picture frames on tables. Again really bad, cheap curtains.

Exhibit 28: An access venue that broken in

Each access point was forced and each door was broken. The Lanza home appears to have been stormed simultaneously. Did they think Adam was still alive and waiting for them?

Even the roller door for the garage (below) is

forced or at least broken. One can understand police forcing a single door as a matter of urgency, but surely not all points of entry.

* The curtains are way too long and cheap, including even the curtain rods, for such an expensive home.

Exhibit 29: The refrigerator filled from the left

The water bottles in the freezer compartment would have expanded to split the bottles if they had only arrive at least for three hours after Nancy had been shot. If the official report were true, Nancy was shot sometime before 9:30 AM and police entered after 12 Noon.

Exhibit 30: Desk set up for right-handed user

The setting here indicates that Nancy was right handed, but the filling of the shelves in both the refridgerators indicates that it was performed by a left handed person, being filled to the left.

* In contrast with Exhibit 27, there is no water bottle to the right of the sand timer on the shelf (4th from the bottom to the left of desk). The chair is in front of desk.

Exhibit 31: The study with no laptop or printer

Here's the study with no laptop or printer and the evaluation form on the Chesterfied chair.

Note only one image of Ryan Lanza in the bookshelf and no modern one of Adam Lanza. Ryan is wearing a graduation gown different to the one in his graduation video.

* Laptop is missing from desk; chair is in front of cabinet, not desk; water bottle to the right of sand timer on bookshelf. Banker box on floor.

Exhibit 32: Workman's tools left on the floor

Workman's tools are on scene before evidence markers are laid down. This is another image which should not have been allowed to escape by the stagers to public scrutiny.

Exhibit 33: Water bottles left on the floor

Stage managers' bottles of water are caught in photos. My (Allan's) guess is that there were three of them.

* I (Kelley) think the house was being lived in as a security measure against anyone gaining access in pursuit of DNA or other evidence.

Exhibit 34: Outdated electronic equipment

The whole house has electricals from 2008 or earlier.

A Dell Inspiron laptop Image 25 and a Brother MFC printer fax from around that era.

Exhibit 35: The paper shredder appears full

The paper shredder is full. What would Nancy have had that required that much shredding? Those setting up the fake scene for a pretend murder, however, have a lot of paperwork they wouldn›t want seen.

Exhibit 36: Ryan and Adam's AAA ID cards

Ryan has a Connecticut AAA card and lives in Queens but Adam has a New England AAA card and lives in Sandy Hook?

Exhibit 37: Back to the Computer Room

Like all other things in the Lanza home the carpet protectors here are either brand new or unused or show no signs of use. These plastic mats are in an unrealistic condition if Adam Lanza was on the computer all hours. The room is too sparsely filled.

There are no books in the bookcase for someone who supposedly shrinks from the world. There are no super hero comics, no computer magazines, no favorite anything anywhere. The games are from 2008 and the machines from the same period. No Spiderman, Star Wars; only a Matrix poster. There is a sack in front of the desk and no boxes.

Exhibit 38: The room has been rearranged

Now we have no sack and stacked boxes. Adam was reported to have a huge spread sheet, where *The New York Daily News* reported that investigators discovered, "a chilling spreadsheet 7 feet long and 4 feet wide that required a special printer, a document that contained Lanza's obsessive, extensive research —in nine-point font—about mass

murders of the past, and even attempted murders."

But none of the photos we have reviewed suggest any kind of research, much less a special printer or a spreadsheet of that size. If it had been in the home, surely it would have been the subject of photographs. But there appear to be no printer, no spreadsheet and no indications of Adam having done any research on mass murders or any other subject.

Exhibit 39: The carpet saver seems unused

Not one scratch or buff or scrape or indent or piece of dust on this carpet saver. It›s not just this. Look for yourself at the photo evidence.

Exhibit 40: And no dust under Adam›s bed

No dust, spider webs or other miscellaneous debris under the Adam Lanza bed. Nothing to suggest it was here for any period of time.

Exhibit 41: A constantly changing down-stairs room

There is no explanation for how the down-staris room came to have so many different states and why they were photographed by a technician and included in a release of evidence to the public--except, of course, government incompetence.

*Boxes have been emptied, sofa is sideways in order to make room to move stuff in. Bed is not made; stuff is on top of armoire.

Exhibit 42: A variation on the messy room

Here's the basement less tidy. Notice the ever-present evaluation paper on the table.

* Green chair has been moved; fewer boxes on bed: some may have been taken upstairs and used to stage tje book shelves, etc. In another picture, the bed has been made and all boxes have been removed.

Exhibit 43: A neater version of the down-stairs room

Here's the basement considerably tidied up with somebody's clothes and bag of food evident. Whose room was this? It wasn't Adam's room or Nancy's bedroom.

Did a forensic's guy break in to set up the house after the incident? Before is even more likely. And he cleaned up for the official visit, but left his clothes behind. Please notice, that the sofa is now flat against the wall.

Exhibit 44: The ever-changing laundry room

The ferns in the laundry room jump around. The ferns are gone here and the coloured box is on the floor. Laundry basket is in front of the front loader.

*The paper towels are on top of ice chest in this photo, in other photo they are on top of fridge.

Exhibit 45: A decidedly tidier version of the basement

The fern and the coloured box move to the top of the washing machine. The laundry basket has has taken some steps to the left.

Exhibit 46: Small things are rearranged

The tube of ointment disappears; a pen moves sideways; the phone and its battery rearrange themselves; the Science Club ID conveniently displays itself.

Since when does a 20-year-old keep phone wallet, etc. in a bathroom cupboard at the lowest level?

Exhibit 47: Inside the Lanza home garage

Notice the evaluation form even in the garage.

Exhibit 48: The broken garage door

The garage door on the right shows Adam Lanza didn›t drive the Honda out of that car space. There›s a box blocking the broken roller door which wouldn't have raised or closed. The Honda couldn›t have driven out of the garage.

There's an evaluation form on the BMW. And of course the man who delivered the oil didn't see the wrecked door even though he had to pass it to fill the oil tank. He didn›t investigate and did not call the police.

Exhibit 49: Wood lice and earwigs in the house

Perhaps a very telling image is this one from the kitchen which has both an earwig and a wood louse at the base of this door. Neither wood lice nor earwigs stay in

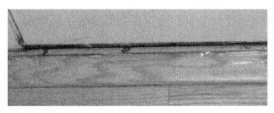

houses during winter. That is their mating season and they seek out the garden in which to mate and live. The image is fabricated.

Exhibit 50: The view looking down the driveway

The faked oil bill has been placed in the letterbox early on a frosty morning as one more fake effect to create the impression that a family was living here, which the evidence presented here refutes.

These exhibits were originally presented by Allan Powell on *"The Real Deal Ep. 80 Explosive New Revelations about Sandy Hook"*, which is available on the Internet.

8

Setting the Stage: Refurbishing the School

by Allan William Powell

Four large trucks supplied by William B. Meyers, a United Vanline franchise holder, delivered the props for the empty school to be window dressed to appear as if it was an active school.

The trucks were from United Van's Connecticut branch. From the state of the leaves on the trees, the last oak leaves are falling so I would say late October or early November.

The trucks unloaded school furniture and props which may have been in storage with William B. Myers since the school was decommissioned and then re-installed at the school to make appear to be a functioning reality. Below are some of those images.

Exhibit 1:
A United Van in the Sandy Hook parking lot

A wet but not freezing day, probably late October or early November, the United truck stands well out of the way waiting to be emptied while another United truck is just visible in the left of the image as it is emptied.

Exhibit 2:
United movers standing by cartons used to transmit props

Here we see some of the United removal staff standing by the empty stacked yellow plastic cartons after the school has been filled with props. A security officer stands guard at the front of the school.

Exhibit 3:
The United agent involved here was William B. Meyer

The sign "Meyer" on the back of the removal truck shows clearly the United agent was William B Meyer. In the background the leaves are brown but not yet fallen.

Exhibit 4:
Three semi-trailers in the background, one in the foreground

Three semi-trailers in the background, one in the foreground. There's a white unmarked FEMA trailer by the portable toilet. Also visible is the portable mortuary referred to by Wayne Carver, Medical Examiner, in his bizarre public speech

about the victims of the hoax. [*Editor's note:* See Chapter 1.]

Exhibit 5:
The empty truck from Bridgeport shows its work was done

This image shows the work done, the empty United trucks from Bridgeport Connecticut. Wm B Meyer has failed to answer any questions I have put to them about the presence of their trucks at the school.

Exhibit 6:
Unmarked FEMA vehicles making back-door deliveries

Unmarked FEMA vehicles arranged deliveries at the back door. [*Editor's note:* We have the FEMA manual for the Sandy Hook event; see Appendix A.]

Exhibit 7: Multiple indications the school had been abandoned

Weed growing and wires hanging loose indicate the fact the school was disused. [*Editor's note:* See Chapters 2 and 3 for more proof that it had been abandoned.]

Exhibit 8: Further signs that the school had been abandoned

Green mould on the wall indicates inactivity at the school, long since abandoned.

Exhibit 9:
Penske Truck Rental also involved in refurbishing the school

Penske truck rentals were also used to move props for the faked shooting into the empty school.

Exhibit 10:
They took photos with the mover's tags still attached

The image bears the name "William B. Meyers" and the notation for the room in which the contents of the yellow labelled bins are to be placed. The label was removed as shown

in the next image when someone realised it would give away the fact that Sandy Hook was staged.

But someone forgot to remove a sticker from a floor mat and it was captured in an image. I»ve sent W.B. Meyers an email requesting that they confirm that the stickers belong to them and if they could tell me when they made the delivery of the props to Sandy Hook. They have not replied.

Exhibit 11:
The MEYER moving sticker identification now removed

Here the William B Meyers sticker has been removed from the classroom sign

Exhibit 12:
Meyer's was responsible for both moving and storage

Over the orange stickers, the label of William B. Meyers can clearly be seen. This indicates that both storage and moving were part of the Meyers› contract.

Exhibit 13:
Vehicles with fake bullet holes were placed in the parking lot

Faked bullet-holed car props were placed in the carpark. The official story in the Sedensky report is that Lanza shot holes on the front glass next to the door and nothing else before he entered. The Sedensky Report also says that cars in

the car park were only damaged from shots fired from inside the classrooms. The only one with any apparent bullet holes in both glass and window frame is Classroom 10.

Other images released in the evidence show that to be false. Additional cars were staged as crime scenes as the drill stagers hadn›t fully decided the scope of the production. A drill is more likely to test a given situation in which participants have been instructed, so here the participants knew the FEMA/DHS drill would involve a shooter but they would not be given exact details of what the drill would involve.

The Lauren Rousseau car referred to in the section on the Lanza home appears in the car park and is shown under a small pavilion as is this vehicle. This vehicle appears to have been struck by a bullet which came through the window of classroom 10, turned left, advanced for forty meters, made a right turn and then a left turn into the rear passenger door. The vehicle has been moved to that location; it has cordon tape trapped under the back wheel.

Exhibit 14:
This vehicle was moved to make for better staging

This vehicle has been moved during the forensic session and appears to have driven over the yellow cordon tape, trapping it under the front wheel.

Exhibit 15:
The Lauren Rousseau car also seen at the Lanza home

This is the Lauren Rousseau car which also was staged as being in the Lanza house driveway. Reflected in the rear passenger door and window is the photographer. The condensation drip of moisture from the exhaust pipe on to the

car park surface indicates that the vehicle has only recently been driven to that location, probably within an hour.

The car from Exhibit 13 would have been shielded from any bullet damage to its right side from Classroom 10 by the Rousseau car, yet a bullet hole in the rear right side passenger door was recorded by the forensic's team.

Exhibit 16:
A bullet fragment was planted in the trunk of the car

The bullet here appears to have been retrieved from a

ballistics testing medium and then placed in the trunk of the Rousseau car.

Exhibit 17:
The Rousseau car was photographed in multiple locations

Here it is under the pavilion. The car has been driven over cordon tape indicating that it has been moved again. The car from Exhibit 13 appears to be beside it, which means the Rousseau car would have been blocking any bullet shown in that exhibit as having hit the rear passenger side door.

Exhibit 18:
A close-up of the bullet holes in the right passenger side.

A bullet coming trough the window of Classroom 10 would have had to have curved over the Rousseau car to hit the Exhibit 13 car. A man is visible in the background at the window through which the bullets were purported to have passed.

Exhibit 19:
Even closer with a forensic identification tag attached.

The stage managers went out of their way to fake their forensic evidence.

Exhibit 20:
These vehicles are cordoned off and not in Sedensky's report

These two cars and a faked bloodstain are cordoned off as part of the pretended shooting. No reference is made by *The Sedensky Report* to any discharge of the Bushmaster in the parking lot other than to breach the window in order to enter the school.

Exhibit 21:
Fake blood has been planted between these two cars

Here›s the faked blood between the two cars. The shadow cast from the eastern sunrise shows that this is early morning.

Exhibit 22:
Notice the forensic tag on the bumper by the license plate

This creates the impression of a thorough forensic investigation of the crime scene.

Exhibit 23:
Here is a bullet fragment but no trajectory of how it got there

A bullet fragment glides conveniently to a halt under a car trunk carpet, but no images of the holes the bullet made in the car trunk carpet exist.

Exhibit 24:
Open school door with no shot-out window glass

This photo taken early on the morning of 14 December 2012 shows the school door open but no window blown out to gain access. Notice the discarded water bottles at front in the gutter. If you look closely you will see an audio-visual

presentation being given on a large screen just beside the American flag in Classroom 8.

Exhibit 25:
A couple of stage managers inside the foyer before the event

Another photo shows a pair of stage managers inside the foyer before the event.

Exhibit 26:
Flag full mast, SWAT vehicle present, windows undamaged

Notice the windows of Classroom 10 are undamaged, the flag is up. Wayne Carver can be seen behind the man in the blue evidence suit. The shot is taken from one of the elevated cameras placed around the car park to record the drill. Leaves are evident on the trees in the background. This is not December. No portable mortuary can be seen, which means this is early morning before the portable mortuary was delivered.

Exhibit 27:
Some Port-a-Potties are already in place early in the morning

Portable toilets were ordered prior to the day and placed in the car park. They appear in the early morning images. The suppliers of the toilets will not answer emails for details on

the supply contract for the potties. Establishing that both the toilets and the mortuary tent were delivered prior to the "massacre" provides one more important proof that this was a planned event. If it›s early morning and Carver is there and the mortuary isn›t, that›s pretty conclusive of planning.

Exhibit 28:
Another car photo early morning before the event takes place

The sun can just be seen rising over the school in reflection on this car rear door. The sunlight has hit the trees on the west side of the car park indicating again that the time of this image capture is early morning and before the incident would begin.

Exhibit 29:
Earlier in the morning before the windows have been "shot out"

One image of a car shows a case of water put down for the boys to help themselves and four windows of a classroom open with three candle shapes in each open window. The end windows have been closed. Other images show  the windows were intact before holes were drilled through the frames to simulate bullet damage.

The sun has yet to rise on the car park but sunlight can be seen on the tree behind the school. This indicates again that it is early morning. The mortuary tent is not in place as it would have been every morning after the shooting had it been real.

Exhibit 30:
The windows have been "fixed" to simulate effects of shots

The mortuary tent can now be seen in the reflection of the window. This means it has been set up some time after the windows of Classroom 10 featuring three candle images apiece were staged to look as though bullets passed through some of them.

Exhibit 31:
The bullet Adam "shot himself with" looks corroded

This image of the 10mm bullet with which Adam Lanza purportedly took his own life shows fragments that appear to be corroded.

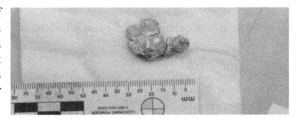

Exhibit 32:
None of the .223 fragments could be matched to the rifle

Other images of .223 bullets recovered indicate they have sufficient land and groove imprints to forensically link them to the Bushmaster, were this a legitimate bona fide forensic investigation. *The Sedensky Report* says

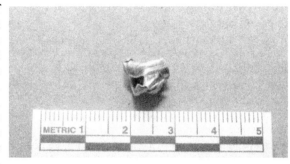

none of the 154 fragments that were recovered could be forensically linked to the Bushmaster. That is simply false.

Exhibit 33:
The office area leading to Nurse Sally Cox's office

She also claimed in another interview that Lanza opened the door and stared her in the face. She says she then jumped under the desk with another staff member and together they stayed there for three hours only calling the police once. The story is highly improbable.

Few public-speaking appearances have been made by Sally Cox. As a crisis actor, she appears to be a loose cannon.

Exhibit 34:
The fraudulent testimony of Nurse Sally Cox exposed

Another image is a view of Nurse Sally Cox's office, which shows she could not have seen the shooter 20 feet away. There is no desk with a view that would have permitted it.

There is also no desk facing the door for her to hide under and watch the shooter, as she claims she did. She also asserted in an interview that she saw his boots through this imaginary hole in the desk. But officially Adam Lanza's footwear was a pair of black shoes.

Exhibit 35:
The mortuary tent and oak tree yet to shed all its leaves

The large tent mortuary doesn't appear in other released photos purportedly taken on the day of the shooting.

Wayne Carver referred to the structure and said autopsies were performed in the tent. Post-mortem examinations for Pozner and Lanza are supposed to have been performed at the Office of the Chief Medical Examiner, not in the Sandy Hook mortuary tent. Images of the mortuary tent show an oak tree in the background, which has yet to lose all its leaves: the time of year is late October.

Exhibit 36:
Moving cars around for the best staging: the blue VW

Multiple images show different parking arrangements for the car props in the school parking lot.

Notice both of the vehicles, including the blue VW, are facing the school.

Exhibit 37:
Now the blue VW is facing away from the school

Now the blue VW faces away from the school. Notice too the man in short sleeves, indicating that it may be much earlier than December. The SWAT team is there but the windows of Classroom 10 are intact. How much proof of fakery do we need?

Exhibit 38:
A door with a broken window was at the back of the school

The Sedensky Report makes no mention of any doors at the rear of the school being involved in the incident, yet two different images of this broken glass exist. The broken door glass appears to be a CGI aspect of the hoax, which did not quite come off. The wired glass doesn't in the real world break as show in the images. This is security glass with a crossed wire through it. It does not shatter like ordinary glass.

Exhibit 39:
A better photograph of the broken door glass in the back

The angle from which this photo was taken makes the broken glass easier to see than in Exhibit 38.

Exhibit 40:
They appear to have faked the image of broken door glass

The broken glass on the doorstep is a CGI image, which could not possible happen in reality. The pieces show that the wire through the glass has shattered as if it

were not wire but glass. This is a physical impossibility.

Exhibit 41:
The fantasy scenario of parallel shots from Classroom 10

Photos exist of the windows in Classroom 10 before and after their doctoring. They show a preposterous line of four freehand shots fired into the aluminium frame. To fire and get that many shots in such straight lines--each exactly at a perfect 90 degree

right angle to the window frame--is overwhelmingly improbable. No one experienced with firearms would find this remotely plausible. One image indicates that the shot ruptured the aluminium inward, which means that it was inflicted from outside. There was no blood splatter from any victim on the inside of the window.

Exhibit 42:
The windows before they were "fixed" to reflect the shooting

This picture shows the window before it was doctored. Notice that there is no reflection in the window of the mortuary tent. This was indeed an elaborate hoax.

Exhibit 43:
The precision with which those holes were created

This image shows how the bullet holes were actually drilled from the parking-lot side of the window. The swarf from the drill has erupted into the classroom side of the window as one would expect from using a drill on an aluminium window frame.

Exhibit 44:
The perps at work drilling the holes in the window frame

This image actually shows the personnel who are at work setting up the window frame with fake bullet holes. It was extremely

revealing that such extensive records were kept.

Exhibit 45:
Cameras to record the drill mounted on cars in the back row

Other images show the extended cameras fixed on cars to record the drill. They›re the little yellow things on extensions from the cars in the back row. The leaves are still on trees so the likelihood that this image was taken in December is very low.

Exhibit 46:
Here's a Connecticut State Trooper setting up his camera

If you look carefully here, you can see the Connecticut State Trooper setting up the camera just to the left of it.

Exhibit 47:
The same photographer worked the Lanza home furnishing

Note the SWAT wagon in the distance in this image waiting to be put out front of the fire station. There is no other reason a SWAT team would attend a forensics site. And there›s the SWAT team in the extreme right of the image their heads visible just above the cars. The man in the evidence overall is obviously aware that he is photographing a complete faked event. He was also in on staging the Lanza home, again being accidentally caught in the image evidence as here.

Exhibit 48:
Police tape up before the window has been blown out

One image shows that someone stuck a chair into the crime scene and the window in the background doesn›t appear to have been blown out yet. There is police tape but "the crime" has yet to be committed.

If I'm not mistaken there is an audio-visual presentation going on in Classroom 12 on a large screen. Indeed, as the second image shows, I am not mistaken.

Exhibit 49:
Wayne Carver waiting for his Mortuary Tent to show up

Here›s Wayne Carver waiting early in the morning for his mortuary tent to turn up. This is early morning before the drill has commenced.

There's a drill executive back near the door waiting for the drill to begin. Note there are no evidence markers down yet on the concrete at the front of the school entrance.

Exhibit 50:
A view from the woods of a school day that will live in infamy

Here's an unofficial image of the stage setting taken from the wooded area. There are two vehicles in front of the school entrance and that telltale chair, too. Why were there two vehicles in an area that ought to be  cordoned off as a crime scene--*if it were a crime scene, that is?*

It's possible that two cars were used for the drill and that one of these was the car that found its way to Gene Rosen's driveway with that broken driver side window for which no alternative explanation has ever been advanced.

These exhibits were originally presented by Allan Powell on *"The Real Deal Ep. 80 Explosive New Revelations about Sandy Hook"* and its sequel, *"The Real Deal Ep. 96 More Sandy Hook"*, which are available on the Internet.

Allan William Powell

Part III

Further Proof
Nobody Died at Sandy Hook

9

Proof from the Social Security Death Index

by Dr. Eowyn, Ph.D.

When a person in the United States dies, his/her death is recorded by the federal government.

The Social Security Death Index (SSDI) is a database of death records created from the Social Security Administration's Death Master File (DMF). Most persons in the U.S. who have died since 1936, have had a Social Security number, and those whose death was reported to the Social Security Administration are listed in the SSDI.

Unlike the Death Master File, the SSDI is available free to the public on several genealogy websites, such as Genealogy Bank. The "state of issue" refers to the state that had issued the individual's Social Security number.

On January 20, 2013, I undertook a search on Genealogy Bank for the SSDI of Adam Lanza — the alleged mass murderer of his mother, Nancy Lanza, and 20 children and 6 adults at Sandy Hook Elementary School in Newtown, Connecticut, on December 14, 2012.

To my astonishment, Genealogy Bank had Lanza's SSDI as December **13**, 2012 — a day BEFORE the alleged mass shooting. (See "SSDI says Adam Lanza died a day before Sandy Hook massacre")

On the next page is a screenshot I took of Adam Lanza's SSDI record on the website GenealogyBank.com. The date (1/20/2013) and time (2:29PM) when I took the screenshot can be seen in the lower right corner of the image.

After the discovery of Lanza's 12/**13**/2012 SSDI went viral, on or around February 2, 2013, Genealogy Bank changed Lanza's SSDI to 12/**14**/2012,

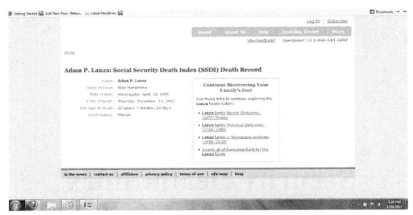

the day of the alleged massacre. (See "SSDI changed Adam Lanza's date-of-death from Dec. 13 to Dec. 14, 2012 !!!")

Another genealogy website, Ancestry.com, was slower on the uptake. Three days after Genealogy Bank had changed its SSDI for Lanza to 12/14/2012, Ancestry.com still listed Lanza's SSDI as 12/13/2012. (See "Ancestry.com still has Adam Lanza's date-of-death as a day before the Sandy Hook massacre")

Lanza's curious SSDI aside, **I *was* able to find on Genealogy Bank the SSDI (of 12/14/2012) of all of Lanza's victims, except one** — that of Ana Marquez-Greene, age 6, whose father is jazz musician Jimmy Greene. In my search for Ana, I had used every variation of her name: Ana Marquez, Ana Marquez-Greene, Ana Greene, to no avail. I hypothesized that the lack of a SSDI for Ana Marquez-Greene may be because her parents had not yet obtained a Social Security card/number for her. (See "Dec. 14 was date of death for every Sandy Hook massacre victim, except Adam Lanza")

But wait!

Remember what I'd written at the beginning of this post — that **the Social Security Death Index (SSDI) is a database of death records created from the federal government Social Security Administration's Death Master File**?

What if I were to tell you that **the Death Master File does NOT contain the SSDIs for any of Adam Lanza's victims**?

In other words, according to the United States Social Security Administration's Death Master File, nobody died at Sandy Hook Elementary School on December 14, 2012.

That's exactly what blogger LivingonPlanetZ of Chemtrails: The Exotic Weapon reported on Feb. 22, 2014.

LivingonPlanetZ refers us to what he calls an "originating website" — a document published on archives.org (date unknown), titled "Sandy Hook – NO DEATHS, NO VICTIMS; According to SSDI Official Master File." (You can also read the document in PDF here or here.)

The anonymous person who uploaded the 107-page document to archives. org had accessed the Social Security Administration's Death Master File, updated through January 1, 2014, and searched for Adam Lanza's victims — in vain.

The document says:

You are invited to search all of these records for the putative 'victims' of the Sandy Hook massacre. The children should all be 6 to 7 years old ("born" 2005-2006), and should have "died" in 2012. The adult "victims" appear in the appendix. (Each entry is followed by a 6-7 digit serial entry number, which demonstrates the continuity of the alphabetical listing – in other words, that they are presented here unaltered.)

I did just that and can verify the claim that none of Adam Lanza's victims is in Social Security's Death Master File. But before I present my findings, here are the Sandy Hook victims (name, birth date, gender, age at death), according to news accounts:

CHILDREN
1. Charlotte Bacon, 2/22/06, female (age 6)
2. Daniel Barden, 9/25/05, male (age 7)
3. Olivia Engel, 7/18/06, female (age 6)
4. Josephine Gay, 12/11/05, female (age 7)
5. Ana M. Marquez-Greene, 04/04/06, female (age 6)
6. Dylan Hockley, 03/08/06, male (age 6)
7. Madeleine F. Hsu, 07/10/06, female (age 6)
8. Catherine V. Hubbard, 06/08/06, female (age 6)
9. Chase Kowalski, 10/31/05, male (age 7)
10. Jesse Lewis, 06/30/06, male (age 6)
11. James Mattioli, 03/22/06, male (age 6)
12. Grace McDonnell, 11/04/05, female (age 7)
13. Emilie Parker, 05/12/06, female (age 6)
14. Jack Pinto, 05/06/06, male (age 6)
15. Noah Pozner, 11/20/06, male (age 6)
16. Caroline Previdi, 09/07/06, female (age 6)

17. Jessica Rekos, 05/10/06, female (age 6)
18. Avielle Richman, 10/17/06, female (age 6)
19. Benjamin Wheeler, 9/12/06, male (age 6)
20. Allison N. Wyatt, 07/03/06, female (age 6)

ADULTS
1. Rachel Davino, 7/17/83, female (age 29)
2. Dawn Hocksprung, 06/28/65, female (age 47)
3. Anne Marie Murphy, 07/25/60, female (age 52)
4. Lauren Russeau, 1982, female (age 29)
5. Mary Sherlach, 02/11/56, female (age 56)
6. Victoria Soto, 11/04/85, female (age 27)

Here are the search results for each of the above names in the Social Security Death Master File (DMF). In the list below, the names of alleged **child victims are bold**; those of **adults are italics bold**:

1. Charlotte Bacon: DMF has 36 individuals named Charlotte Bacon, none of whom is Sandy Hook's Charlotte Bacon.

2. Daniel Barden: DMF has 6 individuals named Daniel or Danny Barden, none of whom is Sandy Hook's Daniel Barden.

3. Olivia Engel: DMF has one Olivia Engel, but she was born on May 18, 1905.

4. Josephine Gay: DMF has 29 Josephine Gay, none of whom is Sandy Hook's Josephine Gay.

5. Anna Marquez: DMF has 21 Anna Marquez, none of whom is Sandy Hook's Anna Marquez.

6. Dylan Hockley: DMF has no one named Dylan Hockley.

7. Madeline Hsu: DMF has no one named Madeline Hsu. The closest, an individual named M. Hsu, was born on Oct. 27, 1940.

8. Catherine Hubbard: DMF has 68 individuals named Catherine Hubbard, none of whom is the Sandy Hook Catherine Hubbard.

9. Chase Kowalski: DMF has no one named Chase Kowalski. The closest, Chas Kowalski, was born on April 10, 1900.

10. Jesse Lewis: DMF has 565 individuals named Jess or Jesse Lewis, none of whom is Sandy Hook's Jesse Lewis.

11. James Mattioli: DMF has no one named James Mattioli.

12. Grace McDonnell: DMF has 38 individuals named Grace or Gracie McDonnell, none of whom is Sandy Hook's Grace McDonnell.

13. Emilie Parker: DMF has 12 individuals named Emilie, Emilia, or Emiline Parker, none of whom is Sandy Hook's Emilie Parker.

14. Jack Pinto: DMF has 12 individuals named Jack or Jacob Pinto, none of whom is Sandy Hook's Jack Pinto.

15. Noah Pozner: DMF has no one named Noah Pozner.

16. Caroline Previdi: DMF has no one named Caroline Previdi.

17. Jessica Rekos: DMF has no one named Jessica Rekos.

18. Avielle Richman: DMF has 5 individuals with a first name that begins with the alphabet A and a last name of Richman, none of whom is Avielle Richman.

19. Benjamin Wheeler: DMF has 206 individuals named Benjamin (or Benjamine, Benjemin, Benj, Benji) Wheeler, none of whom is Sandy Hook's Benjamin Wheeler.

20. Allison Wyatt: DMF has 4 individuals named Allison Wyatt, none of whom is Sandy Hook's Allison Wyatt.

ADULTS

21. Rachel Davino: DMF has no one named Rachel Davino.

22. Dawn Hochsprung: DMF has no one named Dawn Hochsprung.

23. Ann Marie Murphy: DMF has 11 individuals named Ann (or Anna) Murphy, 4 of whom are named Ann Marie Murphy, but none of them is Sandy Hook's Ann Marie Murphy.

24. Lauren Russeau: DMF has no one named Lauren Russeau.

25. Mary Sherlach: DMF has two Marian Sherlach, but none named Mary Sherlach.

26. Victoria Soto: DMF has 50 individuals named Victoria Soto. The closest is a Victoria G. Soto who was born about 1985, married in Texas on July 2, 2011, but is not dead.

LivingonPlanetZ posted about the document "Sandy Hook – NO DEATHS, NO VICTIMS; According to SSDI Official Master File" on February 22, 2014.

It is noteworthy that a month later, Social Security Administration changed its policy on the public's access to its Death Master File. On the website of the Social Security Administration, it says **beginning March 27, 2014, the public can have only "limited access" to its Death Master File**. To gain access to the DMF, we the American people must now jump through several hoops:

- One must be "certified" (via having one's application approved) to be granted "limited access".

- Only certain people are eligible to be "certified". One must have a "legitimate" fraud prevention interest, or have a "legitimate" business purpose pursuant to a law, governmental rule, regulation, or fiduciary duty in order to be certified under the program. (The critical word "legitimate" is undefined, which means Social Security Administration's bureaucrats decide what "legitimate" means.)

- Those who are "certified" for access to the Death Master File must pay a hefty annual per-person subscription fee of $995.

Then there's this cover-their-posterior all-purpose qualifier by Social Security Administration:

This [Death Master] file includes the following information on each decedent, if the data are available to the SSA: social security number, name, date of birth, date of death. ***The SSA does not have a death record for all persons; therefore, SSA does not guarantee the veracity of the file. Thus, the absence of a particular person is not proof this person is alive.***

But wait!

We don't just have to depend on Social Security's Death Master File data to know that no one died at Sandy Hook Elementary School on December 14, 2012.

How do we know that?

The Federal Bureau of Investigation (FBI) tells us so!

Adan Salazar reports for Infowars, Sept. 24, 2014, that **recently released FBI crime statistics show that no murders occurred in Newtown, Connecticut, in 2012**, despite reports that 20 schoolchildren, 6 faculty members, and Nancy Lanza were killed or, in the case of Adam Lanza, committed suicide on December 14, 2012.

In contrast to the Connecticut report, the 2012 FBI crime report for the state of Colorado shows that 29 murders occurred in the town of Aurora that year, a figure that takes into account the 12 people who died in the Century Theater during the midnight premiere of *The Dark Knight Rises* on July 20, 2012.

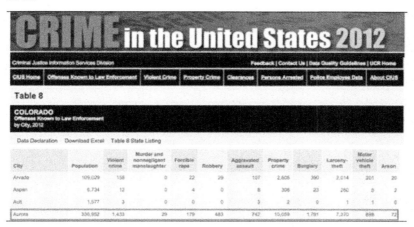

To conclude, **no one was killed on December 14, 2012 at Sandy Hook Elementary School in Newtown, Connecticut**. More perverse still, **according to the Social Security Administration's records, none of the alleged Sandy Hook victims ever lived!**

As the author of "Sandy Hook – NO DEATHS, NO VICTIMS; According to SSDI Official Master File" puts it:

ALL of the identities of the "children victims" of the supposed Sandy Hook massacre, are purely fictitious identities, with no record of either birth or death. As to the adult "victims", the only one with an identity possibly verifiable from the intact SSD Master File, is Victoria G. Soto. The other identities may or may not have been assumed by real people at some time; but the identities themselves are nevertheless fictitious. Secondary copies of the Master File, or perhaps earlier versions, appear to have been altered or "corrected", to include the fake identities. Such altered copies appear to be in use by popular genealogy search websites, though inconsistently.

H/t Nicholas K, Kelleigh N, Victoria M.

This appendix originally appeared as *"No one died in Sandy Hook: Testimony from Social Security Death Master File"* (26 September 2014), *fellowshipoftheminds.com*

Dr. Eowyn Ph.D.

10

CT Crime Data
confirms FBI Report

by Dr. Eowyn, Ph.D. & Jim Fetzer, Ph.D.

"According to the Connecticut State Crime Report for 2012, there were 27 deaths in Connecticut that did not occur in any community or jurisdiction in Connecticut. But if no one died in Newtown, no one died at Sandy Hook"– Jim Fetzer

Brasscheck TV claims **Sandy Hook FBI Hoax** that the victims of the Sandy Hook massacre *really are* in **Viral nonsense** the FBI's Consolidated Crime Report, if you know how to read it.

He (the author) claims that those who believe this is "the smoking gun" of Sandy Hook have committed a mistake, because the numbers are there under a special "State Police" designation.

He even suggests that Wolfgang Halbig and Alex Jones have been taken in, which is especially surprising since the one he refers to as "W" is a former state trooper himself. Someone has blundered, but that would not be Wolfgang. Sandy Hook is a subdivision of Newtown. Murders in Newtown should be reported under "Newtown", not under a "State Police" designation.

Search for Brasscheck TV: "Sandy Hook FBI Hoax: Viral Nonsense"

Murders are offenses under the law and should be reported for the community or jurisdiction that has the legal authority to investigate and prosecute them, even if the investigation were conducted by the CT State Police. *Otherwise, how would any community know what crimes were committed there?*

The Connecticut State Police are an organization, not a community or a jurisdiction. Like everything else about this event, there is nothing normal or consistent or coherent about it. And it therefore comes as no surprise that the FBI report has been confirmed by the state's crime statistics for 2012:

Crime in Connecticut 2012

Arrest Statistics for Year 2012																Agency:	Connecticut Total	
	Murder	Neg. Manslaughter	Forcible Rape	Robbery	Aggravated Assault	Burglary	Larceny-Theft	Motor Vehicle Theft	Arson	Simple Assault	Forgery/Counterfeiting	Fraud	Embezzlement	Stolen Property	Vandalism	Weapons Charges	Prostitution	Sex Offenses
<10	0	0	1	1	1	3	7	0	0	25	0	0	0	0	5	3	0	2
10-12	0	0	6	7	26	42	74	5	4	218	0	2	0	3	40	14	0	30
13-14	0	0	13	47	66	95	364	16	11	790	2	11	4	8	127	52	0	48
15	0	0	4	61	53	95	362	31	11	666	0	7	1	6	96	28	0	18
16	0	1	4	78	76	95	435	39	10	705	2	8	2	14	119	36	1	20
17	3	0	6	99	89	165	586	39	6	733	12	14	3	28	109	36	0	26
Tot <18	3	1	34	293	311	495	1828	130	42	3137	16	42	10	59	496	169	1	144

Go to "Crime in Connecticut COMPLETE for 2012" and on page 26, you will find the data that I am publishing here. *At the intersection of "Murder" with "<10" (below 10 years of age) for 2012, you will find the number "0"!* But that does not quite settle the matter, because the number "27" appears under the heading, "State Police Misc." buried on page 415:

Crime in Connecticut 2012   **Offense and Arrest Data**

Offense Statistics for Year 2012	Agency or Area:	State Police Misc. *			Pop:	3,067,466
	Offenses		Clearances		Value Stolen	
Index Offense	Number	Rate[2]	Number	Pct.	Total	Average
Murder[3]	27	0.9	27	100.0%	$0	$0
Rape	2	0.1	0	0.0%	$0	$0
Robbery	4	0.1	2	50.0%	$215	$54
Aggravated Assault	52	1.7	40	76.9%	-----	-----
Burglary	16	0.5	2	12.5%	$12,669	$792
Larceny	203	6.6	41	20.2%	$445,901	$2,197
Motor Vehicle Theft	74	2.4	34	45.9%	$702,519	$9,494
Arson	35	1.1	0	0.0%	$1,645,012	$47,000
Crime Index Total[1]:	378	12.3	146	38.6%	$1,161,304	$3,072

[1] Arson not included   *Included in State Police total.   **Value Recovered:** $243,497
[2] All rates per 100,000 persons; crime rate of rape per 100,000 females is 0.1
[3] Includes 27 victims of Newtown mass shooting

If you put the data on page 415 together with the data on page 26, then *according to the Connecticut State Crime Report for 2012, there were 27 deaths in Connecticut that did not occur in any community or jurisdiction in Connecticut. But if no one died in Newtown, then no one died at Sandy Hook, because Sandy Hook is in Newtown.*

Twenty-seven people cannot have *died in Connecticut* and also *not have died anywhere in Connecticut* in 2012. The Connecticut State Police, who orchestrated this event, have been caught and are looking for a way out. The FBI is playing along, because Eric Holder, the US Attorney General, was a crucial player in the hoax.

A more interesting analysis

A far more sophisticated discussion of The FBI's Consolidated Uniform Crime Report for Connecticut may be found in *Global Research*, "The Sandy School Massacre and FBI Data Anomalies" (27 September 2014), by Jason Kissner. Jason cites an article by Adan Salazar that appeared on *infowars. com* to critique it and explain why its author got it wrong. He even notes that Connecticut reports zero murders for children below the age of 10 in its own report on crime in 2012:

FBI SAYS NO ONE KILLED AT SANDY HOOK
Agency publishes crime report showing "0" murders occurred in Newtown in 2012

Image Credits: Wiki Commons

Kissner identifies himself as a "criminologist", who would appear to be in an appropriate position to explain why "the data entry identified by Salazar in no way whatsoever supports the claim that the FBI says no one was killed at Sandy Hook. " But of course it does. Since the FBI's data is confirmed by Connecticut's data, but no location for those deaths appears in the state report, it supports the inference no one died, since if they died they had to have died somewhere.

Kissner says, "There could conceivably be real issues as to why the Sandy Hook murders weren't scored in the Newtown 'Agency or Area' even if it is true that the Connecticut State Police managed the 'investigation.'" Because the Newtown event was scored under the "State Police Misc." heading and the FBI received the data from Connecticut, it placed a "0" in the Newtown row. Which means the claim that the FBI says nobody was killed at Newtown is not supported by the FBI's data point. But does Kissner really think people can die in Connecticut without dying somewhere in Connecticut?

After all, murders are reported in the communities or jurisdictions in which they have occurred, not on the basis of the agency or organization that investigates them. Since these "murders" allegedly took place in Sandy Hook and Sandy Hook is a subdivision of Newtown, they should have been reported under "Newtown", not under "State Police Misc." The only reason to cite any murders under "State Police Misc." is to obfuscate that no one died in Newtown in 2012.

Did the CT State police retract data?

When Kissner turns to an article in USA TODAY, however, he comes up with some striking information, which is that the data originally submitted by Colorado on the Aurora "Batman" shooting as well as the data originally submitted by Connecticut about Sandy Hook were both retracted at the request of local authorities, which were in the case of Sandy Hook, the Connecticut State Police:

"The records are voluntarily submitted by police agencies, and FBI officials say the Connecticut State Police and Aurora police departments initially provided the information on the year's two largest killing incidents – only to request that it be deleted.

In Aurora, Sgt. Chris Amsler says his department provides data to the Colorado Bureau of Investigations monthly. The FBI database contains information on 18 other homicides in Aurora in 2012.

"We checked our records and found that all data related to the theater shooting was submitted," he said, adding that investigators were still trying to figure out why the incident was later deleted from FBI records.Connecticut's homicide count is correct, but the FBI's detailed supplementary material includes only the shooting of Adam Lanza's mother at her home in December 2012, just before Lanza went to the elementary school. Lt. Paul Vance says his department submitted a six-page report on the Newtown school victims to the FBI but later identified a mistake. Updated data was provided too late to be reflected in the database, Vance says, but the information should be added soon."

As Kissner observes, what sort of "mistake" could possibly have justified the CTSP to request the retraction of data on homicides? The "supplemental homicide report" (which is the "supplementary materials" mentioned here) is as simple as it gets, but *the mention of the suspect's mother, Nancy Lanza, suggests that information about her may have been in error–which given the latest research about the alleged victims, could very well have justified the retraction–along with the data on every other purported victim.* The school was closed by 2008 and no one died there in 2012.

Sandy Hook "smoking guns"

This report is not "the smoking gun" of Sandy Hook, because the word "the" implies there is one and only one. There are many "smoking guns" for Sandy Hook, including that the school had been closed by 2008, that there were no 469 children being evacuated, that the Shannon Hicks' "iconic" photograph was staged, that the "official report" by Danbury State's Attorney does not connect the suspect to his alleged victims or the weapons he is supposed to have used and that Wolfgang has exposed the "script". The FBI report is important because it encapsulates the problems with Sandy Hook:

> *The FBI crime report is making an impact with the public, no doubt, because it represents the federal government and the authority of the state (not just of Connecticut, but of the United States). We tend to confound authority with truth, when truth is the authority–and where "authorities" lie to the American people all the time: about Lee Oswald, the Gulf of Tonkin, Iraqi soldiers dumping babies out of incubators in Kuwait, about 19 Arab hijackers, about Osama bin Laden, about Saddam Hussein, about Sandy Hook and about the Boston bombing–the authorities are lying to us all the time!*

> *What is incredible is that we still tend to believe in our government, no doubt because the very idea that it would kill 3,000 of our fellow citizens to promote a political agenda is beyond our comprehension. They have experts on mind control and the dissemination of false information to instill fear into us and manipulate us for political purposes. The young Kuwati girl who testified before Congress is an appropriate illustration, since it was an emotional appeal like the emotional appeal of 20 first-graders being massacred at school.*

The statistical records for crimes in states should be straightforward and unambiguous, as Jason Kissner observes: it's a simple spread-sheet with the intersection of kinds of crimes and locations where crimes of that kind could have been committed. *Had there been a murder of 20 children and seven adults–including Nancy Lanza as the twenty-seventh–then those numbers would have appeared in their proper place.* It is a federal crime to report false statistics to the FBI, so the CTSP tacked on a new category of "State Police Misc." as though that solved the problem. But perhaps Nancy Lanza also poses special problems, which have caused them some concern.

What about Nancy Lanza?

Another line of proof concerns the woman alleged to be Adam Lanza's mother, Nancy. There is more than one theory regarding her identity. One, which identifies her with Annie Haddad, has been featured in "A sampler of Sandy Hook videos", where I explained that studies about her tend to disappear from the internet as rapidly as they are posted. In this instance, you can find this one by clicking on this link. Both "Nancy Lanza" and "Annie Haddad" as appearing to be the person also known under the last name "Champion".

This theme is developed further in a new book by Dennis and Sabrina Phillips, *Making a Killing: The Unofficial Story of the Sandy Hook Massacre* (2014). According to the *Tampa Bay Times*, when Nancy Lanza's mother, "Dorothy Hanson", was reached for comment after the shooting, she was "Too distraught to talk." During some initial research, they came across an obituary from the *St. Petersburg Times* back in the year 2000. It was for an "Eleanore Champion" and it's the one of the only obituaries connecting Nancy Lanza to the Champion name.

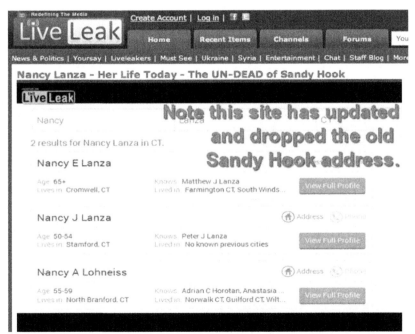

For more, search YouTube for "Nancy Lanza: Her life today — The Undead of Sandy Hook".

An alternative account can be found here: *In the horror story of Sandy Hook, Nancy Lanza, Adam's mother, has been somewhat of a mystery and met a rather awful end, according to the official tale. It would appear that perhaps Nancy never died. The real "Undead" of this false flag. Another part of this farce known as the Sandy Hook Massacre. The absurd photographs from INSIDE the Lanza house would be enough to show normal people that her death was faked. However, here we will provide several additional layers of proof that she obviously is still living her life today. In fact, it appears that Nancy and Peter are back together again... sans "Adam", of course.* (For more, see Chapter 7.)

The situation with regard to Sandy Hook boggles the mind. The Connecticut State Police submit information to the FBI that asserts 27 people died in Connecticut, but at the same time denies that they died anywhere in Connecticut. That is absurd and revealing. The objective of disinformation is to create enough uncertainty that everything is believable and nothing is knowable. But we have a mountain of proof that the school was closed by 2008 and that no one died there in 2012. Even Obama officials in the Department of Education have confirmed it. And Dr. Eowyn offers more proof that no one died in her brilliant study of the Social Security Death Index (Chapter 9), which has apparently been shut down so students and scholars cannot compare the data it provides with the claims being made by local, state and federal authorities.

This chapter is an expanded and revised version of an article originally published as *"Sandy Hook: CT crime data confirms FBI report"* (28 September 2014), *veteranstoday.com.*

175

11

Are Sandy Hook skeptics delusional with "twisted minds"?

by Jim Fetzer Ph.D., & Kelley Watt

"Noah Pozner's death certificate is a fake. But if Sandy Hook had been real, there would have been no reason to fake it. QED"–Jim Fetzer

Someone calling himself "Lenny Pozner", who purports to be the father of the alleged Sandy Hook victim, Noah Pozner, has launched a vicious attack upon those who are skeptical of the "official story" of the Sandy Hook event.

A response has been published by *AbleChild*, observing that the problem has arisen because the "official report" from Connecticut authorities, especially the *Sandy Hook Final Report* authored by Danbury State's Attorney Stephen Sedensky, was a shoddy piece of work that raised more questions than it answers. This exchange deserves serious consideration, not least of all because Noah Pozner appears to be the only alleged "child victim" for whom their birth and death certificates have been released by their "parents". There is no stronger case.

That makes the Noah Pozner case of special significance as an acid test: *if Noah really died, that defeats the critics' claim that "no children died at Sandy Hook"; but if Noah did not die, especially if Lenny's 'proof of death" turns out to be fake, then this effort to defeat the critics will have backfired badly*. And it is very straightforward to demonstrate that *AbleChild* is right about the "official report".

The "official report" on Sandy Hook

At this point in time, it is relatively trivial to demonstrate that the "official report" on Sandy Hook that was authored by Danbury State's Attorney

Stephen Sedensky does not establish a causal nexus between the shooter, his victims and the weapons he is alleged to have used. It suffers from the shortcomings of concluding that there were no fingerprints on the .22 rifle that was allegedly used to shoot his mother and, even more surprisingly, that of the large number of shots that were fired from the 5.56 calibre Bushmaster (close to 150 rounds), none of the bullet fragments could be matched to the weapon:

[53] "No positive identification could be made to any of the bullet evidence submissions noted ... ... in 5.56 mm caliber. The physical condition of the bullet jacket surfaces were severely damaged and corroded. They all lacked individual striated marks of sufficient agreement for the identification process. The test fires also exhibited a lack of individual striated marks on the bullet surface for comparison purposes. This condition can be caused by fouling in the barrel of the rifle and the ammunition itself. The Bushmaster rifle cannot be eliminated as having fired the 5.56 caliber bullet evidence examined," quoting from the 6/19/13 Forensic Science Laboratory report.

Under these circumstances, it would have been impossible for the alleged shooter, Adam Lanza, to have been convicted in a properly conducted court of law for his alleged offense, because n*o causal nexus has been established between the purported shooter, his weapons and the 20 children and seven adults he is supposed to have killed*, which one might have naively supposed was the point of the investigation. But if that was its goal, then its objective was not achieved. If there has ever been such an abysmal failure in the annals of forensic investigation, I would love to hear about it. This is absurd!

The staged photos for the fake event

We have published several studies of the celebrated Shannon Hicks' "iconic photograph", which seems to show children being evacuated from Sandy Hook. But now we have additional proof it was staged, where the children were rearranged into a different sequence to create the "best shot" to convey the false impression that a real emergency was taking place. Here is addition proof that this was a hoax:

And a new video study offers further proof that this was only a drill, where the author is very patient and circumspect in arriving at the conclusion that it was a hoax and no children died. But, of course, if he is correct–and the evidence is over-whlemingly on his side–than Lenny Pozner has no case and we should not be concerned about the "parents of the victims" at Sandy Hook, because there were none.

One of his best observations concerns what a real evacuation would have looked like, which would have been something a lot like this:

When you combine the missing 469 children being evacuated from the school, the absence of EMTs hurrying into the school to rush those little bodies off to hospitals were doctors could pronounce them "dead or alive", the denial of access to the bodies by their parents, the lack of urgency about what was taking place–*including rearranging the children to take a staged photograph*–there really is no room for doubt that this was a drill, which even Obama Department of Education officials have confirmed.

Lenny Pozner's vicious attack

Lenny entitled his commentary, *"Our Grief Denied: The Twisted Cruelty of Sandy Hook Hoaxers"*, and begins with this image and two paragraphs that follow here, which commit fallacies that I spent 35 years teaching undergraduates to avoid. After all, if none of those children actually died on 14 December 2012, then they are not "committing lies" or "spreading misinformation" as the author of this assault claims.

The most obvious is that of *begging the question* by taking for granted the issue under consideration, namely, whether or not 20 students and 6 adults were murdered by Adam Lanzan at Sandy Hook Elementary School on 14 December 2012:

More than a year and a half after Adam Lanza brutally murdered 26 women and children at the Sandy Hook Elementary School in Newtown,

Photos of Sandy Hook Elementary School victims sit at a small memorial near the school on Jan. 14, 2013, in Newtown, a month after the horrific massacre that claimed 20 children and six women at the school. (Getty Images / January 15, 2013)

parents and relatives of the victims still relive the terror of that fateful day along with the daily anguish and torment they suffer over the loss of their loved ones.

Worse, they have to suffer the onslaught of delusional conspiracy theorists, commonly called hoaxers, who claim Sandy Hook was a "false flag" event concocted by the government as a pretext to gun confiscation.

As a parent of one of the murdered students, Noah Pozner, I have worked to debunk and stop the cruel and hateful hoaxers who use the Internet to spread their lies. Recently, some hoaxers have stepped up the intensity of their twisted campaign in an effort to draw more people into this destructive tale of misinformation and continue to disrupt the lives of victims' families.

Equally important, however, is the *appeal to pity*, which, in this case, entails the alleged grief that the victim's parents have had to endure, where what the "Sandy Hook hoaxers" is only cruel if those 26 children actually died that day.

We can only feel their grief if their children actually died, where none of their reactions were remotely like the genuine grief expressed by the parents of dead children in Gaza.

We have no responses remotely comparable from the alleged "parents" of dead children at Sandy Hook. Just as you can search in vain for the missing children, you can search in vain for reactions from them to the alleged deaths of their children. Try Robbie Parker, father of Emilie, meeting the press, for example; or try Anderson Cooper interviewing the parents of Grace McDonnell. Search for any parent displaying real grief. It's not there.

Children killed in Gaza playground shelling

Israel denies striking Gaza's main hospital and a playground, where seven children have been killed.

Noah Pozner's "death certificate"

Upon first consideration, Lenny's "death certificate" for Noah Pozner looks authentic, where questions only arise when you take a closer look. For it to have been published by his father, Lenny, is a significant development, since it is the first concrete proof we have that any child actually died at Sandy Hook. As I have emphasized, there have been extraordinary efforts to suppress information about these 20 deaths:

As Dennis Cimino has observed, *why would they need to use different typewriter ribbons on that certificate for different fields of it? and why is the certificate clearly with shaded areas that are not uniform like authentic death certificates are? You can clearly see that the typewriter clarity is blurry in some fields and clear and crisp in the others, meaning that, while the blurry ones may have been done with a typewriter, the clear sections were photoshopped into the document.* His observations have been reinforced by those sent to me by Bob Sims:

(1) I am rather surprised, according to the copy you posted, that any branch of government was still using typewriters at all, when computers can do it so much better. However, the use of a typewriter in this case makes it much easier to spot fraud.

(2) For starters, can you see any reason for the government typist to change the ball back and forth on the IBM machine I must assume was being used, because I cannot think of a reason to go to the extra trouble, and what for?

(3) For example, look at the very top in Box 3, where the date is posted. Why is that type clearly smaller than the rest of the page? You would have to change the ball for this, but for what reason?

(4) Now look at the capital "A" in Box 12 for Residence (Alpine). It is identical to the capital "A" in Box 22 for Mailing Address (Alpine). It is also identical to the capital "A" in Box 33 for Funeral Home. This is totally as expected, is it not? Read on.

(5) Note that the capital "A" in question above in three different boxes has a small flag at its pinnacle. Compare that to the capital "A", without the small flag in Box 4, Time of Death, Box 26, City or Town, Box 27, County of Death, and Box 39, Time Pronounced, and in Box 46, Time of Injury.

(6) Compare Box 1, "Noah," with Box 7, "November," and you will clearly see that the spacing between the "N" and the "o" is quite different.

(7) Compare Box 1, the "N" in "Noah," with Box 26, the "N" in "SANDY." They are clearly different.

(8) Compare Box 1, "Samuel," with Box 11, "Sandy," and again, the spacing between the "S" and the "a" is clearly not the same.

(9) In fact, the entire spacing in Box 1 is unlike any other in the forged document.

(10) Compare the name "Pozner" in Box 1 with "Pozner" in Box 20, clearly not the same.

Noah Pozner's death certificate is a fake, which we have proven on a dozen or more different grounds. But if Sandy Hook had been real, there would have been no reason to fake it. QED

Moreover, Noah Pozner's "death certificate" states that *"No autopsy was performed"*, while the "official report" states, *"All the victims were given autopsies"*. We know they cannot both be true. It would be tempting to presume that one of them is accurate and the other a mistake. But insofar as they are both predicated on the presupposition Noah Pozner and 19 other children actually died at Sandy Hook, they both appear to be false. *We have no authentic proof that any of those children, including Noah Pozner, actually died. None–for the obvious reason that none of them died!*

Is "Lenny Pozner" Noah's father?

One of the more intriguing developments related to the Pozner case is that the man who calls himself "Lenny" and poses as Noah's father initiated contact with one of the members of the Sandy Hook research group, with whom I have collaborated in publishing several articles, including *"Top Ten Reasons: Sandy Hook was an elaborate hoax"*. I interviewed her and Kate Slate together on *"The Real Deal"*, *(radiofetzer.blogspot.com)*: 24 March 2014. Here is what "Kelly from Tulsa", as honest as the day is long, wrote me about her "conversations with Lenny":

I received an email message several months ago from Google+ stating Lenny Pozner was following (cyber stalking) me, so I hit the reply button and said to Mr. Pozner, " Why are you following me on Google+, is it because I don't believe anything about the official story?" Mr. Pozner wrote me back stating he had indeed lost his son and the death certificates were available to prove it for $19 from the Newtown Clerk's office and I told him that the death certificated were not available and that the town had them sealed and I didn't believe it was really Noah's father otherwise he would have known that and I wasn't going to waste my time talking through emails to someone posing to be Noah's father.

To make a long story short we emailed back and forth until late in the evening when he stated he was tired of using the keyboard and could we talk on the phone. I gave him my cell number and we talked until 3:00 am and proceeded to talk everyday for the next 5 weeks, often multiple times on the same day.

I would say we spent 100 or more hours on the phone back and Roth over a 5-week time period. We laughed, we shared photos and I got the impression he was a soft spoken likable guy, at the same time, I never got the impression he lost his son nor was he able to convince me even though he tried somewhat hard.

Noah Samuel Pozner
Obituary

POZNER, NOAH SAMUEL
Noah Samuel Pozner, on December 14, 2012, a victim of the of the tragic events of last Friday at Sandy Hook Elementary School. Noah was born in Danbury, CT. son of Lenny and Veronique Pozner. How do you capture the essence of a six year old in just a few words ? Noah was an impish, larger than life little boy. Everything he did conveyed action and energy through love. He was the light of our family, a little soul devoid of spite and meanness. He will be forever missed by his mother, father, siblings Danielle, Michael, Sophia and twin Arielle, his grandparents Marie, Dirk, Ivan, Deanna and Lena, uncles and aunts, Arthur, Stephan, Alexi, Patricia and Victoria. May you fly to that peaceful valley and wait for us there. Funeral services will take place on Monday December 17, 2012 (TODAY) at 1:00 PM from The Abraham L. Green and Son Funeral Home 88 Beach Road in Fairfield, with interment following at B'nai Israel Cemetery on Moose Hill Road in Monroe. Memorial contributions may be directed to the planting of trees in Israel.

Guest Book

"Hi Sweet Angel, I think of you so very often and..."
- Pat Davis

 View   Sign

More Photos

View all 61 photos

ABRAHAM L. GREEN
AND SON
88 BEACH ROAD FAIRFIELD, CT

The first time we spoke until the wee hours of the morning: I asked him to produce the following items (by the way, this call began on Friday night and went until Saturday morning) a death certificate for his son, his son's birth certificate showing he had been born, a photo of his wife in the hospital with Noah and Noah's twin sister as well as Sandy Hook report card.

The following Monday he sent me an email telling me to check my inbox and sure enough, much to my surprise, he had posted all the things I asked for on his lenpoz.com website. However, the photo was not of his wife in the hospital, nonetheless, he did post a photo of Veronique with the two newborns in her arms. The death certificate I believe stated he was "never married" which I thought odd.

Speaking of his wife I asked him about Veronique working for the State Department in some capacity to disarm the country of Switzerland and he told me she never worked for the State Department but was a nurse, to which I asked for her nursing certificate (which he sent). Since Veronique's mother worked for the UN, I decided to call the office in the US Embassy and disguised myself as a foreigner to ask for Mrs. Veronique Haller. I was told that "she had left her post in 2013" (after she had been discovered working there for gun control in Switzerland).

On Noah's birth certificate, it states that Veronique was born in Switzerland, but Lenny told me it was a different "Veronique Haller". I told him I felt he was lying to me and I believed it was his wife. I told Lenny that the name "Veronique Haller" was unusual and for it not to be the same person stretched the imagination but he said "Veronique" was a very common name overseas. Whatever!

Like I said, we talked for around 5 weeks and I felt we had developed a friendship of sorts. We laughed many times as he had a very good sense of humor, but my overall impression from my gut told me he was not being truthful and over and over my mantra was, "Your son did not die and on top of that you are much too old to have children that young." He asked me how old I guessed him to be and I said I was "around 61" and he said he was 47 which I did not believe. So I asked him for a driver's license, which he immediately sent before I could practically finish my sentence; but it had expired in 2009 and the photo did not look like the Lenny I had seen on lenpoz. com. In fact, we laughed, because I told him he looked like a Columbian Drug Lord–and he agreed.

Our friendship came to an end rather abruptly because I told Lenny that I was going to make a donation to his Noah's Ark website (to which he sent me the correct address) since there were several official and unofficial donation websites set up on his son's behalf. I explained that, since I did not believe his son nor any others died at the school as the result of any shooting, there *would probably be a class action lawsuit claiming fraud and that, unless I had made a donation, I could not expect to be a part of that suit. I also told Lenny that a friend of mine agreed with me and had just made a donation. The next day he returned her money because if a lawsuit does ensue, he did not want her to be a beneficiary.*

*He wrote me one last email after that, which said, "Fuck You Bitch", and that was the last I heard of my friend, Lenny Pozner. I found it rather strange that, every day–even numerous times a day–I would let it be known that I thought he was lying, yet he never once got upset or mad. When I brought up the money issue was when he ended our friendship. Sad! Go figure! Meanwhile, **Noah's mother has claimed that she has released a photograph of his body.** But no one I know can find it. So where is it?*

For those who base their conclusions upon logic and evidence, there is no doubt that, as *Paul Preston was told by his contacts in the Department of Education of the Obama administration, it was a drill and no children died,* which was done to promote an anti-gun agenda. Yet the charade continues. Not only were *stories and photos published predating "the massacre",* but even *NPR is running stories about the traumatic effects for the Sandy Hook first responders.* No children died–not even Noah Pozner, it would appear–yet the charade continues without end.

This chapter originally appeared as "Are Sandy Hook critics delusional with 'twisted minds'?" (6 August 2014), *veteranstoday.com.*

[Editor's note: Although Appendix C, *The Sandy Hook Timeline,* includes reports from the media, contemporaneous at the time, that copies of the death certificates had been released under pressure from the press to *The New York Post,* none of us has been able to obtain copies--nor do we know of anyone else who has succeeded. Professor James Tracy, for example, wrote to *The Post* asking for copies and received no response. This appears to have been yet another false report like that from the *Hartford Courant,* which claimed that it had receive the *FBI Report on Sandy Hook.* But there appears to have been no FBI investigation of Sandy Hook, where that, too, appears to have been just one more in an endless stream of lies, deceit and deception surrounding Sandy Hook.]

Every grain of Sandy Hook: *Snopes.com* & Plausible Deniability

by Sterling Harwood, J.D., Ph.D.

In the time of my confession, in the hour of my deepest need
When the pool of tears beneath my feet flood every newborn seed
There's a dying voice within me reaching out somewhere
Toiling in the danger and in the morals of despair.

Don't have the inclination to look back on any mistake
Like Cain, I now behold this chain of events that I must break
In the fury of the moment I can see the master's hand
In every leaf that trembles, in every grain of sand.

***

I gaze into the doorway of temptation's angry flame
And every time I pass that way I always hear my name
Then onward in my journey I come to understand
That every hair is numbered like every grain of sand.

***

In the violence of a summer's dream, in the chill of a wintry light
In the bitter dance of loneliness fading into space
In the broken mirror of innocence on each forgotten face.

***

Sometimes I turn, there's someone there, other times it's only me
I am hanging in the balance of the reality of man
Like every sparrow falling, like every grain of sand.

~ Bob Dylan, "Every Grain of Sand," from the album *Shot of Love* (1981)

1. A Brief Introduction to a Brief Critique of a Brief *snopes.com* Essay

I have to admire the folks at *snopes.com* for at least seeming at first to have a plausible answer to every question they address about Sandy Hook in the *snopes.com* 15-page entry on the subject. Since, however, plausibility is a matter of degree, let me raise some brief questions about how the answers at *snopes.com* could be more plausible or less implausible when going beyond initial appearances, and let me point out a few puzzles of the official story which *snopes.com* has yet to answer at all as far as I know.

2. Slicing & Dicing Dr. Carver: What Could Come Crashing Down on the Heads of the People of Newtown?

Let's start with slicing and dicing Dr. Carver. H. Wayne Carver refused to let parents of the 20 dead children at Sandy Hook identify the victims by direct viewing of the bodies. *Snopes.com* diverts attention away from this startling fact by explaining away a closely related fact. Carver said one can control the situation better by using instead photographs of the dead to identify the victims, depending on the photographer. *Snopes.com* said that what Carver meant was that one can use a photograph of the face to identify the victim without showing wounds to the body of a child. This, however, hardly depends on the photographer; this depends instead on the shooter and where he shot the child. If the shooter shot the child in the face or even shot the identifying features of the child's face off, then the photographer wouldn't matter one little bit.

What is *snopes.com* implying here? Are they implicitly saying that some photographers will be insubordinate to Dr. Carver and photograph only blood and guts and refuse to take a photo of an un-bloodied face if there is one? That's just implausible. It's also pretty implausible that all 20 sets of parents would accept a mere photograph for identifying their child as dead. I have serious trouble imagining how even one parent much less 20 sets of parents could be talked out of being with their child right after the tragedy. Ask yourself: *Would you allow some stranger to keep you from your dead child just by showing you a bloodless photo of your child?* It strikes me as most implausible.

Suspiciously convenient, if not implausible, is Dr. Carver's role in changing the law about a year before the Sandy Hook massacre to allow keeping the names of murdered minors secret. The names of the murdered minors did come out within about a day or two anyway, but why have such a law except to give the authorities unneeded time to get their story straight? I can think of no other plausible reason to change the law in Connecticut that had stood for hundreds of years allowing the public to know the names of murdered minors. Dr. Carver is worth additional investigation if only due to his cryptic remark that he hopes future disclosures don't come crashing down on the heads of the people of Newtown (search YouTube.com with the key words of Carver's name and "crashing down on the heads of the people of Newtown"). *Over what disclosure could there possibly be negative consequences crashing down on the heads of the people of Newtown?* No investigation or piece of journalism has yet pinned Dr. Carver down on that.

3. I Never Promised You a Rosen Garden: Enter a Gene Rosen or Two, Slow-responding Humanitarian or Fast-talking Phony?

Next up for your consideration is one Gene Rosen, or actually two Gene Rosens. Again *snopes.com* does a great job of plausible denial by diversion to a related issue. The main issue is why Rosen and a bus driver would babysit six children traumatized by seeing their teacher shot dead in front of them without calling the police to take custody of the children immediately. Instead, *snopes.com* focuses on explaining that Gene Rosen was mistaken for another Gene Rosen who is a member of the Screen Actors Guild. *Snopes.com* knows this because an Internet search *snopes.com* did shows that the acting Rosen is only 62 years old and has lived outside Connecticut (and not inside Connecticut) but that the non-acting Rosen is found on another Internet search by *snopes.com* to be 69 years old and to have resided only inside Connecticut. Whether Rosen, however, was an actor or not is secondary to the main issue of whether his story is phony. *Again, would you sit idle for half an hour if six children and a bus driver wandered into your yard and told you a tale of a murder going on, or would you immediately dial 911?* Rosen's tale is implausible and *snopes.com*'s answer to skepticism about it is a marvelous feat of distraction to a related but secondary issue of Screen Actors Guild membership.

4. There Are Unidentified, Armed Men in the Woods Behind the Massacre: So Rest Reassured?

Now consider the case of what *snopes.com* admits is an unidentified man seen with a gun in the woods near the school on the day of the massacre, as reported in the *Newtown Bee* newspaper. *Snopes.com* reassures us that a reliable local law enforcement source says that the armed man at or near the scene of the crime was only an off-duty tactical squad police officer from another town. But this so-called (implicitly anyway) innocent explanation raises about 100 more questions than it answers. What was his name? Why can't we know his name? Why was he armed? Why was he armed when he was off-duty? Why did he decide to spend his off-duty hours prowling the woods where a massacre was to occur or had just occurred? What did he see, if anything, from the vantage point of the woods or wherever else he traveled in the area that day? To whom did he report, if anyone? With what weapon or weapons was he armed? Did those weapons match those of the accused killer by any chance? Did the man fire his gun? If he fired his gun, did he hit his intended target? What was his rank? What was his level of training? What was the name of the other town he was from? Was he called in from out of town by any law enforcement officials in Newtown?

And of course we could go on. This so-called innocent explanation of an armed tactical squad officer from out of town just happening to be there strikes me more than a bit as being as alarming an explanation as the following hypothetical one: *Oh, don't worry about that armed, unidentified man we saw in the woods behind the massacre; he was just a highly trained off-duty CIA sniper who was just visiting from Hong Kong.* What?! At least if he were from the CIA I'd know why his name was hidden, but tactical squad officers are not undercover officers, so there's no reason at all to hide his name. You can listen to a police scanner and go to wherever the SWAT team is called and take photographs with a telephoto lens of all the tactical squad officers. So avoid confusing tactical squad officers with undercover officers and CIA agents whose names must be kept secret.

Now consider the case of another unidentified man. This time the man was detained, handcuffed, and pinned to the ground. He might have been armed but *snopes.com* evidently thinks that is so unimportant that it fails to say one way or the other. But don't worry, *snopes.com* reassures us that police determined he was just an innocent passerby. *Snopes.com* gives no citation to any source it has for that reassurance. *Snopes.com* fails even to rely on the prestigious *Newtown Bee* here, as it relied on before in trying to reassure us about the mysterious, armed tactical squad officer. Further, *snopes.com* fails to identify which police officer or officers made that determination that the handcuffed man was just an innocent passerby. *Snopes.com* also fails to give the handcuffed man's name or physical description at all. Furthermore, if the guy is so innocent, then why refuse or fail to release his name so the free press of this mighty country can double-check to see if the police might have made a mistake in making their determination of his alleged innocence.

Police do make mistakes, you know. The man's name should be recorded in a police report anyway if the police were engaged in due diligence and so his name should come out eventually anyway unless the police reports themselves are being sealed because there was some sort of intelligence operation going on at Sandy Hook around the time of the massacre. Fortunately, *The Los Angeles Times* on December 14, 2012 reported the man's name as Chris Manfredonia. The story is that police released him because he said he was a parent who had come to the school that day to help his six-year-old daughter and other students make gingerbread houses. There are, however, two more suspicious facts: 1) Manfredonia was wearing camouflaged clothes when spotted in the woods behind the school; and 2) Manfredonia's home address is "directly behind" the other murder scene, the home of Adam Lanza. (See, Sophia Smallstorm, "Unravelling Sandy Hook," youtube.com, starting at about 24:44 into the video, last retrieved 9/24/15.)

5. Robbie Parker & What He Was Robbed of in the Massacre: Not His Sense of Humor

Now consider Robbie Parker (see the YouTube.com clip of his CNN press conference), the laughing father of a freshly murdered child. *Snopes. com* assures us that not all grieving parents grieve the same and, besides, we don't really know what makes people laugh anyway. But we do know what makes it implausible that you would laugh: learning that your child was murdered suddenly and violently by a madman at school. The odds that you would laugh the way Parker does when going up to the microphone are just extremely low. How many other laughing fathers of murdered children have you seen on video or otherwise? Further, it isn't just Mr. Parker's laugh: he also takes a deep breath and seems to right himself the way actors do before starting a scene. *Snopes.com* reassures us that no one from any crisis actor firm has yet been identified as being an actor at Sandy Hook.

But is that because there were no crisis actors at all or only because the secret that crisis actors were used is being so well kept, perhaps because the actors are under contract to keep their identities secret? It is incredibly weak of *snopes.com* merely to say that no crisis actor has yet been identified. I would expect *snopes.com* also at least to say that it has picked up the damn phone and obtained denials from all of the crisis actor firms that any of their actors were working in Newtown on the day of the massacre. How many crisis acting firms could there be to call, anyway? Finally on this point, *snopes. com* suggests that maybe the two parents of Sandy Hook victims laughing so soon on video after the respective murders might just be having a crazy reaction. That's possible, but given how these two parents, Mr. Parker and Ms. Lynn McDonnell, were in the rest of their statements to the media, it surely is implausible. They simply don't appear crazy yet they laugh, smile broadly, and shed no tears.

6. Logical Puzzles in the Official Story Unaddressed by *Snopes. com*

Now I want to turn to puzzling issues that the 15-page entry on *snopes. com* for Sandy Hook fails to answer at all as far as I can see. Another liquid missing from the scene, besides the tears of any parent, is blood. (See, for example, Sofia Smallstorm, "Unravelling Sandy Hook," youtube.com, last retrieved 9/23/2015, and Peter Klein, "Banned Documentaries, Episode 2, What Really Happened at Sandy Hook?," youtube.com, last retrieved 9/23/2015.) *Snopes.com* has no answer I have seen yet for the lack of any photographs or video of blood from the murder scene or from any of the scenes where others were, according to the official story at least, non-fatally injured. Plenty of blood from, for example, the Manson murders, the OJ murders, Columbine and other murder scenes seems to come out but none at all come out from Sandy Hook.

In the aftermath of the Oklahoma City bombing, one color photograph of a fireman holding a bloody, mortally wounded child even won some prestigious awards for photojournalism, and it is a haunting photograph indeed with deep symbolism on several levels. We even see photos of, for example, the dead face of Marilyn Monroe, the dead face of Elvis Presley or the dead face John Lennon leak out but yet we see no leaked scenes of blood or dead faces from the Sandy Hook massacre of 26 plus the shooter's shooting of himself to death. In fact, we don't even see blood on any non-fatally wounded people, though there were some, according to the official story at least. Further, we see no blood on any emergency medical technician, law enforcement officials or health care personnel. And this is in the age of cell phone photography, video-cameras, and helicopters with cameras that can zoom in for close-ups. *Isn't the lack of blood implausible, especially given how many people were filmed milling around the parking lot of the school soon after the massacre?*

Snopes.com also has no answer I have seen so far for the fact that there are gaps in the Internet and email usage at the school that suggest the school was not in use regularly but was used only for a drill. Speaking of Internet usage, another implausible fact, if the Sandy Hook massacre is totally un-staged rather than any sort of psychological operation or drill, isn't it implausible for there to have been Internet donation pages set up for some of the victims so soon after the murders of the particular victims were confirmed? Indeed, one chapter in this book documents how some donation sites were launched some days *before* the massacre. (See also, Sofia Smallstorm, in the YouTube. com video "Banned Documentaries, Episode 2: What Really Happened at Sandy Hook?" at about 59:25; last retrieved 9/9/15).

How is such a launch possible, much less plausible? Ask yourself if you would set up such a page asking for money in honor of your dead child in the wake of the violent murder of your child or whether that would be an implausible use of your time so soon after learning of your child's violent murder at the hands of a madman? Is this a case of advance knowledge of some kind of risk or operation, as appears to be the case of San Francisco Mayor Willie Brown getting at least 8-hours of advance warning to stay off commercial airlines just before 9/11? (See, Phillip Matier & Andrew Ross, "Willie Brown got low-key early warning about air travel," SFGATE (*San Francisco Chronicle Online*), published 4:00am, Wednesday, September 12, 2001.)

Snopes.com also has no answer yet for a young boy interviewed by Dr. Oz on the Dr. Oz show (see the fascinating YouTube.com clip from Dr. Oz's show) who says that *the Sandy Hook emergency was only a drill.* Dr. Oz changes the subject immediately instead of doing the more plausible and straightforward thing and asking the boy why he thought it was only a drill or who told him that it was only a drill. I find Dr. Oz's changing of the subject so fast downright suspicious but maybe Dr. Oz just lacks an enquiring mind or was just obeying a producer's shout into Dr. Oz's earpiece to move along to another subject. Maybe a producer shouted into Dr. Oz's earpiece: Don't pay any attention to the man behind the curtain or the Sandy Hook victim who said it was a drill, Dr. Oz.

7. Conclusion: Too Much Implausibility & Too Many Unanswered Puzzles in an Official Story of a Massacre Years Old Now

Maybe, just maybe, *snopes.com* will eventually conjure up plausible explanations to every logical puzzle posed by the official story of Sandy Hook, but *snopes.com* has failed to do so yet and it has been years since the Sandy Hook massacre. *Snopes.com* does an admirable job of summarizing the official story but the official story itself is far from admirable. The official story is an implausible mess with unanswered puzzles sprinkled over the top. Re-investigate!

EPILOGUE

The Nexus of Tyranny: Tucson, Aurora & Sandy Hook

By Dennis Cimino

In the immediate aftermath of the Newtown staged hoax in Connecticut, many of us began to finally take harder looks at the hoaxes staged in Tucson, Arizona, and in Aurora, Colorado, to see if we could find links connecting them.

They appear to have been carried out by Attorney General Eric Holder and POTUS (aka Barry Soetoro) as a calculated and nation-wide smattering of "terrorist attacks" of an OPERATION GLADIO variety, plotted and carried out to strike fear into the American public and create an hysterical response against the 2nd amendment. Their secondary purpose seems to have been to further demonize 9/11 Truth, as was evident in the closure of facebook accounts of most of the prominent 9/11 Truth figures who were involved in publicizing Israel's role in the mass murders of 9/11, which occurred in the immediate aftermath of the Newtown hoax.

The key begins in Tucson where the acting Sheriff, Clarence Dupnik, and his auxiliaries, staged the elaborate hoax that a federal judge and a Congress woman named "Gabby Giffords" were shot, the judge fatally. While Gabby may have been seriously seriously wounded, I have found multiple indications that suggest this, too, may have been a hoax. Evidence of purely FEMA-staged acting was apparent in the fact that, when you do careful analysis of the photos of the scene, you can find many significant clues.

One is a FEMA coach, kneeling by a stretcher, cue-card in his *non-gloved hands*, reading that, with a small plastic cup of fake blood there, at a site where allegedly real human beings were shot by an orange hair whacko named 'Holmes' that is so psychologically goofy looking you can barely stand to look at him, let alone realize he is like the rest, another Greenberg Zionist actor, participating in one of a series of hoaxes. Here we have one of these FEMA crisis actors reading a cue card, no gloves, at the side of an allegedly wounded person at the scene:

What is particularly telling in the photo of Giffords with an allegedly grave head wound, nobody seems concerned. All backs are turned. In real life if you had a potentially mortally wounded person being taken by an ambulance to a hospital, every one of those people would have been focused on her. Look at them. Nobody cares. Nobody is concerned. Not one person seems in a hurry to move her to the ambulance either. You know *this is a drill*, because of the lack of concern and urgency in these people around this simulated victim or "VicSIM".

Closer examination of the stretcher that Giffords is on, is that no blood is present, and her aide who stated he had "used his own hands to pressure point stop a head wound bleed" oddly has no blood on his gloved hands at all. Neither do any of the EMT personnel transporting her to the ambulance. As many of you might know, head wounds bleed profusely yet Giffords has no blood on her except a small red patch on a rag wrapped around her skull. If the lightbulb hasn't gone on for you yet, it should when you see photos of two of Dupnik's elderly Sheriff's Auxiliary, pretending to be victim relatives at the alleged but simulated crime scene. They appear to be accomplices to an act of treason by Clarence W. Dupnik, the Pima County Sheriff.

In the case of the Aurora, CO, hoax staged fraud, we have an FBI agent standing behind the Chief of Police of Aurora, watching the Chief read his cue card in his head, while Special Agent Jim Yacone smirks in satisfaction when the Chief says he is not prepared to comment about how the shooter may have gotten into the theatre. In the immediate aftermath of this shooting hoax, we have a number of witnesses talk about at least two individuals being involved and flash-bang grenades being thrown into the theatre from different directions by two individuals.

Clearly, on a day like this, no FBI agent has the right to 'smirk' about anything the Chief of Police might divulge, nor would there be any reason for many witnesses to talk about the fact that clearly the assault on the theatre, all staged and a hoax, came from both sides of

the theatre and was carried out by more than one person. So, here again, if Holmes was the man, who were his accomplices? We know someone came in from both sides and threw flash bang grenades into the small theatre. One man could not do that. (Search YouTube for *"FBI Agent, Chief Oates answer questions about Aurora shooting")*

In the Newtown, CT, shooting, where we have been told 20 children and 6 adults were slaughtered, many very big and inexplicable similarities were evident, looking rather like a repetition from Tucson and Aurora, least with the use of Greenberg's actor cadre, the crisis actors from FEMA. We have Dawn Hochsprung, who was allegedly killed shielding children from the lone gunman, giving an interview to The Newtown BEE newspaper that morning.

Clearly this is not merely a misunderstanding here: *no reporter would give an interview and not clarify who that was they were talking to.* Yet Hochsprung was alive enough to give that interview in the aftermath of a shooting in which she died trying to shield children from bullets. Not possible.

The CNN SWAT TEAM Video

We have CNN video of SWAT team members running to the school door through a column of previously arranged orange traffic cones. Expecting someone important that day, were they? Especially since this was footage intentionally shown by CNN of a drill that had actually been staged at the school months before.

A bigger clue is that the crack sealant used to seal the driveway in some of the shots was nice and shiny and fresh, but not long thereafter, it's dull and dirty and aged. That cannot happen in one day. So we now know that the earlier drill was used by CNN (actually shot at St. Rose of Lima Elementary School, approximately 14 miles southwest of the closed Sandy Hook school, based upon information we now have that has matched up the helicopter vs.

Google Earth view and beyond a reasonable doubt shows CNN effectively had to be in on the scam!) in more than one non-live shot of what allegedly took place on December 14th, but clearly did not. It was obviously a hoax. All of it. Purposely staged to deceive the American public to grab our guns.

In the helicopter footage which is now disappearing from YouTube, you see at around 7 AM a helicopter hovering over the scene with a DETROIT fire truck in the footage. EMS is staged far back at the Fire Station and 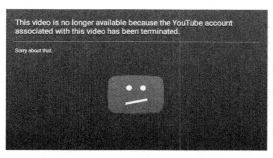 almost nobody is closer than 100 yards or so from the school, and with this video being about two hours before shooting happened, it elicits many questions again about 'how' and 'why' we are able to see it on a day when we were told that a kid got the drop on a security door and nobody was forewarned that he was attempting to gain entry.

Crisis Actors and the Coroner's Press Conference

Now it has been firmly established that many crisis actors were used in Newtown, the most notable one is Robbie Parker, who is told 'just read the card' and has to get into character to act 'distraught' when moments before he is seen smirking and laughing, very much like FBI agent Yacone had in Aurora at the Chief of Police press conference.

Phelps aka as Sexton, from FLORIDA from a photo account that was quickly removed by them once they were identified as ACTORS

I don't know about you, but nobody can explain away his very poor acting here, and nobody can explain the "just read the card" scenario, either. In virtually all of the follow up interviews of parents,

199

they are all dry eyed and not puffy faced, although they are said to have lost their children. This is acting. By crisis actors. By Greenberg crisis actors.

Later that day we have the coroner, Wayne Carver, who is oddly out of character, telling us that all of the vicSIMS were shot using the long rifle, the .223 caliber one and that some vicSIMS had been shot more than ten times. Nobody bothered to ask Wayne why nobody was airlifted to Danbury General for possible salvation as it is not possible that nobody would survive any shooting involving 27 people, under any remote stretch of the imagination. Someone would have been found clinging to life, yet no triage existed that day to ascertain this, and someone mysteriously, not this flakey-acting coroner, had decreed that all were 'dead' on the scene.

This again is not possible. That is not proper code BLUE protocol. You triage. You air lift. You try to save people. Not at Newtown, where they all died instantaneously and were declared DEAD by someone other than the medical examiner that day. By whom? By what authority?

Search YouTube for *"Medical Examiner FULL Press Conference - Sandy Hook School Mass Shooting"*

James Tracy has a brilliant critique of Carver's performance here, where, if ABC/ NCB/CBS are correct in their reporting (that the body was found with only handguns and the rifle had been left in the car), then what precisely are we to make of Carver's contention that they were all shot with the Bushmaster?

What is more likely: that ABC/NBC/CBS, who confirmed their report with federal and state officials, are wrong about the body having been found with only handguns in the vicinity? or that Carver–who did not even know how many of the dead were boys and how many were girls–is wrong about them all having been shot with the Bushmaster?

Bear in mind, if multiple shooters had been involved, then both reports could be true, where Adam Lanza's body was places with hand guns in the vicinity and other shooters slaughtered the children, if, indeed, any children were actually murdered at all. There is even a report that Carver himself has admitted that it was "a hoax".

More Fraud and Fakery

United Way forgot to check the schedule before they had set up the fraudulent "fleece America" site to get money from bleeding hearts who wanted to donate to the HOAX fund to pay these crisis actors. Yep, on 11 December this donation site was set up by United Way. That's mighty clairvoyant thinking there to be so prepped. And the brochure for telling families how to talk to their kids just happened to be released that day, when anyone in the brochure printing business knows that the laying up of a brochure and the production takes days not just an hour or two. Yet it was done on December 14th. And there is evidence it was produced on 12 December, two days before the shooting, meaning again that this was a hoax--and an act of treason.

We have photoshopped photos by FEMA presumably or the FBI, showing Robbie Parker's fake family all sitting in a Christmas card scene that do not make sense (Chapter 5). Ironically, the same dress is worn by the vicSIM girl–although some maintain that

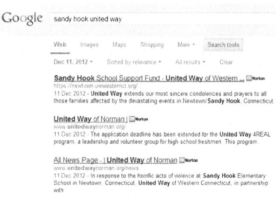

she is actually her sister–when being photographed with President Obama, but we are told that dresses can be used by any child. By the way, all of them are smiling, possibly because that photo was taken during the DRILL months before not on the day alleged. This, in turn, raises serious questions as to whether President Obama himself is complicit.

Add to the fact that two weeks before this, Eric Holder, the U.S. Attorney General, met with the Lt. Governor and Governor of the State of Connecticut and during a press conference held by the Governor with his Lt.

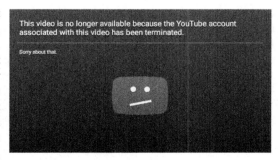

Governor there, they admit this freely, implicating themselves in this hoax and lie perpetrated on the American Public on not just this occasion, but in Tucson and Aurora. What we have is a series of hoaxes staged by the dept of JUST US here, which were interspersed across various parts of the Continental U.S. to do two things: (a) grab guns and end the 2nd amendment. (b) demonize all independent 9/11 investigators and others who would so decry these as staged events.

A Multiplicity of Hoax Shootings

The evidence bears this out that not only was the government involved, but by virtue of CNN airing the drill video months before as live video they too are implicated, as is Anderson Cooper and many others in MSM, including a british scumball gun grabber named Piers Morgan who demands we disarm. We have proven these evemts were purposely staged and that no people were truly harmed or killed in any of these events.

We know that Gabriel Giffords and a Federal Judge were not shot in Tucson without blood being everywhere, yet not one EMS person on the scene there had any blood. You can pretty much rest assured that nobody died in Aurora either, that crisis actors were again used and, per the smirking FBI agent and perpetrator named James Yacone, behind the Chief of Police, this too was a deception.

We can prove the long rifle alleged by Wayne 'fake coroner' Carver in Newtown was found in the trunk of a black Honda that evening, and we can prove that rifle rounds not shotgun shells were ejected onto the pavement behind that car by someone not in law enforcement, by the manhandling and grandstanding of the weapon that night on the helicopter video we all have. We can prove that per their own admission the authorities have now morphed this weapon into an exotic and odd foreign made shotgun when it clearly was not.

It's not relevant any longer whether it was a shotgun, a zip gun, or a b.b. gun, because the likes of Lt. Paul Vance of the CT. State Police, has now said that both long guns that were taken to the crime scene had been locked in a vehicle and outside of the reach of a shooter who died the day before, and could not have used them because they were found in the vehicle long after any rational person could so justify this cordoned off

with crime scene tape, search hours and hours later in darkness. That was not by accident. (Search YouTube for *"Connecticut police threaten to prosecute anyone who challenges Sandy Hook narrative")*

It was on purpose, filmed from the roof of the school using just enough flood lighting to make positive identification of the weapon almost impossible other than it was not a pistol. Regarding the weapons in the car, they could not have been used by any shooter that day, so they are now excluded forever!

Add to this the incredible threat by the CT State Police to charge and incarcerate anyone debunking the hoax and a President without tears declaring our need to give up our 2nd Amendment rights.

CT State Emergency System Hijacked

We can now prove that the entire CT State emergency communications system was 'hijacked' and 'unplugged' on December 14th., 2012, per an elaborate frequency change plan implemented merely 5 hours in advance on that morning, effectively supplanting and replacing normal police and EMS with FEMA/DHS 'shadow' command center personnel, where it turns out that they (the perpetrators from FEMA) made one critical mistake that they hoped nobody would catch. But last night, I caught it.

During the listening to the plethora of radio scanner audio recordings, I finally had a chance to hear the infamous plate run of the black Honda. I had for weeks taken for granted that others who heard it would have validated it as either fakery or reality but nobody caught the fact it is in it's entirely, contrived.

Police and Dispatch, nation wide, use a very time honored ALPHA PHONETIC System to enunciate alpha numeric data between the officers and the dispatchers. It is different from what military use, and it is so ingrained and dyed into the wool of real law enforcement and dispatchers for a good reason. Any error can cost not only the officer his life, but potentially cost others their lives either by sending people to the wrong address or by implicating the wrong person in a crime, or missing a criminal during a CODE TEN run on the person through the system.

During the course of the running of the black Honda, this ALPHA PHONETIC police and dispatch protocol was totally out the window and not used at all. I listened to that audio last night in utter disbelief. Between the alleged officers running the plate through dispatch, and the dispatcher herself, the data was read to and fro like any normal citizen would read data on a radio. They did not use the ALPHA PHONETIC protocol that is ingrained in both the officer and the dispatcher. While other questions have been raised about these communications, this one is decisive:

12.14.2012   9:46:50 AM

9:46:50 AM
Unknown if shooter has been located

Search YouTube for *"Sandy Hook Police Audio Timeline 'Actual Scanner Recording'"*

Suppose for the record that had the officer deviated and read data to dispatch improperly, the dispatcher would have read it back with PROPER PHONETIC enunciation to the officer under any and all circumstances, not as a correction of the officer but to make it clear that to all on the circuit who are listening that they pay attention to the data readback, as many backup units in the vicinity may need that data to properly B.O.L.O. find a car they need to intercept. (B.O.L.O. is "Be On Look Out', by the way.) So on 14 December 2012, we know that 5 hours earlier, a comprehensive frequency change plan for emergency communications in Connecticut, State Wide, was implemented. It wasn't just a coincidence.

As it would now appear, a 'shadow' dispatch center went into operation on December 14th., presumably run entirely by FEMA and DHS or Mossad possibly, because they used non trained, non familiar with the ALPHA PHONETIC protocols police use, to do radio transmissions that day, which now clearly must have all been staged for us like the rest of this hoax was. This is a strong allegation to make, but I make it now based on the way this information was transferred by clearly non law enforcement personnel, intentionally in a way that was interceptable and recorded by someone, if not wholly fed to us via calibrated feed or leak by the perpetrators of the hoax.

It is pretty clear that the entire emergency radio apparatus of Connecticut was unplugged altogether on December 14th., with possibly a back channel to allow non-hoax or non-drill emergency information to be handled by real law enforcers and real dispatchers. As is now certified by this analysis, clearly there is evidence of circumvention just as NEADS was circumvented and not allowed to have live radar feeds from radar facilities on 9/11, but had data that was 26 seconds OLD, for good reason: that being to cull out and remove real targets that the perpetrators needed never to be intercepted, while loading the system up with pre recorded exercise radar tracks and artificial targets to confuse not just military but CIVILIAN ATC personnel on 9/11.

So back to this hoax in Newtown CT, for example, when a police officer calls in 'A B C D' to dispatch, he or she phonetically enunciates it as; "ADAM BAKER CHARLES DAVID" over the radio, and the dispatcher will read back the same PHONETIC information for clarification. On December 14th., the plate data was not read to and from dispatch like this at all. The way the officer and dispatcher read this data was; 'A B C D' AYE BEE CEE DEE' and that is clearly not correct and never ever done because it is too easy to mistakenly misunderstand transmissions coded thusly.

This is now a record, not conjecture, not speculation, but stuff everyone has in their possession that was disseminated and not challenged by Lt. Vance of the CT State Police or other law enforcers now for several weeks, had it been not their transmissions. Why is this such an important issue? Dispatchers and Law Enforcement personnel are trained and trained and trained and trained. Even in high stress environments which they train in simulations, by the way, they are ingrained to not deviate from these procedures.

So it is important to point out here that the people on the radio in Connecticut that day clearly were not law enforcement or dispatcher personnel. They could not have been. They so grossly deviated in the data reads over the radio that no law enforcer or dispatcher would so deviate like that. Absolutely never. Much of these recordings clearly are indicative of non law enforcement personnel on radios. Persons without intensive training as to how to report information to dispatchers and other officers. Other parties familiar with the normal POLICE alpha phonetic system also concur with my evaluation that these are not police nor are they trained dispatch personnel on these recordings.

FEMA or DHS Personnel in Charge

They are FEMA personnel most likely or DHS personnel, or maybe even Mossad agents, given the dynamic of how much control they have here in the U.S., in direct collusion with this government. They provide intelligence to the acting director of DHS, Janet Napoletano, and they are integral to most of the fusion centers in the U.S., *effectively legitimizing a foreign secret police force on U.S. soil who's sole purpose is to spy on and harass American Citizens*, who, for many reasons, do not like what is going on in this hijacked by Israeli spies, nation. The 33 frequency change modification to the communications plan for Connecticut that went into effect 5 hours before the staged hoax went down, happened for a reason.

It entirely circumvented all normal radio and police functions in Connecticut on this day. The screen shots of these 33 frequency changes,

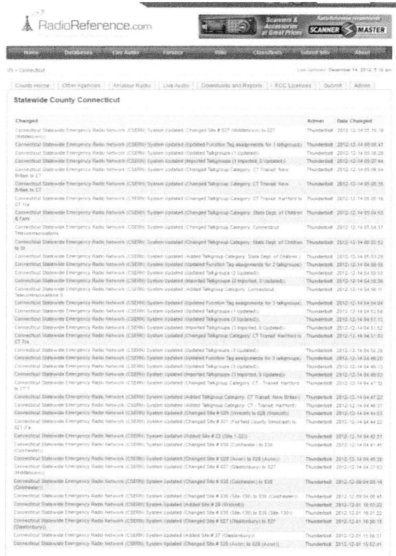

which were made just hours before the event, and of the 'dummy' non-named frequency allocation to one "phantom" that would not normally be blanked out like this in any normal frequency allocation chart, are published here.

To whom does it belong? DHS? FEMA? FBI? This is the de-facto smoking gun that virtually all scanner radio traffic heard on police scanners or whomever provided these to us, are STAGED. And here is a scan of the Connecticut Statewide Emergency Radio Network at the time:

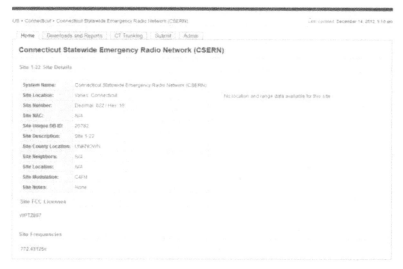

For comparison, here's a parallel scan for the Fairview County Simulcast, which under normal conditions it would resemble:

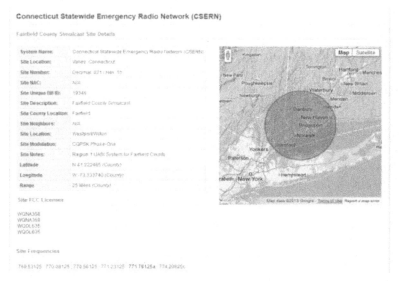

Plus there was an addition that day of one more communications site for which the data is mysteriously absence altogether, please see next page.

It would not be unreasonable to conclude that Site 1-22 was the DHS or FEMA master control site, which was monitoring every communication related to Sandy Hook that day and make sure that no information that would blow its cover got out.

A Series of Escalating-in-Violence Staged Events

We now have more proof that virtually all of this was a staged, canned, very treasonous hoax run by the highest levels of Connecticut State Police, FEMA and DHS who had oversight over all of this on 14 December 2012. Now these sweeping frequency allocations changes make perfect sense. Not unlike on September 11th, where all of the ATC to AA-11 radio broadcasts were found to be fraudulent, scripted and non-reality. This was no different.

And now we have one more proof positive that this was a huge massive deception perpetrated on everyone on December 14th, just like Sept 11th was, and Tucson was, and Aurora was, and perhaps even the Sikh Temple shooting in Wisconsin and the Clackamas Mall shooting were. Probably all run by this corrupt illegitimacy known as the Federal Government and their eager for the money (as Project Longevity bribe recipients).

Search YouTube for "Parents and children smiling and waiting to be interviewed about Sandy Hook mass school shooting"

Something is desperately wrong when so many Americans cannot distinguish between reality and crisis actor fantasies.

Now is the time for every single American to come to grip with the hard reality, which is that our Federal Government has become an internal enemy, which has been hijacked by powerful interests who will cover up any degree of mass murder, treason, and looting that is committed here, especially by Zionists who are promoting the interests of Israel and not those of the United States. Each and every one of us has a choice, which is simple: *RESIST!*

AFTERWORD

Analogies with the London 7/7 Subway Bombings

by Nick Kollerstrom, Ph.D.

The Predator has struck, one more time. We seek for its identity: *what is it?* I here compare two different events, perpetrated by the Enemies of Mankind, seven years apart.

1. Scene of crime remains concealed: no media access

No-one has been able to get into the Sandy Hook elementary school to verify if there are any bullet-marks, bloodstains etc, then on January 2nd the children were transferred to another school some miles away: we assume the old Sandy Hook Elementary School will remain sealed off, and will be demolished.

Perhaps a shootout DID NOT ACTUALLY HAPPEN THERE, it was just an illusion. Kids heard bangs, that's all we can say. The new school will be patrolled by security guards permanently: presumably to maintain the kids in a state of sufficient trauma to prevent them talking, or remembering the wrong sort of thing.

No bodies, only some duffle bags (Daily Mail)

209

The Mail Online 6 January shows this image, subtitled: 'Chaotic scenes at the school as police work to secure the area and bodies are carried out of the school.' But look carefully, no bodies are here, only some duffle bags–and some are doubting whether this is the school car-park.

In the London Bombings, the three train carriages were kept absolutely out or bounds then destroyed one year later: the blown-up bus was taken up to *Sevenoaks Military establishment*, where only the military can see it.

2. CCTV switched off

The Sandy Hook Elementary School was in an up-market area of Connecticut, shown by the large majority of its children being from Jewish families. It would have had high-security equipment including CCTV cameras. We have as yet not been shown images from the time of the crime (curiously vague, but said to have been three minutes around 9:45 on 14 December). There are no images of a 'crime scene' with bullet-marks in walls or through windows. (See Ch. 8.) No wounded persons being interviewed.

During the London Bombings, as also for 9/11, the CCTV was switched off: no pictures, from the most heavily CCTV'd city in the world (until 3 years later when some rather dodgy ones were released).

3. The patsy perpetrator(s), clueless and unmotivated, are themselves killed so they cannot defend themselves. Dead, they can be given all the blame.

There is no reason to suppose that the 20-year old autistic Adam Lanza had any expertise or practice in using guns, still less that his Mother went herself to a firing range or belonged to a rifle club and brought her son along. The car allegedly driven by him to the school turned out to belong to a shady felon, with FBI ties.

Would or could any young man shoot his mother, take her car, drive it to a school to which he does not belong, be dressed in black, shoot his way into the school with several guns and kill virtually every target he aims at?

How could anyone believe such a story? He kills himself–and then goes over to his car and puts the rifle he has used back in the book. There is no conceivable motive for this physically quite impossible sequence of events.

The four alleged London bombers knew nothing about chemistry, never had any interest in it, and had no bomb-making skills that anyone ever heard about. Once dead they had no-one to defend their name against the official fictions. Not one of them had an animus against British society, to motivate any antisocial act.

4. An ever-changing story

If a story is being made up, then different agencies will be spinning it, so it will never be very coherent. The Sandy Hook story became incoherent at the moment when CNN News announced that four pistols had been found in the school: presumably because the official coroner had averred that each of the 28 bodies had an average of seven bullet-holes in them, so they needed four pistols to credibly sound as if two hundred bullets had been fired. One young lad is not going tobreak into the school with four guns–after shooting his own Mother.

The story of the rifle used–the Coroner averred that all injuries had been made with the rifle, then it was found to have been placed in the back of a car outside the school–can never make any sense.

First we were told she was a teacher at the school, and Adam went to that school, then later it emerged: A former school board official in Newtown called into question earlier reports that Nancy Lanza had been connected to Sandy Hook Elementary School, possibly as part of the teaching staff. "No one has heard of her," said Lillian Bittman, who served on the local school board until 2011. "Teachers don't know her."

The 7/7 London bombings was truly an ever-changing story, with a narrative that relied heavily upon journalistic amnesia and credulity over the latest bit of unattributed gossip. Notably over what explosive had been used, which kept changing. The State lies to its own people. The State participates in killing its own people.

5. Terror-Drills being run

On 17 September 2010, HSEEP Homeland Security Exercise and Evaluation Program had a drill with FEMA at the Sandy Hook Fire Department, which is near to the Elementary School. On the day of the event, starting at 9.00 am, a FEMA exercise 'Planning for the Needs of Children in Disasters' took place in Connecticut not far from Sandy Hook. Some conjecture that this got moved and happened at the school, which would account for the presence of Federal troops there seemingly much too early. There is probably a lot more of this to come out. There is a picture on the Web of children of Sandy Hook forming a chain and being told to close their eyes– that is what a kiddie terror-drill looks like–from a couple of months earlier.

"Sandy Hook has a recent history of federally staged Terror Drills. A mock school shooting drill was being conducted in Putman County only miles away on the very same day as the Sandy Hook events on December 14."

The London Bombings had four main terror-drills leading up to it, the last of these by Peter Power on the very morning at the same three tube stations.

6. Guilty culprits announced too soon.

At 9:53 AM, no more than ten minutes after the reported shooting ceased, the Associated Press published a story, "Official with Knowledge of Connecticut School Shooting Says 27 Dead, Including 18 Children." Neighbours of Nancy Lanza said that around 9:15 AM they saw police surrounding the house, taping off the neighborhood and telling everyone to evacuate. Yet, they supposedly did not learn the identity of the shooter until c. 11:30am. They identified the bodies of the "shooter" and his mother before the body identifying process even started, with names, occupations, "health issues", marital status and residency. (See Chapter 7.)

On 9/11, news items started alluding to Osama Bin Laden about an hour after the event. On 7/7 Tony Blair announced that it was an Islamic crime at 5 pm on that day. The total of 52 dead was announced much too early, in fact while two of them 'not yet dead' were still in hospital.

7. Film pre-announcement of the event.

The Batman film '*Dark Knight Rises*' alluded to Sandy Hook region of Gotham City, as a portion of the city of Gotham during a setup of one of the bad guy's dirty deeds in that movie. Earlier promotions of the film the year before did not (Alex Jones discovered) have that Sandy Hook reference. The 2000 film '*The Sandy Hook Lingerie Party Massacre*' has the killer strike in the aftermath of a hurricane.'

Or, the ritual sacrifice of 22 children is portrayed in '*The Hunger Games*' by Suzanne Collins, who, remarkably enough, resides in Sandy Hook.

The London bombings were prefigured in the film '*V for Vendetta*' about an Underground train primed to blow up. It was filmed in the months leading up to 7/7, so Warner Brothers had free run of the London Undergound tunnels. Its launch had to be postponed because it was too similar to what had just happened. Likewise '*the Descent*' a horror movie scheduled to open the day after on 8 July, about people trapped underground and dying: its launch had to be postponed. Compare the classic film '*The Matrix*,' where after 17 mins one sees 11 Sept 2001 on Anderson's passport ID.

8. Families not allowed to see bodies of loved ones.

At least one family had the experience of not even being allowed to see the body of their loved one. "They told me, 'You can't see (the body),'" Gilles Rousseau told Radio-Canada, the French-language CBC." They would just be shown photographs. 'Where are the Sandy Hook Bodies? Many are wondering, are there any bodies?

There was a bizarre aspect to the 7/7 tragedy, in the way families had to wait often over a week just to be told whether their loved one was dead, and then would be not allowed to see the body – with phoney tales that it might upset them too much – or else shown them embalmed with a policeman standing by.

9. Families not allowed to speak

On December 19 the Connecticut State Police assigned individual personnel to each of the 26 families who lost a loved one at Sandy Hook Elementary. "The families have requested no press interviews," State Police assert on their behalf, "and we are asking that this request be honored–a *de facto* gag order. What is it so terrible they might say?

In the 7/7 London bombings, 'grieving parents' would always be wheeled out to support the government narrative, but one could never get to speak to any of them.

Search YouTube for "7/7 Ripple Effect"

10. Identity Theft

Adam Lanza was a vegan because he 'didn't want to hurt animals'. Nancy Lanza 'was a wonderful, beautiful, elegant woman who loved life, and most importantly she loved her son, Adam' a friend has testified. They lived on a street named after the great Indian Yogi Paramansha Yoganada: what did this mean to them?

The Mother has been hyped as an Apocalypse-expecting gun-toting food-storing freak (as a prelude to demonising gun-owners in America, the whole point of this exercise).

Sid Khan especially of the 7/7 Four was a rising star of Beeston, and after his death he became the most thoroughly demonised of the Four. Seemingly endless terror-tales were woven around him. SidKhab was especially proud of his reputation for non-violent conflict-resolution (see my online talk, about MSK as a 'local action hero') Wherever false-flag terror is perpetrated, it is important to try and rescue the identity of the person who gets blamed and demonised (eg for the Bali Bomb of 2002, someone called Amrotzi, who was a quite sensitive and intelligent young man).

11. Actors used

At least one 'grieving parent' at Sandy Hook looks as if he was acting a part. People are suspecting work by *'Crisis Actors.org'*: "Trained players and actors making it real,' available for 'active shooter drills.' They bring 'intense realism to simulated mass casualty incidents.'

The London bombings had some actors spotted on the street that morning, presumably part of the 'terror drill' scheduled for that morning http://www. youtube.com/watch?v=cW089fj94vY 'Wounded' actors were especially noticed around Tavistock Square.

12. Deaths not real

'Even more unusual are the observations of Facebook pages of the deceased being created days or even months prior to the shooting, further suggesting the synthetic and premeditated nature of the event.

For example, on March 23, 2011 a Facebook site was established, titled "RIP Emilie Parker," for the daughter of Robbie Parker, now well-known after the soliloquy delivered on CNN and preceded by a gleeful chuckle and query as to whether he should read the lines provided him.' One may doubt whether any of the 28 'deaths' at Sandy Hook Elementary School were real.

The London bombings had one definite not-real-death, viz Myriam Hyman (but there may have been others). She's on the plaque at Tavistock Square but no way did she die there.

THE BIG DIFFERENCE

Normally when fabricated terror happens, the story is fake but the deaths are real. It is the dead bodies which give the air of gravity and solemnity, so that Those Who Create Delusion will be believed. The London bombings had dreadful scenes of carnage, seen by real witnesses.

Sandy Hook appears to have at most only two dead bodies: Adam and Nancy Lanza. On that morning, the local hospital went into lockdown and cleared four trauma rooms, but received only three patients, two of them dead children (according to the official story) and one mildly wounded adult.

We saw locked-down kiddie-coffins in funeral services, but is that enough? The situation may remind us of 9/11, when airports that morning were waiting for the grieving relatives–but none came. The security forces averred that they had removed the bodies from the school in the middle of the night: had they?

But as the chapters of this book (based upon evidence that has only become available since I composed this essay) demonstrates quite convincingly, nobody died at Sandy Hook.

This chapter is a revised version of *"Sandy Hook: Analogies with the London 7/7 Bombings"* (6 January 2013), *veteranstoday.com*

Appendices

APPENDIX A

The FEMA Manual
for Sandy Hook

FOR OFFICIAL USE ONLY
Federal Emergency Management Agency

Exercise Plan	Emergency Response For
Mass Casualty Drill	Mass Casualties Involving Children

Federal Emergency
Management Agency

Site Activation Call-down Drill
Exercise Plan

[MASS CASUALTY DRILL]

Exercise Date: 12/14/12   Publishing Date: 10/08/12

FOR OFFICIAL USE ONLY

Exercise Plan	**Emergency Response For**
Mass Casualty Drill	**Mass Casualties Involving Children**

FINAL

INTENTIONALLY LEFT BLANK

Federal Emergency Management Agency

Exercise Plan	**Emergency Response For**
Mass Casualty Drill	**Mass Casualties Involving Children**

PREFACE

National Preparedness is sponsored by FEMA and the Department of Homeland Security. This Exercise Plan was produced with input, advice, and assistance from the National Incident Management System (NIMS) exercise planning team, which followed the guidance set forth in the Federal Emergency Management Agency (FEMA), Homeland Security Exercise and Evaluation Program (HSEEP).

The Plan gives officials, observers, media personnel, and players from participating organizations the information necessary to observe or participate in an all hazards preparedness exercise focusing on participants' emergency response plans, policies, and procedures as they pertain to specific scenarios. The information in this document is current as of the date of publication, 10/08/2012, and is subject to change as dictated by the National Incident Management System exercise planning team.

The Preparation for Mass Casualty is a *classified exercise*. The control of information is based more on public sensitivity regarding the nature of the exercise than on the actual exercise content. Some exercise material is intended for the **exclusive** use of exercise planners, controllers, and evaluators, but players may view other materials deemed necessary to their performance. The Exercise may be viewed by all exercise participants, *but the Controller and Evaluator (C/E) Handbook is a restricted document intended for controllers and evaluators only*.

All exercise participants should use appropriate guidelines to ensure the **proper control of information** within their areas of expertise and to protect this material in accordance with current jurisdictional directives. Public release of exercise materials to third parties is at the discretion of The Federal Emergency Management Agency and the Preparation for Mass Casualty exercise planning team.

FEMA

This page is intentionally left blank.

Federal Emergency Management Agency

| Exercise Plan | Emergency Response For |
| Mass Casualty Drill | Mass Casualties Involving Children |

HANDLING INSTRUCTIONS

1. The title of this document is *Mass Casualty Drill Involving Children Exercise Plan (ExPlan)*.

2. The information gathered in this ExPlan is *For Official Use Only (FOUO)* and should be handled as sensitive information not to be disclosed. This document should be safeguarded, handled, transmitted, and stored in accordance with appropriate security directives. Reproduction of this document, in whole or in part, without prior approval from The Department of Homeland Security is prohibited.

3. At a minimum, the attached materials will be disseminated only on a need-to-know basis and when unattended, will be stored in a locked container or area offering sufficient protection against theft, compromise, inadvertent access, and unauthorized disclosure.

4. For more information, please consult the following points of contact (POCs):

Agency POC:

Tom Romano
Federal Emergency Management Agency
860-256-0844 (office)
thomas.romano@ct.gove

Exercise Director:

Not Available

223

FEMA

This page is intentionally left blank.

Federal Emergency Management Agency

Exercise Plan	Emergency Response For
Mass Casualty Drill	Mass Casualties Involving Children

CONTENTS

FOR OFFICIAL USE ONLY
Federal Emergency Management Agency

Exercise Plan
Mass Casualty Drill

Emergency Response For
Mass Casualties Involving Children

This page is intentionally left blank.

226

Federal Emergency Management Agency

Exercise Plan	**Emergency Response For**
Mass Casualty Drill	**Mass Casualties Involving Children**

CHAPTER 1: GENERAL INFORMATION

Introduction

The Preparation for Mass Casualty is a drill designed to establish a learning environment for players to exercise emergency response plans, policies, and procedures as they pertain to a mass casualty incident involving children. A drill is used to validate a single specific operations or function of a single agency/organization and can be used to practice/maintain skills.

This Exercise Plan (ExPlan) was produced at the direction of the Department of Homeland Security with the input, advice, and assistance of the Preparation for Mass Casualty planners.

Confidentiality

The Preparation for Mass Casualty is a *classified exercise*. The control of information is based more on public sensitivity regarding the nature of the exercise than on the actual exercise content. Some exercise material is intended for the exclusive use of exercise planners, controllers, and evaluators, but players may view other materials deemed necessary to their performance. This ExPlan may be viewed by all exercise participants, *but the Controller and Evaluator (C/E) Handbook is a restricted document intended for controllers and evaluators only*.

All exercise participants should use appropriate guidelines to ensure the proper control of information within their areas of expertise and protect this material in accordance with current Department of Homeland Security directives. Public release of exercise materials to third parties is at the discretion of the Department of Homeland Security and the Federal Emergency Management Agency and the Preparation for Mass Casualty Planning Team.

Purpose

The purpose of this exercise is to evaluate player actions against current response plans and capabilities for a mass casualty incident response.

Target Capabilities

The National Planning Scenarios and the establishment of the National Preparedness Priorities have steered the focus of homeland security toward a capabilities-based planning approach. Capabilities-based planning focuses on planning under uncertainty, since the next danger or disaster can never be forecast with complete accuracy. Therefore, capabilities-based planning takes an all-hazards approach to planning and preparation which builds capabilities that can be applied to a wide variety of incidents. States and Urban Areas use capabilities-based planning to identify a baseline assessment of their homeland security efforts by comparing their current capabilities against the Target Capabilities List (TCL) and the critical tasks of the Universal Task List (UTL). This approach identifies gaps in current capabilities and focuses efforts on identifying and developing priority capabilities and tasks for the jurisdiction. These priority capabilities are articulated in the jurisdiction's homeland security strategy and Multi-Year Training and Exercise Plan, of which this exercise is a component of.

Federal Emergency Management Agency

Exercise Plan	Emergency Response For
Mass Casualty Drill	Mass Casualties Involving Children

The capabilities listed below have been selected by the Preparation for Mass Casualty planning team from the priority capabilities identified in the Federal Emergency Management Agency's Multi-Year Training and Exercise Plan. These capabilities provide the foundation for development of the exercise objectives and scenario, as the purpose of this exercise is to measure and validate performance of these capabilities and their associated critical tasks.

CORE CAPABILITY RESEARCH INITIATIVE

The *LLIS.gov* team strives to provide useful and pertinent information to the whole community. In order to deliver relevant lessons learned and innovative practices to our users, the *LLIS.gov* team is focusing its research on Core Capabilities, as defined in the National Preparedness Goal. The *LLIS.gov* team uses the results of State Preparedness Reports (SPRs) to identify the capabilities states have self-assessed as both high-priority and low-proficiency.

The *LLIS.gov* team has already conducted research on Mass Care Services, Cybersecurity, and Community Resilience, and will soon begin research on Housing. The goal of this research is to gather lessons learned, innovative practices, and resources from subject matter experts at all levels of government, NGOs, and the private sector and share them with the whole community. Click on the pages below to view the gathered resources, and please consider contributing your expertise.

List The Target Capabilities To Be Exercised:

- Mass Prophylaxis
- Mass Death of Children at a School by Firearms
- Suicide or Apprehension of Unknown Shooter
- Use of Media for Evaluation
- Use of Media for Information Distribution

Exercise Objectives

The Preparation for Mass Casualty exercise planning team selected objectives that focus on evaluating emergency response procedures, identifying areas for improvement, and achieving a collaborative attitude. This exercise will focus on the following objectives:

This is a list of sample objectives that apply to this exercise. Drills traditionally have 1 to 3 specific objectives.

Site Call-Down. Ability to contact and ensure facilities are available for emergency response functions.
1. Measure the time needed for the jurisdiction to contact owners or managers of Emergency Dispensing Sites during a mass casualty or incident involving children, in accordance with MOUs.

228

The FEMA Manual for Sandy Hook

FOR OFFICIAL USE ONLY

Federal Emergency Management Agency

Exercise Plan   **Emergency Response For**
Mass Casualty Drill   **Mass Casualties Involving Children**

2. Measure the time needed for the jurisdiction to receive access confirmation from owners or managers of Emergency Dispensing Sites during a mass casualty incident involving children, in accordance with MOUs.

3. Measure the percentage of sites that are available for use during a mass casualty incident involving children, in accordance with MOUs.

FOR OFFICIAL USE ONLY

Chapter 1: General Information   1-3   Sensitive Document

FEMA

CHAPTER 2: EXERCISE LOGISTICS

Exercise Summary

General

The Preparation for Mass Casualty is designed to establish a learning environment for players to exercise their plans and procedures for responding to an incident involving children as casualties. The Preparation for Mass Casualty will be conducted on 12/13/12, beginning at 8:00 am. Exercise play is scheduled until the Exercise Director/Controller determines that the exercise objectives have been met. Everyone must sign in with controller upon arrival.

Assumptions and Site Call-Down Instructions

This section contains the basic instructions on how to conduct this drill using both a manual and automated call-down system. These assumptions and instructions are derived from specific CDC guidance and should result in the necessary output for data collection. *For more details, please see: Chan, Edward, et al. Working Paper: Operational Assessments for SNS Readiness. Santa Monica: RAND Health, 2008.*

Assumptions constitute the implied factual foundation for the exercise and, hence, are assumed to be present before the start of the exercise. The following general assumptions apply to the Preparation for Mass Casualty:

- *Site call-down list to be tested.* Jurisdictions have different lists of sites that would be called in an emergency. Example site call-down lists include EDSs and warehouse locations. Site call-down lists should be kept up-to-date, readily accessible, and usable. Jurisdictions should select one or more of these lists for use during this site call-down drill.

- *No-notice/no-availability drill.* To collect the best possible performance metrics, site call-down drills should not involve prior notice to those being called; however, *the drills need not require actually making the site available for use* by the health department.

  - *No-notice.* Given that the purpose of the assessment is to estimate the percentage of the sites on the calling list that are reachable and available on a given day, we recommend the drill be conducted on a no-notice basis. At most, only the players who are required to initiate the site call-down procedure should be notified of the drill, but even they need not be warned beforehand. If using an automated calling system, only players who must activate the automated system need to be notified.

  - *No site activation required.* To reduce the burden associated with gathering performance metrics, *sites on the call-down list are not required to actually make their site available for use* by the health department.

- **It is critical that this message is conveyed to the contacts receiving the site activation call.**

230

Federal Emergency Management Agency

Exercise Plan	Emergency Response For
Mass Casualty Drill	Mass Casualties Involving Children

- *Calling equipment*. Players should have access to all calling equipment and any call response monitoring technology that would be used during a real emergency in order to track the call responses received.

  - *Automated calling system*. Jurisdictions using automated calling systems should collaborate with the provider of their calling system to perform the site call-down drill.

  - *Manual calling system*. Jurisdictions using manual calling systems should run the drill using the same equipment and facilities that would be used during a real emergency. If this is not practical, the drill should be conducted using equipment and facilities that are as similar as possible.

- *Response method*. Jurisdictions should determine the method by which sites on the call-down list will acknowledge receipt of the call-down message and report their ability to make their site available.

  Automated calling system

  - *If an automated response function is available*. Sites on the call-down list should follow the instructions of the automated calling system to acknowledge receipt of the call-down message and report whether or not they are able to make their site available. Typically, persons called can enter a number on their phone after a prompt.

  - *If an automated response function is not available*. Upon being called, sites on the call-down list should acknowledge receipt of the call-down message and report their ability to make their site available. The response can be in the form of an e-mail, phone call, or text message to a phone number specially designated for this purpose. Another option is to set up a call center to receive responses. Only responses received within a predetermined amount of time should be recorded for use in the performance metrics.

  Manual calling system

  - During successful phone calls, the caller can manually record receipt of the call-down message and the ability of each site on the call-down list to make their site available.

- *Protocol for non-respondent follow up*. For the purposes of this drill, the following non-responses indicate that the site on the call-down list has *not* acknowledged receipt of the call-down message:

  - Busy signal
  - No answer
  - Voicemail
  - Wrong person answering but correct person is unavailable
  - Wrong number.

Jurisdictions should determine the protocol for how callers or automated calling systems should handle non-responses.

Federal Emergency Management Agency

| Exercise Plan | Emergency Response For |
| Mass Casualty Drill | Mass Casualties Involving Children |

Exercise Participants

The following are the categories of participants involved in this exercise; for purposes of this call-down drill, participants include the following:

• *Players.* Players are the personnel who do the calling during the exercise. The players in the exercise should be the people who would do the calling in a real emergency.

• *Exercise Director/Controller/Evaluator.* This position has the overall responsibility for planning, coordinating, and overseeing all exercise functions. He/she monitors the status of play and the achievement of the exercise design objectives.

They declare when the drill starts and ends and manage the flow of the drill. This is the only participant who will provide information or direction to the players. However, because the drill focuses on the collection of time-based metrics, they should *not* intervene in timed activities while the drill is in progress.

He/she is responsible for timing the overall drill, gathering individual call data collection sheets, computing metrics, and taking notes to identify areas for improvement.

For an automated calling system. He/she should remain unobtrusive and not intervene with player action.

For a manual calling system. He/she should not intervene with player action. Ideally, the evaluator should be able to listen in on the calls that the players make

Exercise Tools

Controller and Evaluator Handbook

The Preparation for Mass Casualty C/E Handbook is designed to help exercise controllers and evaluators conduct and evaluate an effective exercise. This handbook also enables controllers and evaluators to understand their roles and responsibilities in exercise execution and evaluation. Should a player, observer, or media representative find an unattended handbook, it should be provided to the nearest controller or evaluator.

Master Scenario Events List

The MSEL outlines benchmarks, as well as injects that drive exercise play. It also details realistic input to the exercise players as well as information expected to emanate from simulated organizations (i.e., those nonparticipating organizations, agencies, and individuals who would usually respond to the situation). For the purpose of this drill, the MSEL will not contain injects, but will instead only contain anticipated actions of the players.

Exercise Implementation

Exercise Play

Exercise play will begin at 8:00 am on December 13th 2012. Play will proceed according to the events outlined in the MSEL, in accordance with established plans and procedures. The exercise

---

Federal Emergency Management Agency

| Exercise Plan | Emergency Response For |
| Mass Casualty Drill | Mass Casualties Involving Children |

will conclude upon the completion of operations and attainment of the exercise objectives, as determined by the Exercise Director/Controller. The exercise is expected to end at 11:59 pm on 12/13/12 and be evaluated on 12/14/12 as a real-time event.

Exercise Rules

The following are the general rules that govern exercise play:

- Real-world emergency actions take priority over exercise actions.
- Exercise participants will comply with real-world response procedures, unless otherwise directed by control staff.
- All communications (written, radio, telephone, etc.) made during the exercise will begin and end with the phrase, *"This is a drill."*

Accident Reporting and Real Emergencies

Due to the nature of this drill, it is not anticipated that any accidents will occur, however, if an accident or real world emergency does occur, the participant is to immediately stop exercise play and attend to the accident or real-world emergency as necessary and notify the Exercise Director/Controller as soon as possible. If a real emergency occurs that affects the entire exercise, the exercise may be suspended or terminated at the discretion of the Exercise Director/Controller.

Communications Plan

Exercise Start, Suspension, and Termination Instructions

The exercise is scheduled to run until the Exercise Director/Controller determines that the exercise objectives have been met.

All spoken and written communication will start and end with the statement, "THIS IS A DRILL."

Player Communication

Players will use routine, in-place agency communication systems. Additional communication assets may be made available as the exercise progresses. The need to maintain capability for a real-world response may preclude the use of certain communication channels or systems that would usually be available for an actual emergency incident. In no instance will exercise communication interfere with real-world emergency communications.

See **Appendix B: Standard Script for Calls** for an outline of the recommended script for calling.

233

CHAPTER 3: PLAYER GUIDELINES

Player Instructions

Before the Exercise

- Participants should be familiar with the appropriate emergency plans, procedures, and exercise support documents.

During the Exercise

- Respond to the exercise events and information as if the emergency were real, unless otherwise directed by an exercise controller.

- All exercise communication will begin and end with the phrase **"This is a drill."** This is a precaution taken so anyone overhearing the conversation will not mistake the exercise play for a real-world emergency.

Data Collection

Data collection responsibilities depend on the calling system used. For an **Automated Calling System**, the drill *evaluator* is responsible for all data collection and analysis. Most Automated Calling Systems have the capacity to generate reports detailing the results of the call-down. The drill evaluator is responsible for extrapolating the following information from the report:

    1. *Recording the drill information*, including date and location of drill, number of players, etc. (see Excel-based data collection spreadsheet).

    2. *Recording the following process time stamps (to the hour and minute):*
        a. When the automated system begins contacting sites on the call-down list
        b. When the automated system completes contacting sites on the call-down list
        c. When all sites have acknowledged receipt of the call-down message and reported their ability to make their site available by a pre-determined target time, or a predetermined amount of time has passed.

    3. *Computing the performance metrics after the drill.*

For jurisdictions using a **Manual Calling System**, the players will record data that must be collected by the evaluators in the post-exercise period. The *players (callers)* are responsible for:

    1. *Recording the following time stamps (to the hour and minute):*
        a. When the player begins contacting sites on the call-down list
        b. When the player completes contacting sites on the call-down list

    2. *Recording for each site on the call-down list:*
        a. Whether the site acknowledged receipt of the call-down message
        b. Whether the site reported being able to make their site available by the target time

The drill *evaluator* is responsible for:

    1. *Recording the drill information*, including date and location of drill, number of players, etc. (see Excel-based data collection spreadsheet).

    2. *Gathering the data collection spreadsheets from each player.*

The FEMA Manual for Sandy Hook

FOR OFFICIAL USE ONLY

Federal Emergency Management Agency

Exercise Plan
Mass Casualty Drill

Emergency Response For
Mass Casualties Involving Children

3. *Computing the performance metrics after the drill.*

Chapter 3: Player Guidelines 3-2 Sensitive Document
FOR OFFICIAL USE ONLY

235

Federal Emergency Management Agency

Exercise Plan
Mass Casualty Drill

Emergency Response For
Mass Casualties Involving Children

CHAPTER 4: EVALUATION AND POST-EXERCISE ACTIVITIES

Exercise Documentation

The goal of the drill is to comprehensively exercise and evaluate the Department of Homeland Security and the Federal Emergency Management Agency's plans and capabilities as they pertain to a potential mass casualty incident involving children. After the exercise, data collected by controllers, evaluators, and players will be used to identify strengths and areas for improvement in the context of the exercise design objectives.

Exercise Evaluation Guides

DHS has developed Exercise Evaluation Guides (EEGs) that identify expected activities for evaluation, provide consistency across exercises, and link individual tasks to disciplines and expected outcomes. The EEGs selected by the Preparation for Mass Casualty trusted agents are contained in the evaluator materials packet along with the C/E Handbook. Supplemental evaluation material designed for the drill may also be used.

Data Collection Spreadsheet and Scoring Metrics

The Centers for Disease Control and Prevention (CDC) and the RAND Corporation have developed a data collection spreadsheet and scoring metrics computation spreadsheet, for assessing site call-down capability.

After Action Report

The AAR is the culmination of the Preparation for Mass Casualty. It is a written report outlining the strengths and areas for improvement identified during the exercise. The AAR will include the timeline, executive summary, scenario description, mission outcomes, and capability analysis. The AAR will be drafted by a core group of individuals from the exercise planning team.

After Action Conference and Improvement Plan

The improvement process represents the comprehensive, continuing preparedness effort of which the drill is a part. The lessons learned and recommendations from the AAR will be incorporated into an Improvement Plan (IP). The *After Action Conference* is a forum for jurisdiction officials to hear the results of the evaluation analysis, validate the findings and recommendations in the draft AAR, and begin development of the IP. The *IP* identifies how recommendations will be addressed, including what actions will be taken, who is responsible, and the timeline for completion. It is created by key stakeholders from the Preparation for Mass Casualty participating agency officials during the After Action Conference.

Federal Emergency Management Agency

Exercise Plan   **Emergency Response For**
Mass Casualty Drill   **Mass Casualties Involving Children**

APPENDIX A: PARTICIPATING AGENCIES

Table A.1 *Participating Agencies*

Participating Agencies
Federal (if applicable)
State (if applicable)
[Jurisdiction A]
[Jurisdiction B] (if applicable)

Federal Emergency Management Agency

Exercise Plan	Emergency Response For
Mass Casualty Drill	Mass Casualties Involving Children

APPENDIX B: STANDARD SCRIPT FOR CALLS

Callers and automated calling systems should use a standard script to ensure accuracy and consistency of messages and to ensure that time estimates taken from the drill reflect the pace of activity in a true emergency.

The script should: **1)** clearly state that this is a drill; **2)** assess ability to make their site available **(by a hypothetical time)**; and **3)** in the case of a calling tree, provide instructions for further calls.

The 'hypothetical time' should reflect a realistic approximation of the time needed to prepare a host facility for the receipt of response staff and supplies.

Sample Call-Down Script

- This is a site call-down drill being conducted by the Department of Homeland Security and the Federal Emergency Management Agency. Your site is on the Department of Homeland Security's list of facilities that may be used in an emergency. If this were a real emergency, you would be asked to make your site available for use by the Department of Homeland Security's health department.

- Again, *this is only a drill*. There is no need for you to make your site available as a result of this call.

APPENDIX B

The 20 Children and their Homes

by Nick Kollerstrom, Ph.D.

Twenty families had children allegedly killed at the Sandy Hook event of 14 December, 2012. Each of these families *owned their own home* in Newtown. Most of them had acquired it relatively recently before the event, a couple of years before.

We here examine patterns in that property acquisition. Seven out of the twenty families were Jewish and the data suggests that they seem to have played some key role.

The FBI's year-summary of crimes had no murders registered in Newtown over that period. Nor have any birth certificates, death certificates or coroner's inquests been to-date produced for the twenty alleged children who died [*Editor's note:* apart from the fake death certificate discussed in Chapter 11.] Therefore their status, as to whether they really lived, remains unclear. Without wishing to prejudge the issue, we shall here allude to them as "SHUC", Sandy Hook Undead Children.

The SSDI Social Security Death Index is closely linked to the database of *ancestry.com,* and is widely regarded as a reliable guide to who really lived and died in America.

It based upon a unique account number owned by each US citizen; plus in addition, parents may apply for their child's SSDI for tax-deduction purposes, so that young children may also have them. All twenty of the SHUC had been given SSDIs, and these recorded their deaths on 14 December, 2012, whereas that for Adam Lanza, their alleged killer, was for 13 December 2012. Did the killer die the day before his victims? This suggests that somebody has, to say the least, tampered with the data.

Where Nightmares Take Form

Newtown came into existence in the 1930's, centered on the construction and staffing of a Psychiatric Hospital (aka Fairfield Halls Military Programming Facility) during WW2. It seems to be a place where storied and mundane history somehow overlap. In the year 2000, a film, *'The Sandy Hook Lingerie Party Massacre'*, had a deranged killer strike in the aftermath of a hurricane.

Then, the ritual sacrifice of 22 children was portrayed in the global bestseller, *'The Hunger Games'* (2008) by Suzanne Collins, who was and is a resident of Newtown: she lives just two streets from where Nancy Lanza (mother of the alleged killer Adam Lanza) is supposed to have lived. (*Editor's note*: On that claim, see Chapter 7). That story had 22 children die, while the 'Sandy Hook Massacre' allegedly had 21 (including Adam Lanza). It premiered as a film in March 2012.

The Hollywood blockbuster, *The Dark Knight Rises* had an area on the Gotham City Map (used in the viral marketing campaign, and in the movie) changed to Sandy Hook. A Mr. Scott Getzinger was the prop master who did this, and he lived in the Sandy Hook school district; his widowed wife still does. He was killed in April 2012 in a car accident in which first responders noted his injuries were "not life threatening". He died in the hospital later that night. His widow is public in her belief that he was murdered.

In July 2012, the Batman film, *'The Dark Knight Rises'*, premiered, alluding to the 'Sandy Hook' region of Gotham City as a portion of the city of Gotham during a setup of one of the bad guy's dirty deeds. Early promotions of the film the year before did not (as Alex Jones discovered) contain that Sandy Hook reference. Then, in 2013, the *'Sandy Hook Lingerie Party Massacre'* was re-released under a new title, *'Jersey Shore Lingerie Party Massacre'*.

Singing at the Superbowl

Fifty days after the event at Sandy Hook, ten of the SHUC were observed singing happily in the Sandy Hook Choir at a Superbowl conference–with Beyoncé! They are identifiable–but curiously they were some years older.

From this students have inferred that the images of the ten six to seven-year-old children put out as having died at Sandy Hook, had actually been taken some years earlier. The table below gives data on these ten SHUC families: the official birthdates are given, but these would seem to be impossible in view of their more mature appearance at the Superbowl.

We will come on later to the property prices, shown on the right-hand side of the table.

Important research on this topic has been done by Dr. Eowyn, who traced each of the twenty SSDI records and these include the states in which they were issued as 'State of Issue.' Only four out of the ten SHUC who sang 'after-death' at the Superbowl had their SSDIs issued by the State of Connecticut (of which Newtown is a part). SSDIs are issued by the state in which the individual was born, not where he or she died.

Child	D.O.B.	SSDI	Parents	Rel.	Property cost $	Date of purchase
Charlotte Helen Bacon	22.2.06	NJ	Joel B.	J	387,500	20.8.07
Avielle Richman	17.10.06	CA	Jennifer & Jeremy Richman	J	560.000	4.21.11
Josephine Gay	11.12.05	Mary	Bob & Michele Gay		0	12.25.09
Ben Wheeler	12.9.06	NY	David & Francis Wheeler	J	365,000	27.7.07
Emilie Parker	12.5.06	Utah	Robert & Alissa Parker		0	2.4.12
Caroline Previdi	-	Conn	Helen J. & Eugene Prev.		0	25.12.09
Grace McDonnell	4.11.05	Conn	Lynn McDonnell		0	25.12.09
Olivia Rose Engel	18.7.06	Conn	Brian Engel		0	12.25.09
Daniel Barden	27.9.05	NY	Mark Barden	J	450,000	10.19.07
Jessica A. Rekos	10.5.06	Conn	Richard & Krista Rekos		530,000	6.23.10

The children's names are on the left, their parents in the centre.

There is evidence of false identity. Sandy Hook appears to have been a virtual-reality event, which set up huge revenue streams of income for certain Newtown residents. Thus 'Avielle Rose Richman', for example, seems to have been Lenie Urbina, whose parents Curtis and Richmond Urbina are both directly associated with the Newtown area synagogue. They seem to have loaned their daughter—or at least a picture of her—for this event: the alleged-parents Jeremy Richman and Jennifer Hensel were thereby able to establish the 'Avielle Foundation' and its smart website on 14 December 2012, the very day of the 'shooting.' This aimed to raise $5m in the first year.

As for 'Ben Wheeler', his purported parents, Ben and Francine Lobis-Wheeler, appear to have had only one child, Nate Wheeler. 'Owen Wright' seems to have been the child whose photos were used, where his mother, Jennifer Wright, was rewarded by his appearance at the Superbowl concert. The next table shows the ten SHUC not observed singing at the Superbowl:

Name	DOB	SSDI	Rel .	Parents	Property Cost $	Property bought on
Dylan C. Hockley	8.3.06	Conn		Nicole & Ian	0	25.12.09
Madeleine F. Hsu:	10.6.06	Conn		John & Donna Arnold	0	7.4.09
Catherine V. Hubbard	8.6.06	Conn		Matthew & Jennifer H.	0	25.12.09
Chase M. Kowalski:	31.10.05	Conn		Stephen & Rebecca K.	0	25.12.09
Jesse M. Lewis:	30.6.06	Conn		Scarlett L.	0	25.12.09
James Mattioli:	22.3.06	Conn	J	Mark & Cynthia M	585,000	3.8.07
Jack A. Pinto:	6.5.06	Conn		Dean & Tricia P	0	25.12.09

Nobody is likely to tell us what differences there are between these two groups; all one can say is that all in this second table have SSDIs from Connecticut. Dr. Eowyn was startled to discover that

the Social Security Death Index (SSDI) is a database of death records created from the federal government Social Security Administration's 'Death Master File' and the latter does *not* have SSDIs for any of the twenty SHUC.

Notice that Dr. Eowyn ascertained that *exactly one* of the children had not been issued a SSDI, as shown here. [*Editor's note:* See Chapter 9.]

Homes Purchased on Christmas Day

Another mystery of the Sandy Hook story—which has a tendency to be ignored because it is so strange—is that most of these families acquired their properties on Christmas Day 2009, *apparently for free* (i.e., the recorded price for these transactions was *zero dollars*). Was this just some computer glitch on the part of local estate agents, as has been claimed? If so, it seems odd that those $0 sale prices were never corrected: how can a city make their budget work with such sloppy documentation?

Seven of the children—James Mattioli, Noah S. Pozner, Ana Marquez-Greene, Charlotte Helen Bacon, Avielle Rose Richman, Ben Andrew Wheeler and Daniel Barden—came from Jewish families and had Jewish funerals. These families did not (bar one or two) get their properties free, but paid around half a million dollars for them. In the far-right column of both Tables, dates of purchase of most of the parents' homes appear as being within two years of the event. *Only* non-Jewish families obtained their homes on Christmas Day 2009 (or at least were registered as doing so.) *and* these largely got their homes free.

It may help to depict these facts with a simple 2x2 table of binary (i.e., yes or no) logic:

House purchases registered In Newtown, of the twenty familes

	Purchased on 12.25.09 / or not	Paid for / Free
Jewish (7)	0 / 7	5 / 2
Non-Jewish (13)	10 / 3	1 / 12

If we divide the families between those registered as acquiring their property prior to Christmas Day 2009, and those who acquired it on or after that date, then *most* of the Jewish families acquired theirs *before* that date (5 out of 7), while conversely only 3 out of 13 non-Jewish families acquired theirs before that date. Four of the Jewish families reportedly acquired their homes in the year 2007.

Two of the Jewish families are recorded as having acquired their Newtown home for free, while *all but one* of the thirteen non-Jewish families did so. Nearly all of the non-Jewish families had this mysterious transaction recorded as happening on Christmas Day 2009—a day when no business is normally conducted—whereas not one Jewish family did this.

The town records show that several of the "$0 sales" were preceded by a sale to the same person a few years before for what appears to be a "market price"—as if the Sandy Hook victim had bought the house previously, then sold it to themselves for $0.00 a few years later— suggesting that the loan was paid off by someone else and the deed remained in the original buyer's name. Some of these homes appear to have been re-sold shortly after the "massacre", where it would be worth investigating to what extent the families moved in a while before the shootings and left not long after.

Did that day have any special significance? If we accept that the Sandy Hook episode was an act of state-fabricated terror, then there is another such episode, namely, the 'crotch bomber' scam, which happened on Christmas Day 2009. This was on a passenger flight from Amsterdam to Detroit and we were supposed to believe that he threatened to blow up the plane.

Do the 'Illuminati'—or whoever else one takes to be perpetrating these state-fabricated terror events—intend to link them up in this way? For comparison, the Madrid railway station bombing happened 911 days after 9/11; and then, before the Boston Marathon race began, there was 26 minutes of silence one for each of the Sandy Hook victims—also for a race over 26 miles. Thus the Marathon was *themed* to link with the Sandy Hook massacres, where the two events had in retrospect quite a bit in common. So that 2009 Christmas Day could appear as being somehow significant, linking one fictional terror event with another.

The central issue in state-fabricated terror of the 21st century is usually false or fabricated identity. Who really were the people involved? Did the twenty families ever really have these little children running around in their back gardens, or not? Vast charity revenues have accrued through these fictional deaths. It is hoped that the schematic approach here taken may assist citizens of America in resolving the complicated levels of deception involved. I suggest that a panel ought to be established for a 'Real Identity of the Sandy Hook Children' study, to examine the photographs and families involved, find their real dates of birth, etc. We need the truth.

APPENDIX C

Sandy Hook School Massacre Timeline

by James F. Tracy, Ph. D.

The following timeline of the December 14, 2012 mass killing of 20 children and 8 adults in Newtown Connecticut attempts to demonstrate how the event was presented to the public by corporate news media.

The chronological assemblage of coverage is not comprehensive of all reports published on the incident but rather seeks to verify how the storyline was to a substantial degree constructed by federal and state law enforcement authorities and major media around the theory that 20-year-old Adam Lanza was the sole agent in the massacre.

This scenario became an established reality through the news media's pronounced repetition of the lone gunman narrative and meme. This proposed scenario significantly obscured the fact that police encountered and apprehended two additional shooting suspects on the school's grounds within minutes of the crime. These suspects remain unaccounted for by authorities but the roles they may have played arguably correlate with the shifting information presented by authorities and major news media on injuries and weapons vis-à-vis the mass carnage meted out in the school.

While the certain detainment of additional suspects was pointed to by alternative news media, including *Natural News*, *Infowars*, *Veterans Today* and *Global Research* in the days following the tragedy, the untenable lone gunman narrative has become firmly established in the public psyche via an overwhelming chorus of corporate media reports and interpretations.

Note: Times of occurrences referenced are Eastern Standard Time and in some instances signify time of publication rather than the specific incident cited. Time of publication does not always correlate with exact time of incident. "n.t." denotes "no time" of publication referenced.

1955
May 17

First Selectman A. Fenn Dickinson of Newtown, a 42-year-old Democrat serving his third term as Newtown's foremost public servant, is killed when a truck backs over him at a road project in Sandy Hook. Dickinson Drive, the road leading to Sandy Hook Elementary, is named after the local leader. "Do You Remember?"*Newstimes.com*, May 22, 2005.

2006
June 26

President George W. Bush signs Executive Order 13407 to establish a Public Alert and Warning System for national emergencies potentially involving the public at large. "It is the policy of the United States," the EO's policy summary reads,

> to have an effective, reliable, integrated, flexible, and comprehensive system to alert and warn the American people in situations of war, terrorist attack, natural disaster, or other hazards to public safety and well-being (public alert and warning system), taking appropriate account of the functions, capabilities, and needs of the private sector and of all levels of government in our Federal system, and to ensure that under all conditions the President can communicate with the American people.

The Department of Homeland Security is designated as the government entity for establishment of the integrated mass communication system. "Executive Order 13407 (PDF)," Government Printing Office, June 2006.

December 4

Attorney General Richard Blumenthal, New York State Police (NYSP)

Superintendent Wayne E. Bennett, and Connecticut Department of Public Safety (DPS) Commissioner Leonard C. Boyle release a 207-page report chronicling shortcomings in the Connecticut State Police (CSP) internal affairs system and recommending reforms thereof. The investigation was requested by state troopers filing whistleblower complaints with Blumenthal's office on the DPS internal affairs process.

Commissioner Boyle also asked the NYSP to investigate those complaints and others received from state troopers about the internal affairs system. The report caps a 13-month joint investigation by Blumenthal's office and NYSP involving 262 interviews, 207 of them with current or former sworn DPS employees, thousands of pages of documents, and 112 formal requests for information. "Attorney General-NY State Police Report Finds Shortcomings in CT State Police Internal Affairs System, Calls for Reforms," State of Connecticut Attorney General's Office, December 4, 2006

2010
September 22
8:00AM-5:00PM

US Department of Homeland Security, Federal Emergency Management Agency and State of Connecticut Division of Emergency Services and Public Protection conduct Homeland Security Exercise and Evaluation Program (HSEEP) Training Course at Sandy Hook Fire Department. The training consists of "instructor-led course presentations" in addition to "small group activities, videos, and group discussions." According to the description, "the course also provides overviews of HSEEP-related initiatives such as technology (e.g., the HSEEP Toolkit) and capabilities-based planning (e.g., Target Capabilities List [TCL]).

This blended approach will give participants hands-on experience that readily translates to real-world exercise skills. Activities include creating exercise documentation, conducting exercise planning conferences and briefings, and practicing exercise evaluation." "September 22: The HSEEP Training Course," Connecticut Division of Emergency Services and Public Protection, n.d.

2011
February 23
n.t.

Connecticut State Senators Steven T. Mikutel, Leonard A. Fasano, Michael A. McLachlan, and Len Suzio introduce SB 1054, a bill "to allow the parents of a child who was a homicide victim to request that the autopsy report not be publicly disclosed." SB 1054: An Act Concerning the Disclosure of Autopsy Reports, Sunlight Foundation/Open States, retrieved March 1, 2013.

February 25
n.t.

In a memorandum to the state legislature's judiciary committee Connecticut Chief Medical Examiner H. Wayne Carver II questions the necessity of SB 1054. "The Office of the Chief Medical Examiner as an institution and I are very concerned about the privacy rights of individuals who are examined through our office and particularly with respect to homicide victims whose family find their privacy and grieving invaded by a curious public.

I believe that the proposed legislation is redundant of current statute, regulations, and practices. The Office of the Chief Medical Examiner does not now and has never released autopsy reports to the general public, let alone autopsy reports of a pediatric homicide victim." Dr. H. Wayne Carver II to Chairman Coleman, Fox and Members of the Connecticut State Judiciary Committee, Office of the Chief Medical Examiner, February 25.

March 9

State Police spokesman Lt. J. Paul Vance, a regional celebrity, announces on WPLR radio that he will try out for the next season of the Survivor television series. Tryouts are next Wednesday at Foxwoods. Vance tells the Connecticut Post that he will "do the interview (with Survivor) and explore the process."

Vance's son, J. Paul Vance Jr. called WPLR's "Chaz and A.J." show earlier to nominate his father as a candidate, and Vance Sr. subsequently called in to say he was up to the "tall order," of trying out for the show. The show's hosts said that wardrobe will be important. "Wear your shirt, with the police hat and a grass skirt," said show co-host Chaz. "State Police Lt. J. Paul Vance to Try Out for 'Survivor'," *Connecticut Post*, March 9, 2011.

August 16

Connecticut Governor Dannell P. Malloy appoints J. Paul Vance Jr. as the state's new claims commissioner. The Republican politician was appointed to the job with a $114,000 salary, where he will more or less decide who can sue the state. Penelope Overton, "Vance Appointed State's Claims Commissioner," August 16, 2011.

October 1
n.t.

Existing law preventing disclosure of autopsies to the press or public is bolstered through passage and enactment of recommendations encompassed in SB 1054 by Connecticut State Senate and General Assembly.

Section 1. Subdivision (3) of subsection (b) of section 1-210 of the general statutes is repealed and the following is substituted in lieu thereof Effective October 1, 2011

(3) Records of law enforcement agencies not otherwise available to the public which records were compiled in connection with the detection or investigation of crime, if the disclosure of said records would not be in the public interest because it would result in the disclosure of ... **"the records of an investigation and examination by the Office of the Chief Medical Examiner of the death of a person under eighteen years of age caused by an apparent homicide, including the autopsy report and other scientific findings."**

SB 1054 An Act Concerning the Disclosure of Autopsy Reports, Sunlight Foundation/Open States, retrieved March 1, 2013.

2012
September

At the start of the 2012-13 academic year Sandy Hook Elementary School Principal Dawn Hochsprung announces in a public letter to families the Newtown School District's new security protocol "in all elementary schools." Under the newly-announced security regimen, "exterior doors will be locked during the day. Every visitor will be required to ring the doorbell at the front entrance and the office staff will use a visual monitoring system to allow entry.

Visitors will still be required to report directly to the office and sign in. If our office staff does not recognize you, you will be required to show identification with a picture id. Please understand that with nearly 700 students and over 1,000 parents representing 500 SHS families, most parents will be asked to show identification. Doors will be locked at approximately 9:30 a.m." "Principal Outlined New Security Procedures at Sandy Hook Elementary," *Hartford Courant*, December 14, 2012, 8:25PM EST.

October 17
9:47AM

Sandy Hook Principal Dawn Hochsprung Tweets photo of emergency drill held at Sandy Hook fire station with Sandy Hook Elementary faculty and students participating. Esther Zuckerman, "The Sandy Hook Principal's Twitter Feed is Haunting," *The Atlantic Wire*, December 14, 2012.

November 7
n.t.

Following Obama's reelection Senator Diane Feinstein is believed to be meeting with relevant federal agencies to lay groundwork for reenacting assault weapons ban. "Senator Diane Feinstein Moves to Ban All Assault Rifles, High Capacity Magazines, and Pistol Grips," *Market Daily News*, November 7, 2012.

November 27
11:00AM

U.S. Attorney General Eric Holder and Connecticut Governor Dan Malloy announce Project Longevity, a joint venture by the Justice Department and State of Connecticut, at a news conference in New Haven, Connecticut. The endeavor is described by one law enforcement officials as "a statewide approach that targets repeat criminals, creates alternatives for potential gang members and rallies neighborhoods against violence." Federal money is being directed to engage Connecticut-based agents, academics and social workers who will work for or with the FBI and the U.S. Bureau of Alcohol, Tobacco, Firearms and Explosives. Dave Ingram, "Project Longevity: Justice Department, Connecticut State Officials Target Gun Violence," Reuters/ *Huffington Post*, November 27, 2012. See also, Erin Logan, "Attorney General Eric Holder Discussing Gun Violence," WTNH.com, November, 27, 2012.

December 10

Newtown Schools superintendent Janet Robinson speaks before the Newtown Board of Finance discusses closing one of the town's schools given the area's 25-year-low in elementary school enrollment. "When asked about space needs," the 12-10 meeting minutes read, "school closing declining enrollment Dr. Robinson said that the Ad Hoc Facilities group vetted every option. Their recommendation was when elementary enrollment is projected to be 1500 a study should be commissioned to begin looking at closing a school." Robinson proposes embarking on a study to determine the feasibility of closure. "Our problem is [that] our parents really cherish their neighborhood schools," Robinson notes, "even though these are not small neighborhoods. So, we have to prepare the parents for this in advance." Janet Robinson, "State of Schools Presentation," in Town of Newtown Board of Finance Meeting Minutes, and 2012-12-10 Board of Finance.wmv (electronic record at 1:18:13) Town of Newtown, Newtown, CT, December 10, 2012.

December 11
n.t.

Adam Lanza reportedly visits a sporting goods store in Danbury and attempts to purchase an assault rifle but was denied NBC reports. Julia Terruso, "Reports: Gunman Had Altercation at School Day Before Shooting," *Star Ledger*, December 15, 2012.

December 13
4:13PM

Connecticut State Representative John Frey Tweets his presence at the Sandy Hook Elem. Holiday concert, 4:13pm. "At the Sandy Hook Elementary School concert cheering nieces Joan and Bridget." *http://twitter.com/johnfrey/status/279378604469657601*
n.t.

The alleged gunman at Adam Lanza has an argument with four staff members at Sandy Hook Elementary School, officials tell NBC. NBC reports that Lanza went to the school on December 13 and was in an altercation with four staff members, three of whom are killed in the December 14 shooting. The fourth person will not be at the school the day of the shooting, NBC says. Julia Terruso, "Reports: Gunman Had Altercation at School Day Before Shooting," *Star Ledger*, December 15, 2012.

December 14
9:00AM

"Planning for the Needs of Children in Disasters" emergency exercise conducted jointly by FEMA and the Connecticut Department of Emergency Services and Public Protection commences 14 miles from Newport in Bridgeport Connecticut. "The goal of the course," the description reads,

is to enable participants to improve their community's mitigation and emergency operations plan specifically regarding the needs of children. The course will provide them with the information needed to address the unique needs of children prior to, during and following disasters. It will also provide them guidance and direction on how to form coalitions and how to become advocates for the unique needs of children in all aspects of emergency management.

Shepherd Ambellas and Alex Thomas, "Sandy Hook Shooting: Active Shooter Drill Confirmed By Law Enforcement Raises Suspicion of False Flag Operation, [News Analysis]" *theintellhub.com,* January 12, 2013.

9:00AM [estimate]

"Active shooter drill" exercise commences by Putnam County Emergency Response Team in Carmel Connecticut, 45 miles away from Newtown. "By grim coincidence, even as the terrible events were unfolding in Newtown on Friday morning," the *Southeast Brewster-Patc*h reports,

> *the Putnam County Emergency Response Team ("ERT") happened to be assembled for regular training in Carmel, and team members were at that very moment engaged in a mock scenario of an active-shooter in a school. The ERT is comprised of specially trained and heavily armed officers from the Sheriff's Office and the Carmel and Kent Police Departments. When news broke of the Newtown shooting, the Putnam County ERT commander called Newtown Police and offered to have the ERT respond to the Sandy Hook school, but that response was not needed because Connecticut police had already secured the scene.*

Ashley Tarr, "Sheriff: Putnam Officials to Talk School Safety This Afternoon, "*Southeast Brewster-Patch*, December 18, 2012.

9:30AM [estimate]

Only 35 minutes away from Newtown an active shooter drill is taking place at a school in Carmel, Putnam County. The operation is conducted by the Putnam County Emergency Response Team ("ERT). "The ERT is comprised of specially trained and heavily armed officers from the Sheriff's Office and the Carmel and Kent Police Departments," the *Southeast Brewster Patch* newspaper reports. "When news broke of the Newtown shooting, the Putnam County ERT commander called Newtown Police and offered to have the ERT respond to the Sandy Hook school, but that response was not needed because Connecticut police had already secured the scene." "Sheriff: Putnam Officials to Talk School Safety This Afternoon," *Southeast Brewster Patch*, December 18, 2012.

(9:30AM [see below])

CNN reports local authorities take the first 911 calls from Sandy Hook Elementary School. "'Sandy Hook school. Caller is indicating she thinks someone is shooting in the building,'" a dispatcher told fire and medical personnel, according to 911 tapes. "Sandy Hook Shooting: What Happened?" CNN, December 14, 2012. (*Recording of fire and law enforcement radio dispatch [below] indicates CNN's 9:30AM time and account of events is incorrect.*)

9:30AM [estimate]

Attorney Joel T. Faxon of Newtown, who serves on the town's five-member police commission and is a strong advocate of strengthened gun control measures, claims he is taking one of his three children to the local middle school. As he approaches the school's front doors, he receives a text message that all the town's schools are on lockdown. This precaution takes place on occasion because of the school's proximity to a state prison. "I told my son, 'Okay, something's going on. Let's get out of here.'" Returning to his vehicle, Faxon sees

the chief of police in his official car, headed to the Sandy Hook school, and I looked at my son and I said, "'Oh my God, there must have been a shooting." The chief doesn't respond to anything other than a very serious incident. Within a minute of that time, I got a news report text from the Hartford Courant, that said police were responding to incident on Dickenson Drive, and I thought, "There's only one thing on that street. And that's the school."

Faxon pulls over to the side of the road. "At that point, literally 50 state police and Newtown police cars went by us, and they all went to Sandy Hook Elementary School. I knew there had been some kind of a catastrophe there," Faxon recalls. Faxon texts Bridgeport police captain James Viadero, who he works on a the police commission with. "He was filling me in on what was happening, in real time." As the story took shape in the news only a single death was reported. Yet Faxon said the numbers the Viadero relayed "were just shocking." Faxon's other son goes to another elementary school and was at the the doctor's office for a checkup.

His daughter, a student at the high school, also in lockdown, was texting her father, "'Daddy, what's going on?' I knew she was safe." Faxon observes ambulances heading to the scene. "There were ambulances going down there [to the school], but there were no ambulances coming back to go to the hospital" with survivors, Faxon said. "Just like in 9/11, when the hospitals were all racing to be prepared for the wounded, who never arrived."

Thomas B. Scheffy, "Joel Faxon Has Been Part of the Gun Debate in His Hometown," *Connecticut Law Tribune*, December 21, 2013.

9:34AM [estimate]

Sandy Hook Elementary School reading consultant Becky Virgalla said she was in a meeting with Principal Dawn Hochsprung, school psychologist Mary Sherlach and other colleagues when the shooter broke into the building. When they heard the commotion Hochsprung, Sherlach and lead teacher Natalie Hammond proceeded into the hall "to check out the noise that we didn't know [were] gunshots at first," Virgalla told Reuters Television at a December 23 Newtown memorial. "The three of them were shot and they yelled back 'shooter, stay put.' And they saved my life and the life of four others who were at that meeting," Virgalla said. "Becky Virgalla, Newtown Shooting Survivor, Says Principal, Others Saved Her in Sandy Hook Rampage," Reuters/*Huffington Post*, December 23, 2012.

9:34AM [estimate]

Fourth grate teacher Ted Varga arrives for work at Sandy Hook. Moments later, according an the account Varga related to the New York Daily News, he and four colleagues narrowly escaped a hail of bullets. "You hear screams and gunshots, but it is still surreal," Varga said. "This is an elementary school. ... I heard someone say, 'Oh my God.' And then you hear shot after shot after shot." Undaunted, Varga ran down a hallway "filled with smoke and the smell of gunpowder," according to the press account, "to escape through an emergency exit and then returned to help three colleagues flee through a window.

An unidentified teacher hid underneath a mound of donated Christmas gifts for the needy, hoping the killer jiggling the door to the conference room would move on. "She heard heavy breathing," Varga says. "She knew it was him. ... It's a miracle we're alive, but it's still such a tragedy. You're exposed to a myriad of emotions that even now I can't really understand." Henrick Karoliszyn, "Five Teachers Escape Death as Massacre Rages in Newtown," *New York Daily News*, December 19, 2012.

9:35AM [Estimate]

In the Sandy Hook library three faculty members hear noises and move 15 or so students to a storage closet in the library filled with computer servers. "Hold hands. Be quiet," one teacher tells the children. One child questions "whether there are pots and pans were clanging. Another thought he heard firecrackers. Another worried an animal was coming to the door," the *Washington Post* reports. "They were children in a place built for children, and the teachers didn't know how to answer them ... 'It's a drill,' said a library clerk named Mary Anne Jacobs." Eli Saslow, "Sandy Hook Massacre: Teachers Sought to Soothe Children in Moments of Terror," *Washington Post*, December 15, 2012.

9:35:52AM

Recording of Newtown and Connecticut emergency fire and law enforcement radio dispatch indicates potential of active shooter situation at Sandy Hook Elementary School. "6-7. Sandy Hook School. Caller indicates she thinks there's someone shooting in the building." RadioMan911TV, "Sandy Hook Elementary School Shooting Newtown Police/Fire and CT State Police," Youtube, December 14, 2012.

9:36:20AM [estimate]

Newtown Bee Associate Editor Shannon Hicks is among the first on the scene at Sandy Hook Elementary. Hicks says she was at the *Bee*'s offices about one and one quarter miles from the school when she heard about a possible shooting on the police scanner. A volunteer firefighter, Hicks is "behind the first dozen police officers," according to John Voket, also associate editor at the weekly. This is because the Sandy Hook firehouse where Hicks is stationed shares a driveway with the school.

When Hicks proceeds down the driveway she begins frantically taking photos of the scene "through the windshield of her car, with one hand on the steering wheel and one holding her camera, Voket says. One well-knonw photo featured in news coverage may have been of the first cluster of evacuating students, Voket further notes. Julie Moos, "How the Newtown Bee is Covering Sandy Hook Elementary School Shooting," *Poynter.org*, December 15, 2012.

9:36:38AM

Newtown and Connecticut emergency fire and law enforcement radio dispatch suggests arrival of law enforcement at scene; "front glass has been broken [unintelligible]. They're unsure why." RadioMan911TV, "Sandy Hook Elementary School Shooting Newtown Police/Fire and CT State Police," Youtube, December 14, 2012.

9:37:15AM

Newtown and Connecticut emergency fire and law enforcement radio dispatch indicates continuance of gunfire at Sandy Hook school. "All units:

The individual that I have on the phone is continuing to hear what she believes to be gunfire." RadioMan911TV, "Sandy Hook Elementary School Shooting Newtown Police/Fire and CT State Police," Youtube, December 14, 2012.

9:37:40AM

Newtown and Connecticut emergency fire and law enforcement radio dispatch indicates law enforcement units and backup continual arrival at Sandy Hook Elementary. RadioMan911TV, "Sandy Hook Elementary School Shooting Newtown Police/Fire and CT State Police," Youtube, December 14, 2012.

9:38:15AM

Newtown and Connecticut emergency fire and law enforcement radio dispatch indicates "the shooting appears to have stopped. It is silent at this time. The school is in lockdown." RadioMan911TV, "Sandy Hook Elementary School Shooting Newtown Police/Fire and CT State Police," Youtube, December 14, 2012.

9:39:05AM

Newtown and Connecticut emergency fire and law enforcement radio dispatch indicates citing of shooter suspects fleeing crime scene. "Reports that a teacher saw two shadows running past the building–past the gym, which would be rear [inaudible] the shooting." RadioMan911TV, "Sandy Hook Elementary School Shooting Newtown Police/Fire and CT State Police," Youtube, December 14, 2012.

9:39:20AM

Newtown and Connecticut emergency fire and law enforcement radio dispatch indicates officers' encounter with and apprehension of additional shooter suspects fleeing scene. "Yeah, we got 'em. He's comin' at me down Crestwood Way! Coming [inaudible] up the left side." RadioMan911TV, "Sandy Hook Elementary School Shooting Newtown Police/Fire and CT State Police," Youtube, December 14, 2012.

9:40AM

Chris Manfredonia, alleged father of a 6-year-old Sandy Hook Elementary student, claims he is on his way to the school "to help make gingerbread houses with first-graders when he heard popping sounds and smelled sulfur." Manfredonia runs around the facility in attempt "to reach his daughter and was briefly handcuffed by police. He later found his child, who had been locked in a small room with a teacher. 'The whole reason we moved here a year ago is because when you drive down the subdivision, it's a happy place,' said his wife, Georgeann Manfredonia.

"'There's a ton of children here and the families are very kind and supportive.'" Richard A. Serrano, Allen Semuals, Tina Susman, "Gunman Kills 20, 6 Adults at Connecticut Elementary School," *Los Angeles Times*, December 14, 2012.

9:40AM [estimate]

First responders initially believe there may be two gunmen and are unaware of the carnage in the school until they find 18 children and a teacher in a classroom closet, a recording of the police dispatch authenticated by police indicates. Tracy Connor, "Call For Everything: Police Scanner Recording Reveals Early Moments of Newtown Tragedy," NBC News, December 19, 2012.

9:40:45AM

Newtown and Connecticut emergency fire and law enforcement radio dispatch indicates "one now in room one who [unintelligible] injury to the foot. [unintelligible] call for an ambulance [unintelligible]. RadioMan911TV, "Sandy Hook Elementary School Shooting Newtown Police/Fire and CT State Police," Youtube, December 14, 2012.

9:45:48AM

Newtown and Connecticut emergency fire and law enforcement radio dispatch indicates officers' discovery of "bodies here" and requests for ambulatory/ first responders' backup. RadioMan911TV, "Sandy Hook Elementary School Shooting Newtown Police/Fire and CT State Police," Youtube, December 14, 2012.

(9:50AM [see below])

CNN reports police and first responders arrive at Sandy Hook Elementary. Police did not discharge their weapons. The gunman took his own life with a handgun. "Sandy Hook Shooting: What Happened?" CNN, December 14, 2012. (*Recording of fire and law enforcement radio dispatch [above] suggests CNN's 9:50AM time and account of events is incorrect.*)

10:14AM

Hartford Courant publishes online Google map of Sandy Hook Elementary School. "Map of Sandy Hook Elementary School," *Hartford Courant*, December 14, 2012.

10:15AM [estimate]

Emergency medical technician Peter Houlahan and other EMTs are told their expertise is not needed inside the school or elsewhere on school grounds. "A person who experiences tragic events will inevitably look back and try to identify that last moment where there was still hope," Houlahan recalls, "that instant before all was lost and their life changed forever.

For the EMS teams staged in front of Sandy Hook Elementary School on Dec. 14, that moment came when the Newtown EMS captain ordered us to stand down, that there was no one left to help, no one left alive." Peter Houlahan, "Sandy Hook EMT and Former Whittier Resident Reflects on Massacre," *Daily News*, December 23, 2012.

[Late Morning]

In a December 14 *Newtown Bee* article unidentified school personnel are commended for their courage. Among them are school principal Dawn Hochsprung, who recounted to *Bee* Editor John Voket[5] how "a masked man entered the school with a rifle and started shooting multiple shots – more than she could count – that went 'on and on.'" The problem with the account was that it conflicted with a subsequent storyline where Hochsprung was the first to be killed by the gunmen.

Original December 14 Newtown Bee *story with interview of deceased Sandy Hook Elementary Principal Dawn Hochsprung. Captured by Bing web spider on 12/13/12.*

From Bingj.com: "Below is a snapshot of the Web page as it appeared on 12/13/2012 (the last time our crawler visited it). This is the version of the page that was used for ranking your search results. The page may have changed since we last cached it. To see what might have changed (without the highlights), go to the current page."

Three days later the paper issued a retraction and revised the story further. No additional explanation was provided concerning what party Volkert interviewed and quoted at the crime scene, suggesting a conflicted attempt to establish the storyline.

10:30AM [Estimate]

"Two unidentified nuns" are photographed by journalist Don Emmert, apparently departing the crime scene at Sandy Hook Elementary. One of the individuals has what appears to be official identification around her/his neck. The photo is carried by the *Chicago Tribune* with the title, "Elementary School Shooting." "Elementary School Shooting," *Chicago Tribune*, December 14, 2012.

10:47AM

Connecticut State Police report assisting Newtown police in a shooting at Sandy Hook Elementary School in Newtown, Connecticut. "The Hartford Courant [<-hyperlink is to a different story] reports there are multiple injures [sic] and unconfirmed reports that one of the shooters is dead while the other is still at large. The school superintendent's office says the district has locked down schools to ensure the safety of students and staff. Crimeside Staff, "Connecticut School Shooting: Police Investigating Reports of a Shooting at Elementary School," *CBS News*, December 14, 2012.

10:47AM

[Famous photo taken by *Newtown Bee* editor Shannon Hicks is distributed via CBS and other national media.]

Connecticut School Shooting: Police Investigating Reports of a Shooting at Elementary School," *CBS News*, December 14, 2012, 1047AM EST.

11:11AM

Reuters' Deputy Social Media Editor Matthew Keys reports that police are questioning a handcuffed suspect in relation to the Sandy Hook School shooting. Matthew Keys Twitter Feed, December 14, 2012.

11:18AM

Reuters' Deputy Social Media Editor Matthew Keys reports that according to the Hartford Courant's Dave Altamari there are multiple victims in the school shooting, including children. Parents are now at the scene. Matthew Keys Twitter Feed, December 14, 2012.

11:15, 11:18AM

Reuters' Deputy Social Media Editor Matthew Keys notes WABC TV live aerial coverage shows "law enforcement at on roof of school at center of shooting."Matthew Keys Twitter Feed, December 14, 2012.

11:23AM

Reuters' Deputy Social Media Editor Matthew Keys reports police have told ABC News that two gunman are involved in the elementary school shooting. Matthew Keys Twitter Feed, December 14, 2012.

11:30AM

A Newtown Volunteer Ambulance Corps dispatcher says a Sandy Hook Elementary School teacher was taken to hospital after being shot in the foot. "There are reports of multiple injuries," CBS notes. The *Newton Bee* reports a student with apparently serious wounds was carried out of the facility by a police officer. The school superintendent's office says all schools in the district remain in lockdown. Crimesider Staff, "Connecticut School Shooting Update: One Gunman Dead, One Teacher Injured at Elementary School," *CBS News*, December 14, 2012.

11:34AM

Police say the shooter is dead and two weapons were recovered from him. "The source says one weapon recovered is a Glock and the other is a Sig Sauer." Children and Adults Gunned Down in School Massacre," *CNN*, December 14, 2012.

12:29PM

Hartford Courant mysteriously publishes online Googlemap of neighborhood where Nancy and Adam Lanza reside, which is 36 Yogananda St. "Map of 46 Yogananda St. Sandy Hook, CT," *Hartford Courant*, December 14, 2012.

12:27PM

Anonymous witness and parent of student says that while attending a meeting with faculty regarding her child she heard "at least 100 rounds" being fired when the shooting began about 9:30 to 9:35AM. "There was a 'pop pop pop' in the hall outside the room. Three people went out of the room into the hall where the sounds had come from. 'Only one person came back.'" The same witness says "she then called 911. She said she never saw the shooter but she later was escorted outside the room past two bodies lying in blood." "Children and Adults Gunned Down in School Massacre," *CNN*, December 14, 2012.

1:35PM

Peter Lanza drives up to his home to encounter *Stamford Advocate* reporter Maggie Gordon in his driveway. Lanza rolls his window down after stopping his blue Mini Cooper in his driveway. "Is there something I can do for you?" he asks. Gordon tells him she is a reporter for the *Stamford Advocate*, and explains that she was informed that someone at his address had been linked to the shootings in Newtown. "His expression twisted from patient, to surprise to horror," Gordon writes. "[I]t was obvious that this moment, shortly after 1:30 p.m. Friday, was the first time he had considered his family could have been involved. He quickly declined to comment, rolled up the window, parked in the right side of the two-car garage and closed the door." Maggie Gordon, "Reporter Broke News to Father of Suspect," *Stamford Advocate*, December 14, 2012.

1:57PM

An anonymous federal law enforcement source informs news media the death toll is closer to 30 than 20, with most of those killed being children. The source, who says he is in contact with authorities on the scene, says the suspected gunman had a connection to the school but would not elaborate. Children and Adults Gunned Down in School Massacre," *CNN*, December 14, 2012.

2:09PM

CNN is "told that 18 to 20 of the dead are children." Children and Adults Gunned Down in School Massacre," *CNN*, December 14, 2012.

2:11PM

An anonymous law enforcement official tells CNN that the suspect's name is Ryan Lanza and he is in his 20s. Children and Adults Gunned Down in School Massacre," *CNN*, December 14, 2012.

2:39PM

Anonymous federal law enforcement authorities say "the shooting happened quickly and happened in a concentrated area." Children and Adults Gunned Down in School Massacre," *CNN*, December 14, 2012.

2:52PM

Father of Sandy Hook Elementary School third grade student Stephen Delgiudice describes to CBS News what his daughter heard over the loudspeaker from the principal's office. This prompted the teacher to lock the classroom door. "We have a pretty good program in Newtown," Delgiudice says. "where basically a code red reverse 911 type of a call, and a, came through. [It said] there's a shooting at the school and naturally I obeyed the speed limit and drove immediately to the school. And ah, y'know it was just mass-mass chaos. I finally got to my daughter—a friend of mine led me to my daughter. I wanted to see her face and hold her, which I did, and once I did that there was a sense of relief, but, uhm, it was just chaos." Crimesider Staff, "Connecticut School Shooting: Father Says Student Heard Commotion Over Loudspeaker," *CBS News*, December 14, 2012.

3:05PM

Connecticut Governor Dannel Malloy explains to the nation that he and his administration had been advised in advance that an event of Sandy Hook's magnitude may soon take place in their state. "Earlier today a tragedy of unspeakable terms played itself out in this community. Lieutenant Governor and I have been spoken to in an attempt that we might be prepared for something like this playing itself out in our state." The remark may be in reference to "Project Longevity," a joint effort of the US Department of Justice and Connecticut announced on November 27 "to reduce gun violence in Connecticut's major cities ... To accomplish this, law enforcement, social service providers and community members are recruited, assembled and trained to engage in a sustained relationship with violent groups." "Connecticut Governor Dannel Malloy: 'You Can Never Be Prepared," ABC News, December 14, 2012.

3:16PM

President Obama addresses nation. "As a country, we have been through this too many times. Whether it's an elementary school in Newtown, or a shopping mall in Oregon, or a temple in Wisconsin, or a movie theater in Aurora, or a street corner in Chicago – these neighborhoods are our neighborhoods, and these children are our children. And we're going to have to come together and take meaningful action to prevent more tragedies like this, regardless of the politics." Children and Adults Gunned Down in School Massacre," *CNN*, December 14, 2012.

3:45PM

There were a total of 27 people dead at the school, Lt. Paul Vance of the Connecticut State Police tells assembled reporters. "Eighteen students were pronounced dead at the scene, and two others died at the hospital." In addition, six adults were pronounced dead at the scene. Children and Adults Gunned Down in School Massacre," *CNN*, December 14, 2012.

3:51PM

A federal law enforcement official informs CNN that "shooter arrived and headed directly toward and to his mother's classroom. That and the other information now emerging – another family member killed, police interviews – lead them to believe his mother was the primary target. But they note he also came armed with clear intention of mass killing." Children and Adults Gunned Down in School Massacre," *CNN*, December 14, 2012.

3:54PM

CNN now reports "three guns found at the scene ... the third weapon found on the scene was a .223 Bushmaster. The other weapons, previously reported, are a Glock, and a Sig-Sauer. No word on the models of Glock or Sig-Sauer." Children and Adults Gunned Down in School Massacre," *CNN*, December 14, 2012.

5:12PM

WUSA 9 News correspondent Andrea McCarren reports of her encounter with Sandy Hook Elementary School nurse's encounter with the gunman as he walked into her office. According to the nurse the two make eye contact before the gunman exited the office to begin his murderous rampage. "And as I walked down the streets of Newtown to get to this location not far from Sandy Hook Elementary," McCarren reports, "I happened to run across a woman who had tears in her eyes and she was being led by two younger women and I asked if she was OK. It turns out she was the school nurse at Sandy Hook Elementary and was for fifteen years. She describes the gunman coming into her office. They met eyes [sic]. She jumped under her desk, and he inexplicably just walked out." Andrea McCarren, "Aftermath of School Shooting," WUSA 9 News, December 14, 2012.

6:34PM

Witnesses attest to seeing bloodied children, hearing as many as 100 shots, and "loud booms." "It was horrendous," parent Brenda Lebinski said, who rushed to the school where her daughter is a third grade student. "Everyone was in hysterics – parents, students. There were kids coming out of the school bloodied. I don't know if they were shot, but they were bloodied." Lebinski said another parent in the school "during the shooting told her a 'masked man' entered the principal's office and may have shot the principal. Lebinski, who is friends with the mother who was at the school, said the principal was "'severely injured.'"

Lebinski's daughter's teacher "immediately locked the door to the classroom and put all the kids in the corner of the room." Nearby resident Melissa Murphy listened to events unfold on a police scanner. "'I kept hearing them call for the mass casualty kit and scream, "Send everybody! Send everybody!" Murphy said. 'It doesn't seem like it can be really happening. I feel like I'm in shock.'"

An unidentified girl interviewed by an NBC Connecticut affiliate says she heard seven loud "booms" while in gym class. "A police officer came in and told us to run outside and so we did." Dan Burns and Chris Kaufman, "Connecticut Gun Rampage: 28 Dead, Including 20 Children," Reuters, December 14, 2012.

6:34PM

Photo slide show of Sandy Hook massacre aftermath posted by Reuters includes shots taken by Reuters-commissioned photographer Michelle L. McLoughlin. This includes an especially famous photo by McLoughlin, "Young children wait outside Sandy Hook Elementary School after a shooting in Newtown, Connecticut, December 14, 2012." McLoughlin is located in New Haven, 49 minutes away from Newtown. Dan Burns and Chris Kaufman, "Connecticut Gun Rampage: 28 Dead, Including 20 Children: Slideshow," Reuters, December 14, 2012.

6:34PM

New York City Mayor Michael Bloomberg calls for greater gun control measures. "We need immediate action. We have heard all the rhetoric before. What we have not seen is leadership – not from the White House and not from Congress," Bloomberg said. "That must end today." Dan Burns and Chris Kaufman, "Connecticut Gun Rampage: 28 Dead, Including 20 Children," Reuters, December 14, 2012.

6:44PM

US officials representing three different lettered agencies separately identify the suspected shooter as Adam Lanza, in contrast to what investigators said earlier in the day. No explanation is given regarding what prompted confusion among investigators. Lanza's older brother, Ryan, was taken into custody for general questioning in Hoboken, New Jersey but was not labeled a suspect. "Children and Adults Gunned Down in School Massacre," *CNN*, December 14, 2012.

7:13PM

Fox News presents "newly released police dispatch audio" of exchange between 911 dispatcher and Newtown Police and Connecticut State Police encountering two shooting suspects on school grounds. "I have reports that the teacher saw two shadows running past the building, past the gym which would be rear [inaudible]." "Yeah, we got him. He's coming at me, down [inaudible]." "911 Call Dispatch Audio Reveals Police Response to Sandy Hook School Shooting," *Fox News*, December 14, 2012, http://www.youtube.com/watch?v=16AfZXH33eQ

8:00PM

CNN's *Anderson Cooper 360°* reports on the Sandy Hook tragedy using video footage from an apparently unrelated event. "At 0:06 in and at 1:02 into the following video on *CNN's* website," the alternative news outlet Intellhub observes, "[y]ou will notice the police running through a cross walk area that simply does not exist at Sandy Hook Elementary. Take note of the rounded curb area that leads into a grassy area of some sort with a tree present in the center of the grassy area. This area does not exist on Sandy Hook Elementary Schools property." CNN, "Tragedy Strikes at Sandy Hook Elementary School," *Anderson Cooper 360°*, December 14, 2012.

[Night]

Police recover long gun from automobile in Sandy Hook parking lot. "Police Find Long Gun in Trunk of Car in Sandy Hook Parking Lot, Newtown Connecticut,"*NBC News*, December 14, 2012.

[Night]

Unexpurgated NBC News video coverage of Connecticut State Police press conference reveals (at 2:32) forensics team recovering *two* long guns from vehicle Adam Lanza's allegedly drove to Sandy Hook Elementary

School. NBC News, "Connecticut School Massacre Briefing from Local Police," Youtube, December 14, 2012.

n.t./various

Sandy Hook students and staff relate their experiences of gunman Adam Lanza's rampage to journalists. The *New York Post* reports Lanza arrived on December 14th "with high-powered handguns shortly after 9:30AM." A student tells WCBS-TV, "I saw some of the bullets [sic] going down the hall, and then a teacher pulled me into her classroom." Newtown resident Brad Tefft says very young children sped past horrific bloodshed to safety. "My neighbor's daughter is in kindergarten at the school," Tefft tells *The Post*. "She was in the classroom when the shooter came in and shot the teacher. She ran out past a couple of bleeding bodies." The Post claims "roughly 100 shots rang out." "It was horrendous," parent Brenda Lebinski, whose daughter is in the third grade, says to NBC. "Everyone was in hysterics, parents, students. There were kids coming out of the school bloodied. I don't know if they were shot, but they were bloodied."

Lebinski informs *The Post* a classmate of her daughter, Sofia, could hear a man in the hallway yelling "f–k you" while her and her classmates huddled closely in a locked classroom. Someone gained control of the school's intercom system and Gunfire could be heard in the background of an announcement. "It really started when she heard gunshots and screams on the intercoms," a relative of a Sandy Hook student tells MSNBC.

A female student says she was in the gym when the attack began, telling WVIT-TV: "The gym teachers told us to go into the corner. I kept hearing these booming noises. We all started crying, so all the gym teachers told us to go into the office where no one could find us." Music teacher Maryrose Kristopik shelters 15 children by barricading the music classroom door as Lanza pounded on it in a fury. "The shooter kept banging on the door screaming, 'Let me in! Let me in!' But he didn't get in," a parent informs the *Daily Mail*. First-grade teacher Kaitlin Roig speaks to ABC, claiming she hid her 14 students in the class lavatory, placing some on the toilet so they all could fit, and moving a storage unit to block the door.

The 29-year-old Roig says she locked the door and told the kids, ages 6 and 7, "to be absolutely quiet. If they started crying, I would take their face and tell them, 'It's going to be OK,' " she said. "I wanted that to be the last thing they heard, not the gunfire in the hall." The sizable law enforcement response from law enforcement arrives on the scene in minutes and officers begin leading children out, holding hands. Officers tried to shield them from the tragedy by telling them to close their eyes.

A 9-year-old boy says to ABC News Radio that a cop entered his classroom asking: "Is he in here? Then he ran out and then our teacher, somebody, yelled, 'Get to a safe place.' So we went to the closet in the gym," the boy recalls. "The police were like knocking on the door and they're like, 'We're evacuating people, we're evacuating people,' so we ran out." Alexis Wasik, a third-grader at the school, claims she saw her former nursery school teacher taken out on a stretcher. "We had to walk with a partner,' the 8-year-old tells media. Natalie O'Neill, Mel Gray, and Todd Venezia, "A Scene of Blood, Horror, and Heroism at Tragic Sandy Hook School," *New York Post*, December 15, 2013.

n.t

CBS correspondent notes how police have a second shooting suspect in custody who they are interrogating. "Well, they have an individual in custody, who they're talking to. I am told they're looking into the person as possibly a second shooter. Now that changes the dynamics here a little bit which goes from—if in fact this turns out to be confirmed—it goes from a lone gunman scenario where somebody has this argument with society and wants to take revenge with the most defenseless people in society to a team of individuals who've gotten together and conspired to do something like this." "School Shooting: Possible Second Gunman in Custody," *CBS News Online*, December 14, 2012.

n.t.

The Associated Press interviews an unidentified Sandy Hook Elementary student who describes seeing a shooting suspect prone on the ground in the school's parking lot. Unidentified student: "And then the police like were knocking on the door, and they're like, 'We're evacuating people! We're evacuating people!' So we ran out. There's police about at every door. They're leading us, 'Down this way. Down this way. Quick! Quick! Come on!' Then we ran down to the firehouse. There's a man pinned down to the ground with handcuffs on. And we thought that was the victim [sic]. We really didn't get a good glance at him because there was a car blocking it. Plus we were running really quick." "Raw: Student Describes Scene at School Shooting," Associated Press, December 14, 2012.

n.t.

Newtown residents who knew the Lanzas and relatives speak to *Hartford Courant* reporters. Andrew Lapple was in homeroom with Lanza, describing the boy as a skinny, somewhat timid kid "who never really talked at all." "Lapple said he played Little League baseball with Lanza," the *Courant* reports, "and remembers he wasn't very good. Instead, Lanza was more of a 'tech-geek,' he said. 'He was always carrying around his laptop holding onto it real tight," Lapple said. 'He walked down the halls against the wall almost like he was afraid of people. He was definitely kind of strange but you'd never think he'd do something like this.'"

Another classmate recalled Lanza as being especially reserved. Kateleen Soy said she was in Lanza's seventh-grade class at St. Rose of Lima School in Newtown. She recalled Lanza entered the class after the school year was underway and departed before the spring term ended. "He was really shy, really painfully shy," Soy said."He was a little hard to talk to." Soy then recalled seeing him in the hallway when they were both students at Newtown High School. "I wanted people to know he wasn't always a monster," Soy said. "He became one, but he wasn't always that way." Former bus driver Marsha Moskowitz recalled the Lanza brothers. "You know the trouble kids, and you figure, 'Pfft, that one's going to be trouble.' But I never would have thought that about them," she said.

Moskowitz encountered Nancy Lanza a few weeks prior and "exchanged pleasantries," the report says. Adam Lanza's grandmother, Dorothy Hanson, 78, told The Associated Press she was too distraught to speak when reached by phone at her home in Brooksville, Fla. "I just don't know, and I can't make a comment right now," Hanson said in a shaky voice as she started to cry. She declined to comment further and hung up. Matthew Kauffman, "Gunman Kills 26 at Sandy Hook School in Newtown," *Hartford Courant*, December 14, 2012.

n.t.

Neighbors and friends of 52-year old Nancy Lanza interviewed by *Hartford Courant* staff say

> she was a kind woman with a sense of humor. Slender, with short hair, Lanza was a fixture at neighborhood events such as the Labor Day parade, and had a special interest in Christmas lights." Lanza's friend and neighbor Rhonda Cullens fought back tears Friday afternoon in the doorway of her home on Founders Lane, just around the corner from the Lanza residence. She said she met Nancy Lanza playing bunco, a popular dice game, with a group of women in the neighborhood, but she hadn't seen her for years since she stopped playing with the group. "She was just a sweet, caring person," Cullens said.

Matthew Kauffman, "Gunman Kills 26 at Sandy Hook School in Newtown,"*Hartford Courant*, December 14, 2012.

n.t.

Larry Barton, a professor at The American College in Pennsylvania who has researched violence in workplaces, public spaces and schools for 30 years says the Sandy Hook massacre may be the largest elementary school shooting in world history. This is because most incidents of this nature involve high school or college students. "This is among the most diabolical crimes, to kill kindergarten-age children," Barton said. "It's very rare." Matthew Kauffman, "Gunman Kills 26 at Sandy Hook School in Newtown," *Hartford Courant*, December 14, 2012.

December 15
6:01AM

New York City CBS affiliate reports 2 handguns found inside Sandy Hook Elementary School "near Lanza's body" and "a rifle in the car in the parking lot. It's not known how many rounds he fired," the reporter notes, "but both guns are capable of carrying high capacity extended clips which can hold up to thirty rounds." An eight year old boy, Bear Nikitchyuk, says he was attempting to deliver attendance reports to the principal's office when he "saw some of the bullets going past the hall that I was right next to, and then a teacher pulled me in to her classroom."

Another child says his teacher told the class a wild animal was in the building. "We had to lock our doors so the animal couldn't get in," the boy says. Newtown resident Janice Markey claims that at sunset she was searching "for her friend's missing child and relayed the awful news. 'They just told us that everybody that's missing–that's presumed missing–is in the school and are dead [sic]. The two that they transported to the hospital are now dead as well." Tony Aiello, "Elementary School Tragedy," cbsnewyork. com, December 15, 2012.

7:05AM

State Police Lt. J. Paul Vance on ABC's Good Morning America with George Stephanopoulos. Vance: This is something that's going to take a significant amount of time. From the onset we've had teams looking into the background of [Adam Lanza], peeling back the layers of the onion, so to speak. We have many, many questions that we need to ask—that we need to explore. Stephanopoulos: Three guns found on site? Vance: We haven't discussed that as of yet, but, uh, in excess of three guns. Stephanopoulos: More than three guns. And we know also that the guns match those of his mother may have had. Have you been able to put that together yet?" Vance: We're—we're—I don't have that information specifically– Stephanopoulos:

Do you know if they were obtained legally? Vance: Again, that's something we would also have to explore during the investigation. ABC News, "Tragedy at Sandy Hook Elementary School," *Good Morning America*, December 15, 2012.

8:00AM

Federal and state officials confirm to NBC News that there were four handguns recovered in Sandy Hook Elementary School. Previous reports indicated that two handguns were recovered. Officials also confirm that Adam Lanza left the AR15 military style rifle in his automobile. "They say now that there were actually *four* handguns inside the school," Pete Williams reports from Newtown, "not just two as we were initially told. Four handguns and apparently *only* handguns that were taken into the school. We knew that Adam Lanza, the man said to be the gunman here, also had an 'assault-style' AR-15 -style rifle that he had had taken to the school, it was in the car he drove there, his mother's car, but we have been told by several officials that he had left that in the car." Pete Williams, Today Show, NBC News, December 15, 2012. Kyle Becker, "NBC Admitted: No 'Assault Rifle' Used in Newtown Shooting," *Independent Journal Review*, January 15, 2013.

8:40AM

Sandy Hook resident Gene Rosen comes forth with story that he encountered six first grade children from Sandy Hook Elementary in his front lawn while feeding his cats. "I thought they were practicing for a play or Cub Scouts, and I went and approached them and it became clear that they were so distressed," Rosen told CBS News. "And I took them into my house, and they were crying and talking, and I got them into my house, and they were crying and talking [sic], and I got them some stuffed animals." "Neighbor Found Terrified Children on Front Lawn after School Massacre," CBS New York, December 15, 2012.

2:38PM

Ridgefield state Rep. John Frey tells the *NewsTimes* that his sister, Tricia Gogliettino was driving to Sandy Hook Elementary School on the morning of December 15 to drop off a gingerbread house she and her first-grade child had completed as a school project. According to Frey, Gogliettino was on Riverside Road about one mile from the school when she claims to encounter five young children running up the road. Gogliettino stops her car to inquire what is wrong. The children reply, "Someone is trying to kill us. We were told to run."

Gogliettino put the children in her car and attempted to contact the school but got no answer. She then calls Newtown police, who requested she bring the children to the police station. Gogliettino remarks that while at the station she was allowed to sing to the five children while calling their parents. She then receives a text that her own three children who attend Sandy Hook Elementary are safe, Frey said. "Someone Is Trying to Kill Us," *Newstimes. com*, December 15, 2012.

3:45PM

MSNBC: "Connecticut Chief Medical Examiner H. Wayne Carver provides an update to the media after he and his team examined the victims' bodies at Sandy Hook Elementary School in Newtown following Friday's shootings." In this exchange Carver and State Police drastically change the story on what weapons were used in the shooting, contending that the Bushmaster 223 was the sole weapon Lanza wielded.

Carver exhibits an amazing degree of deferral to law enforcement and overall lack of knowledge about the postmortem operation he has just presided over. For example, a reporter asks, "Were [the students] sitting at their desks or were they running away when this happened?" Carver responds, "I'll let the guys who—the scene guys talk—address that issue. I, uh, obviously I was at the scene. Obviously I'm very experienced in that. But there are people who are, uh, the number one professionals in that. I'll let them—let that [voice trails off]."

Shortly thereafter another reporter asks, "How many boys and how many girls [were killed]?" Carver shakes his head slowly, "I don't know." "Medical Examiner: Rifle Primary Weapon Used in Shootings," *MSNBC,* December 15, 2012.

4:32PM

List of Sandy Hook Elementary victims is released. "Police Release Names of Newtown School Shooting Victims," *Hartford Courant*, December 15, 2012.

5:22PM

Robbie Parker, father of slain Sandy Hook first-grader Emilie Parker, makes emotional public statement televised on CNN's *Situation Room with Wolf Blitzer.* "I can't imagine how hard this experience must be for you, and I want you to know that our family and our love and our support goes out to you as well," CNN recounts Parker saying, as it chronicles its news event.

"Fighting back tears with his voice cracking," CNN reports, "Parker asked Saturday night that the tragedy 'not turn into something that defines us, but something that inspires us to be better, to be more compassionate and more humble people.'" Chelsea Carter, "Shooting Victim's Dad: 'The World is a better place because she's been in it,'" CNN, December 17, 2012.

8:55PM

Federal authorities confirm there is no record of Adam Lanza using local Newtown shooting range. Michael Isikoff and Hannah Rappleye, "Mom of Suspected Shooter-First to Die—Was Avid Gun Enthusiast, Friend Says," *NBC News*, December 15, 2012.

8:55PM

Federal officials claim Lanza took three weapons to Sandy Hook Elementary, a Glock and Sig Sauer, and a Bushmaster .223-caliber semiautomatic assault-style rifle. Authorities remain unclear on whether all guns were used in the attack. Michael Isikoff and Hannah Rappleye, "Mom of Suspected Shooter-First to Die—Was Avid Gun Enthusiast, Friend Says," *NBC News*, December 15, 2012.

9:15PM

"An official with knowledge of the investigation" informs the Associated Press that three weapons were found inside Sandy Hook Elementary on or near Adam Lanza's body—a Bushmaster .223-caliber rifle, a Glock 10mm pistol, and a Sig Sauer 9mm pistol. "Three other guns have also been recovered, but it was not clear where they were found, the official told AP. They were a Henry repeating rifle, an Enfield rifle and a shotgun." Matt Appuzo and Pete Yost, "Connecticut Shooter Adam Lanza's Guns Were Registered to Mother Nancy Lanza: Official," Associated Press/*Huffington Post*, December 15, 2012.

11:31PM

Adam Lanza's aunt Marsha Lanza describes Nancy Lanza as "meticulous" and "self-reliant," pointing out that she kept three guns in the home "for self-defense." "She would never leave the guns out," Marsha Lanza asserts. Josh Kovner and Edmund H. Mahoney, "Adam Lanza: A 'Quiet, Odd' Loner Living on the Fringes,"*Hartford Courant*, December 15, 2012.

11:31PM

Law enforcement officials state the murder weapon was one of three guns owned by Nancy Lanza: a semiautomatic rifle or two semiautomatic pistols. Josh Kovner and Edmund H. Mahoney, "Adam Lanza: A 'Quiet, Odd' Loner Living on the Fringes," *Hartford Courant*, December 15, 2012.

11:31PM

Investigators believe Adam Lanza's behavior was consistent with Asperger's syndrome, a disorder within "the autism spectrum ... marked by difficulty with social interaction. Many with Asperger's are otherwise high-functioning people. There is no pre-disposition toward violence, experts said." Josh Kovner and Edmund H. Mahoney, "Adam Lanza: A 'Quiet, Odd' Loner Living on the Fringes,"*Hartford Courant*, December 15, 2012.

11:44PM

Law enforcement authorities provide press with detailed information on event which becomes bedrock "official" storyline that Adam Lanza murdered 20 children and 6 adults at Sandy Hook Elementary School. After shooting his mother twice in the head while she lie in bed Lanza proceeded to Sandy Hook Elementary where he "fired a half-dozen thunderous rounds from a semiautomatic rifle to open a hole big enough to step through in one of the school's glass doors." He entered the school and shot Principal Hochsprung and school psychologist Mary Scherlach who after hearing the "sounds of gunfire and shattering glass, bolted into a corridor from a conference room across the hall from the classrooms ...

The first classroom Lanza reached was teacher Kaitlin Roig's. Alarmed by the gunfire, Roig hid her students in a bathroom and closed her classroom door. Lanza passed by Roig's classroom in lieu of substitute teacher Lauren Rousseau's, shooting all 14 children who investigators believe were huddled and clutching one another in fear, in addition to Rousseau and a special education teacher who happened to be in the room. Lanza next arrived at teacher Victoria Soto's classroom, who is believed to have hidden her 6- and 7-year old students in a closet. When Lanza demanded to know where the children were, Soto tried to divert him to the other end of the school by saying that her students were in the auditorium.

As six of Soto's students attempted to flee Lanza shot them, Soto and another teacher in the room. Searching for survivors police found the remaining seven of Soto's students still hiding in the closet. They told the police what had happened. The two teacher's aides who were killed were Mary Anne Murphy and Rachel Davino. It was unclear which aide was in which room when they were killed. The first officer arriving at the school found Lanza's body near the door of Soto's classroom. The intense violence lasted about 10 minutes. Lanza fired at least three, 30-round magazines with deadly accuracy. Two of the people he shot survived. All of the victims were shot multiple times. 'I did seven (autopsies) myself with three to 11 wounds apiece,' Chief State Medical Examiner Dr. H. Wayne Carver III said Saturday. 'Only two were shot at close range. I believe everybody was hit (by bullets) more than once.'" Edward H. Mahoney and Dave Altimari, "A Methodical Massacre, Horror and Heroics,"*Hartford Courant*, December 15, 2012.

n.t.

ABC News interviews Sandy Hook Elementary student Ella Seaver who experienced the December 14 event.

Reporter: "What do you remember? What happened?"
Seaver: "We got to school, did everything we needed to and then we heard all this racket at, uhm, our classroom. And we were, like, all scared. Then we heard them say, 'Go in your cubbies.'"
Reporter: "Everybody went to their cubbies?"
Seaver: "Mm-hmm."Reporter: "Did you hear any more bad noises?"
Seaver: "Yes."
Reporter: "And while it was going on your teacher was reading you books and keeping you calm?"
Seaver: "Yeah."
Reporter: "You have a good teacher, don't you?"
Seaver: "Mm-hmm."
Reporter: "D'you love your teacher?"
Seaver: "Yes."
Reporter: "Did she–your teacher–seem nervous?"
Seaver: "No." [Shakes head.]
Reporter: "She just kept her calm and read you a story?"
Seaver: "Mm-hmm." Reporter: "Do you remember which one?"
Seaver: "Uhm, she read us The Nutcracker and another book that was about Christmas."

ABC News, "Connecticut Shooting Parents Seek Information About Loved Ones At Sandy Hook," December 15, 2012.

n.t.

Students at Sandy Hook describe the aftermath of the shooting to reporters. "[A]s reporters converged on the school," the *Hartford Courant* reports, "the children generally seemed more composed than their parents." While news of the incident circulated through Newtown students' parents are said to have filled streets as they converged on the school area. "Police evacuated the children to a nearby firehouse," the Courant reports, "and tearful parents were led into the same building. Most came out relieved, clutching and caressing their children. A few came out empty-handed and grief-stricken. "I saw policemen — lots of policemen in the hallway with guns," 9-year old fourth grader Vanessa Bajraliu, recalls. "'The police took us out of the school. We were told to hold each others' hands and to close our eyes. We opened our eyes when we were outside."

Bajraliu's brother, Mergim Bajraliu, 17, "a senior at Newtown High School, was at his nearby home when he heard shots, he said. He went to a neighbor's house. 'Then we heard sirens,'" he says. Barjraliu says he ran to the school and saw a young girl being carried out that looked badly injured. Bajraliu says another girl had blood on her face. Bajraliu claims he found his sister and whisked her away.

Richard Wilford said his son Richie, a second-grader, heard what he says sounded like "pans falling" when gunshots allegedly rang out. "He said that his son told him that his teacher went to check on the noise, then returned to the classroom, locked the door and told the students to stand in the corner. 'What does a parent think about coming to a school where there's a shooting?' Wilford said. 'It's the most terrifying moment of a parent's life. ... You have no idea.' Third Grader Alexis Wasik, 8, tells reporters police accounted for every occupant of the school before students were escorted to the nearby firehouse. "We had to walk with a partner," Wasik says.

One child departing from the school claims there is broken glass everywhere. A police officer ran into her classroom, she remembers, and told students to run outside and don't stop until they get to the firehouse. Parent Audra Barth, who was leaving the school with her first-grade son and third-grade daughter, tells how a teacher put first-graders into the restroom when bullets came through the window. A 9-year-old fourth-grader, Brendan Murray, says he was in his gym class when he heard "'lots of banging.›" Teachers then hustled students into a nearby closet where they remained for about 15 minutes before police officers appeared and directed them to leave the building. The boy says the students then ran down a hallway and police could be seen at every door. "'Lots of people were crying,›" he recalls. "Newtown Families Grieve As Medical Examiner Works to Identify Victims in Sandy Hook Shooting," *Hartford Courant*, December 15, 2012.

December 16
6:44AM

"We too are asking why. We have cooperated fully with law enforcement and will continue to do so. Like so many of you, we are saddened, but struggling to make sense of what has transpired."—Adam Lanza's father Peter Lanza said in a statement. Jonathan Dienst, "Conn. Shooting Suspect Adam Lanza's Father: 'We Too Are Asking Why,'" *NBC News*, December 16, 2012.

10:30AM

On CBS's *Face the Nation* Bob Orr remarked that at least two computers at the Lanza residence were "smashed to smithereens." CBS correspondent and former FBI agent John Miller noted "that subpoenas have been issued for all of the shooter's email accounts and his mother's accounts, including all of the 'sent' mail and 'received' mail over a long period of time.

Miller said that Lanza's mother, Nancy, had battled with the school system and eventually took her son out of the schools and home-schooled him." Christopher Keating, "Newtown Update: CBS Says Two Computers 'Smashed to Smithereens' In Lanza Home in Newtown; Subpoenas for All Emails of Mother and Shooter," Capitol Watch, *Courant*blogs, December 16, 2012, n.t. [Such programs are typically taped the preceding Friday afternoon.-JT]

12:12PM

Connecticut State Police Lt. Paul Vance states Adam Lanza possessed "an extraordinary amount of weaponry ... In addition to an assault-style rifle and at least two handguns, he also had a shotgun in reserve in the car he drove to the school."

Lance claims that when Lanza's body was found he "still had 'hundreds of rounds' of ammunition in multiple magazines, after having already fired hundreds of rounds inside the school." M. Alex Johnson, "Very Heavily Armed Gunman Shot Mother Multiple Times Before Killing 26 at Connecticut School, Police Say," *NBC News*, December 16, 2012.

12:12PM

Details emerge on Adam Lanza enrolling at Western Connecticut State University in 2008 at age 16. Lanza successfully completed six courses "including website production, data modeling, Philosophy 101 and ethical theory — and compiled a solid 3.26 grade-point average."

University officials claim Lanza presented no disciplinary concerns. M. Alex Johnson, "Very Heavily Armed Gunman Shot Mother Multiple Times Before Killing 26 at Connecticut School, Police Say," *NBC News*, December 16, 2012.

[Afternoon]

President Obama travels to Newtown to address grieving community and repeatedly allude to gun control legislation in an 18 minute speech. "We're not doing enough. And we will have to change. Since I've been president, this is the fourth time we have come together to comfort a grieving community torn apart by mass shootings, [the] fourth time we've hugged survivors, the fourth time we've consoled the families of victims ... Are we really prepared to say that we're powerless in the face of such carnage, that the politics are too hard? Are we prepared to say that such violence visited on our children year after year after year is somehow the price of our freedom?" Daniela Altimari, "We Must Change, President Tells Nation," *Hartford Courant*, December 16, 2012, 11:16PM EST.

4:52PM

Alex Israel was in the same class at Newtown High School with Adam Lanza, who lived a few houses down from her. "You could definitely tell he was a genius," Israel says. "He was really quiet, he kept to himself." Lanza's former bus driver regarded Lanza as "'a nice kid, very polite' like his brother." Another former classmate remarked that Lanza "was just a kid" — not a troublemaker, not antisocial, not suggesting in any way that he could erupt like this." Michael Martinez and David Ariosto, "Adam Lanza's Family: Mom Liked Parlor Games, Guns; Dad, a Tax Exec, Remarried," *CNN.com*, December 16, 2012.

8:06PM

Connecticut State Police Lieutenant J. Paul Vance tells the *Huffington Post* that Adam Lanza specifically used the Bushmaster .223 rifle to carry out all of the Sandy Hook murders. "Adam Lanza used a semiautomatic Bushmaster .223 rifle during his rampage through Sandy Hook Elementary School on Friday," the Huffington Post reports, "firing dozens of high-velocity rounds as he killed 20 children and six adults ... Lanza, 20, carried 'many high-capacity clips' for the lightweight military-style rifle, Lt. Paul Vance, a spokesman for the Connecticut State Police, told The Huffington Post in an email. Two handguns and a shotgun were also recovered at the scene. John Rudolf and Janet Ross, "School Shooter Adam Lanza Used Military-Style Bushmaster Rifle," *Huffington Post*, December 16, 2012.

8:06PM

Senator Dianne Feinstein announces that she intends to introduce legislation reauthorizing a federal assault weapons ban originally passed in the early 1990s during the Clinton administration that was allowed to lapse in 2004. John Rudolf and Janet Ross, "School Shooter Adam Lanza Used Military-Style Bushmaster Rifle," *Huffington Post*, December 16, 2012.

n.t.

Several dozen Newtown residents found "Newtown United," later named "Sandy Hook Promise." The group appears devoted to using the Sandy Hook Elementary massacre to campaign for gun control and raise awareness of the potentially negative effects of violent video games. Amazingly, less than one week after its inception a select number of founding members—including one 16-year-old who formerly attended Sandy Hook School–travel to Washington, D.C. to meet with federal legislators. Michael Dinan, "Newtown United: Grassroots Group Seeks to Curb Gun Violence," *Newtown Patch*, December 22, 2012.

n.t.

Health science and investigative writer Mike Adams observes that much like the Tucson Arizona, Aurora Colorado, and Wisconsin Sikh temple shootings, mass media are scrubbing their coverage and doctoring the storyline to obscure the fact that there were additional suspects and probable shooters at the crime scene. Mike Adams, "Newtown School Shooting Already Being Changed by the Media to Eliminate Eyewitness Reports of a Second Shooter," *Natural News*, December 16, 2012.

n.t.

As news of Newtown massacre spreads popular music stars and actors use social networking sites to state their opinions on the tragedy, with many attacking the National Rifle Association (NRA) and calling for gun laws to be revamped. "How many times do we have 2 (sic) hear 'gunman kills'. FK (f**k) The NRA!" Pop superstar Cher Tweets to her followers. "We cant cure gun violence completely, but we can bring it down to the LEAST Murders by GUN in a Civilized Country! I know people kill people, but HOW MANY FEWER CHILDREN WOULD THIS CRAZY MAN HAVE KILLED WITHOUT HIS THREE fkng (f**king) GUNNNNNNNNS (sic). He couldn't have done this kind of damage without 3 guns, multiple clips &tons of ammunition no matter how crazy he was." Actor Zach Braff writes,

"No one is saying you can't have your gun, crazy angry gun guy. But most of the country is tired of how easy it is to get a gun. Sane people, we mustn't let up on our politicians when this tragedy fades front the top story. This time lets not get silenced by the NRA." Singer Cyndi Lauper opines,

"Really so sad today in CT. Why does it have to be so easy to carry guns? Just so sad all the way around." Actress Sophia Bush writes, "We need to reform our laws AND our way of thinking. It shouldn't be easier to get a gun than to get mental health care." Actor Sean Astin Tweets, "The last minutes of this awful day pass… My anger about gun violence & failures regarding related mental illness challenges rages in my soul". "Cher and Cyndi Lauper Join in Calls for Tighter Gun Control," *Daily Express*, December 16, 2012.

n.t.

Rabbi Shaul Praver of Adath Israel in Newtown, Conn. accompanies a grieving Veronica Pozner, mother of slain six-year-old Sandy Hook victim Noah Pozner into the funeral home where her son rested. A sheet covers Noah's corpse up to his neck, and a social worker counsels Pozner not to remove it. Pozner grieves as Rabbi Praver consoles her. Praver tells the press he did not know Noah or his twin sister, Arielle, another Sandy Hook student present during the shooting, yet Praver bar mitzvahed the family's oldest son and taught the oldest daughter. "Remembering Noah Pozner, Newtown's Jewish Victim," *Chicago Jewish News*, December 21, 2013.

December 17
11:32AM

Connecticut State Police announce they have taken over all crimes scenes connected to the Sandy Hook Elementary School shooting for an indefinite time as their investigation proceeds. "[We have] seized the crime scenes under search warrant [and are] holding on to them indefinitely," Connecticut State Police spokesman Lt. J. Paul Vance told reporters at a morning press conference. David Lohr, "Sandy Hook Crime Scene: Police 'Indefinitely' Seize All Sites Connected to Shooting," *Huffington Post*, December 17, 2012.

12:51PM

Divorce records reveal the parents of Adam Lanza had joint custody of their son and that Lanza's father paid yearly alimony totaling $240,000 in 2010, $265,000 in 2011 and $289,800 in 2012. Nancy and Peter Lanza's divorce cited irreconcilable and was made final in September 2009. The divorce decree designated Adam Lanza's primary residence with his mother in the Yogananda Street address which Peter Lanza quitclaimed to Nancy. Peter was designated as solely responsible for the cost of college for Adam and brother Ryan and for buying Adam a car. Nancy Lanza seldom discussed domestic affairs with friends. She was otherwise regarded as very open and generous. Allaine Griffith, "After Divorce, Lanzas Had Joint Custody of Adam," *Hartford Courant*, December 17, 2012.

12:51PM

A spokeswoman for the Bureau of Alcohol, Tobacco, Firearms and Explosives is uncertain whether Nancy Lanza brought her son to the range or whether he ever fired a weapon there. Allaine Griffith, "After Divorce, Lanzas Had Joint Custody of Adam," *Hartford Courant*, December 17, 2012.

1:09PM

Sandy Hook Elementary nurse Sally Cox tells ABC of her encounter with gunman on the morning of December 14 as she crouched underneath her desk. "I could see him from the knees down, 20 feet away, his boots were facing my desk," Cox said in an interview on *Good Morning America*. "It was seconds… and then he turned and walked out and I heard the door close."

The 60-year-old staff member then heard "loud popping noises" outside the infirmary. Cox was joined by a school secretary and together they dialed 911 before hiding in a supply closet. Lauren Effron, "Sandy Hook School Nurse Hid From Shooter, 'His Boots Were Facing My Desk,'" *ABC News*, December 17, 2012.

1:15PM

Funerals for massacre victims begin in Newtown, with first being for 6 year old Sandy Hook first-grader Jack Pinto. "There are many ways to measure what was lost Friday morning at Sandy Hook," the *Washington Post* observes, "a school shooting that has spurred a national debate about public safety and a speech by the president. But no accounting of the damage was as searing as the one that began Monday, when parents stepped behind lecterns and spoke about the children they would miss." Eli Saslow and Steve Vogel, "Funerals for Newtown Massacre Victims Begin," *Washington Post*, December 17, 2012.

1:26PM

Two witnesses in Sandy Hook school shooting are unidentified adults. "There are two adults that were injured in the facility—in the school—and suffered gunshot wounds and are recovering," Connecticut State Police Lieutenant J. Paul Vance stated. "Our investigators will in fact speak with them when it's medically appropriate, and certainly they will shed a great deal of light on the facts and circumstances of this *tragic* investigation that we're undertaking." [Vance's emphasis] "Key Witnesses in Connecticut School Shooting are Survivors,"*Hartford Courant*, December 17, 2012.

4:00PM

A special broadcast of Dr. Mehmet Oz's syndicated television program is devoted to the Sandy Hook Elementary School massacre. Oz asks "Louie," a Sandy Hook 3rd grader, "what you remember from that day." "I remember that a lot–a lot of policemen were in the, uhm, school," Louie responds. "Uhm, well, a lot–I was like [pause] hiding under–when we were having a drill we were hiding under, like … " As Louie hesitates and takes several deep breaths, his mother nudges him while Oz taps the boy on the shoulder and changes the subject. "Take your time. There's no hurry. Let me ask you, What would you like to say to your teachers?" Semuj1,Hurry–D/L Dr. Oz Interview, Sandy Hook Third Grader Louis 'Having a Drill' – National TV," Youtube, February 4, 2013; See also The Dr. Oz Show, "Dr. Oz Visits Newtown," n.d.

6:39PM

New York City Mayor Michael Bloomberg unveils "Demand a Plan" campaign, sponsored by the Mayors Against Illegal Guns bipartisan coalition that requests Congress and President Obama move immediately on gun control measures. Bloomberg calls Washington's inability to act a "stain on our nation's commitment to protect our children." Carlo Delaverson, "NYC Mayor Launches Campaign Against Gun Violence," *NBC News*, December 17, 2012.

n.t.

Truckloads bearing more than 60,000 toys and stuffed animals begin arriving in Newtown, filling up the gymnasium at Edmond Town Hall in the center of the township. "When I realized that it was getting so large, I thought that we should get this to the children before the holidays," Newtown Social Services caseworker Ann Benore says. Benore organized the toy giveaway for all Newtown children and families. A special collection of toys are reserved for student survivors of Sandy Hook Elementary School massacre. Toys are first examined by a group of local police officers in the gym. "Children ooh and ahh as they enter," the report notes, "and are handed bags. They walk through and choose cuddly bears or games, or both." Volunteers on hand, some of whom have traveled from out of state to offer their services, instruct children on how to make Christmas ornaments. In one area, teacher Christina Morse Scala helps residents draw and create sculpture with recently donated art supplies. "It allows them to express without having to use words. It gives them an opportunity to reflect, bring them to a safe place," Scala observes. Diane Orson, "Toy Donations Pour Into Newtown," National Public Radio, December 24, 2012.

n.t.

ABC correspondent Katie Couric interviews Sandy Hook residents Rob and Barbara Sibley whose son Daniel was a Sandy Hook Elementary. Barbara Sibley claims to have arrived at the school after the assailant(s) forced his way in yet before shooting commenced.

When I got out of [my] car and started walking toward the building I noticed a car in the, uh, drop-off area in front of the entrance–like a black hatchback, had all the doors open and black sweatshirts strewn around it. And again I thought, "That's really odd. You don't usually see that, uhm, at the school." And then I walked to the doorway and there was another mom standing there. And all the while I'm thinking to myself, "The building is so quite, and why is it so quiet" [sic]. And, uh, I said to her, "Is something going on?" And she said, "I don't know, but look." And she pointed and I looked, and, uhm, next to the door where there's a buzzer–you have to buzz into the building–the whole plate glass window to the right of the door was shattered, and there's glass everywhere. And we looked at that and we said, "Well, this is really strange." And as soon as, uhm, those words kind of came out of our mouth [sic] uhm, we started hearing gunshots. I knew that it was gunfire but y'know I didn't–I just ran y'know? I just ran.

Barbara Sibley then explains how shortly thereafter she witnessed the orderly evacuation of students from the school, was reunited with her son, and was invited by him to walk down to the fire house. "One Family's Story of Survival,"CatieCouric.com, December 17, 2012.

n.t. [Date is estimated]

Facebook establishes a special liaison between itself and Newtown families and affiliated organizations seeking to memorialize the victims on its platform. According to the *Hartford Courant*, "shortly after" the December 14 shooting, the popular social media site "set up a special process for them where they have a direct line to someone at Facebook," Facebook spokeswoman Jodi Seth says. "That is unique for Newtown. Every piece of content that has been escalated to us through the families and foundations has been reviewed, every email has been responded to, and action is taken in line with our terms of service," Seth says. The Facebook representative further notes that Facebook is in daily contact with Tom Bittman, chairman of Sandy Hook Promise, a local group established as a response to the incident. Jenny Wilson, "Facebook Will Scrub Newtown Victims' Memorial Pages," *Hartford Courant*, February 25, 2013.

December 18
3:51PM

The parents of Sandy Hook Elementary substitute teacher Lauren Rousseau are informed they cannot view their daughter's body. "They told me, 'You can't see (the body),'" Rousseau's Canadian father Gilles Rousseau informed listeners of Radio-Canada, the French-language CBC. "Because most people he shot, it was two or three shots in the face, point-blank."

Mr. Rousseau further said the bullets used were powerful enough to tear through the school's walls and leave numerous holes in his daughter's car parked outside. Lise Millette, "Lauren Rousseau, Teacher killed in Newtown Shooting, Mourned by Canadian Family," *Canadian Press* via*Huffington Post*, December 18, 2012.

6:00PM

Infowars reporter Rob Dew utilizes overlooked excerpts from CBS and Associated Press coverage of the massacre to explain how there were additional shooter suspects apprehended by law enforcement on the morning of December 14 that have been left unaccounted for and since dropped from public view. Rob Dew, "Sandy Hook 2nd Shooter Coverup," *Infowars Nightly News*, December 18, 2012.

7:59PM

Teresa Rousseau, mother of slain Sandy Hook teacher Lauren Rousseau, states that her daughter's 2004 Honda Civic was "riddled with bullet holes" when law enforcement authorities removed it from the school's parking lot. Henrick Karolizyn and Larry McShane, "Mother of Substitute Teacher, Lauren Rousseau, Killed in Newtown Massacre Stunned: 'We Survive War, She Dies Teaching,'" *New York Daily News*. Also, excerpt of newscast, "Lauren Rousseau's Car is Riddled with Bullet Holes in Sandy Hook Parking Lot," n.t. or date.

December 19
10:11AM

Law enforcement authorities claim Adam Lanza was equipped with three weapons as he entered Sandy Hook Elementary School on December 14: a Bushmaster AR-15 rifle and two handguns — a Glock 10 mm and a Sig Sauer 9 mm. A shotgun was left in his car. Authorities say Lanza used one of the handguns to take his own life but have not disclosed whether it was the Glock or the Sig Sauer. "In fact," CNN observes, "many details remain unknown about the weapons Lanza used that day to kill 20 children, his own mother, six other adults and then himself." Steve Almasy, "Newtown Shooter's Guns: What We Know," CNN, December 19, 2012.

1:07PM

Connecticut Medical Examiner H. Wayne Carver II says he will work with a University of Connecticut geneticist to determine what prompted Adam Lanza to act. "I'm exploring with the department of genetics what might be possible, if anything is possible [sic]," Carver says. "Is there any identifiable disease associated with this behavior?" David Owens, "Obama Calls for New Proposals for Gun Control in Wake of Newtown Massacre," *Hartford Courant*, December 19, 2012.

11:16PM

Hundreds attend wake of Sandy Hook Principal Dawn Hochsprung, including U.S. Secretary of Education Arne Duncan, US Senator Richard Blumenthal and US Senator-elect Chris Murphy. Matthew Kauffman, "Communities Say Farewell to Four More Victims of Newtown Shootings," *Hartford Courant*, December 19, 2012.

December 20
1:42PM

US Attorney General Eric Holder makes unannounced visit to Newtown to meet with Sandy Hook first responders following a meeting in Washington with Vice President Joe Biden, presumably to discuss forthcoming gun control legislation. "Holder to Meet with First Responders in Newtown," Frederic J. Frommer, Associated Press/*Hartford Courant*, December 20, 2012.

n.t.

Fox News Radio reports that investigators speaking with the *Hartford Courant* say 20-year-old Adam Lanza's electronics may not offer much in terms of evidence or motive. They say his cellphone "had little-to-no phone calls or text messaging communications history on it. He also destroyed his computer in such a way as to prevent a forensic investigation of it." "Investigation Continues Into Newtown Shooting," Fox New Radio, December 20, 2012.

n.t.

Further analysis by alternative news media points to additional Sandy Hook shooting suspects overlooked by corporate media. Niall Bradley, "Sandy Hook Massacre: Official Story Spins Out of Control," *Veterans Today*, December 20, 2012; James F. Tracy, "The Newtown School Tragedy: More Than One Gunman?"*Global Research*, December 20, 2012

December 22
12:13PM

The fourth meeting of the new community group Newtown United is attended by US Senator Richard Blumenthal and Senator-elect Chris Murphy, presently a congressman representing Connecticut's 5th district that includes Newtown. Blumenthal and Murphy encourage Newtown United to develop its support network nationally and to fight for strengthening gun control measures. "I think this horrific tragedy has changed America in a way that it's ready to stop the spread of gun violence," Blumenthal says. "There has been a seismic change in public consciousness and the political landscape." Murphy similarly remarks, "We have to talk about the celebration of violence in this country." Newtown resident and energy consultant David Stout emphasizes that guns are not at issue as much as responsible use of them.

Some in attendance want the group to be more aggressive. "Now is the time to push," Jason Petrelli says. "We can't sit back. We can't get trapped in this room. It's time to push right now." Before departing Blumenthal congratulates Newtown United, saying: "Here you have been hit with the most horrific tragedy within recent memory except maybe 9/11, and its impact on the town could have been divisive and destructive, but instead it has brought people together in a way that has been incredibly impressive." The major point that both Blumenthal and Murphy continually emphasize is that Newtown United must find a way to capture and sustain interest in overhauling gun legislation in the face of one major enemy: time. "The other side is waiting for time to pass," Murphy reminds those in attendance, referring to the gun lobby. Michael Dinan, "Newtown United: Grassroots Group Seeks to Curb Gun Violence," *Newtown Patch*, December 22, 2012.

n.t.

Money, toys, food and other gifts continue to stream in to Newtown from around the world. Some parcels are delivered with decorations made by schoolchildren. The United Way of Western Connecticut reports the official fund for donations had $2.6 million as of Saturday, December 15. In addition, other private funds are set up. Former Sandy Hook student Ryan Kraft, who once babysat Lanza, sets up a fund with other alumni that has collects almost $150,000 and is designated for the Sandy Hook PTA. Area officials are uncertain what they will do with all of the funds collected. Pat Eaton-Robb, "Toys, Money, Food Pour In From Around the World as Connecticut Town Mourns Shooting Victims," Yahoo News/Associated Press, December 22, 2013.

December 23
11:01PM

Spiritual and psychological leaders in the Newtown community come forward to make public pronouncements and assist in the mourning process. "This will never leave you and should never leave you. Your tears are proof of your love. The trick is, you've got to find a new form for your love," observes Dr. John Woodall, a psychiatrist and Newtown resident. Woodall is founder of The Unity Project, an organization that has collaborated with the US State Department to assist in recoveries from tragedies including 9/11, Hurricane Katrina, the war in the former Yugoslavia and conflicts in Uganda involving child soldiers.

The Unity Project, according to Woodall's blog, "develops essential core skills for personal, community and organizational transformation in order to prepare young people for a well-rounded, happy and productive life as members of a global community."

Dr. Woodall says it's not possible to answer the question of why the Dec. 14 tragedy happened. "The only helpful question to ask is what next?" Woodall says. Jesse Washington, "After Newtown, Connecticut, School Shooting, Healers Say: Decide for Change, For Good," *Cleveland Plain Dealer*/Associated Press, December 23, 2012.

December 25
n.t.

Scarlett Lewis, mother of 6-year old Jessie McCord Lewis who was slain at Sandy Hook Elementary on December 14, returns to the grade school classroom where her son perished after a grief counselor told Lewis that "Native Americans consider the place where the dead are slain to be sacred ground,"

"I went because Jesse lived that. He was there. I wanted to honor him and be at the place where he lost his life. ... It was devastating, the destruction and damage. I've been going to that school for 12 years. The front doors and the side glass were completely blown out and gone and covered with plywood, but you knew what was under it. ... And then, the first two classrooms were completely gone. The windows were all

blown out. The only other family who had been there was Miss Soto's family. [Victoria Soto was Jesse's teacher]. ... So we took a piece of glass because there was glass scattered all over and we had a little ceremony. We said we're going to carry around a piece of glass and we're going to remember Jesse's bravery. Whenever we feel like we can't do something, we're going to think about our piece of glass and think about what Jesse did running into harm's way."

Tina Burgess, "How One Sandy Hook Mother Lives on After Her Son's Death,"*Examiner.com*, January 6, 2013.

December 26
n.t.

Connecticut State Attorney General Stephen Sedensky files court plea to postpone release of contents yielded through five search warrants. Sedensky argues that unsealing such findings might "seriously jeopardize" the investigation by divulging evidence heretofore known only to other "potential suspects." Pointing to "information in the search warrant affidavits that is not known to the general public," Sedensky also contends that opening the warrants would "identify persons cooperating with the investigation, thus possibly jeopardizing their personal safety and well-being." Ralph Lopez, "Sandy Hook DA Cites 'Potential Suspects,' Fears Witness Safety," *Digital Journal*, February 5, 2013.

7:20PM

Witness to shooting Becky Virgalla interviewed by Connecticut news media. [Video of interview at *Hartford Courant* website has since been taken down.] "Witness to the Sandy Hook Massacre," *Hartford Courant,* December 26, 2012. See Deborah Lutterbeck, "Witness to the Sandy Hook Massacre," Reuters, December 23, 2012.

December 27
2:00PM [est.]

The University of Connecticut men's basketball team visits Newtown to visit with kids, hang out, play some ball, etc. Head coach Kevin Ollie recently said that he wanted the team to be able to "do something for the kids." At the request of Newtown officials there is no media being permitted for the basketball team's visit. The team's enthusiasts anticipate the team will remark on the visit at a subsequent news conference. David Borges, "UConn Visiting Newtown This Afternoon," *New Haven Register*, December 27, 2012.

n.t.

The *Newtown Bee* reports a "reliable local law enforcement source" asserts the "man with a gun who was spotted in the woods near the school on the day of the incident was an off-duty tactical squad police officer." Adam Gorosko, "Police Union Seeks Funding for Trauma Treatment," December 27, 2012.

December 28

Attorney Irv Pinsky asks State of Connecticut Claims Commissioner J. Paul Vance Jr. for permission to file $100 million dollar lawsuit on behalf of unnamed 6-year-old Sandy Hook student for negligence and trauma suffered after hearing screaming, cursing, and gunfire over school's intercom system. As a result, the "child has sustained emotional and psychological trauma and injury, the nature and extent of which are yet to be determined," the proposed claim asserts. Pinsky's claim also alleges "that the state Board of Education, Department of Education and Education Commissioner had failed to take appropriate steps to protect children from 'foreseeable harm.'" Mary Ellen Godin, "Claim Seeks $100 Million for Child Survivor of Connecticut School Shooting," Reuters, December 28, 2012.

December 23-30

Adam Lanza's body reportedly turned over by Connecticut Medical Examiner to father Peter Lanza "sometime last week." "Father Claims Adam Lanza's Body,"*Hartford Courant*, December 31, 2012, 3:38PM.

December 29
n.t.

As part of their investigation Connecticut State Police will *not* recreate what took place in Sand Hook Elementary on December 14 or interview any of the surviving students. Instead, police consider recreating the Sandy Hook School massacre parking lot scene to determine if the bullets fired into the lot were strays the gunman fired in teacher Victoria Soto's first grade classroom, or if he was firing directly at arriving officers. Investigators have completed trajectory work in the classroom but wish to line up the police cars and see if some of the bullets were potentially aimed at them. No police cruisers were hit and no officers. The partial re-creation will in all probability be the last analysis state police conduct on school grounds before concluding that portion of the investigation. Dave Altimari, Jon Lender, and Edmund H. Mahoney, "Police to Re-Create Scene Outside Sandy Hook School," *Hartford Courant*, December 29, 2013.

December 31
3:12PM

Connecticut Attorney General says $100 million claim against state on behalf of 6 year old Sandy Hook student is "misguided," and maintains that "a public policy response by the U.S. Congress and the Connecticut state legislature would be 'more appropriate' than legal action." Edith Honan, "Connecticut Attorney General Says Newtown Legal Claim Misguided," Reuters/*Hartford Courant*, December 31, 2012.

2013

January 1
11:49AM

State Attorney General George Jepsen says lawsuit brought against state lacks a "valid basis." According to a report Jepsen said "the claims commissioner's office was not the appropriate venue for a discussion about the shooting." Amanda Falcone, Request to Sue State for Newtown Shooting Has No Basis, Attorney General Says," *Hartford Courant,* January 1, 2013.

2:42PM

The Washington Post reports that the Lanza family has retained a public relations firm to deal with the press. "When the *New York Post* reported as fact a comment on a fake Facebook page seeming to belong to Adam's older brother," the *Post*'s Bonnie Goldstein notes, "the Lanza family "spokesperson" Errol Cockfield refuted the story." Cockfield works for Edelman, purported to be the "world's largest PR firm." He previously worked as communications director for Eliot Spitzer when Spitzer was New York's governor. Until spring of 2013 Edelman was chief of staff for a New York state legislative leader. Bonnie Goldstein, "Massacre Message Management is New PR Task," *Washington Post*, January 1, 2013.

2:29PM

New Haven attorney Irving Pinsky withdraws claim on behalf of traumatized Sandy Hook student after receiving new evidence. "If the state were liable in this instance, where would the state's liability ever end?" State Attorney General George Jepsen said. Brian Dowling and Hilda Munoz, "Attorney Withdrawing Request to Sue State in Sandy Hook Shootings," *Hartford Courant*, January 1, 2013.

January 2
9:10PM

Jean Henry, a processing technician for the Connecticut Office of the Chief Medical Examiner is placed on a paid leave pending an investigation of an incident on December 16 where she permitted her husband, an unauthorized employee, to view the body of alleged mass killer Adam Lanza. Jon Lender and Dave Altimari, "State Worker Placed on Leave After Showing Husband Adam Lanza's Body," *Hartford Courant*, January 2, 2013.

January 3
[Morning]

Sandy Hook students return to classes 7 miles south of Newtown at Chalk Hill School in Monroe Connecticut. The school was closed about two years ago and recently cleaned and painted to accommodate students. Amanda Falcone, "Sandy Hook Students Back in Class," *Hartford Courant*, 5:18PM EST, January 3, 2013.

6:18PM

Connecticut State Attorney's Office and State Police refuse to give timeline for Sandy Hook shooting investigation. "It cannot be stated too often how invaluable and necessary the work of the United States Attorney's Office, the Federal Bureau of Investigation, the United States Marshals Service, the Bureau of Alcohol, Tobacco, Firearms and Explosives and other federal agencies was and is to this investigation," State Attorney General Stephen J. Sedensky III said. Christine Dempsey, "No Timeline for Newtown Shooting Probe," *Hartford Courant*, January 3, 2013.

Governor Dannel P. Malloy announces intensified gun control measures and mental health protocols and intervention through establishment of the Sandy Hook Advisory Commission. The "expert panel that will review current policy and make specific recommendations in the areas of public safety, with particular attention paid to school safety, mental health, and gun violence prevention." "We don't yet know the underlying cause behind this tragedy, and we probably never will," Malloy said. "But that can't be an excuse for inaction. I want the commission to have the ability to study every detail, so they can help craft meaningful legislative and policy changes." The committee's initial report is due to the Governor by March 15. Governor Daniel P. Malloy, "Gov. Malloy Creates Sandy Hook Advisory Commission to Address Key Areas in Violence Prevention" (press release), State of Connecticut Governor's Office, January 3, 2013, n.t.

New York City Mayor Michael Bloomberg meets privately in his office with former Arizona Congresswoman Gabrielle Giffords, who was almost fatally shot at a constituent meeting in Tucson in January 2011. The sit-down was not listed on Bloomberg's public schedule and a Bloomberg aide refused to state what was discussed. Holly Bailey, "Bloomberg Meets with Gabrielle Giffords on Gun Control," *Yahoo News*, January 3, 2013, n.t.

January 4
3:40AM

Former Arizona Congresswoman Gabrielle Giffords visits Newtown families who lost loved ones in the Sandy Hook shooting. John Christoffersen, "Wounded ex-Rep Giffords Meets with Conn. Families," Associated Press/ *Yahoo News*, January 5.

January 6
6:27PM

Police say Adam Lanza used a pair of earplugs during his alleged December 14 shooting spree. Investigators surmise Lanza may have developed the habit while frequenting gun ranges "or to muffle children's screams during his shooting rampage." "'It's just weird [that he popped in earplugs] given what he was about to go do,' a source said. 'It's not like he had to worry about long-term protection of his hearing because he had to know he wasn't coming back out of the building.'

Police say Lanza was wearing an olive green utility vest packed with 30-round magazines for the Bushmaster .223 rifle. Lanza left a 20 round capacity shotgun in the trunk of the car he drove to the school. Authorities say each gun was "registered to his mother, Nancy Lanza, and appear to have been bought legally between 2010 and 2012 … Police also found bullets outside the school in the parking lot, including some in at least three cars belonging to school personnel, including Rousseau's car." David Altimarti and Jon Lender, "Sandy Hook Shooter Adam Lanza Wore Earplugs," *Hartford Courant*, January 6, 2013.

January 7
6:45PM

Corporate media begins broad defense of official Sandy Hook narrative against widespread and varied skepticism in alternative media with prominent *South Florida Sun-Sentinel* article centering on Florida Atlantic University communications professor James Tracy. In a series of essays on his personal blog, Tracy questions conflicting and unusual information on the incident's coverage in mainstream media. Mike Clary, "FAU Prof Stirs Controversy by Disputing Newtown Massacre," *South Florida Sun Sentinel*, January 7, 2013.

n.t.

The Sandy Hook Shooting: Fully Exposed, a 30-minute video distributed via YouTube debuts and will garner 8.5 million views within the first week of its release. Max Read, "Behind the Sandy Hook Truther Conspiracy Video that Eight Million People Have Watched in One Week," *Gawker.com*, January 15, 2013.

January 9
3:49PM

Salon.com political reporter Alex Seitz-Wald begins series of articles profiling and critiquing Sandy Hook "truth movement." Alex Seitz-Wald "Meet the Sandy Hook Truthers," *Salon.com*, January 8, 2013.

January 11
8:00PM

CNN anchor Anderson Cooper launches blistering attack on Florida Atlantic University Professor James F. Tracy for "spinning conspiracy theories" and declining to appear on his cable news program, *Anderson Cooper 360 Degrees*. "His name is James Tracy. This is a picture of him," Cooper fumed a la Geraldo Rivera, as a photo of Tracy appeared on screen. "This is what he looks like. James Tracy is his name. Now, he claims the shooting did not happen as reported and may not have happened at all."

Earlier that day, CNN and Cooper sent their regional reporter John Zarrella to Tracy's place of employment, where he accosted the dean of his college to ascertain Tracy's location, eventually interviewing the university president. Zarrella and his crew then proceeded to Tracy's residence where they taped and aired video footage while telephoning for an on-camera interview. Tracy spoke to Zarrella via telephone and issued this statement, a portion of which was read on-air, informing Zarrella that his family preferred Tracy retreat from the limelight.

Throughout the segment Cooper appeared indignant that he and CNN's journalistic efforts in the wake of the December 14 tragedy would be questioned. "To suggest that reporters on the ground didn't work to find out what happened there on the ground is beyond crazy," Cooper opined.

"Everybody asked questions. That's what we do." According to Cooper, an invitation to appear on the program remains open. Anderson Cooper and John Zarrella, "KTH: Exposing Newtown Conspiracy Theory," *Anderson Cooper 360 Degrees*, January 11, 2013.

January 13
12:55PM

Newtown city officials convene community to float proposal of demolishing Sandy Hook Elementary School. "Newtown First Selectwoman E. Patricia Llodra said that in addition to the community meetings, the town is planning private gatherings with the victims' families to talk about the school's future. She said the aim is to finalize a plan by March." "Newtown Weighs Fate of Sandy Hook Elementary School Building," Associated Press/ *New York Post*, January 13, 2013.

n.t.

Attorney Alexis Haller, Noah Pozner's uncle, authors and submits a detailed memorandum to the Obama Administration's White House Task Force on Gun Violence on behalf of the Pozner family. " The eight-page document "proposes a range of [state, federal and local] legislative reforms to help prevent another targeted school shooting … The proposals … are based upon conversations within the family, consultations with school security experts, independent research related to prior school shootings, and discussion with legal professionals to focus on criminal law."

The statement urges linking gun control measures to mental health diagnoses, federal grants for school security system upgrades, and mandatory lockdown drills at public schools. Alexis Haller, "Memorandum from The Maternal Family of Noah Pozner to The White House Task Force on Gun Violence," January 13, 2013.

January 14
10:07AM

Probate records are filed for Nancy Lanza, the mother of Sandy Hook school shooter Adam Lanza. The estate's value is not reflected in the probate. No will is recorded. Ryan Lanza asks for an attorney to be appointed as temporary administrator in order to track assets and determine whether Nancy Lanza had a will. Dave Altimari, "Nancy Lanza's Probate Record Filed," *Hartford Courant*, January 14, 2013.

January 16
11:20AM

Anderson Cooper *AC360* producer Devna Shukla contacts Professor James Tracy via email and invites him on Cooper's program. "Our offer still stands to have you on AC360," Shukla's email reads. " We can send a truck to any location of your choice. We can pretape or have you on live at 8pET." "AC360's 180, "*memoryholeblog.com*, January 31, 2013.

3:17PM

James Tracy responds via email to *AC360* producer Devna Shukla, "Does this Friday at 8PM work?" Shukla does not respond. Tracy forwards the email to Shukla twice over the next forty eight hours. Apparently Cooper's "open invitation" for Tracy to appear on AC360 has been revoked. "AC360's 180," *memoryholeblog.com*, January 31, 2013.

January 18
n.t.

"To eliminate any confusion or misinformation" Connecticut State Police reiterate the weapons found at the Sandy Hook Elementary School crime scene. "#1. Bushmaster .223 caliber– model XM15-E2S rifle with high capacity 30 round magazine; #2. Glock 10 mm handgun; #3. Sig-Sauer P226 9mm handgun; #4. Izhmash Canta-12 12 gauge Shotgun (seized from car in parking lot)." Lt. J. Paul Vance, "Update: State Police Identify Weapons Used in Sandy Hook Investigation[sic]; Investigation Continues," State of Connecticut Department of Emergency Services and Public Protection, January 18, 2013.

January 24

The16-member Sandy Hook Advisory Commission established by Gov. Dannel P. Malloy to study the Newtown massacre and make recommendations for legislative and public policy changes begins work forty days after the event. Taking its lead from President Obama's January 16 Executive Orders ostensibly intended to "curb gun violence," the study group appears poised to link firearms ownership with "public safety" and mental health. "Gov. Malloy tells the commission that its tasks were both critically important and extremely difficult — to balance Second Amendment rights with public safety, to improve school safety, and even to help find ways to 'reduce the stigma of mental illness. I believe that responsible, law-abiding citizens of our state have a right to bear arms — but that right cannot come at the expense of public safety,' Malloy said. 'We need to develop a common sense way to regulate access to guns.'" Connecticut is presently among states with the strongest gun laws and law enforcement authorities maintain that Adam Lanza's mother legally obtained the weapons used in the massacre. Jon Lender, "Sandy Hook Commission Begins Work," *Hartford Courant*, January 24, 2013.

January 28

Parents of three children killed in the Dec. 14 Sandy Hook Elementary School massacre testify through the day and into the night on proposed tougher gun laws. They appeared before state legislators serving on the Bipartisan Task Force on Gun Violence Prevention and Children's Safety. An estimated 2,100 people attended the public hearing at the state Capitol complex. "Noah was our 6-year-old force of nature," Veronique Pozner said of her son who was slain in the shooting. "He lies forever motionless in the earth. He will never get to attend middle school or high school, kiss a girl, attend college, pick a career path, fall in love, marry, have children or travel the world. This is not about the right to bear arms," Pozner said. "It is about the right to bear weapons with the capacity of mass destruction. ... The time is now. Let the state of Connecticut become an agent for change. Assault weapons should be comprehensively banned. ... The equation is terrifyingly simple: Faster weapons equal more fatalities."

Although the parents shared their grief and a desire for a specific government intervention, they were divided between the two camps: gun owners and firearms industry representatives, and proponents of stronger gun restrictions. Mark Mattioli, father of James, another child killed, said new gun controls are not right response to the massacre. "I believe in simple [and] few gun laws," he said. "I think we have more than enough on the books. We should hold people individually accountable for their actions and we should enforce laws appropriately. And I would say we're not currently enforcing them appropriately." Jon Lender and Christopher Keating, "Parents of Massacre Victims United in Grief, Divided on Gun Control," *Hartford Courant*, January 28, 2013.

n.t.

The *New York Times* publishes an emotional piece featuring the accounts of several Newtown police officers who were first to arrive on the scene at Sandy Hook Elementary on the morning of December 14, claiming that the officers reached the school in three minutes. "The gunfire ended; it was so quiet they could hear the broken glass and bullet casings scraping under their boots," the story reads.

The smell of gunpowder filled the air. The officers turned down their radios; they did not want to give away their positions if there was still a gunman present. They found the two women first, their bodies lying on the lobby floor. Now they knew it was real. But nothing, no amount of training, could prepare them for what they found next, inside those two classrooms. "One look, and your life was absolutely changed," said Michael McGowan, one of the first police officers to arrive at Sandy Hook Elementary School on Dec. 14, as a gunman, in the space of minutes, killed 20 first graders and 6 adults. It is an account filled with ghastly moments and details, and a few faint instances of hope ...

The stories also reveal the deep stress that lingers for officers who, until Dec. 14, had focused their energies on maintaining order in a low-crime corner of suburbia. Some can barely sleep. Little things can set off tears: a television show, a child's laughter, even the piles of gifts the Police Department received from across the country.

According to the article, the officers proceeded "from room to room, urgently hunting for the killer before he could do more harm." This partially contradicts the official story that Lanza fatally shot himself in the head in teacher Victoria Soto's classroom "when authorities were closing in" [*Hartford Courant*, 3-13-13].

Ray Rivera, "Reliving Horror and Faint Hope at Massacre Site," *New York Times*, January 28, 2013.

January 30
n.t.

Witnesses of the December 14 massacre, including parents, educators and first responders, testify at Newtown High School before state legislators serving on the Bipartisan Task Force on Gun Violence Prevention and Children's Safety. Redding CT Police Chief Douglas Fuchs states: "By 9:45 that morning I found myself with two other Redding police officers and Redding EMF standing in the parking lot of Sandy Hook School." First reports of shots being fired at Sandy Hook was at 9:35AM.

The distance from the Redding Police Department to Sandy Hook Elementary is 11.9 miles and takes 26 minutes to travel at legal speed. Assuming Fuchs and his cohorts were traveling at twice the legal speed (120MPH) to the school it would take them 13 minutes to arrive at 9:45AM. This is assuming there were in fact calls for backup to surrounding communities. Mark Follman and Brett Brownell, "WATCH: Newtown Parents Speak Out," *Mother Jones*, February 8, 2013.

n.t.

Marshall K. Robinson, forensic scientist for the Bridgeport, Conn. Police Department condemned proposed assault weapon and high-capacity magazine bans and pointed out the small number of crimes committed by high-capacity weapons. Robinson makes his remarks at the Connecticut State Capitol before theGun Violence Prevention Working Group convened at the Connecticut State Capitol in response to the Sandy Hook Elementary School shooting. Robinson also spoke in opposition to statements from many of the other 1,300 speakers in attendance advocating for banning high-capacity AR-15 and AK-47 firearms.

The forensics expert pointed out that less than two percent of the firearms he has examined since 1996 that have been linked to violent crime in Bridgeport have been the caliber of AR-15 or AK-47 weapons. Patrick Howley, "Forensic Scientist at Newtown Hearing Slams Assault Weapons Ban," *Daily Caller*, February 4, 2013.

7:40PM

CBS News broadcasts interview of Nicole Hockley, mother of Sandy Hook shooting victim Dylan Hockley, who was also a neighbor of Nancy and Adam Lanza. "That house was kind of a black spot in the neighborhood," Hockley recalls.

No one spoke about them. I've never heard a neighbor speak of them. Perhaps if there was more engagement within a community with neighbors looking out for each other, supporting each other, then maybe they would have gotten help in a different sort of way. But to everyone on your street except for one house, and that happens to be a house with people that–or a person who does this–that's kind of hard to swallow. So there is some regret there.

Michelle Miller, "Lanza Home a 'Blackspot' in Neighborhood," CBS News, January 30, 2013.

February 18

Public Broadcasting Service begins a week-long series of programs on the Sandy Hook Tragedy intended to bolster the official version of events that Adam Lanza was the sole assailant in the school shooting, thereby prompting a national discussion on the relationship between mental health, school safety, and gun control. "In the wake of the Newtown tragedy," the taxpayer-supported entity announces, "PBS continues its coverage with a series of specials from PBS NewsHour, *FRONTLINE, Washington*

Week, *NOVA*, *Need to Know* and more, looking at gun laws, mental illness and school security." PBS.org/WNET, "After Newtown Special Programming," February 18, 2013.

February 19
n.t.

Lieutenant J. Paul Vance of the Connecticut State Police, the principal agency investigating the Newtown mass shooting doesn't think that alleged shooter Adam Lanza was attempting to mimic Norwegian killer Anders Breivik or other mass murderers. "It's someone's theory, but not ours," Vance told ABC News. "It's not anything official that we've garnered." Vance continued, "I can't substantiate that at all and, quite frankly, that did not come from us. It's nothing that came from us and we are the official agency investigating." Shushanna Walshie, "CT Police: Reports Lanza Emulating Other Shooters Unsubstantiated," ABC News, February 19, 2013..

n.t.

Newtown officials move to restrict public access to all death and burial records of Sandy Hook massacre victims. Town Clerk Debbie Aurelia and her staff vow to "do something about" requests for evidence of the tragedy, particularly from the press. Aurelia turns to State Representatives Dan Carter and Mitch Bolinsky and the leadership of the state association of town clerks to develop a bill prohibiting release of actual death and marriage certificates except by "legally entitled immediate family members or their representatives." Aurelia and her staff support such legislation with in-person or written testimony on February 20 at a hearing of the Public Health Committee at the Capital's Legislative Office Building.

In her solicitation Aurelia writes, "From the horrific tragedy in Newtown, awareness has come that we need to protect the personal information of all residents in our towns. Over the past seven weeks the media has repeatedly contacted my office requesting copies of all the death records. They want to know where the victims are buried and how they died. These records contain home addresses, who identified the deceased and their address, burial location and mother's maiden name." Aurelia expresses frustration at receiving requests for death certificates and other proprietary information from the *New York Post* , the *Connecticut Post* , the *Associated Press,*the *Hartford Courant,* and other news outlets. "Some are also requesting all my e-mail correspondence and text messages related to 12/14," she said. John Voket, "Town Clerk, Staff Supporting Access Restrictions to Vital Records," *Newtown Bee*, February 19, 2013.

February 21

A bill is introduced to the Connecticut State Legislature to restrict access to death certificates of decedents younger than 18 years of age by State Rep. Mitch Bolinsky, a freshman Republican lawmaker from Newtown. "I was shocked, dismayed and deeply disturbed when, on Dec. 17, I got a call from the town clerk about the prospect of having a reporter standing beside her during one of the greatest tragedies in the history of the United States in Newtown looking for death certificates of children." Bolinsky said. Christopher Keating and William Weir, "Lawmakers Seek to Restrict Access to Death Certificates," *Hartford Courant*, February 21, 2013.

Week of February 25

Newtown School Superintendent Janet Robinson steps down for position as superintendent in Stratford, Connecticut. School board chairwoman Debbie Leidlein disagreed with Robinson over various policy issues. In the summer of 2012, by a 4-3 vote, the panel declined to extend Robinson's three-year contract. This tension apparently subsided after the December 14 mass shooting because of Robinson's steadfast leadership in the wake of the tragedy. "Superintendent's Move to Stratford Best Resolution to Months of Acrimony [Editorial]" *Newstimes.com*, February 28, 2013.

February 27
1:56PM

Neil Heslin, the father of a boy murdered at Sandy Hook Elementary School is overcome with grief in front of a US Senate Judiciary Committee hearing on a proposed assault weapons ban. "Jesse was the love of my life. He was the only family I had left. It's hard for me to be here today to talk about my deceased son. I have to. I'm his voice," Heslin says. Heslin's son, Jesse Lewis, 6, was among the 20 children and six teachers and school administrators murdered at Sandy Hook Elementary in Newtown, Conn., last December.

Heslin tells of the last moments he spent with Jesse before dropping him off at school on December 14th. "It was 9:04 when I dropped Jesse off. Jesse gave me a hug and a kiss and at that time said goodbye and love you. He stopped and said, I loved mom too." Heslin and his wife are separated. Another witness at the hearing was Dr. William Begg, a physician present in the emergency room the day of the massacre. "People say that the overall number of assault weapon deaths is small, but you know what? Please don't tell that to the people of Tucson or Aurora or Columbine or Virginia Tech, and don't tell that to the people in Newtown," Begg said as his noticeable grief elicited a round of applause from hearing attendees. "Don't tell that to the people in Newtown. This is a tipping point. This is a tipping point and this is a public health issue. Please make the right decision." Arlette Saenz, "Newtown Parent Sobs at Senate Gun Hearing," ABC News, February 27, 2013.

March 4

In its March 4 issue *The New Yorker* magazine publishes a fawning profile of the *Newtown Bee*'s staff and the weekly newspaper's coverage of the Sandy Hook massacre. The article references "conspiracy theorist" Scott DeLarm's photographic essay, "An Inquisitive Couple's Visit to Newtown, Connecticut," published here and at GlobalResearch.ca in late January. "A man from Ottawa, who contributes to a Web [sic] site called Global Research," the piece reads,

> *showed up at the Bee office, and interrogated [Bee editor Curtiss] Clark about a sentence in an article that referred to a second suspect who was later released. Clark directed him to the police department. When the man continued to demand information, Clark said, 'I don't intend to discuss this any further,' turned his back, and shut the door to the newsroom, a rare occurrence at the Bee ... Clark tries to be gentle with "local crackpots," but he wasn't willing to extend the courtesy to people from out of town. He and John Voket hoped to find a psychologist who could explain to readers why people insisted that covert forces were at work in the massacre. Clark had a feeling that the conspiracy theorists were troubled by the same mystery as the journalists who lingered in town. There was almost no information about the months that led to the shooting. Lanza appeared to have no friends and had smashed his computer's hard drive, and in recent years his mother had invited few people inside their home. It was still a crime without a story. "They need some architecture to make sense of this randomness," Clark Said.*

Rachel Aviv, "Local Story: How a Local Newspaper Covers a National Tragedy,"*The New Yorker*, March 4, 2013.

March 5
n.t.

Sheila Matthews, co-founder of the national parents' rights organization AbleChild, and Newtown resident Patricia Sabato collect hundreds of signatures from Newtown area residents calling for the release of the complete autopsy/toxicology results and medical/psychiatric records of alleged shooter Sandy Hook School shooter Adam Lanza. The appeal to Newtown and Sandy Hook community members is enthusiastically received. The activists send the petition to lawmakers and hand-deliver a letter to the State's Medical Examiner, H. Wayne Carver II, M.D., requesting that Lanza's autopsy/ toxicology and medical/psychiatric history be made public. The petition is accompanied by two full pages of federal and state law supporting the release. Kelly Patricia O'Meara, "Was Connecticut Shooter, Adam Lanza, On Psychiatric Drugs? Medical Examiner Snubs Official Request for Toxicology Report," Citizens Commission on Human Rights, March 15, 2013.

n.t.

Major media outlets criticize what they deem undue secrecy surrouning the Sandy Hook School shooting investigation. Representatives of news media including the Associated Press assert such records as those obtained through search warrants of the Lanzas' house and cars should be unsealed, saying the public has the right to see such records. It is only necessary to withhold such records when an investigation might be compromised through disclosure. "There seems to be absolutely no reason that they would need to. It's not going to jeopardize the case in any way," says Linda Petersen, chairwoman of the Freedom of Information Committee of the Society of Professional Journalists.

Attorney William Fish, who represented news media in high-profile cases in Connecticut where evidence was sealed in Connecticut, also argues the sealing is likely unjustified as no prosecution is likely. He conceded, however, that "it's not a surprise to me that a court has in fact sealed the records just because it's so horrible." John Christoffersen, "Connecticut Massacre Records Secret, Media Seek Access," Associated Press / Yahoo News, March 5, 2013.

March 13
4:50AM

Filmmaker Michael Moore makes an appeal on his blog for the release of crime scene photos of the Sandy Hook shooting. Moore believes that the shock effect of such imagery will bring about the end of the National Rifle Association and cause a wave of support for bolstering nationwide gun control measures. "And when the American people see what bullets from an assault rifle fired at close range do to a little child's body," Moore argues, "that's the day the jig will be up for the NRA. It will be the day the debate on gun control will come to an end. There will be nothing left to argue over. It will just be over. And every sane American will demand action."

The famous director invokes photos of Emmett Till's corpse and the victims of My Lai to link Sandy Hook and pro-Second Amendment groups to racism, the civil rights struggle, and American imperialism. Dorrie Carolan, co-president of the Newtown Parent Connection, remarks that carrying through with Moore's idea would be a "horrendous offense" to families of the Sandy Hook victims. "Sandy Hook Families Rip Michael Moore's Call to Release Crime Scene Photos, "*FoxNews.com*, March 15, 2013.

n.t.

Before carrying out the Sandy Hook massacre Adam Lanza conducted research on numerous mass murders, sources close to investigation inform the *Hartford Courant* newspaper. The *Courant* earlier reported investigators finding news articles concerning Norwegian mass murderer Anders Behring Breivik at the Lanzas' Newtown home. Sources now say investigators recovered articles and related documents on other mass murders in one of two bedrooms he occupied in the house.

Dave Altamari, Edmund H. Mahoney, and Jon Lender, "But two sources said that law enforcement computer forensic specialists are continuing efforts to obtain information from the damaged hard drive. Investigators are also using all means to obtain information from Internet service providers and any other relevant entities to obtain records showing how Lanza used his computer, including what sites he visited, what research he conducted and with whom he corresponded. Dave Altamari, Edmund H. Mahoney and Jon Lender, Adam Lanza Researched Mass Murderers, Sources Say," *Hartford Courant*, March 13, 2013.

n.t.

Sources reveal that law enforcement computer forensic specialists are proceeding with efforts to recover information from Adam Lanza's damaged hard drive. Investigators are also pursuing all avenues to gain information from Internet service providers and other pertinent entities to find out Lanza used his computer, including the websites he visited, the research he conducted and who he communicated with online. Dave Altamari, Edmund H. Mahoney and Jon Lender, Adam Lanza Researched Mass Murderers, Sources Say," *Hartford Courant*, March 13, 2013.

March 14
n.t.

Thomson Reuters deputy social media editor Matthew Keys, who provided minute-by-minute account of the Sandy Hook shooting aftermath via his Twitter, is indicted for purportedly conspiring with hacking group "Anonymous" to break into *Tribune* website in December 2010 shortly after his termination from the company. Keys, 26, is being charged with three hacking-related counts and could up to 10 years in prison for the alleged incident. Victoria Kim, "Thomson Reuters Editor Matthew Keys Faces Hacking Charges," *Los Angeles Times*, March 14, 2013.

March 17
8:11PM

Unnamed law enforcement officials say to have uncovered a painstakingly thorough 7-foot-long, 4-foot-wide spreadsheet with names, body counts and weapons from previous mass murders at the Lanzas' Newtown residence. 'It sounded like a doctoral thesis, that was the quality of the research,' claims an experienced law enforcement officer who wants to remain anonymous. "He didn't snap that day, he wasn't one of those guys who was mad as hell and wasn't going to take it anymore," the source said. "He had been planning this thing forever. In the end, it was just a perfect storm: These guns, one of them an AR-15, in the hands of a violent, insane gamer. It was like porn to a rapist. They feed on it until they go out and say, enough of the video screen. Now I'm actually going to be a hunter." Mike Lupica, "Morbid Find Suggests Murder-Obsessed Gunman Adam Lanza Plotted Newtown Conn's Sandy Hook Massacre for Years," *New York Daily News*, March 17, 2013.

March 19
3:58PM

Newtown residents want to legally acquire firearms at twice the rate as usual in the three months following December 14, Newtown police say. Officials received 79 permit applications from the population of 27,000 in the three month period following the Dec. 14 massacre. "A good percentage of people are making it clear they think their rights are going to be taken away," Robert Berkins, records manager for Newtown police. In the past applicants have been hunters, target shooters and business owners. Now, however, police see a broader variety of applicants. John Christoffersen, "Newtown Gun Applications Jump After Sandy Hook Shooting," *Huffingtonpost.com*, March 19, 2013.

March 20

A 28-member task force assembled to decide the fate of Sandy Hook Elementary School will decide on the fate of the school structure within the span of several weeks. The task force "will review a set of options assembled by a team of construction specialists, engineers, architects and land use agents assembled by Newtown Land Use director George Benson." The committee intends to make a recommendation to the Board of Education by mid-May, a GE Capital report from Selectman Pat Llodra states.

In a prelude to the decision public task force meetings will take place "4 or 5 times" from early April to mid-May. "I received a great deal of information on guiding principles from many conversations with various constituent groups and recently asked several additional groups to provide their feedback on the guiding principles," said Llodra. "I reached out to parents of the victims, parents of the survivors, Sandy Hook School faculty and staff, and Sandy Hook School parents."

Following the December 14 shooting local leaders say they are engaging residents and specialists in an ongoing conversation about the questionable future of the building. In January leaders initiated a series of public town hall meetings to solicit opinions from the community. The same officials say they also met privately with Sandy Hook Elementary staff and family. Davis Dunavin, "Task Force to Talk Future of Sandy Hook School Building," *Newtown Patch*, March 20, 2013.

March 21

Alissa and Robbie Parker, parents of 6-year-old Emilie Parker who died in the December 14 massacre, tell *CBS This Morning* they met with Adam Lanza's father Peter Lanza for over, inquiring on his son's medical and mental health history, as well as other concerns. "I felt strongly that I needed to tell him something, and I needed to get that out of my system," Alissa Parker said. "I felt very motivated to do it and then I felt really good about it and prayed about it. And it was something that I needed to do."

Otherwise no information is presented on what was discussed or at what time the meeting took place. The Associated Press reports no answer at the Parkers' home phone on the morning of March 21. A message from AP for comment from Peter Lanza is given to a spokesman for the Lanza family. "Parents of Newtown Victim Met with Killer's Father," CBS/Associated Press, March 21, 2013.

March 23
12:31PM

President Barack Obama uses his weekly radio address to call on Congress to pass a ban on military-style assault weapons and restrictions on ammunition sales. "These ideas shouldn't be controversial – they're common sense. They're supported by a majority of the American people. And I urge the Senate and the House to give each of them a vote," the president declares. Obama has campaigned for a national program of stricter gun control measures since the December 14 Newtown massacre last year claiming the public wants strengthened laws to curb mass shootings.

Senate majority leader Harry Reid introduced firearms legislation earlier in the week that excluded the assault weapons ban, saying there were insufficient votes to pass such a bill. The National Rifle Association and its congressional Democratic and Republic allies oppose such measures. Paul Harris, "Obama Urges Assault Weapons Vote Despite Senate Decision to Drop Ban," *UK Guardian*, March 23, 2013.

March 24
n.t.

Since the December 14 massacre over 40 organizations raise about $15 million, $10.2 million of which is given to the United Way of Western Connecticut. The money is purportedly collected to assist victim's families, traumatized students and first responders, establish memorials and potentially help rebuild the school. The money collected is now given to a local foundation that announces it will be in charge of who receives money and what other concerns funds will be directed toward.

At the weekend a group of 50 parents and family members directly affected by tragedies at Aurora, Columbine, the World Trade Center or Virginia Tech publicly declare that following past events such charities failed to provide aid to the neediest, requesting that funds be sent directly to victims and victims' families. "From this point on, virtually every substantive decision is guaranteed to displease someone," says William Rodgers, Newtown's second selectman and a nonvoting director of the newly-formed Newtown-Sandy Hook Community Foundation. Peter Applebome, "Tragedies of the Past Offer a Guide as Newtown Aid Goes Unspent,"*New York Times*, March 24, 2013.

March 25
8:59AM

Newtown Bee Associate Editor Shannon Hicks responds to query from memoryholeblog on whether the multiple photographs she took at Sandy Hook Elementary as the shooting transpired have been shared with law enforcement or will at any time be made publicly available.

"The photos I took on 12/14 have not been shared with anyone," Hicks said in an email. "We have no plans to do so, either. I would appreciate it if you consider this our final contact," she continued. "I have enough work to do without getting involved in the kind of 'research' that continues to hurt those who live in Newtown." Shannon Hicks to James Tracy /*Memoryholeblog. com* [email in possession of author], March 25, 2013.

March 26
5:46PM

News media and Connecticut state political representatives anticipate release of crime scene evidence by the state attorney's office on March 28. Whether or not this new information will bring the General Assembly closer to voting on a package of gun control bills is still not clear. Chief State's Attorney Kevin Kane is anticipated to release portions of the Sandy Hook investigation on Thursday morning. Kane and Danbury State's Attorney say they have briefed lawmakers but will not take questions from the press. "There may or may not, his words not mine, be things within that information that would be helpful to us," observes Rep. Larry Cafero. Mark Davis, "Sandy Hook Details to be Released," News8 WTNH.com, March 26, 2013.

March 27
3:20PM

Fire destroys the Newtown house of a family whose children survived the Dec. 14 Sandy Hook Elementary School massacre, rendering them homeless. Friends organize to help the family of Hans and Audra Barth. Two of the three Barth children attended the school, the 7-year-old being in first-grade teacher Kaitlin Roig's classroom. Roig allegedly saved her 15 students by locking the classroom door and barricading them in a bathroom. "They lost everything," a friend helping to collect donations for the family says. "The house is going to have to come down, the fire department told them." The Barths' daughter is a third-grader Sandy Hook third-grader. Their youngest is 2. Fire Chief Bill Halstead said no one was home when firefighters responded to the blaze shortly after 3:20 p.m. The fire originated in the basement near a washing machine, yet a precise cause is not known, officials say. John Pirro, "Fire Destroys Home of Sandy Hook Survivors," *Stamford Advocate*, March 28, 2013.

4:54PM

Superior Court Judge John Blawie approves Danbury State Attorney Stephen Sedensky's request to redact for an additional 90 days details from search warrant applications related to the investigation of the December 14 massacre. With several motions Blawie removes the name of a "citizen witness" referenced in various parts of the search warrant applications for Nancy Lanza's house and car. A press report cites a lack of clarity on whether Sedensky is referring to more than one witness.

The State Attorney also asked for omission of serial numbers of several items retrieved by investigators from Lanza's 36 Yogananda Street home in

Newtown, in addition to phone numbers and credit card numbers related to the case. John Pirro and Libor Jany, "Judge Approves Redaction of Details in Lanza Search Warrants,"*Newtimes.com*, March 27. 2013.

n.t.

The National Day to Demand Action on Gun Control is to be marked by President Barack Obama holding an event in the White House East Room with mothers, victims of violence and law enforcement officials who support gun control. Over 140 events are scheduled in 29 states and are intended to target lawmakers on spring break.Vice President Joe Biden says on March 27 how an anticipated Senate April vote on background checks and more draconian penalties for gun trafficking are only the start of the White House's campaign. Limits on "military-style-assault weapons" and high-capacity magazines will not be a part of the Senate bill.

"That doesn't mean this is the end of the process. This is the beginning of the process," Biden remarks during a conference call organized by Mayors Against Illegal Guns with thousands of gun control advocates listening in. "The American people are way ahead of their political leaders," Biden contends. "And we, the president and I and the mayors, intend to stay current with the American people." Nedra Pickler, "Joe Biden: Gun Control Votes 'Only the Beginning,'"*Huffington Post*, March 27, 2013.

March 28
n.t.

In a speech at the White House President Barack Obama tells parents of gun victims that the US needs to be ashamed if the Newtown massacre had been forgotten. The speech is part of National Day to Demand Action, organized by the New York City mayor Michael Bloomberg's Mayors Against Illegal Guns campaign. Gun control activists complain that Obama failed to take advantage of the Newtown victims' deaths as an opportunity to speed such legislation through Congress.

Obama dismisses the criticism. "Less than 100 days ago that happened. And the entire country was shocked, and the entire country pledged we would do something and this time would be different. Shame on us if we have forgotten. I have not forgotten those kids. Shame on us if we have forgotten," the President says. Obama wants the Senate to vote on gun control measures upon its return from its Easter break on April 8. Ewen MacAskill, "Gun Control: Obama Invokes Memory of Newtown in Emotional Plea," *UK Guardian*, March 29, 2013.

10:33AM

Search warrants held under wraps for 114 days reveal that authorities found a large cache of guns, more than 1,000 rounds of ammunition, Samurai swords and knives in Sandy Hook Elementary School shooter Adam Lanza's home. The extensive list of weapons and related artifacts were recovered in a search of the residence on December 14. Still, areas of the warrants were blacked out, including the name of a witness who told police that Sandy Hook Elementary was Adam's "life." The following is a list of the astounding array of weapons and ephemera law enforcement authorities claim they recovered from the Lanza residence:

- A copy of Adam Lanza's Sandy Hook report card
- Two rifles, including the .22 rifle allegedly used to kill Nancy Lanza
- One BB gun
- Several thousand dollars worth of computer equipment and video gaming consoles
- A receipt to a gun range in Weatherford, Oklahoma
- One gun safe in Adam Lanza's bedroom
- Ammunition inventory that fills nearly two pages, including full boxes of shotgun shells with buckshot, hundreds of rounds .22 rifle ammo, and numerous boxes of handgun ammunition
- One instruction manual for the Bushmaster used in the shooting
- 12 knives
- Three Samurai swords
- One bayonet
- Eye protection, ear muffs for a gun range (unspecified number)
- One pair Simmons binoculars
- Paper targets (unspecified number)
- Adam Lanza's National Rifle Association membership certificate
- Unidentified medical records
- Printed email conversations (unspecified number)
- Books about living with Asperger syndrome (unspecified number)
- Three photographs of a dead person covered in plastic and blood
- One bank check to Adam Lanza from his mother for "the purchase of a C183 (firearm)" [A C183 is in fact a digitalcamera.-JT]
- One military-style uniform in Adam Lanza's bedroom

Families of the victims briefed March 27th about details of the search warrants expressed their hope for more stringent gun control measures "It was obvious his intention was to do a lot of damage and he was certainly capable of doing that…considering the amount of ammunition he had," says Mark Barden, father of slain first-grader Daniel Barden. "As a parent, I would think that [Nancy Lanza] probably could have made different choices with how she came to spend her time with her son. Fishing comes to mind," Bardan remarks. Barden says he hopes the release reminds the public of the grotesque and horrific nature of the tragedy. "When people forget about it they do nothing," Barden observes.

Commenting on the snapshot they've gotten into Lanza's life, Barden remembered his own son's kindness and said Daniel used to sit with the lonely kids in class. "I think if there were a Daniel Barden in Adam Lanza's class this may not have happened," he says.

Nicole Hockley, the mother of slain first-grader Dylan Hockley, was among family members who were briefed. "I haven't spent a great deal of time pouring through them," she notes. "Everything I learn about the investigation is painful because it reminds me of the pain of that day and that Dylan and the others aren't ever going to come back. I'm much more focused on the need for change," says Hockley. "The search warrants contents aren't as important." Dave Altimari, "Lanza Had Arsenal of Guns, Ammunition, Swords, Knives,"

Hartford Courant, March 28, 2013. See Reuters original story, Mary Ellen Clark, "Connecticut Gunman Had Large Weapons Cache," *New Hampshire Union Leader*, published at 10:33AM, March 28, 2013.

11:20AM

The National Rifle Association contests any association with Adam and Nancy Lanza. Itemized findings from search warrants posted online from search of Lanza home references a "Adam Lanza National Rifle Association Certificate" discovered in a blue and white duffel bag that also contained a "'Blazer' .22 cal long rifle (50 rounds)," as well as eye and ear protection, cartridges and "numerous paper targets." "There is no record of a member relationship between Newtown killer Adam Lanza, nor between Nancy Lanza, A. Lanza or N. Lanza with the National Rifle Association," the NRA responded "Reporting to the contrary is reckless, false and defamatory."

A review by Politico of the NRA's website indicates the organization offers many "education and training programs," in addition to "online templates for certificates. Organizations around the country also offer what they bill as NRA certificates upon completion of certain classes," Politico reports. "A spokeswoman for the NRA confirmed to POLITICO that it is possible to possess a certificate from the NRA without being a full-fledged member of the organization." Katie Glueck, "AdamLanza, Mom Had NRA Certificates,"*Politico.com*, March 28, 2013.

11:14PM

Iran, Syria and North Korea prevent adoption of the first international small arms treaty to regulate the $70 billion global market, arguing that it the agreement is flawed and fails to ban weapons sales to rebel groups. British UN Ambassador Mark Lyall Grant immediately sought to bypass the move by sending the draft treaty to Secretary-General Ban Ki-moon to put it to a hasty vote in the General Assembly.

UN diplomats say the 193-nation General Assembly can put the draft treaty to a vote as early as Tuesday. "A good, strong treaty has been blocked," Britain's chief delegate Joanne Adamson observes. "Most people in the world want regulation and those are the voices that need to be heard. This is success deferred," she says.

US delegation head Assistant Secretary of State Thomas Countryman tells reporters, "We look forward to this treaty being adopted very soon by the United Nations General Assembly," believing there will be a "substantial majority" in favor. Louis Charbonneau, "Iran, North Korea, Syria Block UN Arms Trade Treaty," Reuters, March 29, 2013.

March 30
6:31PM

Msgr. Robert Weiss of St. Rose's Catholic Church in Newtown has served eight funeral Masses for Sandy Hook Elementary victims. "This tragedy has brought more people to our church," Weiss says. "And where once a mom would bring her daughter to Sunday Mass while dad took his son to a ballgame, whole families come together now. There's an amazing unity. The mantra in town, with green and white signs — the school's colors — in store windows and bumper stickers is now, 'Newtown Chooses Love.' The common decency is overwhelming."

Weiss looks at a poster of the children and educators slain on Dec. 14 behind him and brushes away a tear, the Daily News reports. "Even a priest who dispatches eight children to their eternal reward sometimes needs a priest himself." Denis Hamil, "Newtown Reborn: A Season of Renewal for a Town in Pain," *New York Daily News*, March 30, 2013.

April 1
4:49PM

CBS News claims to have obtained college transcripts from Western Connecticut State University and a photo of Adam Lanza taken for his college identification card. "CBS News Obtains Adam Lanza's College Records," CBS News, April 1, 2013.

April 2
11:51AM

Mark Mattioli, whose six-year-old son was killed in the December shooting, lauds the National Rifle Association for a "comprehensive program" the organization proposed to confront gun violence in schools. "I wanted to take a minute and applaud ... the NRA for coming up and spending the time and resources on putting a program like this together," Mattioli says. "If you look what took place in Sandy Hook, mental health is a huge component of that. We need to focus research attention, research. We need the kids to be safe." Molly Reilly, "Mark Mattioli, Father of Sandy Hook Victim, Praises NRA School Safety Plan," *Huffington Post*, April 2, 2013.

2:02PM

Through a large majority the UN General Assembly adopts an agreement to control the conventional weapons trade. Member states vote 154 to three (Syria, Iran and North Korea), with 23 abstentions, to control the $64bn annual market. The US forced a vote on the proposal after the three upstart nations stood in the way. Russia and China abstain from the vote at UN headquarters in New York. Loud cheers are heard in the chamber as votes are counted. The treaty is the first legally binding international agreement regulating the conventional weapons trade. Yet it allegedly provides for states to recognise "the legitimate political, security, economic and commercial interests ... in the international trade in conventional arms" Amnesty International and the International Red Cross laud the agreement for its contribution to "humanitarian concerns." Ian Black, "UN General Assembly Passes First Global Arms Treaty," *UK Guardian*, April 2, 2013.

April 3
n.t.

President Barack Obama travels to Connecticut Monday to intensify pressure on Congress for passage of a wide-ranging package of gun control laws. Obama speaks at the University of Hartford with Sandy Hook

Elementary victims' invited to attend. This is the president's second trip in one week to Connecticut before traveling to Colorado shortly thereafter. Nendra Peckler, "Obama Plans to Promote Gun Control in Connecticut," Associated Press/Yahoo News, April 2, 2013.

April 4
n.t.

Governor Dannel P. Malloy signs into law far-reaching 139-page bill restricting firearms and ammunition magazines similar to the ones allegedly used by Adam Lanza at Sandy Hook Elementary. The law adds over 100 firearms to the state's assault weapons ban and establishes what lawmakers call "the nation's first dangerous weapon offender registry," in addition to eligibility rules for buying ammunition.

Accompanied by family members of Sandy Hook victims, Malloy signs the bill shortly after the General Assembly spent 13 hours deliberating legislation that will give the state some of the most stringent gun laws in the country next to California, Colorado and New York. "This is a profoundly emotional day for everyone in this room," Malloy announces. "We have come together in a way that few places in the nation have demonstrated the ability to do."

House Majority Leader Joe Aresimowicz: "I pray today's bill — the most far-reaching gun safety legislation in the country — will prevent other families from ever experiencing the dreadful loss that the 26 Sandy Hook families have felt." Susan Haigh, "Connecticut Governor Signs Sweeping Gun Limits Into Law," Associated Press/Yahoo News, April 4, 2013.

n.t.

Bureau of Alcohol, Tobacco, Firearms and Explosives revokes the federal firearms license of East Windsor, Connecticut gun store owner David LaGuercia. Mr. LaGuercia's shop allegedly sold guns used in the Newtown school massacre and another mass shooting in Connecticut. ATF spokeswoman Deb Seifert says she cannot be more specific on why LaGuercia's license, originally suspended December 20 and 60-days with opportunity to appeal, was permanently revoked. "It's been revoked," Seifert said. "It's final at this point."

The ATF will not say whether there is any criminal investigation into Riverview Gun Sales. ATF agents raided the outlet in December, just days after the Dec. 14 massacre. Lee Higgins, "Newtown Massacre: Gun Dealer's License Yanked," April 4, 2013.

April 7
4:00PM

Members from seven families of Sandy Hook Elementary victims representing "Sandy Hook Promise" appear on national television to offer remembrances of their loved ones and discuss avenging their deaths through the pursuit of more rigorous gun control legislation. Connecticut legislators "have passed almost everything we were hoping they would," David Wheeler, father of 6-year-old Ben Wheeler says. "And they have done it in a bipartisan way which is a great message to send out to the other states and to the federal government as they begin this process." Scott Pelley, "Newtown Families on Gun Control," CBS News, April 7, 2013.

April 8

President Obama appears before supportive audience of 3,100 at University of Hartford in Connecticut to invoke memory of Sandy Hook School massacre victims and promote gun-control. "If you're an American who wants to do something to prevent more families from knowing the immeasurable anguish that these families here have known, then we have to act," Obama intones. "Now's the time to get engaged. Now's the time to get involved. Now's the time to push back on fear and frustration and misinformation. Now's the time for everybody to make their voices heard, from every statehouse to the corridors of Congress." Republican Senator Mitch McConnell of Kentucky says that he will unite with at least 13 other Republicans opposed to the gun control legislation recently passed by the Senate Judiciary Committee. Peter Applebome and Jonathan Weisman, "Invoking Newtown Dead, Obama Presses Gun Laws," *New York Times*, April 9, 2013.

n.t.

A literary agent for *New York Daily News* reporter Matt Lysiak proffers a book proposal by the reporter on the Sandy Hook School massacre. Lysiak aided in breaking a story that collected alleged emails written by Adam Lanza's motherprior to Lanza's shooting spree. "Far from being the random act of insanity most have portrayed," the book's synopsis reads, "the shooting that shocked our nation was a meticulously well-thought out premeditated attack years in the making by a violent video-gamer so obsessed with 'kills' that he was willing to go to any length to achieve the top score …

Drawing on hundreds of interviews, thousands of pages of police files, psychologists, and going over a decade's worth of emails from his mother to close friends that chronicled Lanza's slow slide into mental illness, this book will be the first comprehensive account of the tragedy." Jason Boog, "Daily News Reporter Shopping Book About Newtown Tragedy," *New York Daily News*, April 8, 2013.

April 11

The Department of Alcohol, Tobacco and Firearms releases records indicating that Nancy Lanza purchased the Bushmaster XM15 rifle on March 29, 2010, and SIG Sauer 9 mm pistol on March 16, 2011, indicating on the federally-mandated ATF paperwork that she was buying the guns for herself. Lee Higgins, "ATF Records Show Nancy Lanza Gun Purchases," April 11, 2013.

April 12
n.t.

The *New York Times* reports broad bipartisan Congressional support for legislation linking increased funding of mental health care measures with emerging gun control legislation.

The US Senate proposes financing the establishment of more community mental health centers, grants that will go to training teachers to detect early signals of mental illness and direct more Medicaid dollars for mental health care. In addition, resources will go toward suicide prevention initiatives and mental health counseling for children who have experienced trauma. The proponents of one bill say an additional 1.5 million people with mental illness would be brought into the system each year.

Supporters of such measures argue increased mental health care will preclude more killers like Adam Lanza from going undetected. "This is a place where people can come together," Michigan Democratic Senator Debbie Stabenow says. "As we've listened to people on all sides of the gun debate, they've all talked about the fact that we need to address mental health treatment. And that's what this does."

Republican Senator John Cornyn of Texas agrees. "This is actually something we can and should do something about. We need to make sure that the mentally ill are getting the help they need." "This is our moment," says Linda Rosenberg, president of the National Council for Community Behavioral Healthcare. "I hate the connection between gun violence and the need for better mental health care, but sometimes you have to take what you can get." Jeremy W. Peters, "In Gun Debate, No Rift on Better Care for Mentally Ill," *New York Times*, April 13, 2013.

April 15
2:50PM

Two makeshift explosive devices detonate at the finish line of the famed Boston Marathon. The 2013 run is designed in honor of the 26 Sandy Hook Elementary School victims with its 26 mile course. It is also attended by several parents from Newtown participating in the event. Yet the six Sandy Hook families present are caught in a milieu of emergency vehicles and carnage. "It was all those same things, the police and fire and all of that. It's severely traumatic," says Lauren Nowacki, one of the Newtown parents in town for the April 15 marathon. "We thought things were finally getting to a good place from the first go-around, and now this."

Nowacki's daughter was at Sandy Hook Elementary on December 14 but was not injured. Nowacki says all of the Newtown marathoners completed the run before the bombs detonated that purportedly injure 170 people and kill three. "Boston really reached out to us," Nowacki notes. "Even after the bombing, the communications director from the race called to make sure all the kids were all right." The Newtown group will now attempt to reciprocate by honoring the victims of the Boston bombings with their own annual race, the Sandy Hook 5k Run. Colleen Curry, "Sandy Hook Families at Boston Marathon Traumatized Again," ABC News, April 16, 2013.

April 16
n.t.

Connecticut Attorney General George Jepsen and Consumer Protection Commissioner William M. Rubenstein release information they have collected on dozens of charities established to collect funds as a result of the Sandy Hook Elementary School massacre. The 43 charities reporting have collected close to $20.4 million and distributed nearly $2.9 million. Charitable purposes include: providing direct financial support or other assistance to the 26 families; creating scholarships and one endowment for Newtown children and youth; memorial trees; a physical memorial; and "to recognize, support and inspire acts of kindness."

The information was collected following issuance of a voluntary request for information by the Attorney General and Commissioner sent March 28 to 69 charities either registered with the state Department of Consumer Protection, or publically identified as receiving donations related to Sandy Hook Elementary. An April 12 response was suggested. "This request was an initial step to provide information to the public, Newtown community and other charitable organizations trying to meet the needs of those affected by this tragedy," Attorney General George Jepsen says. "My office will be following up with the charities that did not respond." State of Connecticut Department of Consumer Protection and Office of the Attorney General, "Attorney General, Consumer Protection Post Information Received From Sandy Hook-Related Charities," State of Connecticut, April 16, 2013.

April 17
n.t.

In a major defeat for the Obama administration the US Senate votes against several proposed laws that would have greatly expanded government control over private firearms ownership. The bipartisan compromise to expand background checks, ban assault weapons and high-capacity gun magazines did not receive the 60 votes necessary and agreed to by both parties. Senators also refuse Republican proposals to increase access to concealed-carry permits. Family members who lost loved ones in the Sandy Hook Elementary massacre sit in the Senate gallery alongside survivors of the Virginia Tech and Tuscon shootings, and yell at Senators, "Shame on you," after the votes. In a dour tone President Obama reinforces this sentiment at the White House. Surrounded by Sandy Hook parents, he says it was "a pretty shameful day for Washington."

Republican and Democratic Second Amendment advocates assert that their votes are based on logic rather than passion. "Criminals do not submit to background checks now," Republican Senator Charles E. Grassley of Iowa. "They will not submit to expanded background checks." Incensed at the Senate's action, Obama claims the gun rights lobby "willfully lied" about the proposed laws, and both parties had "caved to the pressure. But this effort is not over." Jonathan Weisman, "Senate Blocks Drive for Gun Control," *New York Times*, April 17, 2013.

April 24
n.t.

Newtown Action Alliance puts together Sandy Hook Team 26 to walk in the National Alliance on Mental Illness (NAMI) 5K fundraiser, scheduled for Saturday, May 18, in Hartford Connecticut. The Sandy Hook Ride on Washington cyclists, who rode on bicycles from Newtown to Washington DC, share their logo and name with the walkers. "We were very inspired by the cyclists taking physical action to make a change," Sandy Hook Team 26 Captain Erin Nikitchyuk says. Each walker has a minimum personal goal of $100, "but our overall team goal is to be among the leading teams," Ms Nikitchyuk remarks. "We feel like it would be very powerful to have a Newtown team showing the world with our team efforts that we support finding solutions to the many complex contributing factors that resulted in our tragedy [at Sandy Hook School]," she says. The team is raising the money it will then give to NAMI in assisting families touched by mental illness, and to educate and advocate on mental health issues. "We saw the worst case scenario [at Sandy Hook Elementary] of what happens when we don't support people who need it," Ms Nikitchyuk notes. "[Adam Lanza] obviously needed more support than society gave him." Nancy Crevier, "Sandy Hook Team 26 Will Walk for Mental Health," *Newtown Bee*, April 24, 2013.

April 27
9:53PM

Newtown First Selectman Pat Llodra and Schools Superintendent Janet Robinson are selected to deliver the keynote address at Western Connecticut State University's undergraduate commencement ceremonies on May 12. Llodra and Robinson have been celebrated for their leadership following the mass shooting at Sandy Hook Elementary School on Dec. 14. Llodra is said to have been "a steadfast force for the community as it has wrestled with everything from the international outpouring of donations to advocacy for new gun laws and decisions on the fate of the existing Sandy Hook Elementary School building.

Llodra has been to Washington on several occasions to address issues that have emerged from the tragedy, while she continued to direct the town in its everyday business and preparation of a budget for the 2013-14 fiscal year. Robinson was recently recognized by the University of Connecticut as Outstanding Superintendent of the Year. She is also a veteran educator and school psychologist who has received national acclaim for her management of the Newtown school system following December 14, 2012. Alongside Llodra, Robinson has been a national advocate for addressing gun violence, mental health issues, and school safety concerns. Nanci G. Hutson, "Llodra and Robinson to Address WCSU Graduates," *newstimes.com*, April 27, 2013.

May 7

Parents of several children slain in the Sandy Hook School massacre travel to Delaware to tout stricter gun control measures. Delaware Governor Jack Markell exhibits photos of Daniel Barden. Anna Marquez-Greene and Dylan Hockley–three of those killed in the shooting.Parents coax Markell and Delaware legislators to pass laws banning high capacity magazines.

"There were 11 other children in that classroom that escaped and are at school today because that shooter had an issue with reloading and gave them enough time to run for their lives," Dylan Hockley's mother, Nicole tells the press. Markell intends to sign legislation expanding background checks to almost all private sales in Delaware. "Parents of Newtown Victims Come to Delaware," ABC 6 Philadelphia Action News, May 7, 2013.

May 10
10:34PM

A task for of 28 Newtown elected officials voted unanimously to tear down Sandy Hook Elementary School and rebuild another structure on the site. The proposal will go to the local school board, then face a voter referendum. A study concludes that erecting a new school will cost $57 million. A total 430 Sandy Hook students now attend a revamped school renamed Sandy Hook Elementary School in the nearby town of Monroe. Officials say groundbreaking can begin in spring and a new building might reopen in January 2016. Dave Collins, "Newtown Panel: Tear Down Sandy Hook Elementary School, Rebuild," *Huffington Post*, May 10, 2013.

May 11
12:09PM

CBS anchor Scott Pelley says in a speech at Quinnipiac University that journalists "are getting big stories wrong, over and over again." The CBS presenter did not hesitate in absorbing part of the blame. "Let me take the first arrow: During our coverage of Newtown, I sat on my set and I reported that Nancy Lanza was a teacher at the school. And that her son had attacked her classroom. It's a hell of a story, but it was dead wrong. Now, I was the managing editor, I made the decision to go ahead with that and I did, and that's what I said, and I was absolutely wrong. So let me just take the first arrow here." Daniel Halper, "Our House is on Fire," *The Weekly Standard*, May 11, 2013.

May 12
12:05AM

Huffington Post publishes Mothers Day-themed piece by Sandy Hook Elementary shooting mothers Jackie Barden, Nicole Hockley, Nelba Marquez-Greene, and Francine Wheeler. When Dylan, Daniel, Ana and Ben came into this world," the women write,

> *each of us, in our own way, promised to prepare them for life as best we could. Every day, approximately 11,000 new American moms will make that same loving promise as they meet their babies for the first time. Within a blink of an eye, these women will become intimately familiar with things like bath time, sunscreen, chocolate chip pancakes, and the healing power*

of multi-colored band-aids. And with each new moment shared, something magical will happen. These new moms will get to experience life when it is lived for others. They will learn more about themselves than they ever imagined. The sacrifices are immeasurable. But so is the joy. Hearts melt with every "Mommy, will you please read me another story?" "Mommy, will you give me another kiss good-night?" "Mommy, I love you."

Jackie Barden, Nicole Hockley, Nelba Marquez-Greene, and Francine Wheeler, "A Mother's Promise," *Huffington Post*, May 12, 2013.

May 13

Toxicology tests conducted as part of the autopsy on Adam Lanza by Connecticut Chief Medical Examiner Dr. H. Wayne Carver II show Lanza had no alcohol or drugs in his body when he allegedly shot and killed 20 children and six women at Sandy Hook Elementary School on Dec. 14. Such an exam looks for traces of most every legal and illegal drug. Lanza had no traces of alcohol or any illegal drugs such as cocaine or marijuana in his body. Nor were there indications of antidepressants or anti-psychotic medications. The tests were conducted as part of the autopsy by state Chief Medical Examiner Dr. H. Wayne Carver II. Sources said his final report has been turned over to state prosecutors and investigators. David Altimari, "Sandy Hook Shooter Adam Lanza Had No Drugs, Alcohol in System,"*Hartford Courant*, December 14, 2013.

May 14
6:14PM

Newtown Town Clerk Debbie Aurelia is refusing to release death certificates for the 26 victims of the Dec. 14 Sandy Hook Elementary School shootings, stating that such information on death certificates might be used by identity thieves. Passage of two bills on the topic are before the Connecticut Legislature pursued ostensibly by the Aurelia are uncertain because the legislative session runs out on June 5 and thus the proposed legislation may not get a vote.

This is the view of Rep. Ed Jutila, D-East Lyme, co-chairman of the General Assembly's Government Administration and Elections Committee. "We're down to three-and-a-half weeks, and there are lots of bills trying to make it through that funnel," he said. "This may or may not be one of those." Jutila has not recently heard from the legislation's proponents and notes there is vigorous opposition to the idea of limits on information available to the public for centuries. One bill would impose a six-month waiting period and the second creates new "short" death certificates with limited information, including the person's name, gender, cause of death, and date and place of death, for issuance to to the public. There are exemptions for next of kin, funeral directors and others. Susan Haigh, "Fate of Newtown Death Certificate Bills in Doubt,"*Newsday*/Associated Press, May 14, 2013.

May 21
n.t.

Connecticut's chief prosecutor and the state's governor's working behind closed doors with legislative leaders on a law to withhold records on the police investigation of the massacre at Sandy Hook Elementary School massacre. Such records would include victims' photos, tapes of 911 calls, and more. The secret move was discovered when *The Hartford Courant* received a copy of an email by assistant state's attorney Timothy J. Sugrue, a top assistant to Chief State's Attorney Kevin Kane. In the communication Sugrue discussed options assessed thus far, which involve possibly blocking release of statements "made by a minor." Jon Lender, Edmund H. Mahoney, and Dave Altimari, "Bill Drafted in Secret Would Block Release of Some Newtown Massacre Records," *Hartford Courant*, May 21, 2013.

June 1
n.t.

A change.org petition addressed to Connecticut state legislators requests the swift passage of HB 6424 that will seal from public view police investigation records pertaining to the Sandy Hook massacre under seal. As of June 3 the petition reaches 40,000 signatures. The petition is ostensibly established by shooting victim parents Nicole and Ian Hockley, Mark and Jackie Barden, and Jimmy Greene and Nelba Marquez-Greene. "We are parents and family members who lost children in the terrible tragedy at Sandy Hook elementary school in December 2012," the petition's prefatory message reads. "We're coming together to urge the Connecticut legislature to pass a law that would keep sensitive information, including photos and audio, about this tragic day private and out of the hands of people who'd like to misuse it for political gain." Keep Sandy Hook crime scene information private: Urge the CT Legislature to Pass HB 6424," change.org, June 1, 2013.

June 5
1:35AM

The Connecticut Senate and House vote overwhelmingly to approve legislation preventing public disclosure of photos and videos of homicide victims and other records in reaction to the Newtown school massacre. The law had been vigorously advocated by parents of Sandy Hook massacre victims. The Senate passes the bill 33-2 after seventeen minutes of debate. At 2:00AM the House approves the bill with a vote of 130-2. The legislation proceeds to Gov. Dannel P. Malloy, who is expected to sign it, and will take effect immediately. The law applies to all homicide cases — not just to the Newtown investigation.

A previous version of the proposal applied specifically to Newtown. The new measure will prevent release of photos, videos, or digital video images "depicting the victim of a homicide, to the extent that such record could reasonably be expected to constitute an unwarranted invasion of the personal privacy" of the victim or surviving family members. Audio records of 911 emergency calls would still be released as public records under the state Freedom of Information Law according to the new version of the law achieving passage. Jon Lender, "Senate, House Overwhelmingly Approve Bill to Withhold Homicide Photos, Other Records, After Newtown," *Hartford Courant*, June 5, 2013.

June 12

Parents of the children allegedly killed at Sandy Hook Elementary travel to Washington DC to lobby Congress for tightening laws on gun ownership, including expansion of background checks. In particular, the families meet with Sen. Joe Manchin, D-W.Va., a co-creator of the unsuccessful background check bill, House Speaker John Boehner and House Majority Leader Eric Cantor. The Newtown families were in Washington one month earlier when the gun bill failed to pass the Senate. Shortly after the Senate voted against the plan, several parents whose children were killed at Sandy Hook appeared alongside President Obama at the White House as he vowed to continue the fight to enact stricter gun laws. Obama and Vice President Joe Biden vow to intensify their campaign for stricter gun control measures. Arlette Saenz, "Newtown Families Return to Capitol Hill as Six Month Anniversary Approaches," ABC News, June 12, 2013.

June 14
9:3oAM

Newtown residents and others congregate at Edmond Town Hall to commemorate the six month anniversary of the Sandy Hook School massacre. Later that day Cristina Hassinger, daughter of Sandy Hook principal Dawn Hochsprung, is escorted by Newtown police on a tour of the school's interior. wanted to see the school where her mother was murdered. Hassinger says she wants to put the pieces together of what happened on December 14th. "We went inside," Hassinger recalls.

We went through the doors into the lobby ... The police officer (who was also with us) turned the lights on as we went through. He was ahead of us, like he'd done this before ... It did smell weird, not strong but it smelled. It was closed off. It smelled really musty. There was no fresh air. It smelled stale. That definitely made it more difficult ... We went down the hall and she (the detective) showed me the conference room where the meeting was that Mom, Natalie (Hammond) and Mary (Sherlach) were in. We didn't go inside. It was empty. Not even the furniture was in it ... We went into the classrooms. There is nothing in the classrooms. They are all completely stripped. No desks. They had ripped out the floors. A lot of the ceiling tiles were missing and the windows were all boarded up ... They still don't know which classroom was attacked first. They aren't sure which. If they do (know), they didn't tell us. She (the detective) was telling us what they think happened. The only witnesses are little kids, and what's trauma and what's real, it's all very muddy.

Dirk Perrefort, "A Daughter's Pilgrimage to Where Mother Was Slain,"Newstimes.com, June 15, 2013.10:00AM [Estimate] "No More Names: The National Drive to Reduce Gun Violence," a nationwide bus tour promoting stricter gun control and observing victims of gun violence, touches off in Newtown Connecticut, the site of the December 14, 2012 Sandy Hook Elementary massacre. The tour is scheduled for 100 days, will traverse 25 states, and is being sponsored by Mayors Against Illegal Guns, a non-profit founded in 2006 by New York City Mayor Michael Bloomberg and Boston Mayor Thomas Menino.

Before Newtown's Town Hall a ticker counts the number of people killed by gun violence since the Sandy Hook shootings. "Over 6,000 have been killed by guns in six months alone," declares Steve Barton, a survivor of the July 2012 shootings in Aurora, Colo., and a speaker at Friday's ceremony. "More than 3,000 will be killed while this bus is on the road if we don't do anything." William Holt, "Bus Tour Commemorating Sandy Hook Takes Gun Control on the Road," *Yahoo! News*, June 14, 2013.

n.t.

Hartford Courant publishes an article promoting "a special report" that is to appear in the paper's June 16 Sunday edition. The piece is accompanied by a video, "'The Ducks of Sandy Hook Elementary' Help Newtown Children Cope," featuring Monroe Connecticut police officer Todd Keeping being interviewed on the significance of toy rubber ducks to recovery from trauma. The teaser calls attention to six month anniversary of shooting and the Newtown community's attempt to deal with the tragedy. "Healing is a slow process with erratic progress," the article observes.

For some, the memories remain jarringly fresh — the acrid smell of gun smoke, the sharp echo of gunshots over the public-address system, the crunch of broken glass underfoot as crying children fled — and far worse for others, particularly students and staff at the school office and near the first-grade classrooms where 26 classmates and educators died. For some students, little sounds can be terrifying — the slam of a dropped book, a car door closing or a raised angry voice. Little things can be reassuring, too. Decorated plastic ducks were among the boxes of teddy bears, toys and school supplies that flooded Newtown in the weeks after the Dec. 14 shooting, filling public spaces and garages and, eventually, warehouses. Sent by Kiwanis members in Colorado, the ducks were plucked from the other donations by Monroe police Officers Todd Keeping and Michael Panza, who provided security at the new school. They put the ducks on windowsills and desks, and in classroom nooks, hoping to ease tension and brighten dark days. "Adults like them. Kids like them," Keeping said. "It just got to the point where I'd hear, 'My kid is riding the bus and looking forward to coming to school again.'"

Matthew Sturdevant, "Inside Sandy Hook School: Six Months Later," *Hartford Courant*, June 14, 2013.

June 18
4:25PM

Death certificates for the Sandy Hook Elementary School victims are released as a result of mounting pressure from news media and a FOIA request after the Newtown Town Clerk's office refused to turn them over to the press. The one page documents indicate that 24 of the 26 victims died from "multiple gunshot wounds," but little more. Bill Hutchinson, "Sandy Hook Elementary School Death Certificates Released," *New York Daily News*, June 18, 2013.

June 30
n.t.

The *Hartford Courant* reports that an internet user believed by law enforcement authorities to be Sandy Hook gunman Adam Lanza frequently posted anonymously on internet message boards and gaming chat rooms. The messages exhibit what

Courant reporters describe as "atechnical prowess about weapons and computers, a 'fetish' for a certain bullet and a near-fixation with correcting Wikipedia articles about mass killers."

The suspected poster further questioned "Connecticut's assault-gun ban, offers a blueprint for his laptop computer and provides YouTube links to a commercial for a laughing doll from the 1970s and for The Rock-afire Explosion, an animatronics band that played in ShowBiz Pizza locations in the 1980s." The Courant further reports that the posts in question "reveal an intense and well-developed interest in high-capacity weaponry and an almost obsessive attention to details both in the user's own writing and his editing of articles about mass murder." Alaine Griffin and Josh Kovner, "Mass Murders Captivated Online User Believed to be Adam Lanza," *Hartford Courant*, June 30, 2013.

July 7
n.t.

An unnamed source close to the State Police investigation of the Sandy Hook School massacre says video and audio from cruiser cameras of Newtown police who responded to the Dec. 14 incident show officers failed to enter the building as about 10 shots were fired by gunman Adam Lanza. "There is no doubt there was some delay," the source says. "The question is whether it was significant or justified." Some Newtown officers have been repeatedly interviewed by investigators seeking to establish a firm timeline for the events. The source claims such interviews have touched a nerve among Newtown officers dealing with what witnessed at the school. John Pirro, "Newtown Police Response to Shooting Under Review," *Stamford Advocate*, July 7, 2013.

July 19
10:37PM

Mayors Against Illegal Guns, an organization founded by New York City Mayor Michael Bloomberg, cosponsors a public vigil featuring mass shooting survivors and relatives of victims from Aurora Colorado and Newtown Connecticut who gather with dozens of supporters in suburban Denver almost a year after the Aurora attack.

Vigil participants advocate for strict federal gun control laws. "Why wait any longer?" asks Carlee Soto, sister of slain Sandy Hook Elementary School teacher Victoria Soto. "The time for change is now."Dan Elliott, "Aurora, Newtown Survivors Honor Theater Victims," *Huffington Post*, July 19, 2013.

July 24
7:14AM

Newtown Chief of Police addresses government officials and law enforcement agencies personnel on the Sandy Hook Elementary School massacre and its aftermath at the Police Executives Conference. Before the presentation Kehoe tells a reporter, "The shooting itself lasted an hour and half to two hours. The officers did very well during the event– but the aftermath is what we weren't prepared for."

The police chief adds that a community such as Newtown has to be "cohesive before a crisis event happens" so that such an event can be navigated through. Lindsay Curtin, "Newtown Police Chief in Wilmington to Talk Crisis Management," WECT 6, July 24, 2013.

July 27
8:49PM

The *Hartford Courant* reports on the contrast between the limited number of details released by law enforcement on the investigation into the Sandy Hook School massacre versus the extent of speaking engagements by Connecticut State Police and Newtown police officers across the country, that can involve sharing graphic details of what they saw inside the school.

In March, Connecticut Gov. Dannel P. Malloy and other political leaders critiqued state police for releasing details of the investigation at out-of-state conferences. A police report has been delayed for months, and state law enforcement officials have attempted to push through legislation intended to keep secret some details of the shooting. Dave Altimari, "While Connecticut Waits, Police Talk Newtown Shooting Across US,"*Hartford Courant*, July 27, 2013.

July 29

Newtown resident Lori Hoagland returns to JFK Airport from a 17-day trip to Turkey expecting to be greeted in the terminal by her husband, Robert, only to later find that he has disappeared without a trace.

Robert Hoagland worked for a Bridgeport law firm involved in real estate-related law. "He was a man doing ordinary life things on a Sunday, preparing for his wife to come home," Lori Hoagland says, noting she spoke to him two days before her return. "And he disappeared. ... It's a total, total mystery." Nanci G. Hutson, "Missing Man Remains a Mystery," *Connecticut Post*, August 21, 2013.

August 1
n.t.

The *New York Times* editorializes on the slow pace of the investigation of the Sandy Hook School massacre. "Connecticut officials continue to keep the public in the dark about the state's official investigation into the shooting massacre at Sandy Hook Elementary School in December," the Times editorial staff remarks, "even as state and local police have been discussing it at forums across the nation, sometimes in graphic detail. Though the fullest possible report was promised after the tragedy, its release has been repeatedly postponed, with authorities advising patience while the public grows increasingly puzzled." "The Slow Motion Inquiry Into Sandy Hook," *New York Times*, August 1, 2013.

August 4
n.t.

Peter Lanza, the father of Newtown shooter Adam Lanza's, puts his Stamford Connecticut house up for sale with an asking price of $710,000. The home is described by realtor Halstead Property as a 2,375-square-foot "ranch cape" on 1.04 acres, with three bedrooms, two-and-a-half bathrooms and a pool in the backyard. It's located on Bartina Lane in the Westover section of town, one of the city's more affluent neighborhoods. Maggie Gordon, "Lanza's Father Moving Out of Stamford Home," *Stamford Advocate*, August 6, 2013.

August 13
n.t.

Over 150 take part in an "Active Shooter/Mass Casualty Drill" at Cal State Long Beach (CSULB). "The blood was just make-up, the screams for help only feigned, and the gunman at the center of it all nonexistent," the online Signal Tribune newspaper reports, "but the more than 150 participants involved in the [event] were taking their assigned duties very seriously."

The exercise can be described as "a multi-agency mock response with participants including the CSULB University Police Department, the Long Beach Police Department, Long Beach Fire Department, St. Mary Medical Center, Lifeline EMS, Pacific College and numerous CSULB departments collaborating to apprehend a non-existent shooter and treat "victims" played by actors.

The emphasis of the drill centered on the CSULB Student Health Center and its staff's ability to perform triage in the field, in addition to university personnel's capacity to communicate with outside agencies, the media and the public. Cory Bilicko, "In Wake of School Shootings at Santa Monica and Sandy Hook, CSULB Conducts Multi-Agency "Mass Casualty Drill," *Signal Tribune*, August 16, 2013.

August 14
5:16PM

Newtown First Selectwoman Pat Llodra writes a letter to the Newtown-Sandy Hook Community Foundation's handling $11.5 million collected after the Dec. 14 Sandy Hook School shooting, suggesting that it to give more money to the shooting victims, especially the families of the 12 children who survived.

"Let me state unequivocally that the amount of money provided to the families of the survivors by the distribution committee is inadequate," Llodra writes. "Twenty thousand dollars will be insufficient to address the wide range of mental health needs for these youngsters and their siblings and parents for years into the future." Llodra's letter is one of many questioning the decision to distribute $7.7 million of the $11.5 million under the organization's control. Dave Altimari, "Newtown Leader Wants More Money Earmarked For Shooting Victims," *Hartford Courant*, August 14, 2013.

n.t.

State police assigned to investigate the Dec. 14 Sandy Hook Elementary School massacre abruptly cancel speaking engagements in California and Texas scheduled for this week and are ordered to focus on finishing the much-anticipated report on the shooting that left 20 first-graders and six women dead. Two weeks ago, the *Hartford Courant* reported that state police and Newtown police were traveling throughout the US to discuss the shooting response at conferences yet releasing little information publicly in Connecticut.

At that time, Gov. Dannel P. Malloy and Danbury State's Attorney Stephen Sedensky defended the travel, saying that police were not discussing details of the investigation and traveling was not slowing down the probe.

Since that story appeared, Malloy's chief of staff met with state police officials and told them "to be more deliberative" in choosing whether to attend any of the conferences to discuss the Sandy Hook investigation. After that meeting, state police officials have stepped up the investigation. Dave Altimari, "Connecticut State Police Cautioned About Discussing Newtown," *Hartford Courant*, August 14, 2013.

August 15
5:19PM

Robbie Parker, the 31-year-old father of Emilie Parker who was slain at Sandy Hook Elementary School, donates books to the Hillsboro Public Library after addressing his alma mater, Pacific University in Oregon a week earlier. "When a married couple brings their first child into the world, it's an amazing change," Parker says.

"She was that person for us. She made us the best possible version of ourselves as individuals and as a couple." Parker notes that Emlie liked to draw and read. "I can't tell you how many times she got in trouble," Parker says laughing, on the nights he'd see her light was still on as she read past her bedtime. Andrew Theen, "Father of Sandy Hook Victims Makes Special Emotional Donation to the Hillsboro Public Library," *The Oregonian*/AM 1360 KUIK, August 15, 2013.

August 16
n.t.

The Sandy Hook Commission established by Gov. Daniel Malloy to make recommendations on gun violence, mental health, and school safety, hears from some of Israel's homeland security officials on the school safety model used in Israel. During a meeting the task force held a Skype conference with officials from a group called The Israel Experience in Homeland Security, suggesting how the Israelis have a very different approach to school security and homeland security in general. Hugh McQuaid, "Sandy Hook Commission Hears From Israeli Security Experts,"*New Haven Register*, August 16, 2013.

n.t.

Eight detectives for the Connecticut State Police have received $139,000 in overtime pay to investigate the Sandy Hook School massacre since January 1, 2013. Almost half has gone to two investigators operating out of Southbury barracks, who claim to have put in over 500 hours of work above and beyond the call of duty in 2013. "There has been absolutely no authorization for overtime for attending any conferences," State Police Lieutenant J. Paul Vance says. "They only get paid overtime when they are called out to investigate any criminal cases and/or they work past their normal work day. They respond to call outs and must be available 24/7."

Dave Altimari, "Overtime for Sandy Hook Investigators Nears $140,000 Since Jan. 1," *Hartford Courant*, August 16, 2013.

August 21
n.t.

James H. Smith, a task force member and the president of the Connecticut Council on Freedom of Information questions the makeup of a task force charged with recommending to state lawmakers how to balance victim privacy with the public's right to know. Smith is concerned the overall membership of the 17-person group appears slanted in favor of keeping certain information from public release. "Sandy Hook Task Force Member Questions Secrecy," Associated Press/*CTPost.com*, August 21. 2013.

August 25
9:00AM

A task force meets that formed after Orange (Florida) County Mayor Teresa Jacobs approached community leaders to establish a body focusing on the mental-health needs of children and young adults to avoid tragedies such as Sandy Hook. "When the Sandy Hook shootings happened, I wanted to respond immediately by getting deputies into the schools," Jacobs says. "But that's treating the symptoms and not the cause. Hopefully, we're coming of age as a society so that we recognize mental illness is not some kind of character weakness, but a legitimate physical illness that has to be addressed and treated." Kate Santich, "Children's Mental Health Commission Debuts Today," *Orlando Sentinel*, August 25, 2013.

August 29

Attorney General Eric Holder announces the U.S. Justice Department's Bureau of Justice Assistance will provide $2.5 million in funds to the Connecticut State Police, the Newtown Police Department and other agencies that assisted following the December 14 shooting that killed 20 children and six educators. The funding provides agencies and jurisdictions for costs of overtime, forensics and security during and in the aftermath of the crime, the Justice Department says.

"Providing support to the law enforcement agencies that responded to the horrific scene that awaited them at Sandy Hook Elementary School is one small action we can take to bring healing to a community that's been devastated," Holder states in the news release. "Just over eight months after this senseless tragedy, those who lost their lives, and those who continue to grieve, remain in our thoughts and prayers." DOJ press release (PDF). Cassandra Day, "Newtown Police to Share in $300K for Sandy Hook Shooting Compensation," *Middletown Patch*, August 31, 2013.

September 4

An attorney with Connecticut's Freedom of Information Commission recommends release of 911 recordings from Sandy Hook Elementary School shooting, coming down on the side of The Associated Press in AP's dispute over records withheld by investigators.

The full, nine-member commission will hold a Sept. 25 hearing before issuing a final decision on whether the recordings should be provided to the AP. A spokesman for the state's Division of Criminal Justice, says its attorneys will argue against the release. "Conn. FOI Officer Urges Relase of 911 Recordings from Sandy Hook School Shooting," *Washington Post* / Associated Press, September 4, 2013.

September 7

Teachers at school districts in southern Orange County California are instructed that if they can't hide or get away from a campus gunman, they should aggressively use chairs, tables, fire extinguishers and even books as weapons to disable a shooter. The revamped policy comes in response to the Sandy Hook Elementary School shooting. "Schools in Orange County Teach Ways to Combat Gunman," KSBY News 6 / Associated Press, September 7, 2013.

September 11

Newtown Police Lieutenant George Sinko, a 24-year veteran, receives a written reprimand from the chief. Sinko's colleagues are upset because they say the lieutenant proceeded to direct traffic at a construction site instead of immediately rushing to the Sandy Hook School massacre event with other officers on the morning of December 14. Some Newtown police officers are displeased with what they see as lenient treatment of the lieutenant and are discussing a vote of no confidence in Chief Michael Kehoe. John Pirro, "Newtown Lieutenant Reprimanded for Slow Sandy Hook Response," *Connecticut Post*, September 11, 2013.

September 13

Ground is broken on a playground in Fairfield CT to honor Jessica Rekos, one of the young children slain in the Sandy Hook tragedy. The playground is being developed by firefighters and community members who wish to volunteer. "Building a Playground for Newtown Victim," WTNH News 8, September 13, 2013.

September 14

Gun rights activists in assert they will vigorously pursue state lawmakers advocating strong gun control measures. Connecticut does not have a provision to recall elected officials, unlike Colorado, where two prominent gun control proponents were just booted from the legislature. "Our recall capabilities are at the ballot box next year," says Scott Wilson, president of the Connecticut Citizens Defense League. "We hope to get some of them out of office. ... The key thing is going to be education [of] the gun-owning community." Connecticut's 200,000 gun-permit holders can be a powerful political force, according to former Connecticut Republican party Chairman Chris Healy. Daniela Altimari, "Colorado Recall Energizes Connecticut Gun Control Foes," *Hartford Courant*, September 14, 2013.

September 24

The State of Connecticut refuses a FOIA request to release Sandy Hook gunman Adam Lanza's medical records because of fears that divulging the specific types of antidepressants he was taking would, "cause a lot of people to stop taking their medications," Assistant Attorney General Patrick B. Kwanashie says. The parents organization AbleChild.org is seeking to secure the release of the information after Connecticut Medical Examiner H. Wayne Carver, M.D. denied the request. "What plagues this investigation is that some are simply fixated on having it remain secret in spite of the urgency of transparency that is clearly needed to protect the public," said Patricia Weathers, co-founder of AbleChild. Paul Joseph Watson, "State of Connecticut Refuses to Release Adam Lanza's Medical Records,"*Infowars. com*, September 24, 2013.

Governor Dannel P. Malloy announces September 24 that the State of Connecticut is pledging support to Newtown to build a replacement of Sandy Hook Elementary School and is poised to approve the first round of funding toward its construction at the September 27 meeting of the State Bond Commission. "The tragedy at Sandy Hook Elementary School is never far from our minds. Over the last several months, we've done our best to move forward in a way that honors the memory of those we lost and meets the needs of residents and the surrounding community," Gov Malloy remarks.

"Healing from an enormous tragedy like this is never easy. There are no simple answers, and the challenges are many. With strong resolve and a determination to move forward, we can do our best to support the people of Newtown." John Voket, "Saturday Referendum Calls Voters to Appropriate $50 Million for Sandy Hook School," *Newtown Bee*, October 4, 2013.

First Selectman Pat Llodra and Interim School Superintendent John Reed partake in a video interview September 24 organized by the *Newtown Bee* to help residents understand the implications of an forthcoming October 5 referendum. "As far as the $50 million [is concerned], it comes without strings, it does not have to be repaid, it has no impact on the tax rate," Dr Reed says. "It is an attempt on the part of the state to make Newtown whole. That means we had seven schools when we started the school year last year, and I think it's the state's judgment that we have seven schools now." Dr Reed says the offer as a "win-win situation for Newtown." John Voket, "Saturday Referendum Calls Voters to Appropriate $50 Million for Sandy Hook School," *Newtown Bee*, October 4, 2013.

September 27

At a meeting of the State Bond Commission, the body approves a $50 million appropriation to the Town of Newtown to demolish and rebuild Sandy Hook Elementary School in Newtown Connecticut. Newtown voters are to vote on the proposal October 5. John Voket, "Saturday Referendum Calls Voters to Appropriate $50 Million for Sandy Hook School," *Newtown Bee*, October 4, 2013.

September 29

Many of children that survived the shooting at Sandy Hook Elementary suffer from witnessing the horrors of that day. "Nightmares are persistent," the Associated Press reports, "and any reminder of the attack — a fire alarm, a clap of thunder, even the sound of an intercom — can stir feelings of panic. At the building in a neighboring town where the survivors recently began a new school year, signs ask people to close doors softly and not to drag objects across the floor. "The worst part is the helplessness," says Hugo Rojas, whose son witnessed the shooting. "You want to take that pain away. You want to be able to take those nightmares away, but you can't." John Christoffersen, "Fear Permeates Young Lives of Newtown Witnesses," Associated Press / ABC News, September 29, 2013.

October 4

The North Carolina chapter of the National Alliance on Mental Health holds its 29th annual conference where Nelba Marquez Greene, a mother of one of the slain Sandy Hook students, gives an address to recommend what can be done to prevent such tragedies from happening again. "NC's Mental Health Advocates Focus on Lessons from Sandy Hook," *The Progressive Pulse*, October 4, 2013.

October 5
6:00AM

Referendum polls open for all registered and qualified voters open at Newtown Middle School to appropriate $50 million in state funding to rebuild Sandy Hook School. Town Clerk Debbie Aurelia-Halstead says mailed in absentee ballots for the referendum will be counted if received by Saturday, October 5. John Voket, "Saturday Referendum Calls Voters to Appropriate $50 Million for Sandy Hook School," *Newtown Bee*, October 4, 2013.

October 7

Crews from the Bestech construction contractor begin work at the Sandy Hook Elementary School site, just two days after residents voted to accept a state grant of almost $50 million to demolish the 57-year-old structure and rebuild a new school. The Bestech construction company has not been formally approved by Newtown officials or the State of Connecticut for such duties. John Voket, "State Action Gets Sandy Hook School Project Off to a Fast Start," *Newtown Bee*, October 14, 2013.

October 11

Newtown receives notice from the State of Connecticut that the town can use remediation vendor Bestech for both remediation and demolition under a "professional services" designation. This means town officials will not have to go out to bid for a separate demolition contractor. According to First Selectman Pat Llodra, the town will now be able to obtain a two-to-three-week jump on work at the site. She says this wholly ensures that both the structure and post demolition debris will be removed by December 14, the first anniversary of the shooting. Mrs Llodra remarks the use of Bestech will minimize the number of workers on the site. Further, a single vendor allows for easier security credentialing, and with fewer workers all under the same vendor, controls to assure no debris or images from the demolition process leave the site will be able to be enforced more effectively. John Voket, "State Action Gets Sandy Hook School Project Off to a Fast Start," *Newtown Bee*, October 14, 2013.

October 12

Nouel Alba, a New York City woman who posed as the aunt of a child killed in the Sandy Hook massacre, faces sentencing on October 15 in federal court in Hartford. She pleaded guilty in June to wire fraud and making false statements. Alba is seeking probation, stating that she's already been punished by the media. Prosecutors are pursuing at least a year in prison sentence.

Authorities claim she made up details about the aftermath of the shooting to solicit donations for a "funeral fund" on behalf of the child's family and the families of other victims of the shooting. "Sandy Hook Shooting Fraudster Seeks Probation," Associated Press / *Boston Globe*, October 12, 2013.

October 14

Newtown officials are requiring contractors who will carry out demolition of the Sandy Hook Elementary School to sign detailed confidentiality agreements that prevent them from publicly discussing the site, taking photographs or otherwise revealing information about the school. "It's a very sensitive topic," Selectman Will Rodgers says. "We want it (the site) to be handled in a respectful way."Demolition of the existing Sandy Hook Elementary School is slated to begin the week of October 21, and be finished before the Dec. 14 anniversary of the incident. Nanci G. Hutson, "Non-Disclosure Required for Sandy Hook School Crew,"*Newstimes.com*, October 14, 2013.

October 18

Officials and family members of persons killed during the Sandy Hook School massacre question the slow drip of information versus a full police investigation report as sources now claim that six-year-old Jesse Lewis in fact acted heroically on December 14.

When Jesse, a student in Victoria Soto's classroom, noticed that Adam Lanza ran out of ammunition, he yelled for his terrified classmates to escape. "Jesse did yell `Run!" and four did run, and two others ran into the bathroom," according to Neil Heslin, explaining what investigators who accompanied him on a tour through the murder scene described to him. "I knew that Soto was the first one shot, and then a little girl, and Jesse was the last one shot. He was clearly looking at Adam Lanza directly in the face. He was only shot once, the only one of the victims who wasn't shot multiple times. His wound, as I've stated before in testimony, was in the forehead above the nose, right at the hairline," Heslin asserts. Ken Dixon, Nanci Hutson, and Eileen FitzGerald, "New Details in Sandy Hook Shooting," *Newstimes.com*, October 18, 2013.

October 25

Demolition of the Sandy Hook Elementary school is scheduled begins today. As asbestos is removed, each wing of the nearly 60 year old building will come down. Bestech, a company specializing in removing asbestos, will continue in its demolition of the school through the weekend. The entire process is expected to take five to six weeks. Fulltime security at the gated entrance insures that no curiosity seekers or media can get to the site. Mark Davis, "Sandy Hook Demolition to Begin Friday," WTNH News 8, October 21, 2013.

October 25

NewsCopter 7 over Sandy Hook Elementary School in Newtown, Connecticut as the school was demolished following last year's deadly shooting in which 26 students and teachers were murdered. (WABC Photo/ NewsCopter 7)
More photos at WABC News 7

Workers begin demolishing the Sandy Hook Elementary School building. Newtown First Selectman Pat Llodra says the small-scale demolition is underway and the project will take several weeks. "The process of demolition is incremental, staged precisely and executed carefully," she notes. "There is no wrecking ball action; it is rather a piece-by-piece, section-by-section removal." "Demolition Begins on Sandy Hook Elementary School Building," Associated Press / WABC News 7, October 25, 2013.

October 29

The State of Connecticut releases the full toxicology report on Sandy Hook school shooter Adam Lanza, confirming that no drugs or alcohol were in his system on December 14, 2012. The report notes that Lanza tested negative for marijuana and had part of his brain taken for genetic testing. "There is no chemical reason or apparent medical reason to explain [Lanza's] actions," former chief state's medical examiner Dr. H. Wayne Carver II says. Carver previously sent a piece of Lanza's brain to geneticists at the University of Connecticut Health Center to study for genetic markers. Carver said he hasn't received a final report, but he doesn't anticipate having to alter Adam Lanza's death certificate. "If I thought there was something through the DNA testing that could have been listed as a contributing factor, I would have added it to his death certificate," Carver remarks. Adam Lanza's death was ruled a suicide. Dave Altimari, "Full Report Confirms No Drugs, Alcohol in Lanza's System," *Hartford Courant*, October 29, 2013.

November 6

Representatives of Svigals + Partners, Consigli Construction, and Diversified Project Management report to Newtown Board of Education on progress at the new Sandy Hook School. "So far it is going very well," says Aaron Krueger, project manager for Consigli Construction, says the project is proceeding according to schedule.

Julie McFadden, project manager for Svigals + Partners for its architect and engineering team, gives an update on everything that has been happening with the project since September. "Our first order of business was to assemble the abatement documentation and the demolition documentation and get that up to the office of school facilities up at the state for their review and approval so that work could get under way," Ms McFadden remarks. Eliza Hallaback, "Project on Schedule–School Board Gets SHS Update," *Newtown Bee*, November 7, 2013.

November 8

Aerial photographs indicate that workers have demolished the wing of Sandy Hook Elementary School where Adam Lanza allegedly killed 20 first graders and six staffers with an assault rifle, new aerial photographs show. The concrete foundation is all that remains, and that will soon be destroyed. The demolition proceeds behind high fences with security guards posted to keep onlookers away. Corky Seimaszko, "Newtown Massacre Scene Demolished as Prosecutor Tries to Block Release of 911 Calls," *New York Daily News*, November 8, 2013.

State Attorney Stephen Sedensky pleas to a judge to block the release of the desperate 911 calls from Sandy Hook Elementary made on the morning of December 14, 2012. The state's Freedom of Information Commission ruled in September that the tapes should be released following a request by the Associated Press. Sedensky argues that a stay of the FOI decision would protect both the families of the victims and the surviving witnesses from unwanted press attention. Corky Seimaszko, "Newtown Massacre Scene Demolished as Prosecutor Tries to Block Release of 911 Calls," *New York Daily News*, November 8, 2013.

November 11

A Newtown, Conn., police officer Thomas Bean and Sandy Hook Elementary massacre first responder says he is unable to return to work because of post-traumatic stress disorder and is in danger of being fired. Bean says he has been suffering PTSD since the Dec. 14 shooting. Bean appears on the NBC TODAY show November 11 with the Newtown Police Union President Scott Ruszczyk and union attorney Eric Brown of Waterbury, Conn. "I can't describe the overwhelming senses of emotions that I had," Bean claims, describing the massacre's aftermath. "That night I drank a lot. The next day I wanted to cut myself. I just felt so numb." Laurie Petersen, "Newtown Officer With Sandy Hook-Related PTSD Claim Faces Dismissal," AOL Jobs, November 11, 2013.

November 16

Danbury State's Attorney Stephen Sedensky says a summary of the long anticipated state police report on the Dec. 14 Sandy Hook Elementary School shooting is scheduled for release on Nov. 25. Sources say the original report will be thousands of pages and the date for that document's release is yet to be determined.

Sedensky and state police detectives met with some of the victims' families on November 14. Another group had a conference call with him on November 15 so he could go over the report. Sources say that report probably will be heavily redacted. David Altimari, "Summary of Sandy Hook Report to Be Released November 25, Families Told," *Hartford Courant*, November 16, 2013.

November 25

A 48-page report is released on Monday by Connecticut state attorney, Stephen J. Sedensky III that provides a graphic profile of Adam Lanza but no reason for his crime. "The long-awaited report does not suggest a motive for Mr. Lanza's actions," the *New York Times* reports, "even as it offers a glimpse into his strange, troubled life. It comes nearly a year after the shooting set off a national discussion about gun control, mental health and violence in American popular culture."

Although Lanza was treated by mental health professionals, according to the report, none recognized anything suggestive of his future behavior."Tutoring, desensitization and medication were recommended," the report says. Joseph Berger and Mark Santora, "Chilling Look at Newtown Killer, But No 'Why,'" *New York Times,* November 25, 2013.

November 26

New Britain Superior Court Judge Eliot Prescott denies a motion by State Attorney Stephen Sedensky III for a stay of release on the 911 tapes of the Sandy Hook massacre. Yet the tapes are to remain sealed until Dec. 4 to give the Sedensky a chance to appeal. The AP has sought the recordings in part to examine the police response to the shooting. "Newtown 911 Calls Ordered to be Released by Judge," Associated Press / WABC New York, November 26, 2013.

December 1

Politico reports that at least 37 states have increased spending on mental health since the Sandy Hook Massacre. In addition, such states are experimenting with controversial new ways of raising awareness on mental health issues. These include training public school personnel and students to spot and report on those allegedly exhibiting mental health symptoms. Stephanie Simon, "Sandy Hook Spurs States' Mental Health Push," *Politico. com*, December 1, 2013.

December 3

Gov. Dannel Malloy's office announces that state employees serving as first responders to the Sandy Hook Elementary School shooting are to receive 40 hours of compensatory time as the result of an agreement struck between the state and six state labor unions. David Dunavin, "12/14 Responders Will Receive Compensatory Time From State," *Newtown Patch*, December 4, 2013.

December 4

Recordings of 911 calls from the Sandy Hook Elementary School shooting are released. They indicate anguish and tension inside the building, also suggesting how town dispatchers responded to the calls. The recordings are released under a court order after a lengthy effort by The Associated Press to have them released for review. Prosecutors had argued that making the recordings public would only cause more anguish for the victims' families. "Newtown 911 Calls Released," Associated Press / *Newsday*, December 4, 2013.

December 10

State records indicate that Sandy Hook School massacre-related charities raise close to $28 million since the Dec. 14, 2012 and possess over $11 million that is yet to be distributed. Sixty-three charities responded to the latest survey from the state attorney general's office seeking updates on money raised since the shooting. The surveys are voluntary and 14 groups had not responded. Dave Altimari, "$28 Million Raised by Sandy Hook Charities," *Hartford Courant*, December 10, 2013.

December 14

President Obama leads a national day of remembrance for the victims of the Sandy Hook elementary school shootings while renewing calls for tighter gun control and heightened mental-health care measures. "We have to do more to keep dangerous people from getting their hands on a gun so easily. We have to do more to heal troubled minds," the president remarks during his weekly radio address."

Obama Remembers Sandy Hook Victims, Calls For Tougher Gun Laws," Associated Press / FoxNews.com, December 14, 2013.

December 22

Al Jazeera America editorializes on the failure of pro-gun control legislators in the US to succeed in the passage of sweeping laws. "Little has been done to close loopholes that might have prevented that gun purchase or lay down rules for the possible next frontier of weapons," Al Jazeera opines. "While Congress has renewed the ban on plastic guns — the only gun-control legislation it moved this year — it fell short of requiring that guns have unremovable pieces of metal to make them more easily detectable." "The Year in Guns: In Wake of Tragedy, More Government Inaction," Al Jazeera America, December 22, 2013.

December 23

The *New York Times* publishes an editorial that scolds the US Congress for failing to pass substantive gun control legislation in the wake of the Sandy Hook School massacre. "Despite lawmakers' copious sympathy for the 26 victims of the Newtown, Conn., school massacre," the *Times*' editorial board writes, "all members of Congress were able to manage in the way of gun safety as they left town was renewal of the ban on the manufacture of plastic firearms. This is a type of arcane weapon that figured not at all in the Sandy Hook Elementary School rampage in 2012, nor in the mass shootings featuring adapted weapons of war that have occurred on average every two weeks somewhere in America." "Congress's Temerity on Gun Safety," *New York Times*, December 23, 2013.

December 27
3:22PM

The Connecticut State Police release their final report on the December 14, 2012 Sandy Hook Elementary School Massacre. The report is "only made available at this website: http://www.ct.gov/statepolicenewtownreport. "The report runs several thousand pages and is heavily redacted "according to law." The report also contains some text, photos and 911 calls received by the State Police on the day of the shootings. The State Police further announce that release "of this document is indicative that this State Police criminal investigation is concluded." "Sandy Hook School Shooting Investigation Completed; Report to Be Released," State of Connecticut Department of Emergency Services and Public Protection, December 26, 2013.

The Obama administration's Justice and Health and Human Services departments propose allowing the federal gun background check database access to some mental health records by giving it an exemption from existing privacy law and "clarify" that people involuntarily committed to both inpatient and outpatient institutions could be prohibited from purchasing guns. The proposed rules are the most recent executive actions following the December 2012 Sandy Hook School massacre. Reid J. Epstein, "White House: New Gun Rules for Mentally Ill,"*Politico.com*, January 3, 2014.

2014
January 6

The U.S. Department of Education announces an award of $1.9 million to Newtown Public School District "to help with ongoing recovery efforts following the tragic shootings at Sandy Hook Elementary School in December 2012." This is the second of two grants totaling $3.2 million, the first being made in May 2013. The grant is through the Department's Project School Emergency Response to Violence (SERV) program. According to the DOE, Project SERVE "awards Immediate Services and Extended Services grants to school districts, colleges and universities that have experienced a significant traumatic event and need resources to respond, recover, and re-establish safe environments for students." "US Department of Education Awards $1.9 Million Grants to Newtown, Connecticut, to Further Support Recovery Efforts," US Department of Education, January 6. 2014.

January 7

Brookfield Board of Education member Gregory Beck steps down following a public outcry after a Facebook post Beck made in November. In the remark Beck said his "26 Acts of Kindness" for the Sandy Hook victims would be to deliver boxes of ammunition to his gun-enthusiast friends. Many people considered the post to be inappropriate and offensive, since the "26 Acts" movement had been dedicated to the victims of the Dec. 14, 2012, shootings at Sandy Hook Elementary School in Newtown. Nanci G. Hutson, "Embattled Brookfield BOE Member Resigns,"Newstimes.com, January 7, 2014.

January 17

Peter Lanza assures the Sandy Hook Advisory Commission that he will disclose at least some of Newtown shooter Adam Lanza's mental health treatment records, and heard from two of the foremost autism experts that the disorder doesn't lead to violent behavior. Peter Lanza "called me during the last presentation," Sandy Hook panel Chairman Scott Jackson said before the commission broke for lunch Friday afternoon. "I'm going to sit down with him in short order" to work out the parameters of a records release. Kathleen Megan, "Adam Lanza's Father Willing to Release Medical Records to Sandy Hook Commission," *Hartford Courant*, January 18, 2014.

January 21

Mark Barden and Nicole Hockley two family members of children lost during the Sandy Hook school shooting and representatives of Sandy Hook Promise appear in Concord New Hampshire to testify before a committee promoting criminal background checks in New Hampshire. HB 1559 requires every gun sale go through a licensed dealer and then, a background check process through the National Crime Information Center, closing a loophole that proponents say put illegal guns onto the streets. Tony Schinella, "Parents of Sandy Hook Victims Promote Background Checks Bill," *Salem NH Patch*, January 21, 2014.

January 25

An email by former law enforcement officer and school safety expert Wolfgang Halbig addressed to Connecticut State Police Lieutenant J. Paul Vance and Newtown Police Chief Michael Kehoe is published on *memoryholeblog.com*. The post initiates an important series of appearances throughout major alternative media outlets where Halbig explains his misgivings on the official version of the Sandy Hook School massacre. Wolfgang Halbig, "Retired Cop and Educator Threatened for Questioning Sandy Hook Investigation," *memoryholeblog.com*, January 25, 2014.

The Berkeley Unified School District in Northern California is spending $2 million on an elaborate school safety plan. The school district hired two security consultants, Edu-Safe Associates and Dimensions Unlimited, at the cost of $70,000 to audit the district's 20 schools. The school board voted two to one to spend money on armed-intruder training, increased video surveillance, campus address systems and the installation of new door locks engineered to prevent people from being locked inside classrooms. "I substitute in the school district as well, so I'm happy to see that they're phasing in new locks on the classroom doors," said Tracy Hollander, president of the Berkeley Parent Teacher Association. Jane Nho, "Berkeley Unified School Spends $2 Million on Safety Plan," *Daily Californian*, January 25, 2014.

January 29

The Town of New Canaan waives reimbursement of $7,623 in costs in responding to the Sandy Hook Elementary School massacre. The funds are designated from the $2.5 million Obama Department of Justice payoff to Connecticut and Newtown-area law enforcement agencies that took part in the event response and are intended for training personnel in emergency response to violent offenders. Police Chief Leon Krolikowski says New Canaan sent officers to Newtown every day from Dec. 14 through Dec. 25. The nearby Town of Darien was eligible for about $17,000 and chose to be reimbursed. Nelson Oliveira, "Town Waives Reimbursement for Sandy Hook Response," *New Canaan News*, February 6, 2014.

February 1

Connecticut Emergency Services and Public Protection Commissioner Reuben Bradford steps down from his post and is replaced by Dora B. Schriro, commissioner of the New York City Department of Correction since 2009. Ms. Schriro is a long time acquaintance of Janet Napolitano when both served in Arizona. "After learning of an anomaly with my retirement and much soul searching," Bradford wrote in a resignation to Gov. Dannell Malloy in December 2013, "I reluctantly tender my resignation effective February 1, 2014. When I accepted your gracious offer to serve as Commissioner almost three years ago, I did so knowing there was a shelf life to the position." Hugh McQuaid, "Bradford Retires Citing 'Anomaly,'" CT News Junkie, December 26, 2013.

February 6

Rhode Island Gov. Lincoln Chafee announces a new safety and security plan for the state's schools, a 320-page document assembled by educators, emergency management officials and law enforcement. The redesign was prompted by the Sandy Hook Elementary School massacre in Newtown, Connecticut. The guide is intended to serve as a tool for local schools when creating their own security plans. "RI Releases New Security Plan," Associated Press / *San Francisco Chronicle*, February 6, 2014.

February 11

Former U.S. Rep. Gabrielle Giffords announces that she is writing a book about gun control based on an essay she wrote that appeared in The *New York Times* in April 2013. The article was her response to the fatal shootings of 20 children and six educators in Newtown, Conn., in December 2012. In the piece Giffords chided senators who blocked gun legislation that included expanded background checks and a ban on assault weapons. "As Second Amendment supporters and gun owners ourselves," Giffords husband Mark Kelly told the Associated Press, "we hope our book rouses the long-overdue conversation our country needs to make responsible changes to our gun laws so that no more precious lives are lost." "Gabrielle Giffords Plans Book on Gun Control," Associated Press / *Boston Herald*, February 11, 2014.

Florida State Rep. Lori Berman proposes a bill that will provide for mental health first aid training for school teachers and staff from Florida Department of Children and Families. Berman hopes the legislation will make spotting problem signs routine."The genesis of this bill was actually the Sandy Hook massacre," said Rep. Lori Berman. "I think it's important for us to invest the dollars and try to address mental health and substance abuse problems when they're in their incipient stages," Berman remarks. The bill has already made it through committees in both chambers. The Florida Education Association says that they'd be open to the training. Matt Galka, "Stopping the Shooter," Capitol News Service, February 11, 2014.

February 12

A new study conducted by Moms Demand Action, a citizens group formed after Newtown, and Mayors Against Illegal Guns, cites at least 44 school and college shootings since Newtown in December 2012. The total death toll from the events over the 14 months since then is 28, surpassing that of Newtown itself. The joint report was released in Washington on Wednesday in an attempt to restart the debate on gun control. "We are a developed country, and we have to ask ourselves what is wrong with our culture and laws that's creating an environment where not only do we have 44 school shootings in the past 14 months – but we are doing nothing about it," says twenty-year public relations veteran and present Huffington Post columnist Shannon Watts, also the founder of Moms Demand Action. Ed Pilkington, "Twenty-Eight Killed in 44 US School Shootings Since Newtown, Study Finds," *UK Guardian*, February 12, 2014.

February 14

NBC News carries a graphic report on the 13th staged mass shooter drill taking place at Missouri's Lincoln County school district over the past year. The Missouri state legislature voted to make live shooter drills mandatory following the Sandy Hook massacre. "All but 69 students have gone home for the day on early dismissal," NBC reports. "These volunteer victims, mostly culled from the school's drama class, are outfitted in fake-bloody bullet wounds, still wet and dripping down their foreheads, necks and chests."

A campus police officer tells participants what to expect: "They'll see 'bad guys with AR-15s' shooting blanks during a simulated 'passing period'—the moments when one class ends and the other begins." In addition, "PVC pipes will be dropped on the floor to approximate [Improvised Explosive Devices]." Freshman Crystal Lanham is delighted to be chosen as one of the gunmen's hostages. "'I just really wanna get shot,' she jokes. 'Is that weird?'" Nona Willis Aronowitz, "Fake Blood and Blanks: School Stage Active Shooter Drills," NBC News, February 14, 2014.

Connecticut State Police announce they will hold a ceremony the week of February 17 to honor more than 200 officers who responded to the Sandy Hook Elementary School shooting. State police officials also intend to honor several trauma psychologists who worked with officers following the shooting at the school. No members of the public will be allowed at the ceremony. Dave Altimari, "More Than 200 To Get State Police Awards For Sandy Hook Shooting Response," *Hartford Courant*, February 14, 2014.

March 4

The Second Annual Sandy Hook Ride on Washington (SHROW) is announced. On March 8that 8:00 am ET, Team 26, a group of cyclists, will embark on a 400 mile journey from Newtown, CT to Washington DC to call for "sensible gun violence prevention." The four-day "rolling rally" includes events in Ridgefield, Ct,Greenwich, Ct., Harlem, NY, Doylestown, Pa., Baltimore, Md., College Park, Md., the Washington National Cathedral, Washington, DC and end at the steps of the U.S. Capitol Building. "From Suburbs to Inner Cities," PR Newswire / *Digital Journal*, March 4, 2014.

March 10

The *New Yorker* magazine publishes a 7,600 essay by New York-based writer Andrew Solomon based on an alleged series of interviews with Peter Lanza. "Since the shootings, Peter has avoided the press," Solomon writes, "but in September, as the first anniversary of his son's rampage approached, he contacted me to say that he was ready to tell his story. We met six times, for interviews lasting as long as seven hours. Shelley, a librarian at the University of Connecticut, usually joined us and made soup or chili or salads for lunch. Sometimes we played with their German shepherd." Andrew Solomon, "The Reckoning: The Father of the Sandy Hook Killer Searches for Answers," *New Yorker*, March 17, 2014.

March 26

Missouri Senator Roy Blunt applauds the House of Representatives for passing a demonstration project of the "Excellence in Mental Health Act," bipartisan legislation introduced in 2013 following the Sandy Hook massacre by Blunt and Michigan Democrat Debbie Stabenow in the Senate. The amendment expands access to community mental health services and strengthens the quality of care provided for those living with mental illness. "Blunt Praises Action on Mental Health Bill," KSPR 33 ABC, March 27, 2014.

April 2

The Newtown-Sandy Hook Community Foundation received more than 1,600 responses to a survey of Newtown residents released on March 31. Most respondents called for mental health counseling and assistance services; a small portion suggested that the house where Adam Lanza resided be torn down. The foundation has been deciding how to distribute more than $11 million in donations made in response to the shootings. "Newtown Residents Want Gunman's House Torn Down," Associated Press / WPVI, April 2, 2014. See also, "Newtown Group Sees Long Term Mental Health Needs," CBS New York, April 2, 2014.

April 5

CNN reports that Spc. Ivan Lopez ranted on Facebook on a variety of topics prior to his shooting rampage at Fort Hood in Texas. Remarks included his outrage at Adam Lanza's mass school shooting in Connecticut. He also expressed tremendous fear after experiencing an insurgent attack in Iraq. Ray Sanchez, "Fort Hood Gunman Vented on Facebook About Sandy Hook Shooter, Iraq," CNN, April 5. 2014.

Enrollment in the Newtown Public School District dropped by almost 250 students in 2013. At Sandy Hook elementary alone, 55 fewer students enrolled that year. School officials commission an enrollment study to find if decreased enrollment is aligned with a larger demographic shift experienced in many suburban school districts or if it is yet another lingering effect of the school shooting. Nanci G. Hutson, "Newtown School Enrollment Declines Post Sandy Hook,"*Newstimes.com*, April 5, 2014.

April 10

A half-dozen parents of the 20 first-graders killed in the Sandy Hook massacre attend the meeting of the Permanent Memorial Commission. The 12-member group has been meeting for the past six months to come up with a fitting tribute to the victims and others impacted by the tragedy. "You are the first group we are reaching out to," Chairman Kyle Lyddy says. "We want to find out what you want and what you don't want." John Pirro, "Memorial Commission Meets with Families,"*Newstimes.com*, April 10, 2014.

April 15

Former New York City mayor Michael R. Bloomberg announces he will spend $50 million in 2014 building a nationwide grass-roots network to influence voting outcomes where gun control is an issue. The multi-billionaire wants to develop an organization he hopes can eventually surpass the National Rifle Association in political influence. Bloomberg thinks gun control advocates need to learn from the N.R.A. and punish politicians who fail to challenge the constitutionally-protected right to bear arms. Jeremy W. Peters, "Bloomberg Plans a $50 Million Challenge to the N.R.A.," *New York Times*, April 15, 2014.

April 22

Certain Republican congressional candidates vying for nomination take issue with President Obama's call to involve the Centers for Disease Control in gun control research. When gun violence peaked in the early 1990s, the CDC increased its funding of firearms violence research. Yet in 1996 it backed off under pressure from Congress and the National Rifle Association. Funding for "firearms injury prevention activities" decreased from more than $2.7 million in 1995 to barely $100,000 by 2012, according to the CDC.

After the Sandy Hook shootings, Obama issued a memorandum "directing the Centers for Disease Control to research the causes and prevention of gun violence." The influential Institute of Medicine lept into action, assembling a report on priorities for research on reducing gun violence. Among the questions that need answers, according to the report: Do background checks — the most popular and prominent gun control policy proposal — actually reduce gun violence? How often do Americans successfully use guns to protect themselves each year? And what is the relationship between violence in video games and other media and "real-life" violence? The Obama administration is now asking that the CDC receive $10 million for gun violence research. CDC's current funding for gun violence prevention research remains at $0. Lois Beckett, "Republicans Say No to CDC Gun Violence Research," ProPublica, April 21, 2014.

April 24

The FBI has releases roughly 175 pages of heavily blacked-out documents from its Sandy Hook Elementary School massacre investigation. Of the 175 pages released in response to a Freedom of Information request by the *Hartford Courant*, 64 were completely redacted and most of the other 111 pages were heavily redacted. The*Courant* submitted the request in January after state police released a report on the Dec. 14, 2012, shooting. The names of all witnesses interviewed by federal agents have been removed and there are no references to attempts by federal authorities to recover information from a computer disk that shooter Adam Lanza destroyed. Dave Altimari, "FBI Releases Heavily Blacked Out Sandy Hook Records," *Hartford Courant*, April 24, 2014.

The Newtown Health District participates in a statewide drill simulating a mass casualty outbreak to gauge how emergency response medications can be distributed. District Director Donna Culbert states she has been working with state and regional officials for several weeks to prepare for the drill. "The state created a scenario for us and plan to drive pallets of (supplies) to our distribution center – which is the high school – and we will be there to receive it," she says. "We will be among dozens of drop off sites – all the 32 hospitals and more than 75 dispensing sites will be receiving pallets during the drill." John Voket, "Newtown Participating in Emergency Medication Distribution Drill Thursday," *Newtown Bee*, April 24, 2014.

May 2

The FBI's active shooter training program for local and state law enforcement officials following the Sandy Hook killings has already saved lives, FBI Director James Comey tells reporters. Comey says the chief of police in Murrysville, Pennsylvania "wanted to make sure that I knew that the FBI's training had saved children" when a student stabbed 25 people at Franklin Regional High School last month. "One of the pieces of training we've been pushing out is tell responders to be sure to keep a path clear for ambulances," Comey remarks. "One of the things we've learned from examining past incidents is the law enforcement responders race up, park their cars at all sorts of angles and race towards the building, completely blocking the roads." Comey also notes how the FBI's Behavioral Analysis

Unit is regularly working with state and local law enforcement to address concerns about individuals who might plot a violent attack. Ryan J. Reilly, "Post Sandy Hook Active Shooter Training Has Already Saved Lives, Says FBI Director James Comey," *Huffington Post*, May 2, 2014.

May 6

Sandy Hook School Truth activists and researchers descend on Newtown to look for answers concerning the event. The group includes school safety consultant Wolfgang Halbig and retired university professor James Fetzer. During an afternoon visit to the Western Connecticut United Way to demand financial records related to the fundraising activities embarked on following the event. The group is turned away by a bevy of police officers. That evening Halbig, Fetzer, and several other activists and researchers attend the Newtown Board of Education's meeting and address the body's members during a public comments section. Nanci G. Hutson, "Newtown School Greets Sandy Hook Skeptics with Silence," *Connecticut Post*, May 7, 2014. See also Jim Fetzer, "The Newtown School Board Meeting and the Meaning of Silence," *Veterans Today*, May 9, 2014.

A 50-pound vinyl peace sign is reportedly stolen from a Mystic Connecticut playground built in memory of slain Sandy Hook Elementary student Grace McDonnell. William Lavin, of "Where Angels Play Foundation," claims McDonnell's mother Lynn found out about the theft when the man who apparently took the sign called her. The thief allegedly tells McDonnell he stole the sign because he believes the shooting at the school was a hoax.

The incident comes less than a week after graffiti was found on another victim's memorial playground. The message found spray-painted Sunday at the Ana Marquez Greene Memorial playground in Hartford read, "Peace to Sandy Hook," using a peace sign and the numeral "2." It was later removed. Ana's mother, Nelba Marquez Greene says she was not upset with the graffiti and plans to raise money for a graffiti board to allow similar condolence messages. "Peace Sign Stolen From Connecticut Playground honoring Sandy Hook Victim Grace McDonnell," Associated Press / CBS New York, May 8, 2014.

May 26

Following an apparent May 23 mass murder at UC Santa Barbara, victim Christopher Martinez's father, Richard Martinez, comes out and blames Congress for not pursuing stricter gun control following the Sandy Hook Elementary School massacre in a highly emotional interview with CNN.

Chris Tognotti, "Congress Should Have Acted After Sandy Hook to Prevent UCSB Shootings, Father Tells CNN," Bustle.com, May 27, 2014.

Following the May 23 shooting rampage by an apparent lone gunman the Associated Press circulates a story that according to experts "mass murderers tend to have a history of pent-up frustration and failures, are socially isolated and vengeful, blaming others for their unhappiness ... 'They all display deluded thinking and a lot of rage about feeling so marginalized,' James Garbarino, a professor of psychology at Loyola University Chicago, said in an email." Because mass killings are uncommon, "scholars say there's no way to predict who has deadly intentions, let alone who will reach a breaking point and take action." Christopher Weber and Alicia Chang, "Experts" Mass Murderers Are Hard to Predict," *Seattle Times* / Associated Press, May 27, 2014.

June 4

CNN's Anderson Cooper discusses gun control on The Late Show host David Letterman. The television news anchor remarks that America "isn't ready" or "isn't willing" to tackle the "gun control problem," adding that if Sandy Hook wasn't enough to spur action, then nothing will. Letterman says he's not "anti-gun," but wanted to know "for the love of Christ, when are we going to do something about this nonsense?" "David Letterman, Anderson Cooper Discuss Gun Control,"*Guns.com*, June 6, 2014.

June 5

In the midst of divorce proceedings filmmaker Michael Moore's spouse Glynn notes that just days after the Sandy Hook Elementary School massacre, Moore was offered financing for an anti-gun film. In an e-mail sent three days after the December 2012 shooting, producer Michael Donovan wrote that he was"personally prepared to finance a film" by Moore about the Newtown, Connecticut killings. Donovan and Moore won the 2002 Academy Award for best documentary feature for "Bowling for Columbine." While Moore acknowledged receiving Donovan's e-mail, court records do not include the director's response to the offer. "Michael Moore, Wife Tangle Over Divorce Dollars," *The Smoking Gun*, June 5, 2014.

June 12

ProTecht, an Oklahoma company, reports that it has seen business grow partly due to the "Body Guard" blanket it markets to keep children safe from high-speed debris flying through the air from the tornadoes. Some parents also see the device as protection against gunfire in the apparent rash of school shootings following the Sandy Hook massacre. "The government is not going to do anything in law about guns, and there is nothing else out there to protect the children," says Stan Schone, who helped develop the blanket. Heide Brandes, "Some Turn to Bullet-Resistant Blankets After US School Shootings," Reuters / Yahoo News, June 12, 2014.

June 15

James Tracy sends a letter to CNN's Anderson Cooper, challenging the recognized cable news anchor to travel with him to Newtown and partake in a genuinely thorough journalistic investigation of the Sandy Hook massacre and its aftermath. In the weeks following the event Cooper sent reporters to Tracy's workplace and residence to question Tracy on his initial criticism of the event's media coverage. Evidence accumulating since December 14, 2012 underlines Tracy's initial skepticism concerning the event's authenticity. In the letter, Tracy reminds Cooper that it could be the story that defines journalistic greatness. "It will call for—indeed require—the public service of news professionals like you to find out what really happened and bring the culprits to justice!" Tracy intones. "Anderson, at the end of the day it's just like you say each evening: we truly need to 'keep them honest.'" James F. Tracy, "An Open Letter to Anderson Cooper," Memory Hole Blog, June 23, 2014.

June 17

Connecticut State Police Major William Podgorski dies Monday at Yale-New Haven Hospital after a brief illness. Podgorski was commander of the state police western district, which includes the barracks in Canaan, Litchfield, Southbury and Bridgeport. He was directly involved in the Sandy Hook investigation and redactions in the official report. Dave Owens, "State Police Chief Dies After Brief Illness," *Hartford Courant*, June 17, 2014.

June 21

Cardenas Hoffman, 30, of Venezuela is arrested in a Miami airport for making threatening phone calls to the residents of Newtown, Connecticut, two days after the Sandy Hook Elementary School shooting. Cardenas purportedly made 96 calls to Newtown claiming to be Adam Lanza and threatening call recipients, according to a U.S. Department of Justice statement. He was charged with a criminal complaint in May 2013 for "threats in interstate or foreign commerce to injure the person of another," the statement said. "Man Arrested for Threatening Phone Calls After Sandy Hook," NBC News, June 23, 2014.

The North Carolina chapter of the National Alliance on Mental Illness hopes to elevate the discussion this week at its annual conference.

NAMI-NC executive director Deby Dihoff says the time is right to discuss mental health, school safety, gun violence, and community solutions post-Sandy Hook.

The 29th annual conference brings together school system leaders, social workers, mental health professionals, judicial and court system representatives, law enforcement, as well as individuals living with mental illness and family members.

Nelba Márquez-Greene, the mother of one of the children killed in the Newtown school shooting, will also discuss what can be done to prevent tragedies like this from happening again.

– See more at: *http://pulse.ncpolicywatch.org/2013/10/04/ncs-mental-health-advocates-focus-on-lessons-from-sandy-hook/#sthash.RfgpE0iG.dpuf* the North Carolina chapter of the National Alliance on Mental Illness hopes to elevate the discussion this week at its annual conference.

NAMI-NC executive director Deby Dihoff says the time is right to discuss mental health, school safety, gun violence, and community solutions post-Sandy Hook.

The 29th annual conference brings together school system leaders, social workers, mental health professionals, judicial and court system representatives, law enforcement, as well as individuals living with mental illness and family members.

Nelba Márquez-Greene, the mother of one of the children killed in the Newtown school shooting, will also discuss what can be done to prevent tragedies like this from happening again.

– See more at: *http://pulse.ncpolicywatch.org/2013/10/04/ncs-mental-health-advocates-focus-on-lessons-from-sandy-hook/#sthash.RfgpE0iG.dpuf* the North Carolina chapter of the National Alliance on Mental Illness hopes to elevate the discussion this week at its annual conference.

NAMI-NC executive director Deby Dihoff says the time is right to discuss mental health, school safety, gun violence, and community solutions post-Sandy Hook.

The 29th annual conference brings together school system leaders, social workers, mental health professionals, judicial and court system representatives, law enforcement, as well as individuals living with mental illness and family members.

Nelba Márquez-Greene, the mother of one of the children killed in the Newtown school shooting, will also discuss what can be done to prevent tragedies like this from happening again.

– See more at: *http://pulse.ncpolicywatch.org/2013/10/04/ncs-mental-health-advocates-focus-on-lessons-from-sandy-hook/#sthash.RfgpE0iG.dpuf* the North Carolina chapter of the National Alliance on Mental Illness hopes to elevate the discussion this week at its annual conference.

NAMI-NC executive director Deby Dihoff says the time is right to discuss mental health, school safety, gun violence, and community solutions post-Sandy Hook.

The 29th annual conference brings together school system leaders, social workers, mental health professionals, judicial and court system representatives, law enforcement, as well as individuals living with mental illness and family members.

Nelba Márquez-Greene, the mother of one of the children killed in the Newtown school shooting, will also discuss what can be done to prevent tragedies like this from happening again.

– See more at: *http://pulse.ncpolicywatch.org/2013/10/04/ncs-mental-health-advocates-focus-on-lessons-from-sandy-hook/#sthash.RfgpE0iG.dpuf* the North Carolina chapter of the National Alliance on Mental Illness hopes to elevate the discussion this week at its annual conference.

NAMI-NC executive director Deby Dihoff says the time is right to discuss mental health, school safety, gun violence, and community solutions post-Sandy Hook.

The 29th annual conference brings together school system leaders, social workers, mental health professionals, judicial and court system representatives, law enforcement, as well as individuals living with mental illness and family members.

Nelba Márquez-Greene, the mother of one of the children killed in the Newtown school shooting, will also discuss what can be done to prevent tragedies like this from happening again.

– See more at: http://pulse.ncpolicywatch.org/2013/10/04/ncs-mental-health-advocates-focus-on-lessons-from-sandy-hook/#sthash.RfgpE0iG.dpuf

Originally published as *"Sandy Hook School Massacre Timeline"* (6 January 2013), *memoryholeblog.com*

James F. Tracy

APPENDIX D

Murder and Homocide rates before and after gun bans
by John Lott

Every place that has been banned guns has seen murder rates go up. You cannot point to one place where murder rates have fallen, whether it's Chicago or D.C. or even island nations such as England, Jamaica, or Ireland.

For an example of homicide rates before and after a ban, take the case of the handgun ban in England and Wales in January 1997. After the ban, clearly homicide rates bounce around over time, but there is only one year (2010) where the homicide rate is lower than it was in 1996. The immediate effect was about a 50 percent increase in homicide rates. The homicide rate only began falling when there was a large increase in the number of police officers

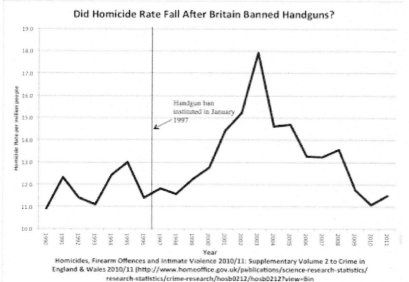

Did Homicide Rate Fall After Britain Banned Handguns?

Handgun ban instituted in January 1997

Homicides, Firearm Offences and Intimate Violence 2010/11: Supplementary Volume 2 to Crime in England & Wales 2010/11 (http://www.homeoffice.gov.uk/publications/science-research-statistics/research-statistics/crime-research/hosb0212/hosb0212?view=Bin

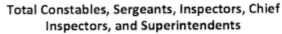

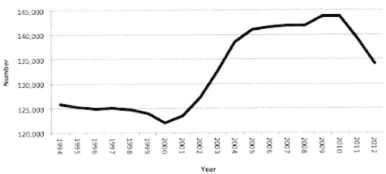

Police Service Strength England and Wales,
Home Office Statistical Bulletin, 2007 and 2012

during 2003 and 2004. Despite the *huge increase* in the number of police, the murder rate still remained slightly higher than the immediate pre-ban rate.

There are a lot of issues about how different countries measure homicide or murders differently, but that isn't really relevant for the discussion here as we are talking about changes over time within a country. Other information for Ireland and Jamaica.

Jamaica's crime data were obtained from a variety of sources. Its murder data from 1960 to 1967 were obtained from Terry Lacey, Violence and Politics in Jamaica, 1960–70 (Manchester: Manchester University Press, 1977). Professor Gary Mauser obtained the data from 1970 to 2000 from a Professor A. Francis in Jamaica and the data from 2001 to 2006 from the Statistical Institute of Jamaica *(http://www.statinja. com/stats.html)*. Jamaica's population estimates were obtained from NationMaster.

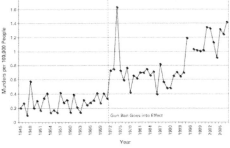

Figure 10.18. Ireland's murder rate. While murder rates in the United States and Jamaica include both murders and manslaughter, Ireland's numbers include only murder. Including manslaughter would probably roughly double the measured murder rate for Ireland for most years. (Murder rate data are not available for 1996.)

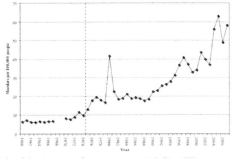

com (http://www.nationmaster. com/graph/ peo_pop-people-population&date=1975).

How about for DC and Chicago (Figures taken from *More Guns, Less Crime*)?

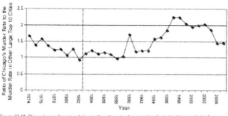

Figure 10.14. Chicago's murder rate relative to the other nine largest cities (weighted by population)

Much of the debate over gun control focuses on what is called "cross-sectional" data. That is crime rates are examined at one particular point of time across different places. Here are two paragraphs from John Lott's *The Bias Against Guns* that explain the basic problem with cross-sectional analysis.

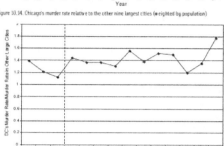

First, the cross-sectional studies: Suppose for the sake of argument that high-crime countries are the ones that most frequently adopt the most stringent gun control laws. Suppose further, for the sake of argument, that gun control indeed lowers crime, but not by enough to reduce rates to the same low levels prevailing in the majority of countries that did not adopt the laws. Looking across countries, it would then falsely appear that stricter gun control resulted in higher crime. Economists refer to this as an "endogeniety" problem.

The adoption of the policy is a reaction to other events (that is, "endogenous"), in this case crime. To resolve this, one must examine how the high-crime areas that chose to adopt the controls changed over time —not only relative to their own past levels but also relative to areas that did not institute such controls.

Unfortunately, many contemporary discussions rely on misinterpretations of cross-sectional data. The *New York Times* recently conducted a cross-sectional study of murder rates in states with and without the death penalty, and found that "Indeed, 10 of the 12 states without capital punishment have homicide rates below the national average, Federal Bureau of Investigation data shows, while half the states with the death penalty have homicide rates above the national average."

However, they erroneously concluded that the death penalty did not deter murder. The problem is that the states without the death penalty

(Alaska, Hawaii, Iowa, Maine, Massachusetts, Michigan, Minnesota, North Dakota, Rhode Island, West Virginia, Wisconsin, and Vermont) have long enjoyed relatively low murder rates, something that might well have more to do with other factors than the death penalty. Instead one must compare, over time, how murder rates change in the two groups – those adopting the death penalty and those that did not.

This appendix originally appeared as "Murder and Homicide Rates before and after Gun Bans", *Crime Prevention Research Center* (1 December 2013).

INDEX

373

Thomas, Alex 252
three semi-trailers in background 140
Till, Emmett 301
Time Magazine xiv Timothy
McVeigh did not blow up the Murrah
Building on his own xli
toxicology reports show Adam not on
alcohol or drugs 319
Tracy responds positively but offer
simply "disappears" 294
Tracy, James F. xxi, xxiv, xxix, xxxv-
xxvi, xlii, xlvii, 19, 92-94, 97-99,
100, 200, 245, 285, 305
Tracy, James sends letter to Anderson
Cooper challenging him to travel
together to Newtown and conduct a
serious investigation 350
trauma-based mind-control 90
triage tarps 105
Trooper One chopper 42
Truth Commission xi
Tucson, AZ 195-197, 278, 278
two long guns from vehicle 265
two unidentified nuns photographed
259
ugly legacy of Barack Hussein
Obama 16

U

UK moves small arms treaty for an
immediate UN vote 310
UN Arms Trade Treaty 87
UN General Assembly moves to
control conventional weapons trade
311
United agent was William B. Meyer
140
United movers standing by cartons
140
United Van in parking lot 139
United Way 201
United Way of Western Connecticut
285, 305
unmarked FEMA vehicles 141
Unravelling Sandy Hook 192

Urbina, Curtis and Richmond 242
Urbina, Lenie 242
US Department of Education 101
USA TODAY 172
used cartridges to plant as props 124

V

Vaidero, James 253
Vance, Lt. J. Paul 21-22, 63-66, 68-
69, 202, 205, 248, 269-270, 276, 279,
280, 328, 342,
Vance, Lt. J. Paul, Adam not
mimicking Anders Breivik 298
Vast stockpile of ammo, weapons,
swords found at Lanza home 308
vechicle moves for better stagine 144
vechicle with fake bullet holes 143
vehicles not in Sedensky's report 146
Vermeule, Adrian ix
Veterans Today xx, 246
vicSims 198, 200, 201
victims missing from SSDI 162
Victoria Soto photos 78
Victoria Soto's photoshopped class
photo 79-80
view down the driveway 137-138
view from the woods of a day in
infamy 157
Virgalla, Beckey 254, 287
Voket, John 255, 258, 298
vote to tear down old school and build
a new one 318

W

Wade, C.W. 51
Washington, Jesse 286
Wasik, Alexis 275
water bottles left on the floor 132
Waterboarding Anderson Cooper xxx-
xxxi
Watt, Kelley xlviii, 41, 44, 63, 177
Watts, Shannon 343
Wayback Machine 34
Wayne Carver can be seen 13

CPSIA information can be obtained
at www.ICGtesting.com
Printed in the USA
LVOW04s0919040316

477771LV00001B/1/P